The politics of grandeur

The politics of grandeur

Ideological aspects of de Gaulle's foreign policy

PHILIP G. CERNY

Lecturer in Politics
University of York

CAMBRIDGE UNIVERSITY PRESS

CAMBRIDGE

LONDON   NEW YORK   NEW ROCHELLE

MELBOURNE   SYDNEY

Published by the Press Syndicate of the University of Cambridge
The Pitt Building, Trumpington Street, Cambridge CB2 1RP
32 East 57th Street, New York, NY 10022, USA
296 Beaconsfield Parade, Middle Park, Melbourne 3206, Australia

First published 1980

Printed in Great Britain by
Western Printing Services Ltd, Bristol

Library of Congress Cataloguing in Publication Data
Cerny, Philip G   1946–
The politics of grandeur.
Bibliography: p.
Includes index.
1. France – Foreign relations – 1958–1969. 2. Gaulle,
Charles de, Pres. France, 1890–1970. I. Title.
DC417.C44   327.44   79–50232
ISBN 0 521 22863 8

Contents

For Marion Kerr

Preface

The argument which is set out in this book was first conceived during a year of study in Paris in 1965–6. The conditions surrounding the 1965 presidential election campaign and the elections of 5 and 19 December of that year, and the context of the foreign policy crises of the day – the French boycott of the meetings of the (European Economic Community) Council of Ministers between June 1965 and January 1966, and the French withdrawal from the integrated military organisation of the North Atlantic Alliance (NATO) followed by the expulsion of American forces from French bases – created distinct impressions. These have been refined, expanded and developed into an extensive reappraisal of the meaning and significance of Gaullist foreign policy in contemporary world politics.

All of this was viewed at the time through the eyes of an American student of political science – accustomed to the rituals and dynamics of politics in a presidential system. It appeared that, as an element common to domestic and foreign affairs in the Fifth Republic, was a single connecting problem, that of consensus-building, or, in other words, of defining and specifying certain rules of the political and governmental game, rules which would come to be taken for granted by most, if not all, of the groups and parties which participate in French politics.

The enormity of this task, and the fragility of previous attempts to start along this path, were made clear not only in ordinary conversation, but also in the dominant themes of literature on French political history. The role of the office of President of the Republic, a role which had expanded and taken on a new symbolic meaning with the accession of General de Gaulle and the inauguration of the Fifth Republic in 1958, appeared to be the key. Indeed, de Gaulle was to state in 1967 that his primary political goal was to ensure that the presidency should become 'second nature' to the French people. Thus, if the new form of authority embodied in the Fifth Republic were, to use Max Weber's

expression, to be 'legitimated', then the most important factor in this
process of consensus-building would be the *image* which was popularly
held and accepted of the role which the president *ought* to play. To look
ahead in the argument, it was necessary to create a 'symbol of the
whole' – a widely held sense that the national constituency of the
president somehow made him the guardian of the national interest –
and to implant and internalise that symbol in the minds and the
behaviour patterns of the French body politic.

Foreign policy was to play a critical role in this process. Achieving
this objective required the linking of the new structure of authority
with the more submerged set of feelings and reactions which are called
'national consciousness'. This is the feeling that a person belongs to an
overarching political association in which not only do its members have
more in common with each other than they have with other groups,
but also, as Aristotle says, the different members of the association feel a
spontaneous concern for the moral welfare of their fellow citizens.
It is a commonplace that war has on occasion in history formed or
reinforced a solidarity of this sort. And foreign policy can, under certain
circumstances, play the role of a sort of war-in-microcosm. Thus the
linkage of foreign policy with a new structure of authority can create a
psychological association of national identity with authority, thus giving
that authority a profound 'legitimacy'. There are inherent dangers to
this strategy, it must be said, and an overambitious foreign policy can
be counterproductive. But if it works it can be extremely effective.

For reasons which will be developed in detail in this book, it is
suggested that such, indeed, was General de Gaulle's intention. Given
his taste for public dramaturgy, his 'certain idea of France', and given
the interrelated roles of the President of the Republic as the only
political figure with a national constituency, as the chief maker of
foreign policy, and as a symbolic head of state, foreign policy was
necessarily involved very closely in the consensus-building process. The
ultimate significance of such a strategy, however, is its effectiveness.
We believe that there is sufficient evidence, both direct and circumstantial, to demonstrate that Gaullist foreign policy was indeed effective
in helping to achieve this goal. Indeed, we feel that our argument stands
up better to historical testing than do the received alternatives. The
implications are potentially significant not only for the study of foreign
policy and international relations, but also for French politics itself.

Short sections of Chapter 2 have appeared previously in *Il Pensiero
Politico*, vol. VII, no. 3 (1974); and a slightly different version of

Chapter 5 has appeared in the *British Journal of International Studies,* vol. 5, no. 1 (April 1979).

I should like to acknowledge a debt of gratitude to those whose help has been forthcoming at the various stages of the book's development. Those who have discussed with me a broad argument which, for a long time, existed only in my head, who have lent me books or articles, who have provided many helpful suggestions or contacts, or who have discussed specific aspects of the argument as earlier sections have been committed to paper, are too numerous to mention by name. My gratitude to them is, however, as full and sincere as ever. But I am particularly grateful to those who have read and commented in detail upon earlier versions of the full manuscript, for their detailed comments have helped immeasurably in the process of tightening up my argument and organisation. They are, especially, Dr Vincent Wright of Nuffield College, Oxford, and Professors Ghiţa Ionescu and Dennis Austin of the University of Manchester. The substance is, of course, my own responsibility.

York   P.G.C.
October 1978

Introduction:
politics and grandeur

Everything begins with mysticism and ends with politics.
Péguy

The foreign policy of France during the years when de Gaulle was the last Prime Minister of the dying Fourth Republic (June–December 1958) and the first President of the Fifth Republic (January 1959– April 1969) had a considerable impact on world politics of the day. It challenged – and occasionally broke – the rules of the game which had been established in the late 1940s and which had set hard in the 1950s. It enraged its opponents at home and abroad, yet it was not revolutionary. It did not spare the *status quo*; yet it did not seek to destroy the entire existing balance of world power, only to modify that balance.

It was far-sighted, in that it was built upon a vision of a post-cold war world, in which the mature nations of the old world and the newly independent states of the Third World would act to counterbalance the political, economic, technological and military hegemony of the two recently emerged 'superpowers', the United States and the Soviet Union, and to loosen the strait-jacket of the nuclear balance of terror. But also, especially with the hindsight of the 1970s, it appears as insufficient, in that it was rooted in a world where the industrialised countries were still reinforcing their economic dominance, when economic growth was high and inflation low, and when global power seemed to be all of a piece – not fragmented, as it is today, into complex circuits of military, economic, cultural and political relationships in which resources are often not commensurate with influence. This was the world before the major upheavals symbolised by the 1973 Yom Kippur War and the quadrupling of petroleum prices which followed, bringing with it a world recession and a painful period of adjustment which has yet to crystallise into a long-term structure of global political relations.

Politically, the world of Camp David is poles apart from that preceding and following the Six-Day War in 1967; that of Angola,

Mozambique and Zimbabwe from that of post-independence Africa in the sixties; that of the 'German problem' since the *Ostpolitik* from that of the building of the Berlin Wall in 1961.

De Gaulle's foreign policy, however, was not defined only by the structure of international relations or by his view of them in isolation. Rather, it was part of a much wider view of man and his world, an ontological perspective on the 'nature of things' which gave coherence to his political action and linked the various facets of his foreign and domestic policies when in power. Janus-like, Gaullist foreign policy has two complementary faces. The first face looks outward to the rest of the world. This was de Gaulle the revisionist, seeking to shake free of cold war constraints and to use to the maximum those capabilities which France possessed to push the reluctant superpowers to recognise that a world of detente would necessarily be a world in which smaller nations' freedom of action and manoeuvre would increase, not decrease, and in which the superpowers themselves would have to shed their ideological pretensions and accept greater limits to their own activity.

The second face looks inward to France, and sees foreign policy as an issue-area among the others. This was de Gaulle the symbolic leader, the founder of a new constitutional order based on a strong and stable executive power, and the guardian of the liturgy of national interest in a country which he saw as historically divided, politically weak, and yet culturally strong, economically ambitious and potentially 'great' – even in a world which it could not, and did not seek to, dominate.

It is the link between these two faces which this book aims to explore. That they were linked has been widely recognised. But the actual substance and content of that link – the underlying ideas, aspirations and goals which gave shape and force to de Gaulle's political action at home and abroad – have never been examined in depth. Polemics have abounded, viewpoints have clashed, and oversimplified stereotypes have been accepted by all too many writers. Words – in particular, the 'key word' with which this study begins: *grandeur* – have been bandied about, occasionally with insight, but rarely with any extended analysis.

Naturally, this has led to misunderstandings and misconceptions, which this book will try to put into perspective and, hopefully, to correct. By integrating the occasional insights of the more perspicacious observers of the General with a philosophical exegesis of de Gaulle's writings and speeches and with a sociological and cultural examination of the setting of de Gaulle's politics and foreign policy, a new synthesis, based upon a new interpretation of the significance of Gaullist policy, is up in the first half of the book and showing how our reappraisal works in practice. Here we find more evidence that, for de Gaulle, *grandeur* was a qualitative, not a quantitative, concept, and that, as a consequence, the Franco-American conflict of the sixties appears in a rather different light. French goals were essentially symbolic and did little to alter the substantive power relationship between France and the United States; however, in wounding American *amour-propre* and in undermining her self-image of altruistically taking on the burdens incumbent upon her as the 'vanguard of the free world', de Gaulle aroused that deep resentment in the United States which stemmed from the loss of face and status and which, in another theatre of American foreign policy, was dragging her deeper and deeper into the Vietnam conflict. The impact of this reaction upon French public opinion was, in fact, to enhance de Gaulle's image and to further his pursuit of national legitimacy for the Fifth Republic and its institutions and processes. And once his symbolic goals had been achieved by means of withdrawing from NATO and the expulsion of American troops from France, relations were rapidly normalised on a bilateral basis. Indeed, although some of the content of French foreign policy has altered since de Gaulle's retirement in 1969 and death in 1970, the presidentialist style and symbolic primacy of the assertion of French independence and *grandeur* have become institutionalised.

It is worth noting, in advance, some limitations which affect our use of the word *grandeur*. In the first place, the word contains significant internal distinctions in its definition and connotation. It can mean, in French, anything from simple measurable *size* or 'bigness', through a sort of 'grandness' with connotations of the *extensiveness* of the influence, power or glory associated with a particular social, political or cultural phenomenon, to a much more profound sense of transcendental moral or cultural value or *worthiness*. The English usage of the term is usually restricted to the second of these three senses, and distortions appear in the comprehension of Gaullist aspirations in the eyes of British and American observers as a result of this perceptual gap. De Gaulle's hopes for French 'greatness', for example, are often interpreted as rather primitive 'dreams of glory' or 'delusions of grandeur'. In the historical personage of Napoleon I the three meanings are most clearly present at the same time. The size of the Empire, the trappings of glory, the extensiveness and intensiveness of French socio-cultural influence on the conquered territories, the very power of France in terms of military capabilities, and the revolutionary moral and philosophical nature of the French 'message', are all summed up in the over-arching image of *grandeur*. Both domestic and foreign observers still look upon the First Empire as a significant paradigmatic epoch for understanding the historical development of French society and politics.

The Gaullist conception of *grandeur*, we shall argue, is a much more restricted phenomenon. In fact, it will appear from these pages as a limitationist ideology, concerned with the search for internal moral unity and worthiness in such a way that these objectives act as a *restraint* on both internal domestic fragmentation and external aggres-siveness and international disequilibrium. Although it has often been pointed out that the Gaullist notion of *grandeur* was a significant symbolic force for the creation of domestic stability and a sense of national identity, only Jean-Baptiste Duroselle claims, as we shall do, that 'even such "politics of greatness" will have an ultimate *domestic* purpose', which is precisely 'to preserve French unity';[3] this comment comes only, however, by way of an aside.

It follows from this assertion that if 'vast enterprises' are conceived mainly as having a domestic purpose, surely the enterprises themselves ought not to be so grandiose as to upset the international system in such a way as to cause other states to attempt to injure France, especially in a world which is highly interdependent and in which French economic and military capabilities are limited. French politics, with this shift of perspective, becomes a dialectic of assertion and conciliation, of revisionism and satisfaction, the purpose of which is to protect and nurture the development of French society and to encour-age the development of a global order which will make this possible. Through a combination of exhortation and limited (mainly symbolic) pressure, de Gaulle sought to support and reinforce structural ten-dencies which he saw as already being present and even inherent in the international system. Chief among these perceived tendencies was the development of an explicitly articulated awareness of the central role of the 'national interest' (itself a function of the domestic 'general in-terest') in creating a viable basis for the peaceful settling of differences in the international arena. His international revisionism was a function of his aspirations for the cultural and social integration and develop-ment of the French people by means of a common purpose, and not the other way round.

The real significance of de Gaulle's idea of *grandeur* is, then, as a symbol, and not as a means to extend French power. It should be seen as a cultural norm, applicable both to domestic French politics and to the moral authority of France in the world. It does not readily fit into the standard paradigms of international relations, whether in terms of power politics – what O'Leary has called the 'billiard ball school'[4] – or in terms of systems theory. It is, in many respects, *sui generis*.[5] This study will not, however, limit itself to an examination of Gaullism as a deviant case. In fact, our main purpose will be to suggest that Gaullist foreign policy represents a particular structured set of analytical categories – what we call a 'syndrome' – which is characteristic of many states in the contemporary world.

There is also a second major limitation on an analysis of *grandeur*. This concerns not so much the content of the idea, but rather its usage. *Grandeur* is but one of a number of words which make up the complex structure of Gaullist ideology, and in this sense our use of it as an overarching analytical concept is clearly artificial or conventional. In his little collection of de Gaulle's sayings, French journalist Jean Lacouture makes clear the limitations in his very brief section 'On *Grandeur*'. Although, he observes, we might expect to find this key word 'everywhere in the Gaullien literature', it has, in fact, become rare; other words, such as independence, have become more frequent alternatives.[6] Lacouture himself, regarding *grandeur* as *the* key word for de Gaulle, ascribes this decline in its usage to a combination of confusion and dissimulation on de Gaulle's part. Thus we can see that, for both Gaullists and anti-Gaullists, the use of the term demands the introduction of a preconception. It is a value-loaded word which reaches its hearers by way of their own conceptions of what it already means for them. Thus we are in that analytical twilight zone where a concept loaded both in the minds of diverse audiences and in de Gaulle's own mind, must be broken down into its empirical elements in a context where the word itself is less observably utilised than intuitively inferred.

Despite these qualifications, however, it is clearly indispensable to use an overarching concept such as *grandeur* in this sort of study. However, we might have chosen 'the nation', 'the state', 'independence', or various other expressions. *Grandeur* does have the advantage nonetheless of underlining the symbolic nature of the ideas under examination. For we are not speaking here of an abstract concept, but rather of a dynamic instrument of political action, an operative ideal. Thus the mysticism which permeates the notion of *grandeur* and looms over it, that shadow of the passions which gives it force but which obscures its essential structure, must give way to politics, wherein lies its source and its objectives.

PART I

Ideological roots and purposes of de Gaulle's foreign policy

France cannot be France without greatness.
de Gaulle, *War Memoirs*

1

The personal equation:
psychology, socialisation and culture

I. The Enigma

Valéry has written that 'A great man is one who leaves others after him in a state of embarrassment.' This, in de Gaulle's case, is not the oft-predicted (but as yet unmaterialised) chaos of *après de Gaulle* in French politics, but the embarrassment of the chroniclers of de Gaulle's political career, who have been forced by the conditions of everyday politics to take a stand on whether de Gaulle was right or wrong, good or bad. He frequently failed to fit into existing categories – 'capitalist' versus 'socialist' in domestic politics, 'imperialist' or friend of the Third World, or ally of West or East in the cold war.

This ambiguity extended to his personality. It was difficult for many observers to know what to expect of him. French journalist André Chambraud once wrote of him:

De Gaulle, the traditional officer, Maurrassian, born in 1890, was made for the purpose of loving colonial France and provincial France [*la France des villages*]. Instead, his historical role has been to precipitate their dissolution, to bring about a withdrawal to the hexagon, to preside over the birth of another France – industrial, urbanised, preoccupied first of all with material progress...a France which he no doubt understands badly.[1]

Foreign observers have found him less complicated. As a consequence of his active questioning of the international *status quo*, he alienated former allies. But neither was he in any sense revolutionary. Thus he often became the target of what James N. Rosenau has called 'devil theories', 'in which the course of events is attributed to a power-hungry individual or to a conspiratorial group'. Such theories are especially attractive in times of tension, when it is easier to blame an individual for undesirable events than to take the time and effort to sift through many complex factors, 'each of which is a necessary, though not a sufficient, cause'; they provide a 'simple and quick explanation', making it possible to both fix blame and cope with anxiety.[2] But they are obviously insufficient, and, in the long run, unsatisfactory.

At home, de Gaulle could not easily be fitted into the categories of 'left' or 'right' as they had tortuously developed since the French Revolution. His nationalism included elements of both right-wing nationalism – authoritarian and hegemonic – and left-wing nationalism – democratic and liberating – both of which had long and mainly distinct histories in post-Revolutionary France.[3]

Often, a particular characterisation of de Gaulle reflected more on the observer than on de Gaulle himself, as the General pointed out in the case of the Republican Party's presidential candidate in 1940, Wendell Willkie:

Because we conferred together in the High Commissioner's office, which M. de Martel had recently provided with a suite of Empire furniture, Willkie represented me as aping the Napoleonic style; because I was wearing the standard officer's summer uniform of white linen, he saw an ostentatious parody of Louis XIV; and because one of my men spoke of 'General de Gaulle's mission', Mr. Willkie hinted that I took myself for Joan of Arc. In this matter, Roosevelt's rival was also his imitator.[4]

Academic critics have often focused upon similar traits of style, along with de Gaulle's politics. Nathan Leites has contrasted his pretensions to grandeur with what he considered to be de Gaulle's true mediocrity.[5] W. W. Kulski placed him outside the bounds of normal politics:

He is a charismatic leader, i.e., a man who, together with his followers, believes that he has been called upon by God or by history (in any event by a supernatural force) to carry out great feats for the benefit of the nation. His vocation is independent of the will of other men. The only rational proof of this vocation is the success of his mission.

To Kulski, not only was de Gaulle's mission irrational, but his chosen vehicle of action – nationalism – was dangerous; international politics 'is not a contest in Christian virtue or a struggle between angels and devils. All nationalism is egoistic because it rests on the assumption that the nation is supreme.'[6]

Indeed, given the great conflicts of the twentieth century and the development of organicist nationalism (particularly its role in German ideology and political culture),[7] the very fact that de Gaulle posits the primacy of the nation-state places him in a 'devil' role in the eyes of many. One American critic accused him of 'an adventurist and irresponsible nationalism' which 'helped bring the world closer to a disregard of the deadly facts of the nuclear age'.[8] By an irrepressible logic, de Gaulle, fairly or unfairly, was seen as a partial reincarnation of that phenomenon of the 1920s and 1930s, the quasi-charismatic (i.e. irrational) authoritarian leader of a nation-state which did not fully conform to the rules of international relations; in other words, in the post-1945 world, a maverick, quasi-totalitarian bull in the delicately balanced cold war china shop.

The resonance of Gaullism – even if witnessed merely by the number and loudness of de Gaulle's critics – has been a major factor both in France and in international relations. At the same time, it has provided a critique of certain existing structural arrangements and practices, and has suggested alternative directions for change. If we are to go beyond 'devil theories' and seek to understand Gaullist ideology and practice, we must seek to separate various strands of personality, culture, conscious rationally guided action and the relationship of all of these factors to the political environment and conjuncture. First of all, we shall turn to de Gaulle's personality.

Personality factors are difficult to assess in politics. When political choices are made by an institutionalised process, personality factors merge with cultural background factors and can often be explained in more generalisable group terms. When choices are made by an individual, that is, when they express idiosyncratic preferences, surface impressions may become clearer and better focused, but underlying motivations take on a greater complexity. A political leader may embody a range of psychological and social experience which cuts across generalised categories and creates untypical perceptual and behavioural personality characteristics.

Personality factors have always been at the core of most observers' analyses of de Gaulle. As Rosenau has pointed out, such factors are both spatially and temporally closest to 'the external behaviours for which they serve as sources'.[9] Furthermore, de Gaulle maintained a strict dividing line between his public and private characters. His public character was theatrical and therefore under the constant scrutiny of journalists. The passing of time and the increasing availability of historical documentation may change this image as the other sets of variables come to be better understood. However, long-standing habits of thought may imprint frames of reference which are hard to change, so that unless certain unspoken assumptions are examined, information which does not conform to expectations may be selected out and ignored. In fact, as will be explained in more detail later, the particular situation in which de Gaulle acted had certain specific permissive characteristics; thus idiosyncratic variables were allowed a wide scope for influencing overall processes, but always within specific arenas and under specific conditions.

Most observers have noted a fundamental dissonance in de Gaulle's character. He is, on the one hand, 'noble, patriotic and dominant', and he somehow does represent the essential France. He is, on the other hand, petty and petulant, founding his policy on long-held grudges, as well as arrogant and unpredictable.[10] British and American observers, in particular, have been hard put to reconcile these contradictory images. Yet Britain and the United States have worked more closely with France, on a global scale, than any other nations. Two sorts of explanations suggest themselves.

In the first place, the very scale of American and British involvement, from the beginning of the Second World War, exacerbated relations. It concerned the most precious of national self-images, during a period of dislocation and change, in all three countries. Britain's Empire and her preference for the 'open sea' over European commitments were coming under pressure both from the supremacy of the anti-colonialist United States and from growing entanglements in Europe which she had previously attempted to avoid. The United States, drawn out of isolation for the second time in a quarter of a century, was torn between traditional distaste for the internecine quarrels of the Old World and an embryonic desire to refashion the rest of the world in the liberal, federalist mould of her own self-image. And France, after twenty years of decline as a Great Power, torn apart internally, having been dependent on the Anglo-American alliance for her foreign policy since the postwar days of Clemenceau, defeated and occupied, counted for little in the perceptions of the United States as to the real content of the problems facing the Allies in the early days of the Second World War.

In his position as leader of the Free French during the war, de Gaulle was in a cleft stick. If he was placating, he would be lost in the scuffle. If unyielding and arrogant, he would be resented and resisted. This anomalous position was to colour the mutual perceptions of the three allies not only during the war, but through reconstruction, parts of the Fourth Republic period, and the entire Fifth Republic. Few would have the forbearance of Churchill:

certainly I had continuous difficulties and many sharp antagonisms with him. . . I knew he was no friend of England. But I always recognised in him the spirit and conception which, across the pages of history, the word 'France' would ever proclaim. I understood and admired, while I resented, his arrogant demeanour. Here he was – a refugee, an exile from his country under sentence of death, in a position entirely dependent upon the goodwill of the British Government, and also now of the United States. The Germans had conquered his country. He had no real foothold anywhere. Never mind, he defied all. . .[11]

But although Churchill excused de Gaulle far more than, for example, did Roosevelt, he was no more disposed to let de Gaulle seriously modify British governmental priorities or to allow him any real say in the overall conduct of the war.

In the second place, it is a fundamental psychological principle that the closer two or more persons or groups are in spatial and temporal proximity, the more their mutual perceptions are attuned to discern faults which, at a distance, might otherwise seem inconsequential. Murders generally occur within the family group; Freudian psychoanalysis puts primary emphasis on relationships with parents in one's early years; and 'good fences make good neighbours'. Indeed, the threat of American and British hegemony was a closer and thus a more clearly perceived threat to de Gaulle's objectives for France, while his obstinacy and arrogance were more closely perceived threats to the Atlantic vision of a world order than even the enemy at times. This was particularly true during the Fifth Republic, when Gaullist policies were frequently thought by Anglo-American commentators to be more disruptive of the world order than Soviet or Chinese policies, as these appeared more and more to be satisfied rather than revolutionary powers. Similarly, de Gaulle used his opening to the East as a means of putting pressure on his Western Allies. In seeking to find explanations for undesirable developments, in a period of stress, contradictions in de Gaulle's personality (contradictions which could plausibly explain why France was both a close ally and a significant threat) were used to reconcile, to explain away, contradictions which were inherent in the structure of the international situation itself. De Gaulle's willingness to question openly the presuppositions of American and British policy merely reinforced these tendencies.

But if the operational environment of de Gaulle's international action served to emphasise idiosyncratic variables, his own psychological environment not only conformed to this situation, but even posited individual factors as being primordial.[12] We shall deal with the more explicit and articulated aspects of this phenomenon when we deal with his theory of leadership in Chapter 3. However, there are three characteristics of de Gaulle's personality which, in a more implicit fashion, demonstrate the way in which idiosyncratic factors influenced his own political behaviour.

De Gaulle's personality can be characterised as self-contained and self-sufficient, eclectic and teleological or goal-oriented.

The first of these tended to be expressed in solitude, or rather, solitariness, and in the maintenance of a manufactured, calculated public personage. He was preoccupied with the idea of solitude and pensive and thoughtful even in his youth; members of his family found him difficult to understand. He kept his private thoughts to himself, except when he sought to express them in a rather didactic literary form.

At Saint-Cyr, the officers' training college, he was described as acting like 'a king in exile'. The chaplain of his division in the last months before the fall of France in 1940 found his profound isolation from his subordinates mystifying, and asked him directly why he was always alone. De Gaulle's reply echoes his inner being:

Solitude, silence, reflection – you know better than I do – without them what would words be, what would they do, even the words of God...? All those who have done something valuable and durable have been solitary and silent people.[13]

Many of his most important initiatives, though long pondered in his mind, have seemed to others to have come merely out of the blue – his flight to London in 1940, his two retirements in 1946 and 1969, his vetoes of British admission to the Common Market, his decision to withdraw from NATO in 1966, and his flight to Baden-Baden and triumphant return on 29 and 30 May 1968.[14] This solitariness has caused misunderstandings, and the apparent suddenness of certain privately nurtured decisions has reinforced others' impressions of his arrogance, petulance and whimsicality, not only in the eyes of his opponents, but also in the view of supporters who have, in some circumstance or other, found themselves on the receiving end.

This capacity for introspection was complemented by his carefully maintained public image. His private life was always scrupulously free from exposure, publicity or scandal. Only because of his strict insistence on privacy and his complete separation of his public – and visible – life from his personal and private affairs, was this possible. The private side of his personality can best be illustrated by reference, first, to his country house, La Boisserie, in the village of Colombey-les-deux-Eglises, where he loved to take long walks and where empty countryside stretched as far as the eye could see; and, secondly, to his retarded daughter, Anne, upon whom he doted – when he was in the Army, he drove miles secretly every night to put her to bed himself (his voice was the only thing that animated her) – and next to whose grave he insisted on placing his own.

Robert Aron has claimed that de Gaulle wished to retire as early as

September 1944 in order not to destroy his image, which he saw as important in itself; he is reported to have said:

As for me, I shall retire...It is necessary to disappear. France may again have need of a pure image. I must leave her that image. If Joan of Arc had married, she would no longer be Joan of Arc. It is necessary to disappear.[15]

De Gaulle's choice of words continually demonstrates 'an obvious solicitude for theatrical artifice'.[16] One of the most influential journalistic books on the Gaullist regime is dedicated entirely to the rituals of de Gaulle's and his followers' public lives.[17] And nearly every book on de Gaulle quotes his own words on the subject, as reported in an interview with David Schoenbrun, which recounts the day of his

discovery that there was a person named de Gaulle who existed in other people's minds and was really a separate personality from myself...From that day on I knew I would have to reckon with this man, this General de Gaulle. I became almost his prisoner. Before I made a speech or reached a major decision I had to ask myself, 'Will de Gaulle approve of this? Is this the way people expect de Gaulle to act? Is this right for de Gaulle and the role he plays?' There were many things I would have liked to do but could not, for they would not have been fitting for General de Gaulle.[18]

This extreme level of detachment would seem to approach a kind of calculated public schizophrenia. Certainly it was calculated, but it also became second nature to de Gaulle, an internalised characteristic of his personality structure. But although he may have seen his public *persona* as a *sine qua non*, he also often felt it as an intolerable burden.[19]

Alongside the introspective and calculated features of his personality was his eclecticism. The range of phenomena towards which he directed his attention was very wide. In the best light, he was something of a Renaissance man; in a less favourable light, he was a dilettante. He is reported as a youth to have preferred the works of Saint Augustine, Pascal and Charles Péguy.[20] This classical emphasis is reflected in his speeches. Among the works which he quotes most often is Goethe's *Faust*, whose hero's fall and later triumph represents the resurgence of traditional concepts of human nature and classical ontology.[21] Another side of his philosophical formation is the influence of the idea of intuition as the only source of knowledge, in the tradition of Descartes, but more immediately in the teaching of Bergson.[22] This cultural background can be seen in his family environment.

The Hoffmanns describe his 'rich and harmonious (*non-conflicted*) cultural legacy', provided by his family, as having three characteristics: inner-directedness; public values; and a 'deep sense of distress about the present'.[23] This background was, of course, very conducive to a taste for history and politics, for his father was a prominent *lycée* professor and an ardent monarchist. In de Gaulle's words, 'My father was a thoughtful, cultivated, traditional man, imbued with a feeling for the dignity of France. He made me aware of her history.' His mother he described as having 'an uncompromising passion for her country, equal to her religious piety'.[24] As the Hoffmanns have pointed out, his entire upbringing, at home and at school, like the French classical tradition and culture, was imbued with the Greek ideal of 'the self-sufficient, self-controlled, and sovereign personality, who controls events, so to speak, from within by force of character'. Thus he sought solutions to his inner tensions by '*transcending* the legacy' which he had received.[25]

And tensions there were in those early years which marked his whole development. For example, the Dreyfus Affair broke during de Gaulle's youth, and although his father remained a monarchist, both he and his sons were appalled at the way truth was twisted by Dreyfus's opponents; they believed in his innocence. While his parents remained staunchly royalist, however, de Gaulle's own attitude towards the monarchy remained ambiguous. One author claims that he was potentially receptive to the restoration of the monarchy on suitable terms as late as 1940.[26] However, another biographer mentions that his family considered him to be a republican as early as secondary school.[27] In any case, this inner tension about the monarchy was resolved, for de Gaulle, by the institution of the presidency. Indeed, de Gaulle characteristically projected his own tensions into goal-directed activity in the outside world. He externalised his actions in order to escape and to transcend those aspects of his family horizons which he found stifling.[28]

From the cultural legacy of his family also came de Gaulle's passion for history. He saw history in every aspect of France, and his life was dedicated to leaving a worthy mark upon history. J.-R. Tournoux provides a rich description of how history and culture were intertwined in the family setting.

At the table there was often discussion on the comparative merits of Caesar and Pompey, on the plays of Racine, Molière and Corneille, on honour and passion. Racine, alas, gave undue importance to passion, while Molière was much too ready to sacrifice virtue; his comedies illustrated baser humanity. So all votes went to Corneille, whose heroes triumphed over the obstacles with which destiny confronted them. 'Remember what Napoleon said,' Henri de Gaulle would tell his sons: 'If Pierre Corneille were alive today, I would make him a prince.'[29]

Regular visits to national monuments were important occasions. Quotations from de Gaulle about lessons of history, or about historical associations, were imbued with a classical notion of the importance of virtue in the doing of great things which build upon each other in creating what is valuable in life; here is the true source of de Gaulle's conception of greatness. Such descriptions abound, but they are exemplified by his description of his thoughts during his triumphal procession down the Champs-Elysées after the liberation of Paris in 1944.

Here, in its turn, was the Louvre, where the succession of kings had also succeeded in building France; on their mounts, the statues of Joan of Arc and of Henri IV; the Palace of Saint-Louis, whose anniversary had occurred the day before; Notre-Dame, the prayer of Paris, and the Ile de la Cité, her cradle. History, gathered in these stones and in these places, seemed to be smiling upon us.

And warning us as well. This same Cité was once Lutèce, subjugated by Caesar's legions, then Paris, which only Geneviève's prayer had been able to save from Attila's fire and sword. Saint Louis, his crusade abandoned, died on the sands of Africa. At the Porte Saint-Honoré, Joan of Arc was repulsed by the city she had just restored to France. Only nearby, Henri IV fell a victim to fanatic hatred. The Revolt of the Barricades, Saint Bartholemew's Massacre, the outrages of the Fronde and the furious torrent of August 10 all bloodied the walls of the Louvre. At the Place de la Concorde the heads of the King and Queen of France rolled on the ground. The Tuileries were to see the destruction of the old monarchy, the exile of Charles X and of Louis-Philippe, the despair of the Empress, and were finally put to the torch, like the old Hôtel de Ville. How often the Palais-Bourbon was the scene of the most disastrous confusions! Four times within two lifetimes the Champs-Elysées was to submit to the outrage of invaders parading in time to their own odious fanfares. Paris, this afternoon, if it gleamed with all the greatness of France, took lessons from its terrible days.[30]

Tournoux informs us of de Gaulle's interest in the ideas of Jacob Burckhardt – history as 'the history of the mind', through the heritage of Greece, Rome and Christianity, expressed through intellectual and artistic joys, spiritual and moral inspiration. But this essentially spiritual heritage was seen as being menaced by 'progress' – industrialisation, haste, thirst for money, centralisation of great states and general levelling. 'But', said de Gaulle of Burckhardt, 'his faith in the life of the spirit preserved him from a hopeless pessimism.'[31]

For de Gaulle, such history is essentially the history of the nation. His belief in the nation was not merely a pedagogical instrument, but 'an essential and deeply ingrained part of his personality and view of the world'.[32] Even his religion was subordinate. Despite de Gaulle's assiduous practice of Catholicism, Emmanuel d'Astier de la Vigerie was convinced that he was fundamentally a monist or pantheist, for whom religion was an external ritual; faith was itself the social order, a Catholic-based morality.[33]

Although we have no way of proving of what de Gaulle's religious faith consisted, it was for him an inseparable component of the sweep of history. As Robert Aron has observed, de Gaulle saw moral or historical truth in everything; no facts were neutral, and their significance for him was 'often more true than the objective truth of the facts themselves'.[34] Charles Morazé derides the type of history which he feels that the General has studied – a history cut off from lessons and deforming facts, ignoring progress and resulting simply from anecdotes and events which can be interpreted as you like.[35] And, given de Gaulle's belief in the inseparability of sentiment and reason,[36] analysed through the social scientist's healthy scepticism of value-free 'facts' and a belief in the psychological primacy of emotional predispositions,[37] we find the source of de Gaulle's concern for greatness. Grandeur is the accolade of history, and history is a moral and cultural epic. It is his role as an historical personality which dominates his self-image.

This self-image moulded his practical experience. He underwent no further profound psychological change, with the possible exception of the weariness of power and disillusionment with political action itself. During his army career, for example, he continually saw military problems as an extension of philosophical and political problems, a perspective which underlay the practical conclusions which he drew about various subjects treated in his books: the overambitiousness of the German military leaders in the First World War;[38] the nature and art of leadership;[39] the role of the Army in the development of the French nation;[40] or the need to create new military elites and to give them better weapons.[41] In the politically effervescent Paris of the 1930s, de Gaulle frequented the discussion circles of many political societies. Though he is often called a Maurrassian partly because of his attendance at the Cercle Fustel de Coulanges, he underwent many differing political influences and had an evident taste for socialist ideas.[42] When he was finally able to approach the Government directly about his ideas on tank warfare, it was to the Popular Front Prime Minister Léon Blum that he looked. Self-contained, seeking to live up to the values imbued in him through his family background by projecting them into political activity, and eclectic in his search for truth, de Gaulle sought goals which would synthesise his experience and action in an historically significant way.

Thus the teleological side of de Gaulle's personality is in a sense an expression of all the rest. It concerns output rather than input. Power, as political scientists tend to agree nowadays, is fundamentally an instrumental variable; it is not an end in itself, though it may become so. And power was least of all an end in itself for de Gaulle. He quotes a letter which President Roosevelt wrote to a Congressman after de Gaulle's July 1944 visit to the United States: 'In relation to future problems he seems quite "tractable" from the moment France is dealt with as a world power. He is very touchy in matters concerning the honor of France. But I suspect that he is essentially an egoist.' De Gaulle comments: 'I was never to know if Franklin Roosevelt thought that in affairs concerning France Charles de Gaulle was an egoist for France or for himself.'[43] If there was any egoism in de Gaulle, he certainly saw it as being for France, not for himself. To left-wing Gaullist Pierre Billotte, the debate about power is false; the true debate is about greatness. 'Greatness is will,' declares Billotte. It involves a need to look outward and not to be consumed in internal quarrels.[44] De Gaulle was pursuing his 'certain image of France', and where a conflict occurred between his own prestige and his conception of the national interest, the latter was always first. Of course, his political action was intended to put the former at the service of the latter in a strategically efficient way.

His early socialisation, as we have seen, was toward monarchism – classical monarchism which saw the king as the only individual whose personal interest was bound up inextricably in the interest of the whole community and not of just a part.[45] But while he accepted the substantive goals associated with this view of monarchism – leadership, continuity, and the need for an embodiment of the collective good – he rejected the actual structure of monarchism as the best or most appropriate means to those ends, and placed greater faith in democracy as an essential part of the process of creating national unity. Popular participation and consultation were an increasingly significant part of his political perspective. On the other hand, his well-developed views on the nature of leadership stressed the manipulation of opportunities and circumstances as the means to his ends. And without a permanent set of long-term objectives, any such manipulation would turn in upon itself and founder in contradiction. Effective action was impossible without thoroughly understood and well-defined goals. In this, his intuitionism was closer to Descartes than to Bergson, but, ultimately, it was probably closer to the classical conception of reason and natural law than to either. 'De Gaulle interests me only as an historical personality', he is reported to have said. His intention was to outmanoeuvre time constraints by understanding the malleability of circumstances and therefore transcending them. The only significant action was that which developed over time in the desired direction, and the only valid judgment was the judgment of future historians. Criticisms levelled at his immediate actions concerned him little.

The teleological side of de Gaulle's character was important for the development of French foreign policy. Foreign policy dynamism, as Joseph Frankel has observed, is often determined by the relationship between the different aspects of foreign policy purpose – the level of aspirations and the content of policy. If the aspirations are either too high or too low for the extant operational conditions, dynamism suffers.[46] Now the simple belief in the nation-state as the fundamental frame of reference for setting policy aspirations says little about what substantive or normative values are to be associated with the nation-state; it is fundamentally a geographical frame of reference, and needs the injection of specific substantive content before it can become an ideology. And these values may have deep internal significance not only for the leader, who may conceive them, 'in all sincerity, as the true goal of action',[47] but also for his followers. Goals are themselves symbols which form part of a rich and immediate experience which can never be captured by cold analysis.[48] Precisely because de Gaulle was a political actor and not a political philosopher – that is to say, he sought to realise his goals through his own action and not merely by changing the minds of other actors – then his own aspirations must be examined at face value when assessing their significance for policy-making and execution.

His goals in the foreign policy field (like his domestic goals) were all the more significant because of their scope. To borrow Wolfers's distinction, they were primarily 'milieu' goals and only secondarily 'possession' goals.[49] Gaullist foreign policy analyst Jacques Vernant distinguishes between policy as 'a simple matter of day-to-day adaptation to an international situation which does not raise any major problems' and policy as 'the global behaviour of the state toward an external environment which poses grave problems and which one seeks to modify in a favourable direction by means of a systematic and continuous course of action'.[50] De Gaulle's policy fell into the second category. As Machiavelli observed, 'There is nothing more difficult to carry out, nor more doubtful of success, nor more dangerous to handle, than to initiate a new order of things.'[51] In de Gaulle's case, aspiration and operation are inextricably intertwined, and the dynamism attributed by even the most hostile critic of de Gaulle to his foreign policy indicates that they were not out of proportion to each other. Whether one agrees or disagrees with de Gaulle, it is nonetheless true that his personality, in all its complexity, is stamped on his policy; and 'No policy is better. . .than the goals it sets itself.'[52]

II. The cultural environment of Gaullist ideology

Many of the cues which de Gaulle received and internalised from his environment, and which were relevant to his choice of goals, un-doubtedly derived from aspects of the French cultural tradition and from culture in the wider sense employed by social anthropologists. His view of history, for example, is to a large degree a received one, although his intensive exposure to it from his father may have abnormally intensified the experience. Indeed, de Gaulle seemed to exhibit a desire to synthesise the various strands of that tradition accord-ing to his own interpretation of the right relationship of its contrasting and even contradictory elements. However, de Gaulle's cultural percep-tion is one which has consequences for the cultural output of Gaullist ideology as well as its cultural input.

Clearly his use of cultural symbolism *via* broadcasting, extensive travelling and the use of other contemporary methods and media of communication between political leadership and public response was a significant element in creating his relationship with social forces generally. The symbolism which he used reflected some sort of com-munity of perception, and the patterns which were thereby manifested are crucial to our understanding of the role of Gaullist ideology as a political tool. In this way we can ask whether Gaullism is a purely conjunctural phenomenon, linked to one man only and therefore both unique (non-comparable) and due to disappear when that man dis-appears, or whether it is a phenomenon more firmly rooted in processes of social and cultural development in France. More precisely, is Gaullism 'destined to overturn the traditional panorama of French political ideologies, that classical division which, since first posited by Thibaudet, categorised the political ideas of France into half a dozen spiritual families or clearly distinct currents of thought'?[53] Could de Gaulle really hope to eradicate 'the contrast between the agitation that sometimes disturbs the surface of France and the reasoned calm of the nation's depths'?[54]

De Gaulle 'appears as the synthesizer of French traditions'.[55] His own viewpoint, here expressed in the opening passage of his *Memoirs of Hope*, the unfinished trilogy which he projected to deal with his years as President of the Republic, constantly emphasises the unity, rather than the diversity, of the French political–cultural heritage:

> France arose out of the depths of the ages. She lives. The centuries call her. But she remains herself all through the long passage of time. Her limits can change without changing her features, her climate, her rivers, her seas, which have marked her for an indefinite time. Peoples live there which have undergone in the course of History the most diverse trials, but which have been drawn ceaselessly by the nature of things, utilised by politics, into one sole nation...she is invested with a constant character which makes the French of each epoch dependent upon their fathers and engages them toward their descendants.[56]

As Edward Kolodziej has observed, de Gaulle applied to France that distinction between Rome and the Romans which was part of the cultural tradition of the Roman Empire: 'Rome was eternal; only Romans lived and died. Men earned a transcendent worth in service to Rome – the eternal city.'[57]

To de Gaulle, the foundation of this transcendent unity is geographical.[58] This raises the question of the relationship of the geographical and the political. For de Gaulle, geography creates certain necessary conditions of unity; it provides certain background conditions or givens which may be more or less conducive to a certain range of political responses. More specifically, the geographical conditions relevant to French development favour a certain kind of balanced harmony.[59] These conditions, however, are neither self-evident nor sufficient for the realisation of the end to which they are suited; they must be 'utilised by politics', i.e. by the conscious action of people in society.

It is well known that de Gaulle blamed the French people for their insensitivity to the natural harmony he perceived. He often spoke of them, in his blacker moods, as '*des veaux*'.[60] This same distrust appears on the opening page of the *War Memoirs*: 'If, in spite of this [underlying potential for greatness], mediocrity shows in her acts and deeds, it strikes me as an absurd anomaly, to be imputed to the faults of Frenchmen, not to the genius of the land.' This distrust derives from his view of France's historical development; French faults can be avoided, if politics is utilised correctly. However, this has not been done in the past.

The French political tradition, to de Gaulle, is schizophrenic. He accuses the French of using too much 'intelligence', and not enough 'instinct'.[61] They cannot match words with actions.

This Frenchman, so orderly in mind and disorderly in action, a logician who doubts everything, solemn but frivolous, a stay-at-home who settles in colonies, an ardent formalist and lover of pomp who can yet sing lustily and 'let himself go', a Jacobin who shouts 'Long Live the Emperor', a soldier defeated at Charleroi who can still attack on the Marne – in short this people so changeable, uncertain, contradictory...[62]

This defect stems from the lack of a unifying vision, a lack of symbols which can bridge this gap between ideals and action, a belief noted by André Malraux in his conversations with de Gaulle after his defeat in 1969.

The General knows (one must go further: he violently resents) that the agony of France does not stem from the weakness of the grounds for believing in her – defeat, demography, second-rate industry, etc. – but from the *powerlessness to believe* in anything.[63]

It is de Gaulle's stress on unifying symbols which has created the base for his political support. André Fontaine has referred to the significance of de Gaulle's association of the defence of the nation with 'the accomplishment of its historic mission', thus allowing it to take on 'an essentially moral and civilising character' and reflecting 'the general interest of all men'.[64] Indeed, this theme is taken up in the statement of the aims of the Gaullist party as set out in 1965:

What, essentially, is Gaullism composed of? Of the combination of *national sentiment* and the *French humanist tradition*, of the *desire for progress* and the conviction that it would not be possible without a strong state, nor would it be desirable unless it were to serve mankind...Gaullism, the modern form of patriotism and democracy, is, in its essence, the affirmation that a certain idea of France has always shaped our destiny.[65]

Thus de Gaulle's ideology does not set out simply to create a set of new symbols. Rather, he seeks to manipulate existing cultural trends in such a way as to create new perceptions of existing symbols.

Such an approach ought to dovetail with certain features of French culture noted by historical, sociological and anthropological observers. Alongside de Gaulle's accusation of too much 'intelligence', we find Curtius describing the French as having a 'juridical spirit'.[66] In the Frenchman's eternal search for the right phrase to express his national character, we find him described as 'particularly self-conscious', lacking in self-confidence, and uncertain about himself and his fellows; 'Perhaps it represents a search for some sort of identity.'[67] These characteristics

reflect French culture's preoccupation with the essential and its emphasis on underlying truths which must be communicated; the real search
is for the right form of words to communicate these truths to those
whose perception of them is lacking or distorted.

Métraux and Mead's description of the way children are socialised
into this way of thinking demonstrates the way it works:

Implicit in such statements is the belief that individuality consists in the development of new variations on old designs. And so, in order to become an individual,
the child must learn the design, must make it his own. In this sense, standards
are not, in the first instance, personal, but exist in the external world and are
learned by approximation; once assimilated, they provide the means for and the
measure of individual self-expression. Congruent with this is the expectation that
the most complex and personally stated idea is communicable if it can be related
logically to the traditional and the known.[68]

However, the underlying truths can only be intuited, not objectively
known. Therefore the process of learning, understanding and expressing these truths requires a merging of presuppositions which are
essentially aesthetic, with a process of thought which is essentially
rational; Descartes's idea of truth is the highest expression of this way
of thinking. Laurence Wylie's description of educational values demonstrates this:

French children are taught that France is a geometrical form. Although they
know that it is not actually a hexagon, they learn to think of their country in this
way. They are taught that history is the rational unfolding of the personality of
France as a nation. It is expected that the individual child will grow up in the
same rational manner, step by step, developing a distinct personality but at the
same time fitting neatly into the rational scheme of society. The traditional
French garden is one in which man has imposed rational forms on nature. The
value, then, for which man should strive in society is the rational organisation of
that society. Good government, like the balanced individual, the strong family,
the attractive garden, is one which is rationally organised.[69]

Such a cultural structure can easily act as an obstacle to social change.
As Wylie points out, the classification of observable units of existence
into well-defined compartments results in a proliferation of labels; the
result, all too often, is that the elaborate symbolism embodied in such
a complex structure comes to stand for the things themselves. External
signs take on more importance than the facts or theories which they are
meant to describe.[70]

These symbols, however, also embody a potential for social and
political change. On one level, different intuitions, leading to different
rational superstructures, can create cognitive dissonance and lead to a

broad questioning of the very foundations of society. Such is the basis of the French ideological tradition, with its dialectic of revolution and reaction. But at another level, these symbols, if manipulated in the synthesising fashion attempted by de Gaulle – particularly the macro-symbols relating to national membership and identity – may potentially act as levers for the particular kind of social change he had in mind, in particular, by strengthening bonds of national sentiment and loyalty to the political association itself, and by giving legitimacy to a new authority structure.

Such a course of action is congruent with a related aspect of French culture – the individual's selfless quest to realise the values inherent in the symbols he represents – which Jesse Pitts identifies as a major cultural source of personal motivation. This is the search for prowess. Distinct from the cruder self-glorification of *machismo*, the French concern for *prouesse* derives from the primacy of underlying truths: 'Prowess is above all the discovery of the predetermined harmony, rather than the imposition of a personal will.'[71] This is a subtle blend; the individual achieves greatness by transcending his individuality through attachment to higher principles. Pitts describes the quality of prowess in more detail. Not concerned with utility, for either the individual or the community, it involves the performance of a 'note-worthy act of valour', done in a spontaneous and unpredictable way: 'it is not a tormented surmounting of oneself, but rather the discovery and demonstration of a harmony between the self and the environment in the service of the divine'. Founded on values derived from the Church, or the traditions of the nation-state, prowess 'consists in the application of these *principes* to particular situations that result in elegant solutions where the immutability of principles, their sacred character, and the talent (grace) of the individual are clearly revealed'. In principle, prowess is available to anyone with deep enough roots in the milieu in which he is acting, for it is not a generalisable but a miraculous solution. And finally, the act 'is validated in his [the actor's] own eyes when the spectator to it acknowledges the irresistible appeal of both the man and the deed'; the recognition of greatness is evoked through the shared values of actor and spectator.[72]

It is within the cultural context of prowess that de Gaulle's pursuit of the greatness of France – the psychological externalisation of the values internalised through his family – takes on political form and social meaning. The individual transcends himself through the pursuit of underlying principles and goals, principles which have a higher moral value and which embody 'the nature of things'. Furthermore, de Gaulle's style closely resembles Pitts's description; the General's observations on the nature of leadership, along with his own cultivation of a style of political action – especially its calculated psychodramatic effects – seem designed to maximise the 'pure image' of prowess on his part (see Chapter 3). And finally, his reactions to public opinion, and indeed his conception of democracy, would seem to place the voter in the role of Pitts's spectator rather than in its traditional context of the 'rational man'. De Gaulle thought his public role futile once his 'contract' with the people was broken; he could have continued to govern after his defeat in the 1969 referendum, but it took away his ability to *faire des prouesses* any longer.

On the other hand, prowess is a concept which involves inherent limitations on objectives, limitations of social solidarity and *mesure*. *Mesure*, a word which de Gaulle also emphasises, is an intrinsic component of French classical thought, 'derived from the Greek idea that the unforgivable sin was defying the natural order according to which each man must keep to his proper place and function'. Thus acts of prowess must not damage the fabric of society; in a stable society, their spontaneity and unpredictability must be restricted to carefully circumscribed situations.[73] But de Gaulle considered the French social order to exhibit glaring weaknesses which prevented the real, true France – the underlying harmony – from realising her potential; this theme runs throughout his entire work. Only 'vast enterprises' will allow her to transcend the mediocrity imposed on her by her social fragmentation, a mediocrity which had led to disaster in two world wars.

Therefore de Gaulle's belief that the order itself was faulted led him to attempt the highest form of prowess of all – the salvation of the state itself and the regeneration of the social order according to underlying natural principles. Prowess of this magnitude was not contrary to, but necessary for, the upholding of *mesure*, for without a regenerated France *mesure* had become simply an excuse for mediocrity. De Gaulle's conception of the necessary acts of prowess involved not allowing these acts to be circumscribed by the *positions acquises* or the vested interests of a 'relatively stable society'; rather, they had to be inspired by goals which he believed to be necessary to restore, and to stabilise, the already damaged fabric of society itself.

Certain key features of French society, furthermore, actually reinforced this approach. French nationality, for example, has always been infused with a cultural sense of insecurity which has called for a conscious effort of justification and legitimation over the centuries. Curtius notes the 'secondary character of French civilisation'.[74] In comparison with the cultural roots and ideals inherent in French civilisation's self-perceived antecedents, Greece and Rome, French culture is both late and derivative. Because of its internal social conflicts, France has never spontaneously conformed to the standards left by the ancient Hebrews and Greeks, who, as Hans Kohn has observed, developed a group consciousness, a separate identity embodied in the whole people, not in the king, the priesthood, or the extent of empire.[75]

This cultural inferiority complex has been exhibited in numerous ways. Curtius speaks of the continuing tendency to *personify* France in cultural terms, to compensate for fragmentation by the use of elaborate and abstract literary images. De Gaulle's references to the 'legendary princess' and the 'Madonna of the frescoes'[76] echo that aesthetic perception of underlying principles upon which the superstructure of French rationality is overlaid. Politics, too, is full of symbolism, deliberately constructed, as in the case of Louis XIV, in order to counter the insecurity and uncertainty of the monarchy or the political system.[77] Even the revolutionary tradition conforms to this pattern. And much everyday political activity in France is organised around and immersed in symbolism. In fact, the different symbols used by political parties under the Third and Fourth Republics when appealing for votes performed a distinct cultural role from those same symbols employed in the parliamentary arena, which was characterised by personal factionalism and coalitional conservatism.[78] The importance of the Bourbon flag for the Comte de Chambord, the significance of the concept of 'Republicanism', the imagery attached to the notion of the Left, all of these are merely examples of the symbolic ideological apparatus which has composed the very elaborate façade of French political life.

Another manifestation of French socio-cultural insecurity is the aversion to the role of *demandeur*. The traditions of French diplomacy emphasise the need for correctness and the belief that to acknowledge a subordinate role will inevitably be counterproductive in the long run. Indeed, almost paradoxically, it is this very inferiority complex which leads to its most often observed characteristic – in an almost Freudian way – to what Kulski calls the 'cultural superiority complex' of the French,[79] while Alfred Grosser speaks of 'Francocentrism', 'cultural nationalism' and 'cultural imperialism'.[80] This is the tendency, visible in French political and diplomatic history, not only to consider French culture superior to others, but also to believe that it should be 'shared by intellectuals of other nationalities so as to raise the cultural level of all Europe'.[81] But, as Znaniecki observes, this mission was only success-ful so long as it was peaceful; when the French attempted to impose their culture, as in the case of Napoleon, the defensive reaction evoked in the Germans and Spanish, in particular, 'stimulated their solidarity against the French'. The peaceful assertion of the French cultural 'vocation' was indeed a significant feature of Gaullist ideology, especi-ally in the stated aims of Gaullist policies concerning the Third World.[82]

Much of the French obsession with education too, can be linked with this persistent felt need to legitimise and justify the social bond. The notion of *civisme* – and the fear of its ever-present enemy, *anti-civisme* – is consciously taught rather than taken for granted. A unique ingredient in French nationalism, according to Kohn, was a Rous-seauean collective personality, based on the general will, and involving public education, active participation, brotherhood and equality. Un-like organicist nationalism, French nationalism has been a nationalism of citizenship, a conscious and conventional construction, in contrast with the metaphysical will or inherent racial consciousness of other nationalist ideologies. It is Renan's 'daily plebiscite', in which indi-vidual will and collective will were symbiotic, not contradictory.[83]

Thus the French inheritance distinguishes the abstract unity of the nation-state from the faults of the actual political system. Pitts distin-guishes between the imperatives evoked by the 'role of the mother-land', which calls forth heroic sacrifice, and the 'role of the state', which calls forth a dualistic reaction, involving, on the one hand, doctrinaire and hierarchical elements (such as duty and obedience), and, on the other, the image of the state as 'delinquent' (the *République des camarades*). Thus the state in the abstract is the good authority, while the government is composed of fools and swindlers and must be checkmated. This analysis reflects a deeper cultural ambivalence to be found in the domestic relationships within the French bourgeois family, which is at once doctrinaire and hierarchical yet expects its members to take part in clandestine delinquent behaviour as an essential part of the wider socialisation process.[84] This ambivalence appears also in civic instruction in French schools, as Greenstein and Tarrow observe:

The emphasis in French schools on nationalism, combined with the lack of emphasis on the actual functioning of the political system, is interesting in that it may lead French children to identify with an abstract entity called 'the State', but to have very little sense of obligation to national governments.[85]

French culture, then, imposes an ideological superstructure of nationalism and *étatisme* on a substructure with often widely deviant standards of behaviour. The value of symbolism is pitched at a very high level, and the French conception of France's mission or vocation takes on a cultural function akin to that played by the Constitution in American political culture or the monarchy in Britain. The difference is that French nationalist and *étatiste* norms are not so much 'dignified' components of the political system, but are much closer to being day-to-day operative ideals. This is especially true for de Gaulle, who eschewed the delinquency and pursued the doctrine.

Such assumptions are found throughout French life and culture. They have been significant in all of the *familles d'esprit* of the French ideological spectrum, left and right, in such diverse perspectives as those of Michelet, Jaurès and Maurras, all of whom saw France as 'the pace-setter for the rest of the world'.[86] They have provided powerful normative determinants of foreign policy behaviour; Macridis attributes French reluctance to adapt to changing international conditions to the strength of this *idée fixe*.[87] The United States has been accused of harbouring a similar view of the world beyond her shores, but where America acted from a position of strength which was seen by many to precede and to justify the American role as vanguard of the 'free world', France tended to exhibit it just as strongly, perhaps even more strongly, at times of weakness: the period of *revanchisme* after 1871; in the Versailles negotiations and settlement following the First World War; and, in 1940, in both the Vichy regime and de Gaulle's Free France.

Furthermore, within this tradition, there was the persistent tension between the notion of the nation declining and dying, and the idea of the eternal nation always re-emerging. This was the tension between the France of Maurras and the France of Péguy, which, according to François Mauriac, was replicated in de Gaulle himself.[88] In this context, the pursuit of *grandes entreprises* becomes an act born of insecurity, and not of grandiose visions or of the desire for aggrandisement. It is a flexible notion, despite its fundamental rigidity; it is a form of justification, and thus it depends upon what has to be justified. French schoolbooks quickly adjusted to the loss of the Empire without losing the underlying tone of national justification.[89] And this classical sense of national *noblesse oblige* can be seen even in the traditional style of French diplomacy, with its classical concept of sovereignty and the diplomatic equality of nations, its emphasis on the elegance of language characterising negotiation and agreement (to which the French language is seen to be most highly suited), its connection with France's long administrative tradition and the feeling of assurance and presence which comes from it, making for hard bargaining when national interests are at stake.[90] These traits preceded de Gaulle, and will, no doubt, continue long after his disappearance.

It is important here to make one fundamental distinction. De Gaulle personified certain characteristic elements of French national culture which abstracted the idea of the unity of the nation, which symbolically expressed what could be called 'national sentiment' or 'national consciousness'. In the English usage, these factors are part and parcel of 'nationalism'.[91] However, as both Pierre Renouvin and Jean Touchard point out, the French word 'nationalism', rather than referring to 'national sentiment', concentrates almost wholly on 'the exaltation of that sentiment'.[92] What we are dealing with here is not nationalist *doctrine*, in the French sense of the word, but simply a cultural tradition (in the anthropological sense of 'culture'), a particular way of expressing the consciousness of common membership in the French nation through common habits of thought and patterns of behaviour.

However, if taken together, these cultural attributes create a pattern which, on the face of it, would seem to be rather conducive to the development of a particular kind of 'exaltation', seeking cultural hegemony rather than military or economic hegemony, the moral superiority of prowess rather than the cruder domination of *machismo*, and emphasising the significance of abstract symbolism in contrast to material capabilities and utilitarian objectives. With the major exception of Barrès's 'cult of the self',[93] we find French nationalism described by various words like 'timid', 'Malthusian', 'gallocentric', 'caring more for dignity than for power', and the like.[94] According to a quotation attributed to Talleyrand at the beginning of the Restoration, '*La France a cessé d'être grandiose, pour redevenir grande.*'[95]

Furthermore, French nationalism, as expressed in actual foreign policy behaviour, was orientated to consolidation, not expansion. Renouvin sums up this interpretation:

French nationalism before World War I was. . .not 'aggressive'. It wanted France's frontiers revised, of course, since it gave pride of place to the question of Alsace-Lorraine, but in the minds of all Frenchmen this was merely a restitution that corresponded to the wishes of the annexed populations. At no point did the nationalists' programme invoke the linguistic argument; it did not forget that German nationalism appealed to linguistic 'kinship' in regard to Alsace, whereas the French argued from the basis of the peoples' expressed preference. Finally, it was careful to avoid launching a radical 'revolutionary' programme, such as the Pan-German and Pan-Slav programmes. In a word, it was conservative.[96]

French civilisation was seen as a civilisation based on moral worth, not on military or economic power. This fundamental epistemological conservatism made its imprint on foreign policy and nationalist doctrine too.

De Gaulle's search for grandeur was also concerned above all with the moral content of the concept and did not seek to challenge, but to realise, the potential harmony which he saw in 'the nature of things'. If de Gaulle was influenced by Maurras, he did not go so far as to believe in the reactionary imperialism of *la France seule*; his ideas had more in common with eighteenth-century French universalism.[97] He saw the grandeur of France as a timeless, continuous process which must regularly be regenerated and brought into meaningful relation with the realities of the contemporary world. Alfred Grosser finds in him, on the one hand, a vision of the past, of 'Eternal France', characterised by a traditional style of diplomacy and military ethic, and a certain nostalgia; and, on the other, a vision of the future in a much changed world in which France, to be true to herself, must find a new and appropriate role. When taken together, these two visions create a vantage point which is beyond any pure and simple analysis of the present conjuncture and which puts the present into a long-range perspective.[98]

Maurice Couve de Murville, de Gaulle's long-time Foreign Minister and Prime Minister, expands and clarifies this perspective; Gaullist policy reaffirms

the elementary fact that the spirit, the feeling, the genius, and, all in all, the soul of our country draws it towards the level of the universal. Over the centuries its vocation has been to witness, to inspire; and its action, its influence, and its prestige have stemmed as much from this vocation as from its political or military undertakings, so that in the long run it cannot be measured by or equated with the victories and defeats or the glories and misfortunes which have beset its history. If there has grown up, according to the famous and now classic expression, a 'certain idea of France', it is indeed in this context that men have conceived it and in this form that it reappears with *éclat* whenever, following an eclipse or even a period of decadence, comes the renewal. Is this not what has most profoundly characterised the eleven years or so which Charles de Gaulle illuminated by his exceptional prestige, and which will remain engraved on the memory, if not in legend? I mean to say that this period has highlighted principles of which France has once again become the herald, principles which are indissolubly linked with each other, and which impose reason and sentiment upon our epoch more than ever. These principles are national independence, the primacy of peace, and cooperation among all peoples.[99]

It is characteristic of de Gaulle that he commented on the foreign policy of Bismarck: 'He knew when to stop.'[100] And François Mauriac emphasises 'that grandeur, or what he calls grandeur, must not be confused with material power or with technical success. If France, diminished as she is in 1964, is still great', thanks to de Gaulle, it is because the French people 'have within them a principle', a 'vocation', or as Mauriac, a Christian, prefers to call it, 'soul'.[101]

Thus de Gaulle's ideology and action reflect a number of cultural features drawn from French society. In seeking to realise, through his personal action, those underlying principles which reflect the predetermined harmony which characterises the geography, history and culture of France, he undertook to achieve acts of prowess which would reveal and renew those principles and those sentiments in the hearts and minds of the French people. Thus would the true greatness of France be revealed and regenerated through shared values which would act as a guide in the future. Externalising his personal tensions and values through the pursuit of these higher goals, he reflected the highest ideas of his milieu. This is the personal equation which led to his pursuit of grandeur.

The philosophical roots of Gaullism

Gaullist ideology was rooted in an ontological world view which derived much of its force from classical natural law doctrines. De Gaulle's writings and speeches provide a large body of evidence containing significant clues to this outlook. Not only does this body of evidence surpass in detail and precision the sorts of psychological evidence available, but it also allows us to explore the complex ramifications of the notion of grandeur as de Gaulle applied it to the political problems facing him as a political actor.

Central to natural law doctrines is the belief that human reason is not merely a psychological process of systematising extrinsic data in a rational manner, but also a means, if trained, of perceiving objective truth. For de Gaulle, reason and common sense allow man to transcend the constraints of ideologies and to understand the nature of things. Modern sociological and analytical writings about the nature of ethical choice are often based upon the epistemological assumption that the choice of ultimate values and goals is in itself not a rational choice, but one which must necessarily be based upon emotion, position in social arrangements, or mere opinion; in this frame of reference, only choices concerning means can be rational.

De Gaulle, in contrast, posits the belief that ethical choice is rational, in the sense of discovering the truth about reality through the use of right reason. Choice, for de Gaulle, ought to be guided by the perception of metaphysical patterns, and ought to involve the orientation of one's action to those patterns. 'For there is in human affairs a sort of obscure harmony by virtue of which the most diverse forms of activity carry the same imprint.'[1] Thus the use of reason allows one to perceive 'the conjunction of superior forces, which the Ancients called "Destiny", Bossuet "Providence" and Darwin "the law of the species", and which, above and beyond the will of men, presides over great events'.[2] This pattern emerges from a conscious development of knowledge of culture and history, and in turn involves a belief in the force of ideas in changing history. He writes:

The power of the mind implies a diversity which one does not find at all in the exclusive practice of one's occupation, for the same reason that one rarely has fun with one's family. The true school of command is therefore the general culture. Through it, thought is set in a position to be trained in an orderly manner, to discern in things the essential from the accessory, to perceive consequences and obstacles: in short, to raise itself to that degree where wider patterns [*ensembles*] appear from nuances *without having prejudged the questions* [my italics]. No illustrious captain has lacked a taste and feeling for the patrimony of the human mind. Behind the victories of Alexander, one always finds Aristotle.[3]

Furthermore, these ontological patterns are seen to manifest a clear substantive content. The natural law reveals itself in philosophy, but also has established the framework within which political action takes place and the goals towards which action is oriented. Originally, society and progress are often born of war, for 'the competition of efforts is the condition of life', and 'man, "limited by his nature", is "infinite in his desires". The world is thus full of opposing forces.'[4]

However, although war may provide the conditions for the birth of society and even civilisation, war cannot be defined by its original structure, or by its practices, for war itself is the embodiment of change and fluidity. Rather, it can only be defined by its goal. De Gaulle's view of the world, like his own approach to political action, is teleological. 'The action of war is invested with the character of contingency. The result it pursues is relative to the enemy. . .'[5] And the goals of war are determined by 'human wisdom'.[6]

The Greek philosopher stated that war is a creative force [*la guerre enfante*]. It is certainly true that its harsh light often puts into clear relief those necessities only previously dimly perceived, and that its devouring activity imposes certain achievements which peaceful epochs reject or delay.[7]

As he said to Georges Bidault in Moscow in 1944, 'War is a surgical operation, necessary to resolve a problem.' To Bidault's reply that the trouble was that war leaders (Louis XIV, Napoleon, Hitler) never knew when to stop, de Gaulle said: 'Bismarck, though, knew when to stop. He told himself in 1871, that Germany was saturated.'[8]

Thus war, or any use of force, must be justified by its objectives. It may have a certain utility, but it is never an end in itself.

Gentlemen, I ask you: is there any state in the world today which is making war for the pleasure of making war? Why do you want the French people to make war, to suffer from war, to fight, for anything except a political policy [*une politique*]?[9]

And war can hinder the pursuit of political objectives, too: 'As long as the knife is allowed to speak, we cannot talk politics.'[10] Therefore, although 'force is necessary to build a state, reciprocally the military effort has value only by virtue of a political policy'.[11] At the core of de Gaulle's view of action, then, is an emphasis on those political objectives which provide its *raison d'être*. He writes:

Often, in our history, our trials have made us greater. This time, too, we can rekindle the flame of our forefathers instead of crying over their ashes. 'It is in flowing towards the sea that the river is faithful to its source.'[12]

And, more specifically:

Alexander's victories were those of a civilisation. It was the barbarian's passionate hunger which caused the fall of the Roman Empire. There would have been no Arab invasion without the Koran, no crusades without the Gospels. The *ancien régime* in Europe rose against France when the Assembly proclaimed: 'Men are born free and equal by law.'[13]

This viewpoint on the use of force, which in an instrumental sense was so vital to de Gaulle's political action, is reflected in his choice of epigraph from Goethe's *Faust* placed at the beginning of the first chapter of *Le fil de l'épée*, which contains de Gaulle's famous 'hymn to force'. He quotes only the words: ''Tis writ, "In the beginning was the Word.". . .I write, "In the beginning was the deed."' (The French translation reads, 'In the beginning was the action.') This is an abbreviation of the passage in which Faust *rejects* higher metaphysical values, and would seem at first sight to imply de Gaulle's own rejection of such values in favour of a certain vitalism, a belief in activity for its own sake. The full quotation, which opens Faust's train of thought and leads to his compact with the devil, runs:

'Tis writ, 'In the beginning was the Word.'
I pause, to wonder what is here inferred.
The Word I cannot set supremely high:
A new translation I will try.
I read, if by the spirit I am taught,
This sense, 'In the beginning was the Thought.'
This opening I need to weigh again,
Or sense may suffer from a hasty pen.
Does thought create, and work, and rule the hour?
'Twere best: 'In the beginning was the Power.'
Yet, while the pen is urged with willing fingers,
A sense of doubt and hesitancy lingers.
The spirit comes to guide me in my need,
I write, 'In the beginning was the deed.'[14]

Here we find a condensation of a continuing epistemological argument, an argument still central to the concerns of philosophy, psychology, and the sociology of knowledge, as to the fundamental relationship between thought and action. If thought is primary, and action derivative, where does thought come from, and how does it lead to action? Can one start with deductive principles of thought, or is knowledge itself an inductive process which must stem from some action? In choosing this passage, de Gaulle seems to come down on the side of the latter. Yet this goes against what we have already had to say about the teleological nature of his ideological universe.

Goethe rescues us from this dilemma in part II of *Faust*, where his hero rejects the evil results of his previous hypothesis with the words: 'Only the master's word gives action weight, And what I framed in thought I will fulfil.'[15] De Gaulle must have been fully aware of Faust's later redemption, and his use of the epigraph would seem not to be without self-conscious irony: what the French already possessed were valid cultural principles (the word); what they lacked was the will to act upon them. In thus putting the cart before the horse, de Gaulle was seeking to restore a balanced harmony in a situation of severe dis-equilibrium, and the outward contradiction would seem to be a con-sciously heuristic one – a method typical of de Gaulle, who saw himself as an educator.

But if the natural world reveals its patterns through man's reason, and if it is ideas which lie at the heart of human actions, then those ideas must take a clear form. That form is the necessity for man to live in society, and, in turn, for that society effectively to seek to promote the common good. This may not be easy, for 'Nature does not move by leaps and bounds. A young tree must not grow in fits and starts.'[16] Rather, 'justice moves forward by slow steps, but [it will come] one day, without a shadow of a doubt. For if "it is necessary for there to be a sun", it is also necessary that there be a justice for the world and for France. Justice, then, will come.'[17]

It will not come through universal ideologies, however, for the 'banner of ideology covers only ambitions'.[18] Rather, it will come through the state, the unique characteristic of which is its ability to personify the whole community and not just one section of it; '. . .nothing effective and solid can be done without the renewal of the state. . .for that is where it is necessary to begin'.[19] All significant political action must start with the state, 'whose role and *raison d'être* is to serve the general interest'.[20]

De Gaulle's conception of this central idea, the 'general interest', can be seen in three ways. In the first place, it expresses a necessarily centripetal force against the centrifugal forces threatening the very existence of society. Thus the general interest is first of all survival. There is a need for a 'common hope' to avoid fragmentation.[21] The danger 'lies much less in edicts launched from ivory towers than in endless examination from which no decision emerges'.[22] Thus the total collapse of the French state in 1940 was the source of the evils of the Second World War. The greatness of France is not simply a search for glory, but rather a necessary factor if France is not to break up. This is the true meaning of the oft-quoted first page of the *War Memoirs*:

But the positive side of my mind also assures me that France is not really herself unless in the front rank; that only vast enterprises are capable of counter-balancing the ferments of dispersal which are inherent in her people; that our country, as it is, surrounded by the others, as they are, must aim high and hold itself straight, on pain of mortal danger. In short, to my mind, France cannot be France without greatness.[23]

In the second place, the general interest is the commonly shared sense of moral values held by the society, personified by the state – a 'common sense'[24] or 'collective harmony'.[25] Such a national sentiment is formed within the context of a particular nation-state, but it reveals character-istics which hold true for every nation. The history of France, for example, is unique, and its study reveals the essence of France. The genius of France is in her *idealism*, 'which from the beginning of time has been the second nature of France, which was and which remains the principal trait of her character and the essential element of her influence'.[26] And inextricably intertwined with this idealism is the juxtaposition of two quite different, but complementary, ideals – that of liberty, and that of classical civilisation.

In de Gaulle's view of the world as it is, the development of civilisa-tion has meant the gradual unfolding of ideals which have a particu-larly spiritual value, and which are coming more to represent the ideals not just of France, but of the world as a whole.

I will not be so presumptuous as to claim to explain here just how during the last two thousand years there has extended over the world the reign of those conceptions, those customs, and those laws which have given to it its soul and shape. You know better than anyone that thanks to those conceptions, customs and laws, and despite differences of language, of religion, of nationality, despite the battles of armies, the rivalry of policies, and the competition of production, a sort of common ideal, a similar notion of what the collectivity owes to each man and, reciprocally, of what each man owes to all the others, has imposed itself on the different peoples as they have evolved over time. At the base of our civilisation, there is the liberty of each person in his thoughts, his beliefs, his opinions, his work, and his leisure.[27]

Thus de Gaulle sees a process of convergence at work in the world, a convergence which is based upon values which are emerging from an unfolding process of historical development which reconciles progress with the underlying principles of the 'nature of things':

at the origin of every discovery and accomplishment there is the human mind, of course with increasing means at its disposal, but itself immutable in its nature and capacity...no advance is ever brought about upon a *tabula rasa*...renewal would be incompatible with renunciation, and, in short, ...progress is inextricably intertwined with tradition.[28]

Central to this development of civilisation is the growing realisation of the need for liberty. In 1943, the inevitable defeat of the Axis powers 'is the proof of the failure of that political, social and moral system, called totalitarianism, which claimed to purchase greatness at the price of liberty'.[29] In this evolutionary process, French civilisation is seen as the democratic civilisation *par excellence*, for it combines a long history of cultural evolution with liberty. For although democracy may give rise to murderous factions, it can also bring people together and make them more conscious of their moral community.[30] This is de Gaulle's notion of *rassemblement*, inherent in his political strategy throughout his career, in which democratic rituals are a concrete symbol of unity. Democracy becomes a kind of culturally rooted tacit consent, which can even exist, in France, prior to the establishment of specifically democratic institutional or participational processes; 'there is a pact twenty centuries old between the greatness of France and the liberty of the world',[31] for 'democracy is inextricably intertwined with the best understood interest of France'.[32]

Indeed, France combines the two factors which together make democracy not only desirable, but also necessary and fitted to her nature: a fruitful and spiritually necessary diversity, with all its creative tension; and a need for unity arising not only out of her exposed position but also from the collective creativity embodied in her classically based cultural heritage and the desire of the French to form a deeper community. The various 'spiritual families' which make up France have these attributes in common, as de Gaulle describes them:

these families respond to the tendencies of the mass of our fellow citizens. Faced with the trials of humanity, minds are provoked above all by care for social justice, by the generous lights which Christianity offers the world, by the desire to be free as far as individually possible, and by the cult of our living traditions. It is necessary, it must be added, to note that these different sources of sentiments and opinions are in no way exclusive and that each Frenchman, whichever way he leans, is more or less linked to the others.[33]

Democracy, then, is not so much a process by which people should be divided against themselves, but rather one by which creative diversity is brought together in a higher synthesis. This higher synthesis is at the heart of the notion of collective harmony. It requires two things: on the one hand, it is only by accepting the limits of classical *mesure* and reason that unbridled ambitions become 'reasonable national ambition'; on the other, it requires that the community as a whole be directed and channelled and inspired by the only conscious instrument for achieving this higher synthesis, the state. Classical measure without the state, and the active ideals it pursues, would be pure conservatism, totally passive. The state without classical measure, on the other hand, would be dangerous and menacing. But taken together, they reinforce harmony and cancel out each other's harmful effects.

The importance of *mesure* is the message of de Gaulle's first book, *La discorde chez l'ennemi*. During his time as a prisoner of the Germans in the First World War, he spent his time studying German military theory and practice, and the philosophy of Nietzsche.[34] His conclusion, which is not startling, is that the Nietzschean justification of the striving for personal power for its own sake (the philosophy of the Superman), when combined with the social conditions of late nineteenth-century Germany and the cult of national power which was the ideological driving force of German unification, partly created by Bismarck and partly succeeding him, had created in the German military mentality a dangerous equation. That equation was between the personal success of individual generals asserting their own ambition, and the higher national search for power and glory. There were, for example, none of the inherent limitations which we have seen in the notion of prowess. The ramifications of this ideology were dangerous both to the countries near Germany, who were targets for this self-justified aggressiveness, and to Germany itself, which would thereby be drawn farther and farther into a situation which she could not deal with. And as the situation became more and more overextended, the result would be more and more vain strivings, more and more indiscipline, especially at the top (which is the focus of de Gaulle's analysis of the German political and military situation as the war progresses), until the structure of the nation would crumble.

Such an argument foreshadows later analyses of the rise of Nazism from the ruins of the First World War. The cause of such snowballing abandon was 'the characteristic taste for enterprises out of all proportion; the passion for extending their personal power, whatever the cost; and the distrust of those limits traced by human experience, common sense and law'.[35] Personal power lost all proportion because it became an end in itself. This de Gaulle explicitly eschewed.

In contrast to the German ideological context, French habits, culture and temperament dispose Frenchmen, according to de Gaulle, to a quite different attitude:

In a French park no tree seeks to smother the other trees with its shade; the lawns accept being geometrically laid out; you do not get the lake trying to be a waterfall or the statues claiming that they alone must be admired. Sometimes there is an air of noble melancholy about such a park. Perhaps it comes from the feeling that each part, in isolation, might have shone more brightly. But that would have been damaging to the whole, and those who walk in the park rejoice in the sound sense which has produced its present splendid harmony.[36]

We have already noted the cultural significance of the Frenchman's garden, a theme mentioned frequently in the literature. Curtius draws out similar themes in contrasting French 'civilisation' with German *Kultur*.[37] The political implications of such proportionality also appear in a comment by Maurice Duverger, contrasting the institutions of the Fourth and Fifth Republics with those of the German Weimar Republic (with its partially analogous presidential system). The French temperament, he asserts, unlike the German, is unlikely to turn to a man like Hitler in a national emergency, for democratic habits are too engrained.[38] This belief is characteristic of the 'positive side' of de Gaulle's mind. As he said of the need for the Free French to continue the war in 1940: 'Common sense, wisdom and skill are on the same side as honour. It shall soon be recognised...that nothing is more reasonable than to fight for France.'[39]

But if the French temperament turns Frenchmen away from the kind of unjustifiable ambition which the lack of common sense and *mesure* permitted to develop in the German character, the faults of the French still exist, but are very different. These faults are not those of megalomania, but, on the contrary, are the result of setting one's sights too low. There is a gap between de Gaulle's idealised and heuristic conception of 'the genius of the land', on the one hand, and the 'mediocrity' of Frenchmen (at times), on the other. What is lacking is an effective French state to turn the general interest into political action. Classical measure without the state results in impotence; but a strong state, bound by natural limits, is the vital necessary minimum for the maintenance of 'political effectiveness'. And political effectiveness, the capacity of a state to pursue a 'political policy', is the standard by which political institutions and structures must be judged.[40]

The positive elements which have emerged from the French tradition have, according to de Gaulle, been the work of the state. 'The state, too, which responds to France, is responsible for her heritage of yesterday, her interests of today and her hopes for tomorrow.'[41] He personally rejected the alternative of his own dictatorship in 1944–6 because of his belief that solid institutions were more important than political power.[42] The construction of an effective state was paramount as a first priority for the achievement of any long-range goals: 'there can be for us no security, no liberty and no effectiveness, unless we accept a great deal of discipline, under the guidance of a strong state, impelled by the ardour of a rallied people'.[43]

But while the state responds to France, it responds to her in a particular way. For, once again, it is reason which leads to effective action, while passions hinder such action: 'sentiment does not suffice for building political edifices'.[44] The pure parliamentary regime may have been suited to the circumstances of the nineteenth century, but it is not sufficient for the needs of today.[45] For while the conditions of the nineteenth century required deliberation – the formation of a rudimentary democratic consensus – those of the twentieth century require action; 'it is the notion of governing, with all that term implies in the way of capacity for action, and not just for deliberation, which it is important. . .to emphasise. . .'[46]

De Gaulle's view of the role of the state, then, is that of undertaking tasks and solving problems as they face the community. Commenting on the failure of the Fourth Republic in this respect, he said: 'Indeed, everybody feels that there exists an irremediable disproportion between, on the one hand, the dimension of the problems which we must resolve, and, on the other, the nature of the regime.'[47] It is therefore necessary to restore 'the strong and continuous authority which is indispensable to every great task facing the state'.[48] The necessary course of future action is clear:

France first measures the mortal dangers which were caused in turn by the slow degradation of public authority and the infamy of personal power. She concludes that it is necessary as soon as possible to establish a new democracy, such that the sovereignty of the people can be exercised totally through suffrage and popular control, and such also that the power charged with guiding the state may have the means to do so with force and continuity.[49]

The actual form of the state is, however, less of a matter of absolute principle than of suiting the institutions of government to the conditions of the time. 'The Greeks once asked the wise Solon: "What is the best Constitution?" He replied: "Tell me first, for what people and at what time in history?"'[50] Later, in criticising those juridical experts who found the 1958 Constitution difficult to categorise, de Gaulle said: 'Let us say, if you like, that our constitution is both parliamentary and presidential, consistent with the requirements of our equilibrium and the traits of our national character.'[51] The importance of the state is in its principle – 'that particular interests are always constrained to yield to the general interest'[52] – and in its conformity to the necessities of governing a particular people in a particular epoch, and not in any universal form.

Though democratic, the state requires elites, not in the sense of a self-interested, self-perpetuating superior social caste, but as trained and public-spirited intermediaries assuring its good functioning and its concern with the general interest. France, as de Gaulle saw her, needed new *cadres* to 'animate and lead this renewed nation in the future', *cadres* which would 'reveal themselves' in 'resistance and combat'. In this way the state would itself be renewed; otherwise the trials of the Second World War would have been undergone in vain. 'France has not undergone [these tribulations]...just to put a new coat of whitewash on her tombstones.'[53] The old elite groups of the right and the left had failed, and needed to be superseded by those whose only concern was the common good.

There is no longer any right or left. There are the people who are higher up and who wish to see the great horizons because they have a very burdensome, difficult, and long-range task to accomplish; and there are those people who are lower down and who agitate in the swamps.[54]

Nevertheless, all Frenchmen are able to call upon a reserve of national spirit. This is the real meaning of his celebrated claim that 'Every Frenchman was, is, or will be *"Gaulliste"*.'[55]

Now the reason, for de Gaulle, why every Frenchman retains a spark of Gaullism is that, for him, Gaullism as an historical phenomenon represents the continuity of France. And this continuity, in itself, is not a static continuity, but an ever-changing and evolving one; new circumstances require an ability not only to adapt, but also to meet new challenges.[56] Indeed, the nation-state is itself the product of a process of evolution, one which at the present time represents the reality of its situation in the world, and which will continue to do so in the foreseeable future. Of course, this reality may be superseded if political necessity along with a viable wider base for political community create new forms of political effectiveness. But there are certain tasks, tasks with a cultural and popular base, which cannot devolve beyond the nation-state until that cultural and popular base also outgrows it. Europe, for de Gaulle, has a kind of cultural reality and legitimacy, but Europe's very reality and legitimacy can be seen in many ways as representing merely an aggregation of various national cultural patterns.[57] Therefore, so long as political attitudes, which have this cultural and communitarian element at their core, remain basically national, so must responsible, accountable and culturally rooted political structures. Only the nation-state is capable of pursuing that higher synthesis of unity-in-diversity which is the goal of all political action.

The nation-state, as a political system, results from the need for political effectiveness. For the state to be effective, it requires a social base, an ability to reflect psychological identity as well as goals. Such a symbiosis between base and structure represents not a Marxian dichotomy of the superstructure imposing itself upon the substructure, but rather a developmental process whereby the need for effectiveness is gradually synthesised with an appropriate territorial or social circumscription. The result is not oppression or conflict, but the gradual realisation of a common consciousness, a common relationship to the nature of things.

This is the sense of the whole, the holistic pattern – the *ensemble* – which reflects the essence of unity-in-diversity, and, thus, of nature.

Human passions, insofar as they remain diffused, realise nothing ordered, nor in consequence effective. It is necessary that they be crystallised in well-defined circumscriptions. That is why patriotism has aways been something local, each religion builds temples, and the cult of arms postulates an *esprit de corps*.[58]

The nation-state has evolved out of the evolution of the world, and represents the matching of needs with constraints. In fact, the nation-state, even for de Gaulle, is not the be-all and end-all. But because of its nature and organisation, and therefore its contact with a more complex and more deeply rooted reality, it provides the only solid base for political action in the contemporary world. 'We are in the epoch of effectiveness, that is to say the epoch of organised *ensembles*.'[59] 'The law of our epoch is no longer the permanent and systematic struggle of interest, but indeed the organisation of our economic and social solidarity.'[60] In the search for such organisation, the nation-state must also be the starting-point. No other structure can be (de Gaulle specifically considers class to be a disruptive rather than a potentially unifying force), for no other structure in the modern world represents the crystallisation of social bonds in the way the nation does. The state, then, is the goal-setter – the active, dynamic, restructuring element in society. But it cannot exist in a vacuum, and requires a national base.

Therefore the nation-state, for de Gaulle, is the proper bearer of political legitimacy. No other level of organisation can claim the same kind of all-pervading loyalty, for no other organisation can possibly express collective consciousness in the same way.

Once a nation is formed, once there are fundamental geographic, ethnic, economic, social and moral elements within it that are the texture of its life, and once, on the outside, it comes into contact with foreign influences and ambitions, there exists for that nation, despite and above its diversities, a group of conditions vital to its actions, and, ultimately, to its existence, and that is the general interest. It is, moreover, the instinct it has of this general interest which cements its unity and it is the fact that the state conforms to [the general interest] or not that makes its political endeavours worthwhile or incoherent. In a modern democracy, oriented towards effectiveness, and threatened as well, it is therefore vital that the nation's will be expressed globally when it concerns destiny. Such indeed is the foundation of our present institutions.[61]

Ultimately, the success or failure of the nation-state depends upon the collective consciousness of the social base. 'The greatness of a people can proceed only from that people.'[62] But the activity of the people must be 'utilised by politics' and organised, if their efforts are to be effective.

Thus the state must guard against centrifugal elements, elements which would act contrary to the general interest, in the nation.

In the history of France, there have always been, in one form or another, feudal fiefdoms [féodalités]. Today, they are no longer found in dungeons, but there are still fiefdoms. These fiefdoms are in the political parties, in the trade unions, in certain sectors of business. . .of the press, of the bureaucracy, etc.

Those who represent this new feudalism [les féodaux] never like a state which really does its job, and which, as a consequence, is able to dominate them.[63]

The disadvantage of older forms of political and social structure is that in this sense they were unable to do their job. Their base was either too small or too diverse and fragmented. But the conditions of the modern world impose upon society problems which certainly go beyond the bounds of the nation-state, and there is an important difference of opinion about how these problems should be tackled. To try to transcend the nation-state by creating supranational structures would, in de Gaulle's view, be self-defeating, for such supranational structures would not have any reality or roots in common consciousness, no instinct for the general interest, *in the present conjuncture*. Problems would merely be papered over, not solved on any firm basis of building for the future. On the contrary, says de Gaulle, it is necessary to build by means of slow steps, gradually perhaps creating wider patterns which in time would develop their own reality. For the moment, however, 'in order for the old but renewed continent to find a balance corresponding to the conditions of our time, it seems to us that certain groupings [e.g. Europe] must develop without, of course, encroaching upon the sovereignty of each member'.[64]

Thus for Europe to evolve into a political structure which would supersede the nation-states, two elements would have to be present: a firmly rooted and established state; and a common consciousness, a cultural unity which exists perhaps in embryo, but which cannot be created overnight. In criticising the setting up of the Council of Europe, and the early European communities, de Gaulle considered that the necessary conditions did not yet exist. These organisations were attempting to operate 'in the domain of speculation', for 'nothing has been rooted in ways of life, nor in laws'. Indeed, 'one cannot yet perceive in Europe today that elementary and popular impetus which permitted, for example, the monarchy to unify France, the Hohenzollerns to form the German Reich, or General Washington to bring into being the United States of America'.[65]

Furthermore, the essence of being a European is in itself conditioned by one's nationality. Europe exists only by virtue of the nations of which she is composed; 'there can be no Europe except by virtue of her nations...'. Because of the effects of her previous development, any 'fusion' of Europe can be only 'confusion' – or 'oppression'. A 'man without a country' cannot be a European. For example, 'Chateaubriand, Goethe, Byron, Tolstoy – to speak only of the romantics – would have been worth nothing in Volapük or Esperanto, ...but there are always good writers in Europe because each of them is inspired by the genius of his country.'[66] The social base necessary for the effective action of the state, then, is more than merely the mutually interlocking structures of the economic system, or of race, or of geography, although these are always important 'objective' factors in creating the perception of common identity. It is rather the less tangible links of culture, civilisation, common ideals and temperament – and the coming together of these in the national consciousness through the medium of politics – which lie at the heart of the phenomenon of nationality.

This view of the internal nature of the nation-state also forms the core of de Gaulle's wider view of the nature of international society and relationships. For international politics can only be defined by reference to this combination of the legitimate action of the state and the nature of social relationships within the national community. International politics, for de Gaulle, was just that: the necessary inter-action of nation-states for their mutual advantage but without endangering their own identity. This is what he meant when he said during the Fourth Republic that he did not wish to *change* French foreign policy, because the Fourth Republic governments had no foreign policy to change. Rather, he wanted to *give* France a foreign policy.[67]

De Gaulle saw the problem of international relations as a dilemma: how to meet contemporary conditions and problems in practice, while maintaining the integrity of the nation-state upon which international society is itself based by definition. In this context, he distinguished three modes of action: sovereignty and independence, necessary for the state to act legitimately; interdependence and the need for collective action; and, standing between these first two, a variegated level at which several distinguishable intermediary modes link independent action and interdependent action in a constructive manner, including mutual non-interference, equilibrium and cooperation. Independence, in the contemporary world with its machines, speed of communication and interchange of ideas, cannot 'have the least connection with isolation',[68] despite its key role in maintaining the legitimacy of the decision-making structure. In this global context, independence means the ability to initiate constructive activity and to express the creativity which derives from social consciousness.

Independence signifies a desire, an attitude, an intention. But the world being what it is – so small, so narrow, so much given to interference with itself – then real independence, total independence, belongs in truth to no-one...there is no state so great, however powerful it may be, which can do without the others. And so long as there is no state which can do without the others, there is no policy possible without cooperation.

But international sovereignty signifies something positive. It signifies that a people takes on its own responsibilities in the world. It signifies that it expresses itself for itself and by itself, that it reflects what it says and what it does.[69]

It is self-evident that an international society based upon the legitimacy of the national community must be characterised by mutual self-restraint and non-interference. This self-restraint is manifested in the balanced structure of global politics; 'in the last analysis and as always, it is only in equilibrium that the world will find peace'.[70] This equilibrium has three characteristics: a balance of power; mutual (mainly intergovernmental) cooperation; and, to assure the stability of the balance, a convergence of values and priorities among the leading states in the international system. De Gaulle's objective in international relations was precisely what one observer has described as 'impossible to conceive of' – an 'international of nationalisms',[71] which alone could combine the two prerequisites of effective power and legitimacy.

A balance of power is necessary, first of all, because of the legitimacy of the nation-states themselves. In the absence of a balance, there would be dominance or hegemony, on the one hand, which would deal one kind of blow to the basis of human society by undermining the responsiveness of the state to the people; or, on the other hand, there would be war, which would be even more dangerous. Of hegemony or war, the greatest danger is of course war, and in times of war full solidarity is absolutely necessary with the side which most closely approximates with national ideals. Thus, in the middle of the controversy about the North Atlantic Treaty Organisation which raged between France and her Atlantic partners in the early 1960s, when the Cuban missile crisis arose in 1962 de Gaulle immediately and without hesitation declared his full solidarity with the United States (despite the fact that the latter had, through the integrated NATO command, mobilised her troops in Europe without consulting her allies).[72] Even in war, however, a certain reciprocity is hoped for, a reciprocity which de Gaulle felt was not forthcoming from the United States during the Second World War despite French sacrifices 'in the service of liberty'.[73]

But at other times, the greatest danger to international society is hegemony. Doing what was possible to help maintain the equilibrium between the Great Powers was a cornerstone of French foreign policy when greater autonomy was regained after the Liberation. It even affected domestic problems, and was offered as the explanation for the exclusion of Communist ministers from the key cabinet posts of Foreign Affairs, War and the Interior in November 1945, at 'a difficult moment in the relations between these two very great powers, a particularly serious moment for the future of peace'.[74] Such a balance of power, however, was not seen as a sterile game of diplomacy, although diplomacy is a very important weapon. Rather, equilibrium is a preliminary condition for the achievement of other objectives. It is an instrumental goal rather than a final objective. It is, above all, the condition of peace, the significance of which was reaffirmed by Couve de Murville: 'peace disappears when there is disequilibrium'.[75] Thus without peace, nothing is possible; without equilibrium, peace is impossible. Peace, too, is therefore an instrumental goal, a condition of the pursuit of more profound aims (a minimal social contract without a Hobbesian sovereign). Peace allows France 'to consider and deal serenely with the important matters which concern her'.[76]

In the modern world, even purely domestic objectives have highly significant international ramifications, a perspective to which de Gaulle fully subscribed. Therefore it is necessary that there exist a means for dealing with these ramifications in a peaceful way which neither disturbs the balance of power nor threatens the legitimacy of the state. That method, for de Gaulle, was 'cooperation'. The concept of cooperation connotes the maintenance of national sovereignty within the international arena, while at the same time establishing a wide series of agreements between governments which allow joint action to be taken effectively. The most widely known form of cooperation approved by de Gaulle was bilateral aid to underdeveloped countries. However, he spoke of cooperation also as the final stage of the thawing of the cold war, as a necessary element of European development (in contrast to his *bête noire* of 'integration', which was seen to undermine the nation-state in the process), and, in fact, as an ideal method of synthesising the necessities of nationhood with those of international problem-solving.

'Cooperation' was the core of his proposals for the reform of NATO in September 1958,[77] of the Fouchet Plan for political cooperation in Europe in 1962,[78] of the Franco-German Treaty of 1963, and of the large number of bilateral agreements signed during his time in office. In a way, it was something of a panacea. But its very existence as a concept depended upon a further element of de Gaulle's view of the world, an element mentioned briefly above and a vital presupposition of much of Gaullist foreign policy: the notion of convergence. In his view of the cold war, for example, de Gaulle foresaw three stages in its thaw – *détente, entente,* and cooperation. The process began with a mere lowering of tensions, *détente* (or relaxation). This stage would be followed by a further transitional period, that of *entente* (or understanding), a mutual recognition by the various nations of each others' objectives – 'the *rapprochement* of minds that is the prerequisite of the future'.[79] And, after these transitional stages, the future lies with co-operation, an active process of common problem-solving deriving from the development of an international 'general interest' and *common* objectives.

For the balance of power is not just any balance of power. It is one which is based upon those universal values which de Gaulle believed to be the culmination of the evolution of civilisation: 'peace and progress' can be found 'only in that liberal balance of the universe, which has always been and still remains – at the price of much blood and many tears – the age-old goal of France'.[80] Therefore, in the modern world, the national interest no longer opposes nations and peoples to each other, but links them together even more strongly so long as none of them seek to achieve hegemony or to dominate others. Further, the achievement of national objectives today requires common objectives.

In order to win the peace, it will not be enough to control gigantic resources. It will not be enough to impose on the victimised peoples rigorous conditions for the security of all. It will not be enough to conclude treaties and alliances. Rather it is necessary that all these riches, all these guarantees, all these pacts, be applied to a general objective, chosen in such a way that all efforts converge on it and that all dreams, all desires, and all devotions take fire and give unstintingly towards its realisation. For today, as always, it is ideas which lead the world.[81]

Even today, the nations of the world are finding a common objective in a 'world which reflects both justice and common sense at the same time'.[82] For 'by reason of modern activities, man's condition tends to become alike everywhere and . . .the virulent opposition of the various regimes is destined to diminish'.[83] All nations must now pursue that which 'man, by nature, desires – a better life, and freedom'.[84] Indeed, the means now exist to achieve these; every country 'must have its share in what modern civilisation can and must bring to men in terms of well-being and dignity'.[85]

France believes that the future of modern civilisation can lie only in the under-standing, then the cooperation, and, finally, the osmosis between the countries that created civilisation and continue to create it, and which have spread it throughout the world and continue to spread it, and, above all, the osmosis of all the European peoples.[86]

Thus the balance of power in the modern world is the vehicle by which nation-states begin to cooperate and to realise their common ideals.

For de Gaulle, then, the problem of adapting to the conditions of the modern world does not require the changing of the political units which make it up, as much as it requires the strengthening of those units so that they may effectively pursue their real interests – which are not necessarily conflicting, but potentially complementary. In the domestic context, too, the nation-states of today, for all their past history and community consciousness, cannot afford the luxury of fragmentation and ineffectiveness. The imperative of the modern world is solidarity at home, and this means both economic *dirigisme* and an attempt to overcome class quarrels through association and participation.[87] This leads us to a tentative discussion of de Gaulle's social and economic viewpoint.

In order to achieve this solidarity, the economy must serve the public good. For progress at home – and not power abroad – is the imperative of the age:

since progress, in the sense that it is understood in the present era, is henceforth the supreme law of any society, the goal towards which we must proceed is well and truly determined for us, while the responsibilities, the means and the behaviour of the public authority must, by necessity, be adapted to the great effort of renovation.[88]

The nationalisation of the major energy and banking enterprises in the postwar period, along with the setting up of the Planning Commissariat, flowed from de Gaulle's, and others', desire to see the economy harnessed to the national interest.

This is not merely a question, however, of changing the ownership of the means of production; it requires a more complex machinery capable of responding dynamically in an ongoing process. 'The economy is a battle which is never definitively won – no matter what one obtains, no-one is ever anything like satisfied, and nothing is ever acquired once and for all.'[89] An entirely new attitude towards economic and social policy is demanded, one which could transcend the social divisions deriving from the division of labour without at the same time meaning an intensification of the class struggle or a movement towards revolution.

De Gaulle's ideas about how the economy should work have been repeated many times. They appear most definitively in this passage from the *Memoirs of Hope*, which is worth quoting in full:

However, for a long time I have been convinced that modern mechanical society lacked a human dimension to assure its equilibrium. The social system which relegates the worker – even if he is comfortably well-paid – to the role of an instrument and a cog in the machine is, in my view, in contradiction to the nature of our species, not to mention the spirit of healthy productivity. Without contesting the accomplishments of capitalism, for the profit not only of a few, but also of the collectivity, the fact is that it bears within itself the causes of massive and perpetual dissatisfaction. It is true that palliatives attenuate the excesses of the system based upon '*laissez faire, laissez passer*', but they do not cure its moral infirmity. On the other hand, communism, although it prevents in principle the exploitation of men by other men, brings with it an odious tyranny imposed on the person and plunges life into the lugubrious atmosphere of totalitarianism, without obtaining anything like the results which are obtained in liberty, as regards standard of living, working conditions, distribution of products, or technological progress as a whole. In condemning both of these opposed systems, I think, therefore, that everything commands our civilisation to construct a new one, which regulates human relationships in such a way that each person participates directly in the results of the enterprise to which he brings his effort, and takes on the dignity of being, for his part, responsible for the working of the collective enterprise on which his own destiny depends. Is this not to transpose onto the economic plane, taking account of the factors which are unique to it, those notions which are, in the political order, the rights and duties of the citizen?[90]

Out of this general condemnation of existing socio-economic systems came that part of de Gaulle's ideology which found the least echo and achieved the fewest results: the 'contracts of association' (a limited form of profit-sharing) in industry and the postwar *comités d'entreprise* (an early attempt at worker participation in decision-making); and the regional and Senate reforms proposed in 1969. The problems of social and economic reform were immediate and concrete. They depended most – more than other types of problems requiring decision – upon the immediate conjuncture and least upon de Gaulle's long-range view of history. This is why, for him, putting the state right came first; establishing the equilibrium of the political system itself took priority. Such social and economic reforms as were desirable had best come later, when the effectiveness of the political institutions would ensure their success, and when the regaining of independence and grandeur in the world would once again allow France to pursue *une politique* which was truly her own. Without the concurrence of an effective state, a consciousness of solidarity, and a sense of mission deriving from a high moral vision, these reforms might merely serve once again to reinforce the *féodalités*. The need was more far-reaching:

French democracy must be a social democracy, that is one which assures organically to each person the right and the freedom to do his own work, and guarantees the dignity and the security of all in an economic system outlined with a view to the development of national resources and not to the profit of particular interests, where the great sources of common wealth belong to the nation, and where the direction and control of the state will be exercised with the regular concurrence of those who work and of those who are enterprising.[91]

But the social problem is never fully elaborated, much less solved, for de Gaulle – just as the economy cannot run itself, and the nation breaks down into quarrelling particular interests, if it is not actively directed towards the higher synthesis. Even this synthesis, in itself, cannot be 'perfect, nor complete – as no human thing can be'.[92] There is a permanent need for the nation to be called back continually to its objectives. On the material foundations of progress must be built the aspiration 'to achieve a higher form of national life, where that which is good and beautiful is respected, protected and exalted; where thought, science, arts, religions and spiritual forces have the high place which their nobility deserves. . .'.[93]

There is a certain resignation and pessimism pervading de Gaulle's ultimate view, however, no matter how much the nation is thus inspired. The then Prime Minister (later de Gaulle's successor as President of the Republic), Georges Pompidou, in an interview with the weekly *L'Express* in 1967, compared de Gaulle to Philippoemen, the last great leader of ancient Greece in its late stages of decline before the Roman takeover. And this attitude is reflected in de Gaulle's actions, or, more particularly, his reactions to events which seemed to contradict his attempt to create this new national spirit, especially in 1946, 1968 and 1969. For the nature of things, while providing the set of axioms and imperatives according to which the world must be organised if it is to survive and prosper – the underlying principles of its working – comes up against real men. This is why de Gaulle, in one sense, preferred France to the French, although he understood that France could only bring the French together and could not fully re-fashion them. 'For, in essence, whatever the frontiers, the races, or the ambitions, it is man which is at the root of everything.'[94] Between the goal and its achievement comes the imperfection of humanity.

De Gaulle's view of the world, therefore, shared the fundamental tension which is common to natural law doctrines – between a teleological insistence upon the existence of higher goals and the necessity of pursuing them, on the one hand, and the limits set upon any such venture by nature and by man himself, on the other. This tension usually manifests itself in a hierarchy of goals which, the more precise they become, the more they become vulnerable to the limitations and complexity of man, flawed by his inner tension between his reason and his passions. For de Gaulle, the nation-state was a teleological community in a world where passions divided men. Reason, common sense, justice and measure were the correct standards of behaviour in a setting where national unity was all too often the product of racism, sentiment and a will to power.

De Gaulle attempted to make certain important distinctions here. The first of these was a nationalism based on classical values, self-restraint, non-interference, mutual understanding and cooperation, rather than upon exclusiveness or organicism. The second was an emotional view of France based, paradoxically, on reason rather than passion – or, more precisely, upon *good* passions or sentiments whose effect was constructive rather than destructive, rallying the people to a better common life rather than imposing a totalitarian order.

These distinctions were difficult to uphold, and their effects difficult to predict. But, finally, permeating the whole, was a sense of Sisyphean obstinacy. The unanswered question of de Gaulle's ideology is whether it was based upon faith or upon an existential determination to succeed; it was most probably both. And common to all of the different emphases of the various aspects of de Gaulle's political thought was the role of ideas and images as active agents of social change. The symbolism of grandeur sums up the behavioural relevance of Gaullist ideology, for, ultimately, the significance of these ideas will not be found in their abstract form, but in their impact upon the social context. This is the meaning of de Gaulle's 'historical personality'.

The dynamics of Gaullist ideology: de Gaulle's theory of leadership and political action

De Gaulle's ideas about political leadership provide the crucial link in any understanding of him as an 'historical personality' – the link between his philosophical and personal *Weltanschauung*, on the one hand, which supplied the purpose and motivation of his action, and, on the other, the policies, strategies and decisions which comprised that action in particular concrete situations and circumstances. Leadership was seen as important because, at crucial times in history, when political structures are weak, unstable or transitional, the intelligent and well-prepared leader can maximise his use of symbolic and manipulative resources in order to shape the course of events. In times of flux and crisis, the skilful leader can often control key aspects of the process in which inputs into the political system – demands, structures of power, influence and support, and culturally rooted predispositions – are converted into outputs – policies, resource allocation, modified or new power structures, and the like.

The central motivation of de Gaulle's action was, of course, his view of the world. And this outlook itself involved assumptions and prescriptions which moulded his leadership style. His view of history, according to Robert Aron, was often divided into two perspectives. The first was a long-range perspective, and it took in the sweep of French history, if not the whole history of civilisation. The second, immediate perspective dealt with day-to-day facts and events, and these often do not fit with generalisations emerging from the first, long-range perspective. When the two coincide, then 'every gesture he makes, every word he says against the background of the present stands out at the same time against the background of history'; such is 'the moment of his very great successes'. However, when the two perspectives are at odds, 'when day-to-day politics fail to correspond with the great visions of history and the great needs of history and civilisation, then there is a clash'; at such times, de Gaulle, in Aron's view, takes the side of history, and lets the present go by the board.[1] But whichever side he took in a particular set of circumstances, de Gaulle always agonised over the gap between these two perspectives, and his action was always directed, in his own mind, towards their intertwining and reconciliation wherever possible.

Thus the essential problem of political action, for de Gaulle, was to reconcile the general and the particular while maintaining overall movement towards a general objective. The early development of this outlook took place in the context of military thought, of strategy and tactics. Ultimately, its logical focus was upon concrete points of conjuncture, when the necessity for action required and demanded the effort of reconciliation. Once the long-range objectives had been formed into overall strategy, and the terrain entered, then the test of the leader's capacity was his ability to deal with crises, and to resolve these crises while maintaining momentum towards the goal. At times of crisis, 'the judgment, the attitude, the authority of leaders depend above all upon the intellectual and moral reflexes which they have acquired throughout their career'.[2] He thus trained his own reflexes towards 'acting for greatness' when 'confronted by the blandishments of mediocrity'.[3] His leadership style involved the attempt to remain on remote heights in order best to withstand the pressures surrounding him, and thus to keep the long-range objective in view.

This concentration on remoteness, while effective in dealing with certain crises, was little suited to the maintenance of the *status quo*, even where de Gaulle himself had been the main architect of that *status quo*. For this reason, in public life de Gaulle found it difficult to ensure that the reactions of others were consonant with his own perceptions, objectives and intentions. His manner, his concern with history and nationhood, and his often tenuous personal position (especially during the Second World War) often produced impressions in others which were quite the opposite of those which he hoped to arouse. These problems, however, were, in a sense, built in to de Gaulle's very style of acting. Certain elements in his own theory of political action – set out mainly in *Le fil de l'épée* – and which echo throughout his public activities, were based upon a carefully calculated aura of ambiguity which was designed to maintain support while at the same time keeping open a variety of policy options and freedom of action. Misinterpretation was bound to occur in such conditions.

De Gaulle's theory of action was intended to make it possible for him to put his philosophy into practice. For him, such a philosophy was insufficient when set out in terms of abstract ideas. And it was not sufficient to await the evolution of the world to a higher form of civilisation in order to realise its objectives. Any such achievement depends upon the conscious activity of men, for, ultimately, the activity of the world is human activity. Thus his ambition was not simply to be right (nor even just to be seen to be right), but in fact to do right as he saw it. And just as the general interest – which existed in itself, but which needed an active element (the state) to carry it out – was useless unless it was turned into action, so a philosophy was useless unless it, too, was carried out. Philosophy demanded practice, just as practice required philosophy.

Now the active element in this theory was leadership. Leadership, to de Gaulle, required two things. In the first place, it required support, and the task of maintaining support required an image which could appeal to both reason and sentiment. In the second place, it required decision-making, and this demanded of the leader a capacity to see the nature of the choice confronted – and the implications of the alternatives – as well as an ability to carry out the decision (and other decisions) once made.

The maintenance of support, then, required above all an image which would allow the leader freedom of action and did not constrain him too closely within its terms. The combination of these factors was not easy to achieve; ambiguities, stilted phrases, awkward gestures and inflexibility often resulted. He had the habit of referring to himself in the third person, saying 'de Gaulle has done such and such', rather than 'I have done. . .'.[4] His concrete policy views were often left in doubt; his hesitation about starting out on the road of social and economic reform, which he had spoken about for some time, was intensified by a lack of public acceptance of this part of his programme (especially on the part of a large section of his supporters). The argument about whether de Gaulle was a man of the left or a man of the right will never be resolved, because it is difficult to be sure just how far he really wanted to go. For, in his mind, the requirements of getting anything done at all were so exacting that a slip might mean a fall.

It was by acting as the inflexible champion of the nation and of the state [in 1940] that it would be possible for me to gather the consent, even the enthusiasm, of the French and to win from foreigners respect and consideration. Those who, all through the drama, were offended by this intransigence were unwilling to see that for me, intent as I was on beating back innumerable conflicting pressures, the slightest wavering would have brought collapse. In short, limited and alone though I was, and precisely because I was so, I had to climb to the heights and never then to come down.[5]

The image, then, was *a sine qua non*, a minimum requirement in the continuous struggle to obtain and to maintain sufficient wherewithal to pursue the long-range objective; it was a means to political power.

Now the means to power, and the use of power, require a strong sense of pragmatism, a pragmatism which stands in basic contrast to the permanence which de Gaulle demanded of motives and objectives: 'To raise oneself above oneself in order to dominate others, and, through this, events, is an effort which does not vary in its essence. But its procedures change radically.'[6] It is not the pragmatism of the opportunist, but the instrumentalism of the actor and rhetorician. According to Alfred Grosser, it is not possible, in studying the behaviour of de Gaulle, to separate 'sincerity, in other words the profound conviction that what one says is true as well as the reality of the emotion, and calculation, that is to say the conscious utilisation of deeply felt emotion and conviction in order to obtain a certain political result. Sincerity and calculation are inextricably intertwined.'[7]

The difficulty of blending long-range goal orientation and pragmatism, and sincerity and calculation, creates continuing tensions and problems for the leader. Principles, and their application, are not always self-evident, and the image must not be betrayed. Doubts and hesitations build up behind the rhetorical and behavioural mask which has been constructed so painstakingly. The drawbacks are obvious; the loss of the April 1969 referendum was characteristic of the pitfalls to which de Gaulle's style was vulnerable.[8] His own testimony expresses his true feelings about his self-chosen form of action:

There I was, obliged as much as ever to be this de Gaulle to whom is personally imputed all that comes to pass directly or indirectly, whose every word and every gesture, even when wrongly attributed to him, become everywhere subjects of discussions of all kinds, and who can appear nowhere without being surrounded by ardent clamours. This manifests the eminent dignity of the leader, but also the heavy chain of the servant.[9]

However, despite these ambiguities, contradictions and drawbacks, the maintenance of de Gaulle's position depended upon the image on which it had been built, and both image and position rested upon two fundamental elements: *rhetoric* and *distance*. A man who set great store by his literary ability,[10] de Gaulle put great effort into his rhetoric. His painstaking writing through bad and worsening eyesight was a continuing strain.[11] It has been said that his vocabulary in public statements is one of the best extant examples of the use of a limited range of classical French words chosen particularly in order to be understood by the man in the street and to evoke the most appropriate response. It was clear, precise and comprehensible, and yet did not give the impression of talking down to his listeners. It was clear as it stood – yet it contained his own form of ambiguity on a very specific level.

He scorned clumsy attempts to utilise rhetoric, and this dislike coloured his views of ideological politics, particularly those of the Soviet Union at the time of the U-2 incident and the abortive summit conference in Paris in 1960:

> But we can discern nonetheless what is excessive and artificial in all the demonstrations organised around these problems, and that is why, once again, we do not allow ourselves to be moved by all the tumult, all the flow of invective, of formal notifications, of threats launched by certain countries against other lands and especially against ours. This is all the more true in that we realise the tactical element that enters into all this staging by those who, so to speak, make it their job to upset others.[12]

However, he was certainly not loath to use rhetoric and its potential for masking his own intentions. The most striking example of his use of dissimulation occurred during an important visit to Algeria in 1958, when his power still depended to a great extent upon the support of the Army and upon the appeasement of the right-wing *colon* population in Algeria who had paved his way to power on the understanding that their desire to keep Algeria French would not be betrayed. He was required to address an Algiers crowd during a time when certain right-wing leaders were beginning to suspect that he might not be the champion they had hoped for.[13] They expected something of him, and, after all, 'One does not sway crowds except by elementary sentiments, violent images and brutal invocations.'[14] As the crowd shouted and clamoured for *Algérie française*, and mixed their shouts of 'de Gaulle' with 'Vive Salan' – a reference to the leader of the Algerian section of the army and one of the engineers of the return of de Gaulle to power in May 1958 as the only way out of an impasse between the insurgents in Algeria and the government in Paris – de Gaulle replied with the phrase: '*Je vous ai compris!*' This ultimately ambiguous statement electrified the crowd and won them over completely; they did not listen to the short speech which followed, and which set out de Gaulle's concrete plans for Algeria in terms which might not have pleased them. On only one other occasion did de Gaulle seem to go farther in committing himself to the goal of a totally French Algeria, and that was a relatively minor incident which some observers have felt to be an uncharacteristic slip of the tongue.

'I have understood you.' This remark has been analysed and re-analysed, especially during de Gaulle's first seven-year term of office as the French Government drew nearer and nearer to an Algerian settlement in 1961–2. 'Understanding' was taken by the French Algerians and their supporters in France (especially those on the extreme right) to imply agreement, or at least a kind of tacit conformity, with their own views; de Gaulle's moves towards autonomy, self-determination and later even independence for Algeria were seen by these groups as a betrayal of their support at the very least, treason against the French nation at most. Our clearest evidence as to their meaning is de Gaulle's own explanation in his memoirs of the period. 'I threw out the words, apparently spontaneous in form but basically well calculated, with the intention of evoking enthusiasm without allowing them to commit me farther than I had resolved to go.'[15] By that point in time, he had already decided that Algeria had at least to be given autonomy – which would mean the end of the social and economic dominance of the *pieds-noirs* – if not yet independence.[16]

But de Gaulle's use of rhetoric was not primarily for purposes of dissimulation. It was also necessary to inspire the people with the proper sentiments – those good passions which were fundamentally constructive in effect. The element of ambiguity is strong here, too, for words such as 'general interest', 'nation', 'greatness', 'independence', 'France', 'progress' and the like, have two levels of meaning. In the first place, they mean what de Gaulle means by them, and in many cases it is crucial to know just where certain concepts – such as the state and the nation – fit into de Gaulle's philosophy if one is seeking to understand what he means. In the second place, however, such words mean something to all men, and, carefully used, they may help to achieve what de Gaulle hoped to achieve on the social plane – to undermine the conflicts and divisions of an earlier era and to replace their fundamental assumptions with a new set of assumptions based upon values and ideals held in common by diverse groups. By introducing a new political language, de Gaulle hoped to produce a new consciousness of common values and thereby to reinforce the solidarity which he thought to be so necessary in the modern world.

His use of the word *grandeur*, as we have already seen, was particularly significant, for on the one level he was using it to re-establish and to validate a conception of greatness which was linked neither with aggressiveness and expansionism (in contrast to the rhetoric of the fascist era) nor with the rhetoric of individual interests and class struggles (the rhetoric of capitalism and of Marxism). Here he was also using it in its classical French sense, of a greatness which is a greatness of soul and not power, of quality not quantity, of morality and not ego. Although he did not use the word as often as has been supposed by some supporters as well as critics, it is one of his crucial rhetorical images. But he was also using it in the second sense described above, as a 'hurrah-word', a word calculated to evoke a favourable image in a wide range of listeners. In this sense, perhaps, de Gaulle's ambiguity was not always successful in achieving his desired end, for there is no doubt that emphasis on such words as grandeur was a two-edged sword, which often was ineffective at rallying support from a wide range of groups, but too often merely reinforced right-wing support from groups who would define 'greatness' somewhat differently. Nonetheless, as we shall see in Chapter 10, the image evoked by de Gaulle's policy had an appeal which, unlike many aspects of domestic policy, did tend to cut across ideological and class boundaries, and a central component of this image was grandeur.

De Gaulle's choice of vocabulary did not always emphasise the same images, however. Recent research has in fact shown that de Gaulle's choice of hurrah-words varied considerably according to the type of speech that was being made. Cruder, more nationalistic images tended to be evoked at times of crisis, while during periods of consolidation not only did his speeches tend to be longer and more precise, but they also emphasised a more moderate and liberal vocabulary. A content analysis of de Gaulle's broadcast speeches between 1959 and 1965 shows that by the application of several analytical criteria, these speeches can be divided into two classes: 'appeals' (*discours-appels*) and 'state-of-affairs' messages (*discours-bilans*).[17] The former tend to be shorter and to occur during periods of political difficulty; the latter tend to be considerably longer, and to occur during times of consolidation. Both types tend to have longer sentences as the years pass, especially marked for the state-of-affairs messages which have considerably longer sentences on average after the Algerian settlement than before. The state-of-affairs messages also tend to manifest a richer vocabulary. All in all, the latter category seems to be a more significant vehicle for de Gaulle's public image over the long term, although the appeals tend to be more linked with critical periods and therefore may evoke more intense immediate responses.

It is interesting, in view of this, to note finally that the different types of speeches contain different key words. The appeals stress the words most often thought to typify de Gaulle's speeches: 'Republic', 'State', 'people', 'I', 'confidence', 'nation'. The state-of-affairs messages, in contrast, have a quite different emphasis: 'our', 'year', 'economic', 'world', 'development', 'progress'.[18] It is possible to hypothesise that this distinction may in fact have been linked to another distinction which has been frequently analysed: that between so-called 'Gaullien' Gaullism, the Gaullism of the 'personal contract' between de Gaulle and France – personal and plebiscitary; and 'legislative' or 'institutionalised' Gaullism – the Gaullism of the Gaullist party both in parliament and in the party organisation. Unfortunately, the two most significant forms of Gaullist explication, the press conference and the televised interview (the latter being prominent in 1965, 1968 and 1969), which are also the longest and the richest in vocabulary, are not even included in the general conclusions of the study cited. They would almost certainly reinforce the general analysis considerably in favour of the state-of-affairs type.

In terms of our general argument about the importance of de Gaulle's image as a key factor in his strategy to maintain support, this analysis of his rhetoric leads to two remarks. Firstly, the most intensive use of crude national symbolism is clearly limited to crises of the state, when their mobilising power is the greatest. And, secondly, the domestic content of his later consolidationist rhetoric implies that domestic milieu goals were in fact the primary objects of his long-term political activities. Thus in terms of de Gaulle's instrumental objective of gaining power, a necessary prerequisite for goal-oriented leadership, those periods which he found to be most constraining and option-limiting were those which required the most stern and uncompromising intransigence – the Algerian period, the crisis period of May 1968 and so on. On the other hand, the flourishing periods of domestic policy-making were 1963–5 and June 1968–April 1969 (between the massive Gaullist victory in the parliamentary elections of June 1968 and de Gaulle's resignation) – both periods when legislative–Gaullist consolidation was greatest and when the President's domestic options were least constrained by his image (though perhaps most constrained by his supporters and colleagues).[19] When we look closer at the image of nationalistic rhetoric, then, we find that behind the surface ambiguity a clearer 'modernising' image emerges, with national symbolism as merely one of the range of linguistic instruments used.

De Gaulle's image, however, was not simply his rhetoric. It derived to a great extent from his own comportment, his bearing, his choice of settings and his attitude towards his work and towards his underlings. And here one can see clearly that to his mind, being on a 'higher plane' – that of those 'who wish to see the great horizons because they have a very burdensome, difficult, and long-range task to accomplish' – is strategically central as well as philosophically necessary. For the maintenance of distance is vital for the maintenance of prestige; and prestige, for de Gaulle, is the crucial instrumental factor which separates leaders from followers. De Gaulle's views on prestige are less esoteric and ambivalent than many other aspects of his thinking, and they are clearly expressed in Chapter 3 of *Le fil de l'épée*. They are also among the most widely discussed elements of his approach. In fact, they are frequently taken to represent an end in themselves, a mystical vitalism more important to de Gaulle than the more sophisticated normative side of his philosophy.[20] However, *Le fil de l'épée* is a book about leadership, about the effective use of means, and not about ends.[21] De Gaulle hints at this by his choice of epigraph for the book, the quotation from Faust which we have analysed previously. Indeed, it would seem reasonable to assume that his book on leadership was meant to be for leaders in general, and not just for those sharing his political and philosophical beliefs. Prestige is part of a strategy, in the way rhetoric is – to maintain support while retaining maximum freedom of action concerning substantive goals and decisions.

De Gaulle regarded prestige as a particularly necessary attribute in contemporary society, for the old bases of hierarchy and elite power have atrophied. Traditional sources of authority, particularly birth, no longer command respect. Unlike Max Weber, however, de Gaulle did not believe that the future lay in the hands of the bureaucratic elite; rather, he accepted the French maxim, '*L'intendance suivra*' – the view that bureaucrats were essentially followers, not leaders (provided that real political leadership existed). In this general vacuum, the military has become in modern society a very important source of political leadership – firstly because it trains for the *use* of leadership and power (and not merely the appearances), and, secondly, because it is dedicated to some conception of national interest and solidarity. In this latter sense it differs from both bureaucratic leadership – which is concerned with formalities and procedures (the core of Weber's argument) and not with normative substance – and business leadership or leadership of other sectional groups – which are concerned with sectional ends rather than with the general interest.

In this transformation of society, this crumbling of old structures, leadership, according to de Gaulle, is required to manifest its value without being able to call upon existing social structures for support. 'The man who commands, whatever his rank, must remember that to be followed, he must depend less upon his elevation than upon his value. He must not confuse power with its attributes.'[22] Thus prestige must flow from his person in times when structures are disjointed. In order to achieve this, the leader must possess a 'creative spark'. However, the creative spark is not in itself enough; it must be combined with a mastery of the leadership art itself. 'For the leader, as for the artist, the gift must be moulded through one's professional skill and experience.'[23] De Gaulle's prescriptions for the attainment of prestige are set out in a classic passage which is often quoted, and which needs to be set out in full to be appreciated:

First of all, prestige cannot exist without a certain sense of mystery, since people have little reverence for that which they know too well. Every religious sect has its tabernacles and no man is a great man to his servants. It is therefore necessary, in one's projects, one's manner, one's mental actions, that an element is retained that the others cannot grasp and which intrigues them, moves them, and holds them breathless. Not, certainly, that one should enclose oneself in an ivory tower, ignore one's subordinates, and remain inaccessible to them. Indeed, on the contrary, to be the Emperor of men's souls demands that one observe them and that each of them might believe that he has been distinguished from the rest. From that time on, when the leader has been adjudged capable of adding all the weight of a singular virtue to the efficiency of known procedures, confidence and hope will redound to his credit in an obscure way.

Such a reserve of the soul usually cannot exist without that of gestures and words. Appearances, perhaps, but according to which the multitude establishes its opinion. Is this so wrong? And is there not a relationship between the inner strength and the outward aspect of an individual? And further, the experience of warriors has never underestimated the importance of attitude. But while, among those who command, the lowest try as hard as they can to behave themselves well in front of their troops, the greatest arrange their interventions very carefully. They make of it an art which Flaubert grasped so well when he depicted in *Salammbô* the effect produced upon hesitant soldiers by the calculated appearance of Amilcar. Every page of the *Commentaries* shows us how Caesar measured his public gestures. And everyone knows the care Napoleon took always to display himself under such conditions that impressed others' minds.[24]

Distance, then, together with rhetoric and gestures, can be skilfully blended to produce prestige; charisma is not a magical quality, but a dramaturgical device, in which the world is the stage. The measuring of words is essential (as is the measuring of gestures and distance); silence is not their antithesis, but simply the other side of the coin. 'Sobriety of speech accentuates the shape of an attitude. Nothing elevates authority better than silence...To speak, in addition, is to dilute one's thought, to drain one's ardour, and, in short, to spread oneself out when action requires that one concentrate one's efforts.'[25] Indeed, there is a 'necessary correspondence' between silence and the giving of commands, which rules out too much talk and demands the Roman *imperatoria brevitas*, conciseness above all. But such silence must complement ardour and decision-making, and these character-istics must be seen by all. Thus leadership requires effectiveness and accountability.[26] Above all, however, leadership requires that the methods and the goal be such that they can inspire the man in the street to forget about his particular interests and dedicate himself to the common good.

It is a question of responding, in effect, to that obscure wish of all men, the infirmity of whose organs make them desire the perfection of the goal – who, limited by their nature, nourish infinite desires and, each measuring his smallness, will accept collective action provided that it holds out the promise of something great...It is the basis of eloquence.[27]

Prestige, then, is the combined product of words, actions and settings.

The content of what is said can often be less significant, of course, than the way it is said; the relationship between form and content, between medium and message, then, is one which can be either mutually reinforcing or mutually prejudicial. As Murray Edelman points out, the content of hortatory political language may evoke different ideological responses from different groups, but its form 'calls out the same responses from the mass audiences exposed to it'. It builds up links of confidence and trust in the public accountability and reason-ableness of policy-makers. Indeed, even the syntactical form of such language increases the intensity of the emotional response. 'Word orders like "Ask not what..." are not used in ordinary conversation or even ordinary speech-making. We associate the unusual deployment of verb, adverb, and accusative pronoun with biblical language and with eloquent oratory of the past, and we respond to the poetry of these associations.'[28]

In addition to the actual form of words, intense responses may be heightened by the settings in which words or actions are used. De Gaulle, both in his prescriptions in *Le fil de l'épée* and in his own uses of symbolic language and gestures, emphasised the need to create a dramaturgical atmosphere which he sees as part and parcel of the prestige of great historical leaders. According to Edelman again, the conscious manipulation of settings has the effect of obscuring the information content of the message presented, yet it gives the message meaning in the eyes of the audience. The artistic or dramatic quality of political settings is carefully contrived and constructed 'to emphasise a departure from men's daily routine, a special or heroic quality in the proceedings they are to frame'. The emphasis is not simply upon the grandness of scale – although 'massiveness, ornateness and formality are the most common notes struck in the design of these scenes' – but rather on the perceptual gap between everyday life and the 'special occasion' upon which attention is constantly focused, giving the impression of proximity to an event of historic significance. It must be manifestly clear that the setting 'is framing a special performance and not ordinary life'. The onlookers thus are drawn into the actor's desired frame of reference rather than their own, 'for the framed actions are taken on their own terms', thus making for 'heightened sensitivity and easier conviction'. Inconsistent facts in the wider environment are filtered out, and it is possible to concentrate a number of different forms of suggestion – 'of connotations, of emotions and of authority'. Such creation of an artificial space is essential to the arts, and it is essential to symbolic politics too, 'although a political setting is too rarely a work of art'. The audience must still be psychologically removed from their social situation and 'injected into an artificial universe or semblance'. Once this has been achieved, its attention can be diverted from cognitive analysis of the environment into a situation where symbols become more meaningful than facts and direct manipulation of the environment. The key is that in such a setting 'there is no tie to consequences at all, no means of verification'.[29]

De Gaulle's advice to military leaders emphasises the need to make the best use of limited means to maximise the impact of meanings in just this way. Later, as politician, his uses of such media as radio, television, elaborately staged press conferences and tours of the provinces manifested an attempt to apply these prescriptions using the latest and most effective techniques available – a reflection of the evolution of his military thought from firepower through tanks to nuclear weapons. Thus the respondent is drawn into the world of the leader, drawn in on an emotive level – and this not only makes it more possible for the process to be stage-managed, but it also intensifies the impact of the very kind of 'good sentiments', the kind of moral values, which de Gaulle sought to inculcate in the French people. It conveys the kind of emotional fervour which puts political argument into a different league, which communicates 'the reality of the battle, the importance of the stakes, the gripping quality of the great drama of state'. Indeed, Edelman continues, it makes the onlooker into a participant, thus becoming 'a medium of self-expression, a rite which helps the individual to reflect in action his own interest in, and relationship to, what Lasswell has called "a symbol of the whole" '.[30] The respondent thus feels that he is able to transcend his own limitations and achieve something noble, something great.

Indeed, *Le fil de l'épée* itself was not merely an analysis of military leadership; it was also meant to stir the French Army out of the lethargy which it had exhibited since the middle of the nineteenth century. It was itself an example of the leader's attempt to use words, to stir and to hold attention, although its impact remained limited at the time. And here, too, the silences are significant. Ultimately, de Gaulle suggests, the significance of the armed forces themselves depends upon the objectives towards which they are turned.[31] The book, however, which has usually been thought to contain the essence of de Gaulle's thought, says nothing directly about the aims and values towards which action must be directed in any concrete political or philosophical sense. All he tells the reader here is that, like a water-plant, the army must push its way upwards from the shadows where it has hesitatingly lain, towards the surface and the sunlight. Its reward, however, was assured, in this search for the light, for 'it is indeed necessary for there to be a sun' – a natural source of values and goodness towards which it is necessary to strive.[32] Thus the underlying assumptions of de Gaulle's view of the world are hinted at, but not specified. They are left to the nature of things.

Prestige, then, and the lessons contained in the essence of military leadership – for de Gaulle's essence is normative and teleological rather than positivist – comprise a fundamental part of de Gaulle's theory of action. They provide conditions necessary for successful action, but, as such, they are of a fairly low order of instrumentality, for the army is merely a tool for either good or bad. On a higher level of instrumentality, one finds that de Gaulle's theory of action rests upon the ability of the leader to make the *right* decisions. Thus it is his theory of decision-making which is at the heart of his prescriptive theory, for it combines an understanding of goals and objectives – which are the *raison d'être* of leadership – with a skilful appreciation of the necessities and constraints inherent in the conjuncture. This is the crux of the problem of leadership, for, as we have seen, the actions of the leader must both be and appear to be effective and responsible. And in order for his action to be effective, the leader must have a particular way of thinking, a thoroughly formed mental set, which is both analytic and synthetic – able to work within the limits of time and space. The leader requires, for this task, the qualities of character and intuition: an ability to see the essence of a problem, the constraints on its resolution and the possible opportunities for action; the capacity to choose the alternative course of action which is best suited to achieving long-range objectives within the perceived limits; and the inner strength to carry through his decision and to accept the consequences.

This sort of leadership involves a conscious choice – and a conscious personal sacrifice – if the role is properly to be played to the full. In de Gaulle's own view of the choice he made, 'My nature warned me, my experience had taught me, that at the summit one can preserve one's time and one's person only by remaining habitually on the re-motest heights.'[33] Leadership has its personal disadvantages, for each leader is rent by an internal conflict resulting from the burdens of leadership. Happiness is not permitted in the solitude which is 'the misery of superior men'. 'It is necessary to take sides, and the choice is cruel', for one has to be surrounded continually by that 'sort of melan-choly which impregnates all that is august: men as well as things'.[34] Leadership requires tremendous perseverance. But perseverance and character, too, like prestige, cannot exist without an integrating thought process which can give them direction and motivation. '. . .The success of great men implies multiple faculties. Character, taken in isolation, produces only foolhardiness and stubbornness. But, on the other hand, the highest qualities of mind will not (by themselves) suffice.'[35] Correct decision-making requires the right combination of these qualities of character and mind. It requires a highly trained *intuition.*

De Gaulle's ideas about political leadership and decision-making draw significantly from the Cartesian concept of action as artistry, of leadership as creativity. It requires a sound knowledge of conditions: the nature, strength and intention of the enemy; the terrain; one's means and resources; the weather; in sum, a whole series of given factors which, between them, present an infinitely varying picture, a vast range of possible combinations. While the task may appear simple at first, in fact it requires more than precise knowledge to turn these contingencies to advantage. It requires not merely intelligence, 'the nature of which is to grasp and to consider the constant, fixed and definite element while shunning the mobile, unstable and diverse elements'.[36] Such knowledge perceives only one side of reality. The other side is movement, and the understanding of movement requires intuition.

Bergson depicts for us, at the same time as he is analysing it, the uneasiness and uncertainty of the intelligence when it comes into contact with moving reality. 'We feel indeed that none of the categories of our thought can be applied exactly to the phenomena of life. In vain, we force the living into one or another of our frameworks; and every framework cracks; they are too narrow, too rigid especially for what we want to put into them. Our reasoning, so sure of itself when it hovers over inert phenomena, feels ill at ease on this new terrain.'[37]

This dilemma highlights, in *Le fil de l'épée*, the value of a military training when it comes to leadership. War, according to de Gaulle, is a good school for the intuition: 'Always there is some surprise shock, some element which has escaped one's attention, some event which has deceived one's judgment.'[38] The exigencies of war demand that the decision-maker transcend mere intelligence and grasp the moving nature of reality.

This is not to say that intelligence can go by the board. It is, of course, necessary as a prerequisite. 'By elaborating the given factors of conception beforehand, it clarifies them, specifies them and reduces the field of error.' And even in the middle of movement 'intelligence from the beginning introduces some fixity into so many uncertainties'. 'In short, in the mind of the man who must act, it prepares conception, *but it does not itself give birth to that conception.*'

Bergson has again shown how, in order to come into direct contact with realities, the human mind must acquire intuition by combining instinct with intelligence. If intelligence procures for us theoretical, general, abstract knowledge of what is, it is instinct which furnishes us with practical, particular and concrete feeling. Without the former, one could not have logical sequences or enlightened judgments. But without the effort of the latter, there could be no profound perception nor any creative impulse. Instinct is, then, in our very being, the faculty which links us most closely with nature. Thanks to it, we can get to the heart of the order of things. We can participate in what it finds there in the way of obscure harmony. It is by instinct that man perceives the reality of the conditions which surround him, and that he puts to the test the corresponding impulsion. There exists, for the war leader, in the matter of conception, a phenomenon analogous to that whose subject is the artist.[39]

Instinct in isolation, however, would merely lead to confusion. Intelligence must come back into its own. 'Grasping onto the basic principles given by instinct, it elaborates them and attributes to them a determined form, in fact a definite and coherent whole.' This is necessary when one has to command and direct a system of complex forces which have no strength without order; and the process as a whole must result in a method for its application. From analysis, it is necessary to proceed to synthesis, which requires reflection and meditation on the same things continually. Intelligence and instinct cannot exist in isolation from each other if they are to result in action, and neither must be neglected. Inspiration is useless without knowledge; but arbitrary and fixed doctrines are equally dangerous.[40]

The need to blend, to measure, judiciously to balance and to integrate intelligence and instinct, however, lead to a further, culminating consideration. Instinct and intelligence, which are qualities of the mind, are little use to the leader, whose responsibilities are so great – for 'in the last resort, decision-making is a moral question'. Thus moral prescription is the centre around which the rest revolves. Not even orders from above can resolve all of the moral problems which a military leader faces, and the higher one gets in the hierarchy, the greater the moral element in decision.[41] At this point we have come full circle. True leadership demands that one be as free as possible to make the kind of moral decisions which are required by a situation. And this kind of latitude can ultimately be found only at the pinnacle of the hierarchy of power. Therefore the leader, to be true to his own calling and convictions, must be willing to make the sacrifices and create the aura and image which are the means to his ends. He must have character and prestige. And ultimately, by implication, he must be a political leader as well. For although the military profession may be a fine school of leadership, and although military organisation may be particularly appropriate to the problems and structures of modern life, nonetheless the legitimacy of a society is expressed not in its weapon, the armed forces, but in its head – in the state. And in politics, although the constraints upon action may be more varied, complex and subtly entangling, the problems to be dealt with are both more fundamental and of higher moral status.

De Gaulle's view of decision-making in politics has certain characteristics in common with his view of military leadership – the elements of mind and character, prestige and rhetoric, are just as basic. The element of morality is present even more strongly in politics, for politics is itself concerned with those normative decisions which are to be made on behalf of society as a whole. De Gaulle's whole conception of political purpose and the role of the state reflects this classical conception of the nature of politics as that species of human activity concerned with the general interest. In politics, for example, one of the more fixed elements of the military art – the enemy – is transformed into a concept which is far less tangible, more variegated and obscure. And the question of goals becomes obscure also, because whereas in war the obvious objective is victory, in politics – especially given de Gaulle's clear commitment to liberal democracy as an expression of national legitimacy and unity – the objectives must be derived from that most tangled of webs, the popular will.

De Gaulle's analysis penetrates to the heart of the dilemma of democracy. For even if the objectives pursued derive in some way from the will of the people, their application must still be effective. And effective application is inevitably vulnerable to charges of autocracy. Furthermore, the opposition is also part of the people in a democracy, and cannot be ignored. Therefore the relationship of the leader to the people is crucial to de Gaulle's view of the correct political regime. The only sure way for the popular will to be translated and effectively converted into political outputs is via the leader – not in any organic way, but through his trained intuition combined with the support which he has been able to attract and to maintain, and, ultimately, through the values and goals which he represents and pursues.

In the last analysis, then, the leader for whom de Gaulle's prescriptions are intended must have two sides to his character. He must be both *within* the social context and yet *outside* it at the same time. He must be a solitary figure, measuring his words, his gestures – and his silences – from a distance; yet the effect of his action must be to draw his audience into *his* world, to show them what needs to be done in the name of the collectivity in its cultural as well as political and economic common interest, and to make that view of the common interest immediate and relevant to them. These are the burdens of the political *prouesse* demanded of the true statesman, for, in the end, it is the sanction – or the disapproval – of the people which determines the success or failure of the venture, for they are the source of legitimacy. And, in the longer perspective, it is their image of his achievement – bright or dim, approving or disapproving, great or ordinary – which will determine the essential characteristics and the prominence of that 'historical personality' which was the essence of de Gaulle's ambition.

De Gaulle's theories of leadership and political action are relevant, however, not merely to an historical understanding of de Gaulle, but further to any analysis of the relationship of his personal efforts to the wider political and social environment and conjuncture in which he acted. For his views, his ambitions, to be effective, they must be consistent with the conditions in which they are applied. As was suggested at the beginning of this chapter, such congruence did not always exist; nonetheless, his overall record of performance suggests that, even where he was only partially successful, he often struck a chord which left an intense and lasting impact and impression upon both his supporters and his opponents. It is possible, in this perspective, to analyse in more detail the specific points at which the intentions, purposes and tactics characteristic of de Gaulle lead into programmes, policies, grand designs, and in a broader sense, into responses to structural and systemic pressures and changes. These provide the real test of Gaullist ideology in action.

National consciousness and the role of France in world politics: the Gaullist perspective

The ideological frame of reference in which French foreign policy must operate, and from which it derives its objectives and thus its dynamism and sense of purpose, is the result of a wider cultural and philosophical environment – of which de Gaulle was a particular product and interpreter. This environment imposes quite specific meanings and operational implications upon concepts such as *grandeur*, the nation, or independence, which characterise its language and its rationale. In this chapter we shall briefly examine three levels at which such concepts are woven into the context in which French foreign policy-making takes place. On the cultural and historical level, we shall look at the various conceptual meanings which can be found in the traditional options of French foreign policy, and the way that they form a larger fabric which de Gaulle was later to perceive and to interpret in his own way. These conceptual meanings will then be set into the domestic ideological structure of French society in order to study the ways in which foreign and domestic policy intertwine on this basic level of ideological perception. Lastly we shall examine the ways in which these conceptions operate as background variables in the way that de Gaulle saw the actual position of France in the world and accepted them as criteria for pitching the general level of aspiration for his overall foreign policy design. In this way we can build up an overview of the interface between Gaullist ideology in the sense of a *Weltanschauung*, which we have been examining so far, and various other background factors which make up the ideological environment of French foreign policy in the post-1958 period.

I. The French Foreign Policy Tradition and Grandeur

French foreign policy has more than once been characterised as being in a state of permanent tension between a desire of the French leaders to avoid foreign entanglements and to cultivate their own gardens,[1] on the one hand, and an outward-looking ambition which derived from both internal and external insecurities, on the other. In the first place, as we have already seen, French policy was always dominated by a cultural element which put cultural values – their protection, development and extension (especially given the French tendency to universalise) – before a search for either economic wealth or pure military power. Secondly, France's geographical situation – both her position as regards other countries and her domestic geographical structure and composition – demanded both an effort to maintain internal cohesion and unity, and a continual vigilance in a regional environment containing several hostile or potentially hostile powers (Britain, Germany, Spain, etc.). There was, as Raymond Aron has observed, a parallelism between the twofold 'vocation' of French policy – continental and maritime – and the vacillation and hesitation of her diplomacy:

With a northern frontier open to invasions and quite close to the capital, France was inevitably obsessed by the concern for an always precarious security. Situated at the western extremity of the small cape of Asia, she could not ignore the call of the sea and the lure of remote expeditions. She divided her forces between a diplomacy of continental hegemony (or of security) and a diplomacy of an overseas empire. She did not succeed completely in either direction.[2]

The results of this ambivalence led not only to an inconsistent foreign policy in terms of expansionism – where and when to extend French power – but also to the predominance of political and cultural *rationales* in setting objectives and justifying actions. In the same way that in the domestic political economy socio-cultural norms and abstract political ideals limited and channelled the development of a more advanced form of industrial capitalism,[3] in the foreign policy sphere the concern with survival and the dominance of the cultural norms by which social cohesion was maintained prescribed a primacy of 'politics' over 'economics'. Even the Napoleonic conquests had as their rationale the spread of French conceptions of civilisation and not French conquest *per se*. The foreign policy of Napoleon III, too, was dominated more by an adventurist support for certain nationalist causes and a desire to contain Prussian expansionism. And the timidity of foreign policy under the Third Republic was set off only by the irredentist *revanchiste* sentiment and by colonial expansion. Even French colonialism was somewhat different from British economic-style imperialism or the German desire for a place in the sun. In Stanley Hoffmann's words:

No economic drive explains the spread of French colonisation. France exported little capital to her colonies and was not much concerned with their economic development. France's colonisation was triple: military, peasant and administrative. The French civil servant rather than the merchant became the symbol of French rule. France would not easily disengage from an empire acquired as a means toward rank and as a way of spreading France's universal values, rather than as a source of wealth; an empire subjected to the French instinct of centralisation, applied to areas where central authority found or brooked no limits to its commands.[4]

French policy towards Europe, too, was always one dominated by an image of an overall *political* settlement which would transcend traditional quarrels while maintaining national identity – from the idealism of the post-Revolutionary period to the visions of Briand, Monnet, Schuman and even, with a different emphasis, de Gaulle.[5] For French independence was political independence, self-determination; not autarchy, nor aggressive military imperialism, nor economic imperialism, but rather a desire to settle once and for all the interlinked double problem of national cohesion at home and national security abroad.

Indeed, Jean-Baptiste Duroselle describes the core of French foreign policy as a tendency towards 'dominant introversionism'.[6] The features of this characteristic quality primarily include territorial satisfaction, a primacy of political factors over economic factors, a will to peace and a decline of the taste for glory which had itself arisen from the drive for internal national cohesion. Indeed, Duroselle notes: 'On this superficial level the taste for glory corresponds to a taste for *panache*, that is, the outer trappings of glory.' These outer trappings of glory did, however, possess considerable symbolic value, and their decline coincided with the claim made in the 1930s by the extreme Right that such symbols belonged to them alone – and not to the Left, which had claimed the banner of national glory after 1815, and which had shared it with the Right at various periods, e.g. the *Union sacrée* of the First World War. On the whole, though, as Dorothy Pickles has pointed out, the Third and Fourth Republics belonged to that tradition which saw France as 'a basically satisfied power'.[7] However, what she describes as a contrasting tradition, the 'dynamic tradition', as we have seen, had never been a full-fledged tradition of hegemony, but indeed had shared many of the cultural attributes of the introverted tradition.

It was the shock of the defeat of 1940 which highlighted and brought home the consequences of French vacillation in the foreign policy field and emphasised the interrelationship between foreign policy and domestic policy. Indeed, in the 1930s, it was foreign policy which was the most salient issue-area of French politics insofar as it demonstrated the incompetence of the political system as a whole when critical decisions had to be made. This is one of the subjects on which de Gaulle himself is clearest in his constant emphasis, which echoes his views on the need for an effective state:

At the time when they were faced by the problem on which, for France, all the present and all the future depended, Parliament did not sit, the government showed itself incapable of adopting as a body a decisive solution, and the President of the Republic abstained from raising his voice, even within the Cabinet, to express the supreme interest of the country. In reality this annihilation of the state was at the bottom of the national tragedy. By the light of the thunderbolt the regime was revealed, in all its ghastly infirmity, as having no proportion and no relation to the defence, honour, and independence of France.[8]

Duroselle catalogues the way in which the war brought home, on the material plane,

the inability of French diplomacy to defend the national interest; the defeat meant the annihilation of the nation's military potential; the occupation meant the inevitable exhaustion of economic resources, that is, ruin; and the small share in the victory meant the near certainty of failure to attain national goals unless they happened to coincide with those of powerful allies.[9]

But the war, and the symbolism of the war (in particular the dual symbolism of de Gaulle's Free French abroad and of the Resistance at home), revealed that political conflicts *other* than the traditional left–right split, and the immobilism associated with it, found a response in French society. Although national symbolism and sentiment seemed to become the property of the Right in the wake of the Dreyfus Affair at the turn of the century, and although in the 1930s the Left rejected them in favour of pacifism, in fact 'the Left was rejecting the surface symbols, not patriotism itself'.[10] Once the war was under way, it became clear that the left–right cleavage cut right across attitudes to the war – pacifism, defeatism, collaboration, flight abroad or internal resistance. Furthermore, the Left felt that national symbols had been 'stolen from the people by the Right', who were to use them, via the collaborationist Vichy regime, to dismember the patrimony of the nation in the interest of sections of the bourgeoisie. In the various Resistance movements, and among the Free French in London, there finally seemed to emerge a national sentiment and a patriotism which could overcome left–right divisions – and it was this ideal which de Gaulle aspired to achieve. This experience and this aspiration are highly significant in the light of postwar developments in France, both in terms of the failure of de Gaulle to establish a new state along these lines and in the attempt to return to the parliamentary synthesis of the Third Republic through the proxy of the institutions of the Fourth.

For again, it was foreign policy which focused attention upon the weaknesses of the Fourth Republic when viewed in Gaullist, *étatiste* terms. This was particularly true as regards France's relations with the United States and the North Atlantic Treaty Organisation, and even more directly, concerning the colonial question. French commitment in Indo-China and Algeria drained the nation of economic resources as well as keeping it at war without a break from 1946 until 1962. And again, positions on the left–right spectrum cut across attitudes on these vital questions.

The influence of world pressures in highlighting these weaknesses becomes more and more evident as one observes the process of development in world politics in the twentieth century. On the one hand, the global nature of power and conflict, and, on the other, the intertwined linkages characterising the world economy, combined to undermine the fragile equilibrium upon which the French regime had traditionally rested. Introversionism, made possible in France by the recognition of German military superiority after 1871, and reinforced by habits of dependence upon Britain and the United States made necessary by the nature of the First World War and the Versailles settlement (not to mention the failure of French intervention in the Ruhr in the 1920s), was shattered once and for all by the collapse of the Maginot Line. As Alfred Grosser has pointed out regarding the foreign policy of the Fourth Republic, France in the 1940s and 1950s was torn apart by both of the major conflicts then dividing the world. The first of these conflicts was that of communism versus anti-communism; the development of the cold war, the division of Europe and integration into the Western bloc through NATO were paralleled in the domestic arena by the existence of a powerful, Stalinist Communist Party and its exclusion from the normal politics of parliamentary coalition-building. The second was that of colonialism versus anti-colonialism; as one of the two major traditional colonial powers, and as one which, in Algeria, thought of its role as more than just colonial given the large and influential population of *colons* whose first home was Algeria but whose nationality and culture were French, France was divided both externally and internally. Furthermore, in both Indo-China and Algeria, the two conflicts both entered into the accounting; by the time de Gaulle returned to power in 1958, they had become fused in the minds of many, particularly in the higher echelons of the army, who felt that they were, in Algeria, fighting not a colonial war against indigenous nationalists, but a holy war for Western civilisation against Communist-inspired barbarians. And, in fighting the National Liberation Front of Algeria (FNLA) as if they were barbarians, the army itself became barbarised. The Fourth Republic collapsed from its failure to deal effectively with these intense and complex challenges.[11]

Underlying these conflicts, however, and linking up with the dominant tradition of introversionism, was, in embryo, a broad reappraisal by public opinion of attitudes on the French role in the world. Roy Macridis describes how introversionism became intertwined with a desire for a new kind of independence based on the strength of a retrenchment towards an independent Europe:

> throughout the period of the Fourth Republic, the public, even if badly informed, reacted with a remarkable degree of unity in favour of neutrality and European cooperation; feared Germany; suspected N.A.T.O. and in general agreed that independence and security can be based only on national strength and freedom of action. Despite an underlying realisation of France's reduced world status the public continued to cling to the image of a strong and independent France. They deplored the reduction of French strength and accepted European unity as an instrument for the realisation of national security vis-à-vis both the United States and the Soviet Union.[12]

De Gaulle's call for a foreign policy based on the renewed *grandeur* of the French nation – of an internal moral revival which would transcend the divisive conflicts of the Fourth (and Third) Republic by drawing France back into the hexagon while increasing her strength and independence and at the same time creating the effective state which would avoid such conflicts and act for the national interest in the future – had a large potential audience. Tradition and conjuncture, the sweep of history and the necessities of the immediate situation, came together in a way that de Gaulle was all too prepared to exploit in order to demonstrate where, in his view, the true interest of France lay.

In terms of French foreign policy experience, particularly in the twentieth century, then, we can discern the development of two factors which are especially relevant to our analysis. Firstly, this experience included a demonstration of the critical weaknesses of the French state and particularly its parliamentary tradition in dealing with the outstanding foreign policy problems of the day, with disastrous results for the state itself in 1940 and 1958. Secondly, from a fusing of introversionist tradition and the circumstances of world politics in the postwar period, there grew up a latent potential for widespread positive public response to a new synthesis of French political traditions through a reappraisal and strengthening of sentiments of national identity and independence – through altering and improving the domestic image of foreign policy among the French people themselves. In this way, permissive conditions developed for the creation of new symbolism based on a new self-respect. Here we have one of the critical conditions for de Gaulle's political action, for the proselytising of *grandeur*. Thus, in Grosser's words, the 'nationalism of resentment' which characterised the last years of the Fourth Republic might be replaced by a 'nationalism of pride'.[13]

II. Grandeur in the domestic arena

The Gaullist conception of *grandeur* is meant to appeal directly to the French person's need for a way to create a more coherent – and more nationally rooted–perspective on politics and society. This 'preoccupation with the idea of achieving a morally coherent world', which is present in 'all practical thinking which is not merely technical in character', generally 'comes to the fore when, in their practical experience, men discover a conflict between themselves as individuals and the natural and social world in which they live'.[14] Thus de Gaulle hoped, in Chateaubriand's phrase, 'to lead them there by means of dreams'.[15] As he said to Jean-Raymond Tournoux on the subject of national ambition in an interview on 8 January 1958 – before his return to power:

You see, the truth is like this: the French no longer have any spur to action. The thing which spurs a people on, is ambition. And France cannot do without a great national ambition.

Under the monarchy, France had the ambition of achieving the unity of her natural frontiers; later, she had the ambition of spreading the revolutionary gospel; under Napoleon I, it was the ambition to dominate Europe; under Napoleon III, the ambition to abolish the treaties of 1815; under the Third Republic, the ambition of *revanche*; and after the disaster of 1940, the ambition of Liberation.[16]

De Gaulle's intention was to provide such an ambition. But the ambition, as Tournoux observes, was for popular consumption.

In the General's judgment, it was important, from the psychological point of view, to obtain for the French – who had been accustomed for centuries to play a great role – the *compensation* of a universal message, capable of masking the decline of a country which, without noticing it, was passing from the rank of a world power to the rank of a nation of the second order.[17]

Although this ambition seems remarkably abstract and unrealistic at first sight, its implications are far-reaching. As Florian Znaniecki has argued, in many situations it is more significant to provide symbols than material goods. Symbols, like other 'ideational cultural products', as he calls them – unlike 'material cultural products', which can be used only by a limited number of individuals – can be used by any number of people who can all 'worship the same deity, accept the same moral standard or norm, reproduce or admire the same piece of literature or music (or), speak the same language. . .' Indeed, products of ideational culture do not wear out; 'only if they cease to be used do they lose their significance and eventually disappear'. They thus constitute 'a more influential and more lasting bond of social solidarity than material culture'.[18] Furthermore, not only can symbols be more durable and more widely shared than material goods, but they can also make sense of experience in a 'morally coherent' way and provide the criteria for choice in a confusing environment. The sense of belonging which they create is not merely imposed; it is also internalised, and becomes a part of an individual's *self*-definition. In Erik Erikson's words:

By accepting some definition as to who he is, usually on the basis of a function in an economy, a place in the sequence of generations, and a status in the structure of society the adult is able to selectively reconstruct his past in such a way that, step for step, it seems to have planned him, or better, he seems to have planned *it*. In this sense, psychologically we *do* choose our parents, our family history, and the history of our kings, heroes, and gods.[19]

By specifying definitions, assumptions and so on in symbolic terms, then, what appears to the individual to be a two-way communication system is set up, in which he seems *spontaneously*, as well as necessarily, involved. It may be possible for the observer, of course, by choosing 'objective' criteria (i.e. by reifying certain criteria), to assert that such a perception on the part of the individual is a false consciousness, but nonetheless it appears to be a truly mutual and reciprocal bond in the way it is experienced.

De Gaulle's primary political aim was to create such a symbolic universe for the French. By integrating traditional French cultural values with the necessities and constraints – and the limited but real potentialities – of the new, reduced French role in the world, he sought not merely to reconcile the French to a loss of power, but, more importantly, to make them aware that a valuable and morally significant role still remained to be played, if they could realise it. In this context, the concepts of national independence and national greatness, and the specific conceptions which de Gaulle constructed to give them substantive content, became the linch-pin of the overall symbolic structure. There are, indeed, several ways in which the concept of nationality can be seen as a particularly appropriate symbolic vehicle for such a task.

In the first place, the concept of a *nation* is multidimensional. Acceptance of a national framework of personal identity by the individual covers each of Erikson's three categories of individual self-definition: economic function, for a national society has a specific economic structure into which the individual is set and in which he sees his immediate economic behaviour; generational position, for national identity has a continuity which links the individual with such anomie-dispelling bonds as ancestral lineage and the sense of creation which comes with posterity; and social status, which gives relationships with others a predictability and structure which enables the individual to make sense of social encounters.

Secondly, the national framework reduces the *distance* between the different needs of the individual. At the psychological level, Herbert Kelman suggests,

the nation gains much of its strength from the fact that it represents the coming together of two important and in some sense contradictory needs: the need to protect those – such as members of one's immediate family – who are close to the self and extensions of it; and the need to transcend the self through identification with distant groups and causes. The nation is close enough to draw on the first of these needs, yet distant enough to satisfy the second.

Particularly important in this context is the linkage between the conception of the nation and sacred objects – including family symbolism (motherland, fatherland) and religious symbolism (the mystical or divine origins of the nation).[20] If a vacuum exists vis-à-vis this sort of overarching and interrelating symbolism, two sorts of consequences may follow: nationalism may flourish as an ideological doctrine;[21] and 'the perception of the state as meeting the population's needs and interests can compensate for a lacking sense of national identity, and can in fact help to create such an identity'.[22] Such conscious substitutes for pre-existing national identity symbols become more significant, in fact, as the size and complexity of the political system increase; 'the larger a polity becomes the less does the concept of the people designate a real community, and the more does it tend to denote a logical construction, or a logical fiction'.[23] Thus the task of creating and maintaining such a symbolic structure becomes more and more essential to the individual's need for self-definition the more the polity grows.

In the third place, the nation-state possesses a sufficient quantity and quality of seemingly autonomous attributes to make it a highly efficient frame of reference for the creation or the evolution of a rich pattern of symbolism which would be hard to duplicate. A common language, common cultural traditions and common historical experience are especially significant. Besides being extremely salient features of the fabric of everyday life – and therefore highly significant factors in socialisation and general behaviour (e.g. language and communication in general act as a *prerequisite* for other manifest behaviours) – they have, or can develop, sufficient interrelation, mutual reinforcement and overall coherence to appear not merely as referential symbols in their own rights, but also as subsets of an overarching *condensation* symbol which they have in common, i.e. the structural framework of the nation-state.[24]

Thus the nation becomes not only the most convenient mediating symbol within the social structure, but also a virtually irreplaceable one, a sort of 'crossroads' or linch-pin symbol which gives 'moral coherence' to the political world in which people live. The very idea of nationhood

implies a consciousness among members of a collectivity of the special bonds that tie them to one another. I find very useful, in this connection, Fishman's (1966) suggestion that an ethnic group becomes a nation when it begins to *ideologise* its customs and way of life. That is, when it goes beyond the conception of 'this is the way we do things' to a conception of 'there is something unique, special, and valuable about our way of doing things.' It is ideologising of this sort that makes it possible to develop allegiance to and invest one's identity in a collectivity that goes beyond – in both space and time – one's primary-group, face-to-face contacts.[25]

National symbolism is wide-ranging, potent symbolism. In France, the conditions were favourable to the development and manipulation of such symbolism, and Gaullist ideology provided both the substantive content and the framework for political action.

Now not only is the nation-state a particularly appropriate structural framework for the development of effective unifying symbols for the recipient individuals or groups who are exposed to such communications, but it also provides the symbol-maker with a range of possibilities as to both the substantive content which can be injected into such symbols and the range and scope of practical activity which can be justified by reference to the symbols. However, once established, the content of symbols takes on an independent meaning, and is not totally manipulable. Once created, they are no longer merely the property of the symbol-maker, but become collective property. The very manner in which they are experienced and internalised by the respondents – through 'the supplying of meanings in vague situations, stereotypes, oversimplification, [and] political quiescence' – 'are in large measure associated with social, economic or cultural factors affecting large segments of the population. They acquire meaning as group phenomena.'[26] In other words, 'symbolisation constitutes objects. . .which would not exist except for the context of social relationships wherein symbolisation occurs'.[27]

Furthermore, symbols are not transferable; they are never wholly arbitrary or empty, 'for there is the rudiment of a natural bond between the signifier and the signified. The symbol of justice, a pair of scales, could not be replaced by just any other symbol, such as a chariot.'[28] Indeed, the style and setting of symbolisation are an integral part of the content of the symbol. In American society, for example, the style of hortatory language used in making appeals for public support derives from a source with specific ideological (to be precise, theological) connotations – the Puritan sermon – which has influenced the content chosen by practitioners of the style.[29] The history of American foreign policy is littered with righteous pronouncements of doubtful practicality but great force and enormous historical impact – Washington's Farewell Address, the Monroe Doctrine, the statements of Woodrow Wilson, the Good Neighbour policy, the Atlantic Charter and so on. Indeed, President Carter's declarations concerning Human Rights are a prime example of this phenomenon. And the settings of the symbol-creating and symbol-reinforcing processes also create *expectations* about content, about what can be taken for granted in the message and what cannot. Settings create the perspective from which the message will be perceived by a mass audience, affecting both their response and 'the emotional aura which accompanies the response'. Most significantly, Edelman argues, settings can create an aura of 'business as usual', and once this aura comes into being, 'it thereafter defines the various specific acts' which will be perceived as 'politically acceptable'.[30]

The settings of Gaullist foreign policy are discussed in more detail at various points in this book, but it is significant to note at this point that settings can themselves both transcend and structure reality. They create associations which are real and immediate in their impact and influence, but which are only vicariously experienced. As Edelman writes: 'It is especially significant that the evoked settings need not have been physically experienced.'[31] In this sense, the concepts of the nation and of national greatness are both a reinforcement of an existing cultural bond and an injection of an up-to-date immediacy which aligns its potential meaning with the realities of the present-day world of experience. This simultaneity of fixed and flexible elements is the key to the significance of Gaullist symbolism; it assures its continuity. In Stanley Hoffmann's words, which echo de Gaulle's theory of leadership: 'What remains fixed is the command itself: like natural law, grandeur is an imperative with a varying content.'[32]

The key to Gaullist symbolism is the perception of France as having a particular – and unique – identity which is internalised by the French people and itself becomes a significant social bond. This is de Gaulle's 'certain idea of France'. Thus it becomes analogous to the British monarchy, the Constitution, the works of Marx and Engels, and the like, as one of the 'dignified elements' of the political community. This quality has been described rather better by Almond and Verba as 'the quality of quasi-sacred community'.[33] Now this symbolism is expressed primarily through specific images linked with foreign policy, especially France's prestige in the world and the need for greatness. This chosen vehicle is particularly significant, because foreign policy in its widest sense – activity deriving from the relation of the French nation-state to other nation-states – has the unique ability to express wholeness in a meaningful and active day-to-day context – a context which is often dominated by experiences of partiality and conflict.

Where a constitution may be the focus of hierarchical domination within a society, and where a monarch may be dignified but passive, and where many political ideologies may emphasise struggle, competition, and coercion of or freedom from others, foreign policy can be both active and an expression of the unity of the whole. Of course, it is certainly not always so; I am speaking of a *potentiality* stemming from the projection of the consequences of internal divisions outward as a kind of sublimation and substitution process. This is William James's 'moral equivalent of war'[34] and becomes transformed into an *institutionalised* expression of solidarity similar to military norms.[35] The significance of such norms lies in their effectiveness at creating unified action, at mobilising people into active collectivities which are not only disciplined, but self-disciplined. As military values, norms and methods become more and more acceptable and legitimate, as J. P. Nettl has observed, 'the greater becomes the compression factor in the process of mobilising commitment; acculturation, though necessarily narrow, can be deliberately and intensely applied, resistance more legitimately broken'. In this sense, phoney war – Sukarno's 'confrontation' policy, or even cold war – 'is an ideal solution; it provides all the domestic social advantages of warlike mobilisation without the economically ruinous and socially dangerous commitment to actual war'.[36]

Thus Robert Bloes compares the Gaullist myths – particularly the myth of the Strategic Nuclear Force – the *force de frappe* – with the American myths of the frontier, the New Freedom, the New Diplomacy, the New Deal, the New Frontier and the Great Society. All of these can be viewed as 'vast enterprises' in the Gaullist sense: 'In effect, the essence of myth is not to have a meaning which is objectively visible, but to draw together human energies outside and beyond the rational.'[37] As Edgard Pisani, a former Gaullist cabinet minister, has suggested in a more personal context, de Gaulle did not want to force France into the predetermined categories of his grand design, but neither did he want to align his design too closely on '*la France-réalité*'; his designs and images were themselves an attempt to link these extremes together, to show that 'France' existed in all of the different manifestations characteristic of her, yet that at the same time these manifestations had a common core and a holistic unity. The French needed an ambition, but that ambition had to be deeply rooted enough to mobilise spontaneously the energies of the people.[38] De Gaulle specifically marshalled foreign policy-related images in his 1965 presidential campaign – using them, according to Pompidou, to justify domestic policies as well as in their own right[39] – and throughout his career his strategy gave a large part to foreign policy themes and their symbolic referents.[40] Their mobilising capacity was, to him, self-evident. Tournoux reports de Gaulle's concern about the removal of the *Domine salvam fac rem publicam* from the Gallican liturgy;[41] the motivation was the same. Grandeur was not just a philosophy, nor was it a vision of an ideal world. Rather it was a means for raising the level of mass politics, an active element in an ideological world.

The process by which such an element was consciously constructed was one with great potential scope. Symbolic thinking, from the vantage point of the symbol-maker, provides great possibilities for the 'determined innovator' to draw together 'elements from a variety of existing myths and other kinds of doctrine...to make a mythical account which is not simply a version of any single known myth'.[42]

The whole might become greater than the sum of its parts. This is the process which Lévi-Strauss calls '*bricolage*', in which the myth-maker 'builds up structured sets, not directly with other structured sets, but by using the remains and debris of events. . .fossilised evidence of the history of an individual or a society'.[43] Here we can see the significance of de Gaulle's conception of French history, which, as has been noted earlier, was of an anecdotal nature. De Gaulle built his 'certain idea of France' out of a kind of *bricolage* of historical anecdotes and into a structured myth with direct relevance and application to contemporary problems.

Once this process has been successfully initiated, its range of impact is wide, for it can combine and blend together that which was previously divided and divisive. According to Harold Lasswell, '*Key signs provide a unifying experience* fostering sentiments that may transcend limitations of culture, class, organisation and personality.'[44] Furthermore, such symbols are not only useful, but necessary, for the existence of sufficient ideological community or consensus to maintain the continued quasi-voluntary cohesion among members of a social group. It is, in fact, the very diffuseness of the symbols themselves which makes them effective. To quote Henry Tudor again: 'In any reasonably civilised society, myths are incorporated into a general ideology composed of several mutually supporting practical points of view.' More sophisticated and abstract arguments thus appear less lucid and compelling than mythical argument.[45]

It is in this context that de Gaulle accused the French of having too much intelligence and too little instinct. The French historical parade of ideologies, parties and constitutions were to him a clear condemnation of too much reliance on abstract principles. Rather, de Gaulle was concerned with the unity of theory and practice, and his abstractions were always conceived from and through practice – or so de Gaulle himself believed. Edward Shils has commented that, in looking at the basis of social consensus, the internal coherence of the ideas contained therein must reflect, and be reconcilable with, the diversity of actual practice in society.

The ambiguity of the central terms and beliefs permits diverse interpretations to be made while those making the divergent interpretations retain some measure of adherence not only to the term or the belief in question but also to a residual element which is consensually shared with others from whom they diverge. Efforts to make the terms and beliefs more explicit and systematic might lead to a situation in which more weight is attributed to the dissensual elements at the cost of the residual consensual element.[46]

In France, in particular, foreign policy presented itself as the only reliable basis for building such a symbolic consensus – especially in the eyes of de Gaulle. National sentiment, in the first place, was particularly meaningful to the French themselves. In the words of Douglas Johnson, 'If they can forget that they are Catholic or anti-clerical, bourgeois or communist, in a Parisian bureau or on a Breton farm, and if they can remember only that they are French, and if they can see themselves as only the children of France, then the greatest difficulty of governing France is over.'[47] But the global environment, too, reinforced such myths. The emergence of new nations, along with the strength of the superpowers – seen in the classical sense of 'Great Power' nation-states – and the rapid growth of ideological and practical 'polycentrism' within their respective alliance systems, have all fed into the regeneration of nationalitarian ideologies and sentiments. And on a third level, too, the individual, seeking to escape from the anomie and alienation of mass society, searches for symbols in a context where the choice of symbols and ideologies has multiplied; the holistic character of national symbolism makes identification with the national collectivity seem the most natural choice. De Gaulle saw and understood these conditions – all the more, because he believed in the symbols themselves. The domestic function of grandeur, then, was to provide a viable foundation for the development of a consensus which French society had previously lacked, although, in de Gaulle's mind, the potential capability for creating such a consensus had always existed. His aim was to pursue and reinforce this capability, and he became an expert at the necessary symbolic *bricolage*.

III. The Level of Aspirations in de Gaulle's Foreign Policy

The pursuit of grandeur, even as a function of an ultimate domestic purpose, means, as we have seen, that foreign policy and foreign policy aspirations had to be, on the whole, the most visible and salient feature of the Fifth Republic's political activity – although it went in tandem with the consolidation of the new political institutions. In consequence, it was necessary that the level of policy aspirations had to be high, and to be seen to be high.[48] As Hoffmann has written, the very notion of grandeur 'implies a will to be an actor, not an object; a player, not a stake; ...it entails a decision to be as ambitious, universal and inventive an actor as world politics in general and one's power base in particular allow'.[49]

In considering the level of aspirations of de Gaulle's foreign policy, however, it is all too easy to see the salience of foreign policy as indicating a primacy of foreign policy in Gaullist values, and to conclude that 'greatness' equals the quality of being 'grandiose'. Even Hoffmann falls into this conceptual trap. For him, it 'involves the subordination of domestic politics to the primacy of international affairs and to the requirements of status: grandeur implies that the nation must be ready to bear the sacrifices such a policy requires. . .'.[50] Now we have distinguished between *the symbolic primacy of the national interest* (expressed in images derived from foreign policy), on the one hand, and the actual primacy of external objectives, on the other. Several factors arise in a consideration of this distinction.

The first of these, one which has already been alluded to, is the distinction between appearance and reality. Many authors writing about de Gaulle perceive a clear gap between what they perceive as the actual level of de Gaulle's external objectives, on the one hand, and the insufficiency of the real policy outcomes, on the other. Significant examples include: de Gaulle's dramatic stand on NATO versus the continuing and close cooperation between France and NATO on the sub-symbolic level; the equally dramatic 'empty chair' clash between de Gaulle and the European Economic Community's Commission in 1965 versus the continuing willingness of France, again, to cooperate on a sub-symbolic level, as well as the symbolic importance but real vacuity of the Luxembourg Agreements of January, 1966; the emphasis on the development of strategic and tactical nuclear weapons versus their various weaknesses and their strategic vulnerability and even counter-productivity; the operations of France in the monetary field, i.e. calling at one time for a return to the gold standard, versus the inevitable primacy of American objectives in some form or other; and the emphasis on detente with the Soviet Union and Eastern Europe versus the small volume of French trade with the area and the small amount of leverage which France could hope to exert there.[51]

Certainly, in the ideological context elaborated by these writers – i.e. the obsolescence of the nation-state in the contemporary world and the capability gap between medium powers and superpowers – these perceived discrepancies would appear to be significant, and would signal a broad and decisive defeat for de Gaulle's foreign policy. However, in the ideological context as we have been developing it here, it would seem to me more than plausible that such a 'defeat' was not only consonant with the symbolic and limitationist nature of Gaullist objectives, but also, in a more fundamental way, insignificant. This is because the true measure of significance was not, in what would at first appear to be a paradox, external successes; rather, the acid test was domestic impact.

If the French somehow came to believe that de Gaulle had restored something of France's lost greatness, if they believed that France once again had a significant moral role to play in the world, if they came to identify with that moral role – and if that identification effectively cut across party, class, regional and other cleavages – then and only then would French foreign policy have been successful. The problem here is that, like de Gaulle's calculated public schizophrenia as to his personal role and image in French politics, his foreign policy, too, was characterised by a calculated and all-important gap between apparent, publicly proclaimed objectives and broader ideological objectives. Towards the end of this book, we shall look at some of the available data on domestic public impact. But for the moment our purpose is simply to point out the gap between the importance of the symbolism and the relatively lesser importance of the outward signs of Gaullist foreign policy.

A second important distinction, one which is closely related to the above, is that between immediate aims, on the one hand, and long-range goals or visions, on the other, in the ways that they affect the general level of policy aspirations. The two may coincide, of course. But, as Renouvin and Duroselle point out, the foreign policy-maker is risking certain 'stakes': 'as a rule, what is at stake – the "national interest" – comprises the whole complex of national objectives, the ideal; whereas the immediate aims are pursued day by day and constitute what might be described as the successive elements of the stake'.[52] For example, familiar to all students of bargaining and conflict resolution are such tactics as 'bidding up' the stakes, which may be used in order to achieve an objective which is, in fact, much more limited than the claimed, or even the most obvious, objective. Furthermore, there is the significant question of time sequences. Clues to the relationship between actual objectives and claimed objectives may appear from the sequence in which the latter appear within the particular configuration of forces existing at a particular conjuncture. For example, it may be worth demanding most when least is attainable, in order to create the setting for a long-range campaign for the attainment of more limited objectives.

De Gaulle's 1958 memorandum about the structure of NATO has been described in this context by J.-R. Tournoux and C. L. Sulzberger.[53] The controversy over whether de Gaulle really wanted merely the restructuring of NATO, or something quite different – e.g., an excuse for France to withdraw from the organisation (and perhaps even the Atlantic Alliance) altogether – has dominated American analyses of de Gaulle in particular. Indeed, it has proved impossible to provide clear and decisive proof either way from the existing evidence.[54] It is even possible, given the nature of de Gaulle's *Weltanschauung*, to posit a kind of holism in his foreign policy, in which the individual elements in the stake become relevant merely to the success and progress of the whole, which is seen to be greater than the sum of its parts. Thus, if the interpretation which can be placed upon the whole is changed, then the parts themselves, taken separately, and being merely secondary features, do not in themselves add up to a sufficient basis for testing (much less proving) the relative success or failure of the whole. Indeed, these separate – instrumental – parts, when taken together, may constitute little more than *capacities* for attaining the overarching objective, and therefore of little value in isolation. After all, power or capacity is not an end in itself in most circumstances. Therefore the attainment of capacities may provide a clue to, but will not necessarily be a cause or determinant of, overall objectives. And grandeur was not a specific policy, but a quality which should characterise all aspects of policy – 'an attitude of dignity and self-respect'.[55]

Therefore, in seeking to identify the general level of aspirations of de Gaulle's foreign policy, a number of traditional clues fall by the wayside. The concept of 'nationalism' is of very little substance here. The concept of the nation-state is not a substantive determinant of the *content* of a doctrine which may be based upon its geographical framework. The historical development of German nationalism and the circumstances surrounding the waging of two world wars were characterised by a particular *kind* of nationalism, but this may be no more significant than the concept of 'society' in determining the content of social doctrines. Indeed, in each case, a particular *conception* of 'nation' or 'society' must be posited. Furthermore, nationalism exists in different forms depending upon the nature of the activity into which it is injected. We are all familiar with the threefold distinction between the psychological aspect (independence, *patrie*, identity, national consciousness or sentiment – depending on the context of the author), the juridical aspect or structural framework (nation, sovereignty, national situation), and the active or instrumental element (state, duty, autonomy, nationalism) which, in somewhat different forms, and emphasising slightly different features, regularly reappears in the literature on Gaullist nationalism. An extension of such criteria would indicate three different dimensions along which aspirations could vary: national sentiment versus nationalism; satisfied versus expansionist; and defined nation versus in search of a nation.[56] Is the nation-state in question isolationist or universalist? If universalist, are its objectives warlike or peaceful? Is it egoist and possessive, or generous and missionary?

These questions are not predetermined by the existence of nationalism *per se*. 'What is common to all cases of nationalism is the attempt to promote these (shared) goals by maintaining or establishing a nation-state as an effective political unit. The nature of the goals involved, however, may vary widely from country to country, from period to period, and from group to group within a given country.'[57] They may include economic development, military expansion or internal democratisation. And these goals will be linked with the domestic social structure. And, in contrast to the tradition of aggressive, racist nationalism analysed by Kedourie, certain writers have identified an alternative model of nationalism – a nationalism based on a search not for domination but for *autonomy*, or, in the word coined by one Egyptian writer, *nationalitaire* – a 'reconquest in depth of identity'.[58]

These polar distinctions would seem to cut across, for example, Duroselle's distinction between 'extroversive' and 'introversive' goals, because 'nationalitarian' goals would include elements of both in a distinctive mixture.[59] Gaullism, as we have seen, is just such a distinctive mixture. André Malraux claimed that French nationalism was more akin to Swiss nationalism than to the German variety, because it involves no will to hegemony, yet it can still be imperial: 'There is the imperialism of what one takes and the imperialism of what one gives' which distinguishes the isolated national consciousness from the universal national consciousness. Thus French nationalism not only displays no will to hegemony, but also desires to share its blessings around and to reinforce the development of autonomy as a general principle for world politics.[60] In this way, Gaullist foreign policy would resolve the apparent contradiction between the need for international solidarity and the desire for independence; this would be true of both European policy and global policy, according to Georges Pompidou.[61] Furthermore, the kind of independence involved requires a willingness to take necessary and unpopular decisions and to face the consequences while at the same time, in the words of Couve de Murville, avoiding 'adventurism'.[62] Independence demands responsibility, a reciprocal and balanced commitment which reconciles French interests with the general interest of the international community, at least in theory.

Probably the most direct statement of the implications of the nation-alitarian principle and its implications for foreign policy comes also from Couve de Murville; it deserves full quotation:

What, then, is this famous French nationalism? Is it that our country expresses national ambitions towards any of its neighbours? Is it that she has shown in any way in Europe or elsewhere the least will of adventure or domination? Is it that someone thinks that France is a risk, however minimal, to peace in general? In reality our country has, with the end of the Algerian affair, resolved the last of her great problems. Her first objective has become her own economic and social development. She has no outside ambitions, other than to participate in the construction of a true Europe, to act everywhere in the direction of equilibrium and of peace, and finally to bring her contribution, and it is proportionally the first, to the struggle against underdevelopment. Naturally she has the worry of her independence, even when it is a matter of alliances, but this care is accom-panied by a strict respect of the independence of all and by a strict policy of non-intervention in the internal affairs of others. Who would disagree with this caring for independence if these two corollaries of which I have just spoken were to be found everywhere?[63]

In the light of this official statement, found in a speech by the Foreign Minister to the National Assembly in 1966, external goals are clearly seen to be based upon a domestic rationale. But even relevant domestic criteria possess a universal dimension which was to make French foreign policy active rather than passive. And in today's world, the realisation of those goals requires decisiveness and active participation in inter-national politics. Thus the search for autonomy is both extroversive and introversive at the same time, and cannot be reduced to either.

One of the consequences of this basic posture is that traditional capabilities are less significant. If power is the capacity to make others do what you would have them do, then it can derive from a variety of sources. Academic writers have usually considered that policy-makers base their judgment and esteem on three criteria (among others): '(1) a nation's level of technology, which is closely related to its (2) immedi-ately available military capabilities, and (3) the reputation it can generate abroad through its day-to-day diplomatic conduct and political, economic and social behaviour at home'.[64] However, a more sophisticated and suggestive typology of power has been presented by Johan Galtung, who makes a threefold distinction between the follow-ing: ideological power (represented by ideology, culture, language); remunerative power (represented by population [labour], land [area] and capital [GNP]); and punitive power (represented by military expenditure, military hardware and software); these, however, represent capabilities, rather than power actually exercised (Galtung calls them types of 'resource power'). Now these forms of power or capability do not, themselves, determine outcomes; they are merely forms of raw material, and their significance depends on how, under what conditions and to what ends they are used; it is difficult to use a sledge-hammer to crack a nut. Resource power can be resisted or limited either by balancing, or by the development of effective autonomy – power over oneself. Thus self-respect may counter ideological power, self-sufficiency can resist dependence upon another's remunerative power, and fearlessness can at times check punitive power. Resource power and its types are the most familiar forms of power. Autonomy is a psychological attitude. Ultimately, however, they are not the only, and not even the principal, forces in determining the nature of the power hierarchy. For the hierarchy itself – the pattern of authority and obligation – contains structural features which favour certain actors over others. These structural features characterise not so much the actors themselves, but their interactions. This *structural power*, which is very close to Rosenau's concept of 'linkages', includes such elements as exploitation (an uneven distribution of opportunities deriving from relative positions in the production process), fragmentation and penetration. All of these depend upon the postulation of different types of relations between a 'centre' and a 'periphery', relations which could not be changed by redistributing resources; they can only be altered by restructuring the way in which costs and benefits are distributed in the system itself. It is dependent upon a division of labour.[65]

The concept of structural power is particularly useful here, even though we are not using it in the sense of explaining dominance or imperialism in the general sense of the global distribution of power which Galtung envisages. Autonomy can be a useful concept, too, in that de Gaulle's foreign policy is generally aimed at developing the psychological capacity for autonomy among the French themselves. Resource power, on which so many studies have concentrated, becomes somewhat less relevant except as a background factor. But structural power, in particular, helps to explain why France under de Gaulle not only resisted power (e.g. emanating from the superpowers) to a notable extent, but also *exercised* power which was not directly due to French capabilities.

Of course, France in some respects exercised resource power. To most of the world, she is one of the exclusive club of very rich Western industrial countries in Galtung's 'centre'. But in economic terms, France, like the rest of industrialised Western Europe, is certainly not at the same level of wealth or development as the United States. For example, in the matter of the development of advanced technology, France would seem to be caught in a development trap not dissimilar in kind (only in degree) from the economic development trap experienced by the Third World. While economic development in the Third World advances, that of the West advances even faster, partially (at least) because of the structure of the world economy which reserves the most important production processes to the 'centre'. Similarly, while technological development in France advances, technological development in the United States advances much faster – creating an ever-widening gap in absolute terms – due to such factors as the expenditure of funds at a much higher absolute level than that in France, leading to a multiplier effect. France, therefore, in order to sustain its own technological development, is put in the position of becoming ever more dependent upon the spin-offs of American technology (licensing, research and development, etc.), thus further reducing the scope for indigenous innovation.[66] The resource power gap widens.

However, for this very reason, France possesses the potential for autonomy, because it possesses the necessary conditions for a consciousness of the need for autonomy. France is aware of her dependence upon the United States and has had sufficient traditional status and independence to reject and resist American hegemony – a potential which was central to de Gaulle's own intentions and actions. On the other hand, France also possesses a vital minimum of resource power relative to the rest of the world, and thus she can escape the worst consequences of the structural trap; the 'underdeveloped' world is not so lucky. She is *both* in the 'centre' (economically) and on the 'periphery' (in terms of military and technological resource power in the global strategic context) at the same time. Thus France, from her position in the global structure of power, can be seen as having the potential resources and leverage to play a 'middleman' role.

Now the ability and the aspiration to play a 'middleman' role – which is here conceived as bringing together the elements of what the French call a *rôle charnière* (hinge) and a *rôle moteur* (active, innovative) – depends upon two factors: the consciousness and willingness of the actor to play such a role; and the vulnerability of the international system at key points in time and space to the influence which can be exerted by such an actor. De Gaulle recognised the first element: 'In order to exercise a national authority, it is not necessary to be a great country. Tito, for example, possesses an international authority because he can wield first of all a national authority.'[67] For de Gaulle, 'from the political viewpoint, there is no lack of historical examples of men who have resisted – and who have won – after having run the risk of the physical annihilation of their country'. This requires, in Tournoux's words, a kind of 'international judo', the weak using the strength of the adversary and turning it against him.[68]

Joseph Frankel points to the position of France between the super-powers, maintaining varied interests and outlets, as a key example of the role which geography can play in influencing views on the nature of the national interest. French experience is not unique in this respect, and the power of such images is potentially great. Collective symbols often emphasise the special role of a group as being 'between' other people, with an historic mission of 'mediating between two peoples, cultures, religions, or civilisations'.[69] But such a role is more complex and more difficult to play than the role of dominator or dominated. It requires continual activity, vigilance and manipulative skill. It demands both decisiveness in the face of risks and the avoidance of 'adventurism' – to be aware of the real limitations on one's sphere of action. Thus, on the one hand, a determination to make the most of this role is required. To de Gaulle, France can and must stay France:

> She must not be weakened by doubt. Intransigence and challenge are the order of the day. Yes, in spite of everything, France has a role to play, if not one of innovation, then at least one of initiation to culture, to humanism, to genius and to the heritage of Rome and Athens.[70]

But such a search for the 'prestige of the spirit'[71] is particularly relevant to the relationship between France's actual capabilities and the potential receptivity of the structural environment. Culture and spirit are, partially at least, rationalisations of the limitations inherent in the middleman role, which is the only way that France could afford to be concerned primarily with domestic development, weak in resource power, and active and influential as an international actor, all at one and the same time.

It is, of course, problematic whether or not the conditions prevailing in the international system were receptive to this level of Gaullist aspira-tions. The effective leverage of an international actor like France will depend upon the nature of the conflict situation. France could act either as a direct power-broker using her (limited) resource power to tip a delicate balance; the French strategic nuclear force was meant to provide this sort of capability. Or she could act as a catalyst, to reinforce pre-existing trends or structural potentialities latent in the existing situation. Independence and grandeur, in either of these senses, 'can be measured, or even approximately evaluated, only relatively' to the power, structural position and degree of conflict or consensus between actors in a particular situation.[72] The essence of the middleman role is not, therefore, to carry out a wholesale restructuring of the international system; nor can it be to assert France's right to be a Great Power equal to the superpowers; nor even to isolate France from the international system as a 'maverick'. Rather, it is to manipulate the potentialities of the system in order to maximise influence while at the same time minimising risk.

Such aspirations require the prior acceptance of the fundamental structural limitations imposed by the system itself, while working for changes which, though dramatic in style, are in fact incremental in consequence. The grandeur of France, to be both effective at home and feasible internationally, requires that France be able to exercise influence disproportionate to her material means. The unique blend of cultural conceptions, foreign policy traditions and interpretations of the actual international conjuncture which underlay de Gaulle's approach to foreign policy provided a response and an initiative which were, within strict limitations, both effective and credible. His symbolic *bricolage* gave France an ambitious, yet not unrealistic, role to play in a changing international environment. This role required a complex equilibration of decisiveness, will and salience – primarily on a symbolic level – with a sophisticated awareness of the circumscribed nature not only of her capabilities but also of her structural position with its limitations and potential opportunities. Such a balancing act, furthermore, while being especially appropriate to France, also reflected the structure of contemporary international relations generally. Having, in this chapter, examined the relevance of the Gaullist perspective to the wider ideological and cultural environment of France, it will therefore be useful to go a step further and to ask whether it is not also representative of a more general phenomenon characteristic of today's world.

Foreign policy leadership and national integration: a framework for analysis

The study of foreign policy leadership is characterised by a number of conceptual and methodological problems, problems which have become apparent in our treatment thus far of de Gaulle's approach to foreign policy. Are we studying de Gaulle, the man? De Gaulle, the ideologist? De Gaulle, the practising politician, acting within a particular social, cultural and political environment? Or are we studying phenomena which are widespread? Is de Gaulle merely a particular and interesting example of a pattern which can be observed elsewhere in international – or domestic – politics? And, if so, how can we evaluate and judge the relative importance of the various factors involved – as well as the significance of de Gaulle and his foreign policy as historical phenomena?

This sort of book, then, is located on the divide between the study of the individual and idiosyncratic, on the one hand, and the structural and patterned on the other. It stands at the crossroads of the internal political system and the international area. And it lends an aura of personalised comprehensibility to complex processes of change and development, integration and disintegration, in the multidimensional political, social and economic environment in which it is set. Its very choice of subject matter seems to assume that political actors, although working within specific systematic constraints, also possess opportunities to make and/or enforce choice under permissive conditions which allow a significant amount of conscious manipulation. Furthermore, studies of this type often take for granted that the nation-state – its politics, culture and historical development – is the most significant unit of analysis; it is generally treated as given, rather than problematic.

Having treated the personal, ideological and cultural variables which relate to de Gaulle's role as an historical actor within a specific and unique context, I will attempt in this chapter to chart a course through the complex waters of generalization – seeing de Gaulle's foreign policy from the perspective of broader analytical categories relevant to foreign policy leadership in the context of national political integration. We shall develop a set of interrelated hypotheses about a particular syndrome or category of political behaviour, namely the attempt to legitimise the authority of the state itself within what Znaniecki has called 'modern national culture societies'.

I. Authority Legitimation, Social Cohesion and the Perception of National Interest

The task of legitimising authority within a political unit is one which has preoccupied both political philosophers and political actors throughout recorded history. Most of the modern industrialised nation-states underwent this process at some time between the seventeenth and twentieth centuries. In most of these cases, the legitimation of the authority of the state either coincided with or was structurally linked with the rise to dominance of that group or class which initiated, implemented and commanded the industrialisation process. This combination of political institutionalisation and economic development has been reified by many observers into a general process which is called 'modernisation' and which has been accompanied by certain structural features.[1] In the present era, this process has been complicated for the 'new states' – mainly ex-colonial territories – not only by influences and imperatives caused by the extended direct rule of these areas from abroad and according to criteria laid down by colonial powers,[2] but also by the structural influences of the international system, which is characterised by an imbalance between the centre and the periphery on a range of levels – cultural, political and economic. An entire literature has grown up around the concept of 'nation-building', whether according to criteria drawn from the Western experience or from various Third World perspectives ranging from the conservative to the radical.[3]

But whatever the dominant group in the legitimation process, whatever the historical and socio-economic context of that process, and whatever its rationale and ideology, authority legitimation is clearly an essential and indispensable ingredient in the transition of society from the condition of being an aggregation of social relations to the state of being a *political* society or community which develops a capacity for collective action and collective decision-making along with a common sense of identity and consciousness of membership in the collectivity. The substantive content of that consciousness and the norms which guide decision-making may vary (what Aristotle called 'friendship' and 'justice' – the two prerequisites of a *polis*), but the process of legitimation is of *a priori* significance for *any* teleological or behavioural theory of the state. It is particularly central to the historical study of any society in which the legitimation process is non-existent, incomplete or uneven; and contemporary societies generate complex, intense and ever-increasing demands upon their structures and resources.

The main task facing the political elites of nation-states in which the legitimation process has not (temporarily or permanently) achieved stability or equilibrium is – in their own eyes – to further the development of that process and to channel it towards their particular objectives. This can happen in comparatively developed polities as well as underdeveloped ones. In the case of de Gaulle, his own view was that his main task was the legitimation of political authority (*via* the state in its reformed condition after 1958) in French society. It has been pointed out that the democratic–political revolution in France, unlike the modernisation revolution in several other countries, was characterised not by the cohesiveness of a modernising elite, but by a fundamental cleavage between opposing elites which prevented the consummation of the socio-economic aspect of the modernisation process.[4] Hoffmann, among others, has pointed out that the very survival of the political system of the Third and Fourth Republics was ensured only by its failure to carry out innovative decision-making and its concentration on maintaining a potentially unstable equilibrium – the 'Republican synthesis' – among the contending forces within French society.[5]

Now, for de Gaulle, the rationale of his attempt to revitalise and to expand the legitimation process was in order that the political decision-makers in France could have sufficient authority to carry out certain functions – activities, tasks and roles – which were inherent in his view of the state. As the rationale for the political system itself was seen by him to derive from the effective execution of those functions, the existence of such authority was seen as a necessary precondition for the state to fulfil the social function which it possessed by definition – i.e. the active pursuit of the 'general interest'. In his view, those tasks which should have been carried out by the state had in effect fallen traditionally to various vested interests (*féodalités*) to the benefit of those vested interests and to the detriment of the national interest. Thus de Gaulle, like many other leaders of states in a process of formation or transition, was searching for a means of legitimating his new political order so that the French state could play a more active normative role in French society. Fundamental to this search is the reinforcement of factors of social cohesion at the level of the nation-state.

It has been suggested that three principal factors which hold political communities together are kinship, ideology and work (relations of production).[6] Clearly, in a nation-state, kinship is a bond which is both too binding in its psychological imperatives and too loose and extended in its socio-biological structure to provide a sufficient basis for the legitimation of authority. History has shown the serious drawbacks of extended racism, and ethnic identity often leads to conflictual rather than consensual relationships by highlighting sub-national – divisive – rather than national loyalties. As for the relations of production, the fact that economic (and even socio-economic) systems frequently do not coincide with political boundaries, but with sub-national class, regional and other boundaries (not to mention extended and complex international linkages), means that only autarchy could be presumed to be a sufficient condition for national cohesion, although a degree of compatibility and/or complementarity of economic roles and functions may be necessary for minimal cohesion.

Ideology, likewise, is often a divisive factor, especially when its internal structure coincides with other than national perceptions and loyalties. For elites and leaders seeking to reinforce national cohesion, however, it is possible to posit that a national ideology, a national consciousness made explicit, can play not only a mediating role, but also an active, architectonic role in focusing legitimacy upon the state. The purpose of an authority-legitimating ideology at the level of the nation-state is to ensure (a) that compliance with the authoritative social order (the state) is *internalised* rather than coerced, and (b) that the exercise of authority takes place within boundaries best suited to the maintenance of compliance; in addition, for teleologically-oriented leaders like de Gaulle, its purpose includes keeping the state aware of and concerned with the carrying out of its proper tasks.[7] It defines normative relationships all round.

If a 'legitimate order' does not exist, or exists only partially (for example, where it is concerned merely with maintaining compliance and not with the way authority is itself exercised), then ideology will be the most appropriate instrument for creating such an order. The 'ideational culture' is that aspect of community cohesion which is most easily manipulated; in contrast, kinship structures tend to be deeply rooted *a priori*[8] and economic structures tend to be extremely complex and thus tricky to manipulate centrally. Ideology, in contrast, is a mental or psychological construct. It exists in intangible, often non-material relationships. It tends to be dominated by condensation symbolism – i.e., its symbols tend to evoke some essential relational characteristics of a wide range of diverse material and ideational experience and perception (rather than any specific and concrete point of reference) – whereas kinship and economy tend to be dominated by more circumscribed referential symbolism. Therefore its impact is the greater insofar as it structures the respondent's frame of reference – the filter by which he distils, colours and makes sense of his world and his experience.[9]

Similarly, ideology involves the expression of language, and therefore can be manipulated; in some cases, this can be done in a very short time, where language provides sufficient common reference points, and provided, too, that respondents are sufficiently receptive. Material variables may be more resistant to rapid alteration. Furthermore, societies can be seen not so much as physical but as historical phenomena – 'societies exist in time more than in space'[10] – and ideology as condensation symbolism can cut across generations as well as across social groups. Ideologies are similar in *content* to political culture, which is the 'particular pattern of orientations' towards political objects which characterises political systems. These orientations ('predispositions to political action'), which derive from historical memories, motives, norms, emotions and symbols, can be broken down into (a) cognitions (knowledge and awareness of the political system), (b) affect (emotional disposition to the system) and (c) evaluation (judgment about the system).[11] In sum, then, if an ideology becomes sufficiently internalised, it becomes either the whole of, or, more likely, a more or less significant part of, the political culture itself, and determines the dominant orientations of the public towards the political system.

Given the significance of the role of the political system itself (especially in modernised societies) as a socialising agent,[12] ideology in all its ramifications can become the predominant factor in creating a 'legitimate order', with a legitimised scope of action, where such an order was previously lacking or undeveloped. This is all the more significant in that nation-states are dynamic, not static, structures; this includes 'purposive efforts to gain new members'[13] by spreading the consciousness of common membership to those who are deemed (by the prevalent ideological or symbolic standards) to be true if not yet conscious members, by using propaganda or organised mass education.

Ideology plays a *continuous* role in this dynamic process, both by linking different elements of the process and by its diachronic nature, persisting and acting over time. This legitimising role played by ideology is all the more important in the modern world insofar as the dominant legitimising principle today is democracy (at least at the level of lip-service). Legitimacy, therefore, has more and more to be achieved (i.e. must be constantly justified to the populace) and is less and less ascribed.

Authority legitimation in contemporary nation-states, then, is a process likely to revolve around ideology, whether as official rationalisation, historical justification, or actual principle and purpose of social and political action. Ideology provides a method of cutting across disparities and cleavages in the search for national solidarity. Nettl goes so far as to suggest that in modern society, interest-specific cleavages, oppositions and so on are 'compensated by the existence of conservative universalist perspectives with regard to nation and society'.[14] Of course, if patterns of political authority do not converge,[15] then latent conflicts may emerge.

This is particularly significant in the case of liberal democratic societies, where the very justificatory ideology of the political system itself posits that many such sub-national groupings should be permitted to exercise certain forms of political and social activity (voting, free speech, competitive parties, representative assemblies, etc.) with little direct legal hindrance (though other hindrances, social or economic, may prevail). In such an environment, the ideological–symbolic process by which authority is legitimated must continue to be strong over time if the endogenous solidarity-producing variables within the sub-national group are not to be reinforced beyond the threshold of 'pluralism' by exogenous factors emanating from the wider social, political and economic environments. Indeed, the maintenance of wider national ideological loyalties need not have a specific referential link with material experience. National solidarity may hide or even justify injustice and exploitation:

Not only does systematic research suggest that the most cherished forms of popular participation in government are largely symbolic, but also that many of the public programmes universally taught and believed to benefit a mass public in fact benefit relatively small groups.[16]

And indeed the cultural memory of class or other microsocieties, the orientations they exhibit towards the political system, are also heavily permeated, if not dominated, by myths and symbols which mediate material experience. Thus, although ideology cannot change the material experience of such sub-national groupings, it can affect the expression and transmission of such experience through language and can impose its own logical (or ideo-logical) structures. It is a common-place of political science that some sort of common ideological umbrella or consensus is a prerequisite for the survival of liberal democratic institutional norms.[17]

It would seem, then, that central to any ideology of legitimation is not simply its substantive content, nor even its instrumental rationale, but its *de facto* acceptance on a behavioural level by those individuals and groups which might otherwise provide the focus for effective dissent and/or disruption of the state decision-making structure. One factor which might lead an individual to support 'his' political system, of course, is satisfaction with government output. However, the authors of *The Civic Culture* suggest from their findings that a more diffuse sense of attachment, less closely tied to performance, may in fact be more significant.

Satisfaction with political output usually varies with system performance. The more diffuse sense of attachment to the system (or what we have called 'system affect'), though in the long run not unrelated to specific output, can be expected to be a more stable kind of satisfaction. It is the kind of 'rain or shine' attach-ment that will enable a system to weather a crisis in its performance.[18]

Kelman distinguishes between 'sentimental attachment' to a system and 'instrumental attachment', and identifies several sub-types of the former: commitment to cultural values reflective of national identity; commitment to the *role* of national linked with group symbols; and commitment to the sacredness of the state.[19] Parsons links a very similar list of factors to the maintenance of institutional stability, adding that a fourth characteristic of stability involves some recognisable order for the integration of sub-systems into the overarching normative com-plex.[20] When such conditions exist, or, as Herz puts it, when there is 'an impression or even a conviction that the unit in question "should be" the one on the basis of which a particular group organises its separate and distinct existence as a "nation", there is legitimacy'.[21] Those characteristics of institutional stability and legitimacy which are most potent tend also to be ideological and symbolic in nature.

Such legitimacy does not simply emerge from the depths. It results from an historical process. It follows from this that the process of authority legitimation involves, first and foremost, the *generation of system affect.*

Thus nation-building – the creation of a set of political structures called a nation-state – proceeds very often by the institutionalisation of commitment to common political symbols. It is not merely that the symbol represents the nation, but that the creation of the symbol is coterminous with the creation of the nation.[22]

These symbols – whether visible symbols like a flag, active symbols like a constitution, or abstract symbols like national myths or consciously constructed ideologies of 'individual freedom' or 'from each according to his ability, to each according to his need' – are institutionalised, given centre-stage in the developmental process of national life, and associated consciously or unconsciously with the real or imagined benefits which may be seen to flow from membership in the national community. This process requires not only the building of specific new symbols, but, as Harold Lasswell has pointed out, also the emancipation of the respondents from old, specific authority symbols: 'They involve a new symbol rival to the old, which is legitimised by a sustaining myth, and executed by an elite which rises to the main posts of income and deference in the name of the new symbol and its mythological elaboration.'[23]

In the cases which we have been discussing, where the legitimation of authority at the nation-state level is uneven or incomplete, the passage from old to new symbols requires a process of political integration, which Claude Ake has defined as 'the progressive focusing of the primary loyalty of the individual on the state and the reduction of intra-state tensions by creating a cultural–ideological consensus'.[24] In the light of what we have already said, this process of political integration can be seen not so much as one of diffusing information about the state as one of transmitting *meaning*. The important factor, again, is not governmental output, but rather 'the *flow* of affect from the individual and the community into the legitimate political institutions'.[25] The key is what takes place in the minds of the respondents, not the political actors. And the integration process is often *contrary to the requirements of governmental performance* as viewed by the political elites, counter-elites or other politically participant groups. As Murray Edelman has pointed out:

Meaning is basically different from information and incompatible with it. Meaning is associated with order – with a patterned cognitive structure that permits anticipation of future developments, so that perceptions are expected and not surprising. . .

Information involves complexity or lack of order: inability to foresee. Unlike meaning, it is transmitted; and what is transmitted is complicating premises. . .
The believer must either retain his belief and the meaning it confers or abandon

it...information destroys meaning...Any datum that can be anticipated does not have to be transmitted, whether it is valid or not. If it is anticipated and still transmitted, it is redundant and therefore not information – not complicating or surprising.[26]

The problem, then, for actors desiring to promote and to achieve political integration is to create channels of communication which communicate meaning without necessarily transmitting too much complicating information. This is why, under close examination, the symbols of nationhood – the accepted explanations which make norms seem obligatory to the respondents – do not stand up to rigorous testing as to their relationship with reality.

It is...clear why all the usual descriptions of a people in terms of a community of languages, or character, or memories, or past history, are open to exception. For what counts is not merely the presence or absence of any single factor, but merely the presence of sufficient communication facilities with enough complementarity to produce the overall result.[27]

It is of course true that the situation is somewhat different where there already exist latent cultural factors which can contribute to and reinforce the integration process. Few societies lack any such factors, but they are often outweighed in new states by centrifugal factors. However, a de Gaulle, even a Stalin or a Mao, can call upon a greater reservoir of cultural supports than an Nkrumah or a Gandhi.[28] This will be more clearly seen to be true in terms of our argument as it will develop below, because of the extent to which *exclusive* common identification (i.e. *vis-à-vis* outsiders) takes on a greater role in the integration process. Nonetheless, whether pre-existing potential supports are present or not, the creation or reinforcement of symbols of nationality is fundamentally a process in which governmental performance and complex structures of logical argument are only significant to the extent that they instil or reinforce a tendency towards norm-oriented responses on the part of the individuals making up the social fabric.

Furthermore, the process does not end with the communication of meaning to the respondents. The respondents' actual behaviour must be sufficiently modified for the new symbols to reflect, as well as to shape, the behaviour of the political system as a whole. The legitimation of authority must be reflected in the way in which authority is exercised, and the way that actual exercise is reacted to by the public. As Karl Deutsch observes:

National consciousness, from this viewpoint, is the attachment of secondary symbols of nationality to primary items of information moving through channels of social communication, or through the mind of an individual. . .To have effect, the secondary symbols of nationality must not merely be attached to selected items of information about individual or social life, or the physical environment. They must be fed back into the making of decisions. On a simple level, they may secure for the items to which they are attached quicker or preferred attention, more frequent or speedier recall, greater weight in the process of decision. On another level, they may change some of the decision-making system's operating rules for whole classes of items – and thus, in a sense, its operating 'values' – with effects on the general behaviour of the system, and even on the pursuit of its goals or on their change for new ones.[29]

Thus the symbols, or the general response to those symbols, must be able to mobilise both actors and public, creating feedback into the system itself.

According to J. P. Nettl, such mobilisation functions tend to be underplayed, unrecognised or the subject of 'outraged denial' in the developed West because they do not fit with the ideological façade of liberal democracy. However, mobilisation is 'one of the most important functions for the achievement of which so many sophisticated Western and Soviet political techniques have been imported into developing countries':

At some stage of historical development, every society undergoes one or several processes of mobilisation; when such mobilisation is political, it creates or develops the growth and strength of the polity, and may well extend the range as well as increasing the saliency of the political system. It is also the major accelerating factor in both the extent and level of political acculturation.[30]

It is, says Nettl, 'in fact the most important, the central, function of many political collectivities, i.e. parties, interest groups, etc.'. Mobilisation in Western countries, however, tends to be characterised by an outward façade, a vehicle whose use is rationalised in instrumental terms other than mobilisation as such. Elections, for example, rarely affect the composition or ideology of political elites, although they may shift the ideological balance slightly. Furthermore, the role of the representative legislator himself is circumscribed by a range of social, economic and political constraints. Yet their representative function, which provides their widely trumpeted and ostensible rationale, is often of little importance compared to their symbolic–mobilisational function – their significance as a ritual act in binding the voters to the norms of the polity and the 'rules of the game'.[31] To Edelman, they provide a setting *par excellence* for the kind of hortatory language which is essential to the integration process with its symbolic, ideological and cultural characteristics.[32] And the complexity of the promises to be made and the groups to be 'aggregated' allows conflicting and even contradictory statements to be aggregated and apparently reconciled because they are brought together under the same symbolic umbrella.[33]

The same is true, but on a larger – societal – scale, when the focus of mobilisation processes is on the nation-state itself. Mobilisation processes 'all relate people tightly together in a distinct and often novel form, by evolving particular structures and by giving people common goals and reference groups'.[34] In doing so, these processes create and reinforce new conscious or unconscious priorities, either as substitutes for old priorities or by developing macro-social priorities where none existed previously. Nettl identifies a number of these mobilisation processes. Legalism, for example, is not only abstract; indeed, 'one of the most successful elementary forms of mobilisation of otherwise unacculturated sections of the periphery of society is the claim for the return of rights believed to have been illegally removed or denied'.[35] In addition, mobilisation through 'an elite-controlled mobilising party',[36] working from the top downwards, is one of the most salient types of mobilisation. In the case of a single or predominant party, 'mobilisation is overt, and every attempt is made to avoid conflict in commitment to party or state – either by having only one party, or by identifying the ruling party from among several with the special aura of such "fused" legitimacy'.[37] The other most salient type of mobilisation is the 'national–constitutional' type. This type can operate either through domestic channels – such as the development plan – or by reference to designated opponents, such as imperialists (in the new states; presumably by other sorts of enemies, national–territorial or ideological, in the developed countries).[38] One of the most familiar of these processes is that represented by the constitution itself, which 'legitimises in morally unquestionable postulates the predatory use of such bargaining weapons as groups possess' while at the same time fixing as 'socially unquestionable' the rule of law and of a 'social order run in accordance with a code that perpetuates popular government and the current consensus on values'. According to Edelman, this fundamental ambivalence 'becomes the concise and hallowed expression of man's complex and ambivalent atttitude towards others', and provides the sought-for 'encompassing principle that will introduce stability and predictability into this explosive clash of interests'.[39] Beyond these general mobilisation processes, of course, there is an historical context – a unique combination of circumstances which can reinforce or undermine mobilisation through specific events, especially events which restructure reality by defeating one group and giving victory to another, or events which restore or reinforce a particular structure of norms or of power relationships.[40]

But in order for these mobilisation processes to be fully effective, they must develop an internal momentum or 'take-off' which feeds back reinforcing and accelerating stimuli (rather than neutral or regressive stimuli) into the system itself. In the case of the political system of the nation-state this 'take-off' occurs when the concept of the national interest becomes widely internalised. In such a situation, 'not only do political actors tend to perceive and discuss their goals in terms of the national interest, but they are also inclined to claim that their goals *are* the national interest, a claim that often arouses the support necessary to move towards a realisation of the goals'.[41] This does not mean that all of the forces at work within the system are moving *by themselves* in the same direction – towards some teleological image of the national interest – but that the aggregate weight of the variables in the system has a cumulative effect on all of the variables.[42] In terms of political legitimacy and internalisation of norms, the image of the national interest would dominate the interrelationships which compose the causal mechanism in the process of change. In this way the very image of the national interest would provide the impetus for, and the direction and boundaries of, *goal-oriented behaviour* within the system. In ex-colonial societies, for example, such images reflect the dilemma of traditionalism *versus* modernisation:

Nationalists alternate between xenophobia and xenophilia; they predict that they will simultaneously 'outmodernise' the West in the future and 'restore' the true values of the ancient civilisation; they argue both for egalitarian and for hierarchical principles at the same time. Nationalism and related ideologies unite these contradictory tendencies in the society under one large symbol. If these ideologies are successful, they are then often used as a means to modernise the society and thus to erase those kinds of social discontinuity that caused the initial nationalistic outburst.[43]

It is of course problematic as to whether it is possible, in the Third World, for nation-oriented mobilisation to achieve the goal of 'development', but such has usually been the theory applied by post-colonial elites themselves. The belief that such mobilisation *can* be effective, however, is the basis for whatever credence is given to the national symbols and therefore to the dominant authoritative structures. In the developed world, nation-oriented perceptions are more thoroughly rooted in historical consciousness, and the relevance or irrelevance of such symbolism is not so obviously demonstrated by reference to economic disparities and the like. But in either case, presuming that the goal of the political actors is political integration of the nation-state within a particular legitimate order, the instruments of mobilisation are marshalled in the attempt to maximise and cumulate responses, expectations and patterns of behaviour which are meant to reinforce identity with macro-social symbols while neutralising or assimilating into the system the maximum number of individuals and/or sub-national groups.

II. Foreign Policy, the Routinisation of Charisma and National Integration

The specific instrument *par excellence* at the disposal of elites hoping to mobilise the population of a legally recognised nation-state towards authority legitimation and political integration is foreign policy. Several characteristics of foreign policy are particularly suited to this task. In the first place, foreign policy of any sort requires 'a definition of the situation' in which some sort of political cohesion of the nation-state as a behavioural unit is, by definition, a built-in, *a priori* assumption of perception, cognition and action. The forms, rituals and often the real interplay of international affairs takes place in a system where the rules of the game specify that the actors are nation-states; therefore the national interest *exists*, 'however vague and nebulous it may appear to be, at least as an important datum'.[44] Thus, no matter what the disagreements about foreign policy may be, they have in common a quite specific operational framework, which is that of the concept of national interest, whatever the content which is explicitly or implicitly included in various conceptions of that national interest.

Secondly, foreign policy is an excellent medium by which to transmit meaning without transmitting information. The distinction which it fosters between the 'we' and the 'them' – and the active ideological thrust which it gives to this distinction – effectively selects out information which may be complicating (so far as national identity is concerned) and thus destabilising. Furthermore, foreign policy symbolism operates in a unique context of combining *remote objects* with *immediate perceptions* of rewards and penalties. The cultural role of war memories, more than the experience of war itself, exemplifies this attribute of foreign policy perceptions. The remoteness of the day-to-day foreign policy situation from the individual, and even from the usual environments of political parties and interest groups, removes any information that could be readily perceived – much less assimilated into a cognitive structure. In Edelman's words, 'there are few or no competing cues available to political spectators':

This kind of monopoly is most evident in international affairs. The negotiation of alliances or the erection of defences and the speeches of officials against an enemy country are the strongest, and sometimes the only, signal to mass publics that the target country is potentially hostile. In this case, as usual, actions are more persuasive generators of opinion than speeches.[45]

Thus the linguistic and ideational content of the manner in which foreign policy issues are generated and dealt with (at both international and national levels) is both more salient and less open to individual or group 'testing' through experience than any other sort of political issue. The general issue-area of foreign policy is potentially an even more powerful form of condensation symbolism than legal rights, constitutions, and so on. This is partly because it is thought to be 'higher' than domestic politics in the sense that it claims to appeal to and to derive from the broadest possible solidarity and unity. The claim of the nation-state to embody the 'political association' which subsumes all others and which was described by Aristotle later became part and parcel of the 'state of nature' conception of international relations.[46] As James Rosenau has argued, 'Whatever the differences among the members, they would seem minimal compared to the distinctions that set them all apart from the members of the other systems that comprise the environment.'[47]

It is also partly because actual cultural memories of international interactions, for the mass of the population, tend to be the more cataclysmic the more they impinge upon the perceived world of the individual or the sub-national group. Everyday foreign policy activity has always been dealt with by leaders and specialists; it is historically about the closest an analyst can come to identifying an approximation to a hypothetical ideal type of elite autonomy in the decision-making process. For the average individual or group, however, by the time they come into direct contact with international issues, these issues are either so diffused as to be informationless (though symbolically extremely meaningful) or so *directly* threatening as actually to subsume the entirety of an individual's perception, cognition and action in the immediate requirements of the historical event. (War is a matter of life and death.) Unlike accidental death, as in road accidents, illness, etc., international conflict dominates the individual's entire frame of reference when he is drawn directly into it. He not only has to face death, but he has also to *justify his and his compatriots' death to himself and to others.*

However, unlike the individual existential act, war is collective. Many are in exactly the same position, and therefore the justification for it cannot be a purely individual justification. It must be a collective justification, based on collective, even universal principles. The cultural residues of such justifications are far more potent, as a result, than those of other issue-areas in the political system. Cultural memories of war last a long time and often dominate entire socialisation processes. They involve issues not simply about how to make life better or worse, but about the very problem of survival itself. Therefore, by the time foreign policy issues become salient and real to the public, meaning is usually quite clear; reactions take place according to cultural predispositions rather than to information, and any new information is selected and organised accordingly.

Thirdly, foreign policy issues, unlike domestic issues, are seen to transcend the complexities of the relationship between the individual and the state which dominates the content of so much ideology and political philosophy. The nation symbolises the social bond itself, transcending the instrumental bond of individual interest-plus-tradeoffs-equals-obligation; obligation is treated as self-evident (except, perhaps, by religious objectors, cosmopolitan elites or capitalist classes – the latter well hidden behind patriotic slogans, however). Common system membership, as such, is usually irrelevant to domestic issues, to which individuals bring a 'multiplicity of affiliations and loyalties. Goals thus become confounded by cross-cutting interests, and the maintenance of a clear-cut priority of values with respect to one's fellow-citizens becomes a delicate and complicated task.'[48] Indeed, going a step further, 'one of the principal functions of symbols of remote objects, like nations and classes, is to serve as targets for the relief of many of the tensions which might discharge disastrously in face-to-face relations'.[49]

The reason that foreign policy can play this role, in addition to its remoteness and its symbolic potency, is that it *appears* to escape the zero-sum perceptual framework of the allocation-of-resources problem which dominates domestic politics.

Foreign policy controversies...do not require the participants to treat each other as rivals for scarce resources. What one actor or group gains, another does not give up. Each participant seeks to persuade the decision-making authority to adopt a particular solution, but none posits a solution that necessitates depriving other system members of some of their possessions or privileges. Thus, since there is nothing material to bargain over, the parties to the issue need never come together or respond to each other.[50]

In the context of national integration, of course, foreign policy issues are inextricably intertwined with the dynamics of group dominance and resource allocation, particularly given the linkages characterising the contemporary international system as a whole. But the point here is that the ostensible framework in which foreign policy issues are usually discussed and treated deals with such allocational problems by negotiation, bargaining and conflict *within* the broad elite strata (both at home and abroad), and the detailed ramifications of such issues rarely need filter down to larger publics.

We have already noted that the problems of political integration vary depending upon the pre-existing degrees of national consciousness; so too with the manipulation of foreign policy issues. In the purely structural sense, then, the process under examination is a conservative one. However, we can identify two qualifications to this conservatism. In the first place, the content which is associated with the symbol of the nation-state may be radical, either in the international sense (e.g. the revolutionary associations of Communism despite the doctrines of 'socialism in one country') or in the domestic sense (the instilling of national – especially cultural – consciousness which is associated with, for example, the Chinese, Korean and Albanian revolutionary regimes). In the second place, the object of this conservatism may be a new, rather than an old, structure. It may involve, as we have pointed out above, the emancipation of people from old symbols (tribal, religious, etc.) and the focusing of a new identity on new symbols (which need not necessarily be 'modern' symbols, just different ones). In this case, foreign policy (and all other symbolic forms of mobilisation) become central to the self-appointed tasks of the new elites, and attempts are made to manipulate the symbolism to a much more intense degree. Thus Sukarno's policy of 'confrontation', Nehru's policy of leadership of the non-aligned nations, and, in a more restricted sense, de Gaulle's policy of *grandeur*, all involve a much greater degree of conscious manipulation of national symbolism than, for example, American concern to defend the 'free world' or Soviet expansion of sea-power, which derive from a pre-existing set of widely accepted national images and rationales. In the latter case, conservatism is a feature of the current situation; in the former case, policy is used to *create* symbols which it will then be possible to be conservative about.

The contemporary international situation can be interpreted as both functional and dysfunctional in this process. In an age of rapidly increasing interdependence at all levels, it becomes more and more obvious that the nation-state framework suffers from severe disadvantages where effective decision-making is concerned. On the other hand, this very fluidity of national and international political structures makes the perception of a focal point – a yardstick by which to make sense of the 'buzzing, blooming confusion' of world politics – all that much more important *if* political stability is taken to be a significant objective.[51] Of course, stability itself can exist at a range of different levels, from the stability of the international system as a whole to the stability of nation-states, local or ethnic sub-cultures, classes, or societies without classes (as yet unrealised but everywhere pursued). Thus the requirements of stability across a series of levels can, and often do, mutually conflict. The pursuit of stability must take place within a wider and more multiform normative complex which lends stability its very *raison d'être*. In this context, the focusing of legitimative and integrative behaviour upon the nation-state involves both a normative judgment – that the nation-state is the most appropriate (or the least inappropriate) social–territorial framework available for the pursuit of preferred goals (when compared with the alternatives) – and a strategic judgment – that it is possible effectively to attempt to achieve those goals through a particular course of action within the framework of the nation-state structure.

This is the stage at which we return to the problem of mobilisation. We have argued that foreign policy is an efficient medium through which to undertake the task of political integration. And the combination of foreign policy with other mobilisation – dominant-party, national–constitutional and so on – may be presumed to be even more efficient provided that the various processes are sufficiently compatible in terms of the maintenance of a low level of disagreement or conflict between the various components of the overall process (different party factions, pressure groups, regional or class interests, etc.) as well as being sufficiently coordinated to follow actively a coherent political strategy. Such is, of course, the source of the effectiveness of Apter's 'modernising elite'.[52] As well as providing the structural linkage between the various mobilisation processes and coordinating them according to the normative pattern which dominates the integration process, a modernising elite can also act as the locus of symbolic perception of the overall process. One need only think of the role of the 'founding fathers' in the United States to see how, on the one hand, social ties, political rationality and coincident economic interests provided the structural core of the integration process itself, while at the same time, on the other hand, the images, the rhetoric and the constitutional authority of this pseudo-revolutionary elite combined to create a popular response which is still significant two hundred years later in symbol and myth.

In the creation of such a significant popular response, it is interesting to observe the role which would seem to be played by *personification*, rather than abstract rationality, in giving substance to the mythical or symbolic image. It would seem that individuals' perceptions of such remote objects and processes are heightened by the possibility of the mediating images taking on readily recognisable personalised forms. One of the ways in which primary contact is significant for an under-standing of more remote or abstract processes is that it creates a frame-work for selecting evidence about the good or bad, acceptable or unacceptable qualities of such processes. To create a broad and viable basis for affective support of such an object and/or process, it must be recognisable to the individual in his own personal terms and in the context of his own personal experience. Thus, for an individual or elite which seeks to create widespread social patterns of affective response to a set of symbols, the personification of the mobilisation processes as being in acceptable hands would seem to be an essential element.

Sometimes the personalised symbol or image provides a façade for the 'real' forces at work behind the scenes. Often, however, where real power is vested in a readily identifiable group or individual, the symbol is merely a more or less distorted image of the real. And when, in a transitional period such as we have specified earlier, this image becomes the most salient aspect of the integration process, a highly efficient method for communicating meaning – while carefully filtering out dysfunctional information – is created. This, I would argue, is the essence of the phenomenon which social scientists since Weber have been attempting to analyse under the rather more confusing term 'charisma'.[53] Like the role of the nation-state as a focal point for creating a coherent and readily assimilable image of the complexities of politics in contemporary international society, the personalisation of leaders creates a *sense of knowing what is going on* in the political system and political life. This sort of mediation was important, of course, when earlier historical forms of the political system operated over great distances with poor communications, particularly during major crises, wars, etc. But in the modern world, 'charismatic' mediation

– the perception of power as personified by a leader – becomes even more important.

The rapid unification of national, regional and transnational structures; the rise of popular expectations of performance in terms of democratic values and living standards; and the bureaucratisation of decision-making, production, distribution, social organisation and the like: all of these processes increase the psychological distance between individuals and primary groups, on the one hand, and social, political and economic institutions on the other. Charismatic mediation, however, cuts across this psychological distance, and creates a sense of comprehension and identification – a sense that despite the advent of mass society, what goes on at the top is still, nevertheless, on a human scale, with recognisable motives and ways of thinking. The individual can *imagine* what is going on, and his sense of alienation from society is thereby reduced. This form of mediation is made practical and feasible by the development of modern methods of communication (the press, radio, television and the cinema) which allow the great mass of the population to become familiar with the existence and the personal qualities of particular 'public' individuals – as well as giving these individuals a means of communicating directly with the mass. 'There is thus created an actor–audience relationship which seems to permit both participation and understanding.'[54] In the contemporary world, such mediation becomes a necessary and ongoing part of everyday life.

The literature on charisma as a significant element in political modernisation is interesting and growing. However, the debate is moving away from the idea that charisma is some sort of supernatural or magical quality inherent in the leader himself, to the analysis of the different attributes and capacities necessary for attaining a status which gives the charismatic leader a kind of aura in the eyes of his followers as well as an ability to transcend constraints normally imposed upon systemic actors. Charisma is no more a quality of the leader as individual than beauty is; rather, it is in the eye of the beholder – and in the way it affects the beholder's behaviour. Often it is this very ability to transcend normal constraints, thus giving the impression of having superhuman powers, which gives the actor charisma. The very existence of charisma, then, depends upon the presence of a political actor perceptive enough, determined enough and possessing enough resources to exploit these conditions in terms of an overall strategy. 'The political analysis of charisma, therefore, must begin not with the leader's personality, but with the vacuum that he fills';[55] this is what

Tucker calls 'situational charisma'.[56] And the charismatic leader is distinguished by the 'normative authority' which he consciously seeks to impose: 'The true charismatic leader accepts his own mystique, his consciousness of his role in history, so that the public or a significant subgroup allows him to relate his personal political goals with a wider moral vision and thereby affect public action.'[57] The reality of charisma is in its perception, and the significance of charisma is in its consequences.

The analysis of charisma, then, must focus not on its appearance but on its causes and properties. Those causes include general receptivity on the part of the public at large or of a strategically significant section of that public, or what Erik H. Erikson has called 'charisma-hunger'.[58] As a reaction to 'alienation, anomie, despair of being able to chart one's own course in a complex, cold, and bewildering world,'[59] charisma may be called upon to minister to fear, anxiety (particularly an 'identity-vacuum'), existential dread and so on. 'Correspondingly, a charismatic leader is one who offers people salvation in the form of safety, or identity, or rituals, or some combination of these...'[60] As Lasswell wrote in the 1930s,

The rulers of yesterday who depended on bread, circuses, and wars to protect them from domestic disturbances are superseded by rulers who are adept at diverting, distracting, confusing, and dissipating the insecurities of the mass by the circulation of efficacious symbols.[61]

The linguistic factor is significant in creating an impact. The leader's use of language creates an emotional impact from both its form and, of course, its setting.[62] Furthermore, charisma usually needs to be authenticated, or proven by symbolic or real performance. Factors in the authentication process include the leader's own sense of 'self-confidence and calling', which must be 'supplemented by extraordinary deeds before the claim of the leader is accepted by the followers'.[63]

Charisma, however, appears in several forms. The emphasis of Weber's analysis, according to Schweitzer, is on 'faith charisma', whereas in the contemporary political context other types – based on the attraction of values embodied by the leader, on purely emotional identification ('natural' charisma), and even 'ephemeral' charisma – are more important. The requirement of exceptional deeds, says Schweitzer, is binding only in the first, providential, type. In 'value' and 'natural' charisma, ethical doctrines and the emotional bond are sufficient during the leader's lifetime in maintaining the followers' belief. Indeed, these ethical beliefs and emotional bonds may continue, after the leader's death, to sustain 'institutional' and/or 'legendary' charisma.[64] The impact and consequences of charisma, then, depend not upon the leader's magical qualities, but on the content and the emotional strength of the bond which is created with the followers. The keys to these qualities are, on the one hand, ideology, in the twofold sense of a system of ideas and a movement based upon the pursuit of those ideas, and, on the other, structural changes which result from the institutionalisation of all or part of the charismatic leader–follower relationship. In this latter sense, Apter specifically links the phenomena of charismatic leadership with the problem of political change: 'Charisma as a normative phenomenon can only affect behaviour when it consolidates itself in a new structural system. When development is small, this is difficult to accomplish.'[65] Or, as Tucker writes: 'charismatic leadership rejects old rules and issues a demand for change. It preaches or creates *new* obligations.'[66]

In this chapter we have been concerned with foreign policy leadership as an instrument of political change in a particular sense – its capacity to inculcate patterns of affective response to symbols of nationhood as superior to membership in other groupings. In this sense we follow Apter in considering charismatic leadership to be not merely a transitional phenomenon in the modernisation process (i.e., involving change from traditional to legal–rational norms), but a more all-embracing phenomenon. The charismatic leader is not so much an intermediate phenomenon who is neither traditional nor bureaucratic, but a linking or bridging phenomenon who can be – or at least be seen to be – *both* traditional *and* modern at the same time. In fact, the content which the charismatic leader introduces into the personal, ethical and organisational characteristics of this transition will mould and shape the respondents' image and perception of the essential relation between the old and the new. Whatever normative changes the charismatic leader effects will depend upon his ability to transcend traditional constraints (this can involve just as much an assimilation and manipulation of traditional norms as their denial) and to induce acceptance of a new order – an order based upon the value complex which is seen to be embodied in the leader's action. The institutionalisation of his new order is called the 'routinisation' of charisma.[67] The typical charismatic leader does not, in fact, content himself with his personal aura: 'Even while their reputations were at their most charismatic, Nehru and Atatürk were fully absorbed in perfecting their organisations. Routinisation proceeded as or even before charisma became manifest.'[68]

Routinisation, then, is not solely the problem of finding a successor (the problem which Weber emphasises). Rather, it is the problem of institutionalising a new set of norms. Here we have come some way from Weber's contention that bureaucratic and traditional authority are rational (because they are bound to 'intellectually analysable rules', on the one hand, and precedent, on the other) 'while charismatic authority is specifically irrational in the sense of being foreign to all rules'.[69] If charisma were such an irrational phenomenon, then its interest to the student of political authority would be marginal; abstract processes of change would be far more important. However, if charisma is taken in its wider sense of meaning personal leadership which takes on an ability to transcend rules *and to impose rules of its own* – and to initiate processes whereby those rules become routinised and institutionalised – then the structural impact and significance of charisma may be greater even (at certain key historical transition periods) than the more mechanistic processes of traditional or legal–rational legitimation of authority. And if, as we have pointed out above, the conditions of modern society make a kind of charismatic leadership into an ongoing process which follows psychologically analysable rules in reducing subjective perceptions of alienation, the ramifications become even greater. And particularly where the processes of national integration and authority legitimation are incomplete, uneven or embryonic – particularly in the case of the new states where citizens are still in the grip of traditional institutions and wary of the state's claim to their loyalty – then the recognition of the authority of the state is facilitated 'if the state's claims are put forward by someone whom the masses respect and trust'. If the masses respect the leader in a way they do not respect the state, then 'this personal respect can be used to buttress the state until it wins its own legitimacy'.[70]

The charismatic leader wins his following by symbolising a capacity to cope, rather than by concrete results. If that impression of capacity to cope can be transplanted onto the institutions of the state, then charismatic leadership becomes a significant feature of national integration. Like the concept of national interest, it can induce a feedback process in which the legitimacy of the leader and the legitimacy of the state reinforce each other in a reciprocal fashion. The effectiveness of charismatic leadership is the ability of the leader to affect this transition from old norms to new, from old institutional structures to new.

In the sense that it transcends this dichotomy of norms, it is beholden to neither, and can produce its own unique blend – through creative *bricolage* – of old and new.

Of course, the actual political capacity of and support for charismatic leadership normally imposes limits, and therefore each charismatic leader is an historically unique phenomenon insofar as both the content of the normative blend and the extent to which he can transcend limits over time and structural space are bound to vary with circumstances. This is what Apter calls 'normative exemption',[71] and once this period ends, if the new normative complex has not been adopted as general systemic practice, the charismatic leader fails and becomes publicly charged with his failure. If he succeeds, then charismatic leadership can affect both the speed and the direction of political change in a way which may dispense with certain intermediate stages or create unique patterns which escape sociological categories. It is thus a particularly significant form of political mobilisation in the process of political integration, although its failure lacks the usual structural safety net which traditional or bureaucratic forms of action provide.[72]

The combination of this extended kind of charismatic leadership with a substantive focus on foreign policy, we would suggest, can be a particularly potent instrument for pursuing the goals of political integration, nation-building and authority legitimation in societies where the nation-state framework is shaky. In both cases we have remote objects, manipulable by elites, of such an intense psychological nature (the associational link with emotional anxieties, etc.; the reinforcement of a sense of 'we' distinct from 'them'; the transmission of meaning with a minimum of complicating information) that together they have a potential impact theoretically far beyond the bounds of instrumental, resource-allocational political conflict. In many new states, anticolonialism provides an even more explosive mixture by including direct racial and economic exploitation in the symbolic framework (although this becomes far more complex in the post-independence period). Whereas the answer in the early 1960s was usually taken to be some form of neutralism, the focal point of externalisation today becomes international racism (e.g. policy towards South Africa) or neo-colonial economic exploitation. But the utilisation of this combination of techniques is not limited to the Third World. One need only think of the role of Adenauer's foreign policy in the creation and institutionalisation of the German Federal Republic, the impact of Washington's Farewell Address on American development in the nineteenth century, and, in our own case study, of the symbolic role of de Gaulle's idea of *grandeur* in foreign policy on the question of public acceptance of the Fifth Republic.

Conclusions

The significance of this syndrome today is that, given the presence of the necessary conditions, it responds to certain salient features of contemporary politics at both domestic and international levels. Essentially, the international system is in a situation where the forces of systematic centralisation – strategic, technological and economic – are developing concurrently with opposing forces of systemic fragmentation – national independence, the breakdown of cold war bipolar dominance, ideological and ethnic cleavages, diminishing raw material supplies and so on. In this context, the autonomy of state elites is diminishing both at home and abroad. Yet the nation-state, if anything, is becoming an even more significant political factor as both the legal repository of sovereignty (and thus a factor of continuity and reference in a fluid environment) and *the only systemic level with direct accountability for its behaviour to a clearly defined and recognised population grouping.* As Raymond Aron has written: 'The political unit defines itself through opposition: it becomes itself by becoming capable of external action.'[73] This is becoming increasingly true in the contemporary world.

In a world where opposition no longer takes the form of a clearly defined conflict situation, but rather operates, as it were, according to a complex matrix of forces, foreign policy leadership becomes a key locus for symbolically charting a course through these forces – or at least, in the symbolic sense, for being *seen* to be courageously and independently *attempting* to chart such a course. The actual relevance of foreign policy leadership will, of course, be limited by the salience of foreign policy to the perception of relevant publics. But foreign policy, at least in its symbolic implications, is more widely acknowledged and seen (*via* more extensive communications media, etc.) than ever before outside of wartime. Its leadership aspect is more significant, too. As Nettl has pointed out, political mobilisation in the new countries tends to be 'from the top of the institutional pyramid downwards, instead of upwards towards authority from a cleavage base'.[74] The community, rather than consisting of an aggregation of individuals and groups formed on the basis of sub-national loyalties, is asserting its primacy in an ever more holistic manner. This is fundamentally different from the essentially constitutional development of national power and cohesion which characterised the ancient and medieval tyrannies or even the bases of support for Robespierre or Napoleon. Those who censure the new states for lack of attention to the forms of pluralistic participation not only miss the essence of their contribution, 'but also miss the functional contribution of, say, the Soviet Communist Party and even the UNR in France'.[75]

Thus it would seem that the scope for such symbolic foreign policy leadership is actually increasing in the world today as the problem of maintaining political stability grows more complex. 'The redefinition of future expectations is in part due to the relatively exclusive pre-occupation of the individual with the fate of the master symbol.'[76] Several authors quoted by Edelman seem to concur that: 'Emotional commitment to a symbol is associated with contentment and quiescence regarding problems that would otherwise arouse concern.'[77] (This statement is, of course, only true insofar as the symbol itself is of a 'functional' rather than a 'dysfunctional' nature with relation to the stability of the political system in question.) Given that the 'master symbol' of the contemporary world would seem to be the independence and moral authority of the 'national culture society', then 'One key to political stability seems to be, therefore, the practice of flexible politics behind the façade of an inflexible commitment to a national mission.'[78]

At the same time, however, such an approach has its limits and dangers. While the nation-state may be the 'master symbol', it will, if conditions do not permit, turn from being a convenient fiction into a highly inconvenient one. The external environment may be a fluid one, but its very fluidity may make it intractable; the internal environment exhibits much greater plasticity for national elites than does the outside world. There may be fewer 'givens' in the international system, but there are also far fewer ways to exert consistent goal-directed pressure without taking large and complex risks. The symbolic location of accountability for the consequences of decisions at the level of the nation-state means that when governmental performance is perceived to have failed – and when this failure is in fact due to unperceived or only dimly perceived international causes which do not bend to domestic manipulation – then the potential for instability is increased also: '. . .sensitivity to transnational activities increases the domestic implications of international transactions'.[79] Furthermore, the demands which may be placed upon a national government as the result of heightened domestic expectations of foreign policy performance may lead even the most determinedly limitationist foreign policy to attempt to provide proof of its effectiveness – leading to adventurism. Such adventurism brought about the fall of Sukarno, for example, when the pressures of 'confrontation' with Malaysia heightened domestic tensions in the long term and became counter-productive, leading to his downfall and the extreme upheaval which surrounded it.

Finally, the style of such symbolic foreign policy leadership may lead to 'opportunity costs' in the shape of a tendency to deal with day-to-day foreign policy affairs on a level of continual crisis management and manipulation. The drawbacks of such a style can be seen in the institutional pressures which can be generated by the regular use of great feats of high politics, with all the tricky stage management and isolation from wider forms of consultation, information and bargaining which may better fulfil the requirements of the particular problem at hand.[80] As an extension of this point, institutional conflicts may develop between the leader and a whole series of other actors within the national political system – diplomats, parliamentarians, pressure groups, businessmen, trade unions, etc. – and tactics may be used which alienate international interlocutors. Opposition forces at home will constantly call for the limitation of 'personal power', and the regularisation of international negotiations may suffer (e.g. de Gaulle's symbolic rejection of British entry into the EEC). Such symbolic use of foreign policy can grease the skids as well as oil the wheels.

Further exploration of the exploitation of foreign policy leadership for the purposes of national integration requires the examination of case studies. Such factors as (a) the intentions and ideology of the leader(s) in question, (b) the vulnerability of the internal environment to a range of integrative pressures, (c) the compatibility of actual foreign policy with the requirements of salience and the avoidance of excessive risk, and (d) the impact of foreign policy symbolism on the domestic plane (orientations of opposition groups, etc. to relevant symbols; in developed liberal democracies, the response of mass publics *via* opinion surveys, and so on) are especially significant in detecting the presence of the syndrome we have been describing. The data, however, are amorphous and open to a range of interpretations, and the symptoms are not, in themselves, self-evident. They are no less real or relevant, however. They provide a starting-point for the rethinking of many traditional categories of foreign policy and of its relation to the international system. This book is an attempt to construct such a study.

On the whole, foreign policy is still generally treated, as a datum, within the traditional context of diplomatic relations. Strides have been made, certainly, in treating the domestic sources of foreign policy, its relation with certain transnational forces such as multinational firms, and its impact upon inter-nation linkages. However, what is needed, in very broad terms, is a cultural science of foreign policy, which treats foreign policy (and, ultimately, international relations generally) as a socio-psychological construct or a socio-cultural system. Insofar as international society is a society in the contemporary world, and not merely a conglomeration of societies, it has its rules, roles, symbols and rituals. In normal 'domestic' society, such factors can be more signifi-cant determinants of behaviour than functions, expediencies, explicit objectives, instrumentalities and so on. The use of foreign policy leader-ship to further national integration is but one aspect of such a re-orientation. The syndrome described here, involving the creation of a set of symbolic stimuli and responses which give the individual a sense of normative identity with the other individuals and groups composing the nation-state, is important not only for the development of domestic political systems, where it feeds back *via* various processes of normative compliance, but also for the international system itself. In the latter case, its detection may enable the observer to make clearer and more relevant distinctions between bluff and genuine threat, between foreign policy objectives which demand reaction and those which do not. Today, widely internalised symbolic objectives like national indepen-dence and socialist revolution are specified by an ever-increasing range of individuals, groups and governments. We need to make better sense of the myriad images and messages, the real and the symbolic conflicts, and the actual sources of cohesion and compliance which are character-istic of such a world.

This book attempts to make a start in an area where conventional analyses of international relations have proven insufficient to get to the core of de Gaulle's activity on the world and the national stage. His political ideas, both as to ends and as to means, though invested with their own historical uniqueness, are nonetheless characteristic of the pattern we have set out in this chapter. The pattern covers a wide range of phenomena, and is therefore flexible. The legitimation of the authority of the French state was not a process which had to take place on a *tabula rasa*, nor were the symbolic structures which characterised French society wholly alien to the authority of the nation-state; in fact, a fertile cultural reservoir was tapped by de Gaulle in the sense that nearly 170 years of post-revolutionary instability and vacillation between authoritarianism and *immobilisme* had created a sense of national mission confronted with a sense of national frustration. France was a national culture society without a viable political system. Therefore it lies at some distance from the experience of the 'new states' of the Third World in this sense. But the structural impediments in, and the complexity of, French society were such that any form of political change required something of a *deus ex machina* to break the deadlock. This de Gaulle quite consciously set out to do. And, in this case, the use of foreign policy symbolism was both innovative – given the divisive conflicts which immobilised French foreign policy in the mid-1950s and created a vacuum for de Gaulle to fill – and expedient – in the context of French domestic politics, which were increasingly volatile and susceptible to nationalistic appeals.

France, furthermore, was in a very different situation from Third World countries insofar as her international relations were concerned. She was enmeshed in a web of relations arising out of the post-Second World War settlements and the imperatives of the cold war, and she was in addition a relatively wealthy country undergoing a rapid transition from a longstanding pre-war situation of economic stagnation to the rapid postwar development of an advanced industrial economy. But although this position may have prevented even the conception of moves towards neutralism or autarchy, and although in the long run it limited de Gaulle's attempts to maintain a degree of strategic and economic independence to a few symbolic areas and minimised Gaullist innovation in the sense of actually changing the international system (i.e. by acting as an independent variable), it also provided de Gaulle with a situation of strength in the context of his overall strategy.

France's ability to possess a nuclear striking force without seriously affecting the bipolar strategic balance enhanced not so much French prestige abroad but Gaullist prestige at home. France's ability to call for independence from the United States without destroying (or even officially withdrawing from) the Atlantic Alliance, despite French withdrawal from the NATO military organisation, gave an impression of effective manoeuvrability which also played to natural French resentment of American economic and military predominance. French provocation of crises in the European Community preserved a certain French sovereignty while allowing economic integration to proceed in a number of more or less significant fields. This ambivalence, and the avoidance of excessive risk which accompanied it, merely served to strengthen the symbolism expressed in de Gaulle's foreign policy. And this was crucial to him in a period when the legitimation of a new set of national political institutions required the maximisation of national symbolism, concurrently with the search for economic modernisation and growth. The relative mobility of French policy was a useful card to play in relations with the socialist world and the Third World as well, although it had little *independent* effect on the evolution of the international system as a whole. De Gaulle was doing, in his own particular context and manner, something quite similar to what certain other leaders were doing, for it was an appropriate response to the interaction of his objectives with the development and structure of the international system.

The first half of this book has been devoted to the personal, ideological and structural context in which de Gaulle's foreign policy emerged and developed. Giving coherence to the whole was his own view of the world and of the role which he was to play. The way in which he played it, and its impact upon France and the rest of the international system, is the subject of the rest of the book.

PART II

The grand design and foreign policy *praxis*: a case study in Atlantic relationships and the domestic impact of Gaullist policy

The positive side of my mind also assures me that France is not really herself unless in the front rank; that only vast enterprises are capable of counterbalancing the ferments of dispersal which are inherent in her people.

de Gaulle, *War Memoirs*

6

Structure and development of the grand design

I. The grand design and its implications

De Gaulle's objective was to pursue a foreign policy which would increase France's standing in the world, ensure her a vital minimum of independence and freedom of manoeuvre in her international relationships, shelter her drive for social and economic progress at home, inculcate a sense of national identity and national interest in the body politic, reinforce and legitimate the new institutional structures of the 1958 Constitution, and yet which would avoid excessive risk from either external entanglements or endemic conflicts over priorities at home. Creating the foundations and the structure of such a complex, and therefore potentially fragile, achievement required, as does a French park, a sense of the balance and symmetry of the whole. It required a grand design.

To be effective at home and feasible abroad, such a politics of *grandeur* demanded that France be able to exercise influence disproportionate to her material means. To make this possible, three conditions were necessary. In the first place, French political elites needed the will to undertake and persist in a balancing act between national ambition and the avoidance of excessive risk or overextension. As a corollary to this, a domestic reservoir of popular support of continuous foreign policy activity, a reservoir based on the acceptance of foreign policy symbolism as central to political cohesion and obligation, was required. Secondly, France must not merely represent the French national interest as acting against the interests of other states, but rather as creating a solidarity of interests with the others. Thus French policy had to appeal to a sufficiently widely accepted general or universal principle to ensure the active or tacit support of other states in international dealings. And thirdly, the French grand design itself needed to be both sufficiently flexible and sufficiently predictive to be able both to follow and to shape the actual course of events in the international system as a whole over time.

The thread which united these three conditions for de Gaulle was the principle of national independence – of which France had to appear as the exemplary champion.[1] As de Gaulle said of 'the idea of self-determination': 'It is the kind of elementary psychological state of mind which is all the more active as it finds the support of the entire world, including the countries that yesterday were colonisers.'[2] Thus the independence and self-determination of states extrapolates Gaullist principles, which are themselves derived from a 'certain idea of France', from the national base into the international system. This is the core of de Gaulle's 'strategic image', to use Frankel's term.[3] As the then Prime Minister, Georges Pompidou, explained in a speech to the National Assembly:

there can be no lasting peace when misery and riches live side by side, when the weak are subjected to the strong, any more than there can be internal peace in social conditions of moral and material injustice. The objectives of such a policy are difficult. But make no mistake, they are the only ones which are profoundly realistic at a time in history when all men are conscious of their dignity. In this perilous world where the internal and inevitable will to power of the great powers has incalculable means at its command, it is necessary for a voice to raise itself to claim the right of nations, feeble as they may be, to respond to themselves and to decide their own destiny. This role today has returned to France. Her genius inspires her to it, her history teaches her to do it, her place among nations and the international prestige of General de Gaulle permit her to do it. Of course, to assume this role brings with it certain inconveniences. But if France discarded it, she would be unfaithful to herself and would deceive the obscure hopes of man.[4]

This bond between the strategic image of French policy and the interests and demands present (if not inherent) in the nature of international politics does not, however, imply either inactivity (as we have seen) or equality between states. Middle powers are normally unable to defend their interests by force, and therefore, if independence is to permit France to defend her interests, not only must it consist of 'refusal to be dependent', but it also requires 'an active, constructive and original policy, the antithesis of "neutralism"...'[5] Academic observers of de Gaulle's foreign policy have sought words to describe this quality. W. W. Kulski calls it 'uncommitment' or 'systematic nonalignment', while Edward A. Kolodziej refers to a 'plural international system' which would create mutually balancing cross-pressures, a 'global grid of interwoven conflict relations', and a 'kind of free marketplace in which France sells and buys its political wares as it pleases'.[6] A semi-official French commentator refers to the transience of stable equilibria in the international environment, the permanence of

competition, and the lack of mechanisms to prevent certain consequences stemming from over-production of weaponry to maintain the
balance.[7] But all this merely means that France, in seeking to increase
her manoeuvrability and to widen her options, must exploit the structural interstices and the margins of the international system.

The Gaullist attack on the *status quo*, however, does not imply that
relations between states can be put on a footing of equality.[8] Indeed, as
Pierre Hassner points out, it is an inherent contradiction of Gaullist
foreign policy that, given its different sorts of objectives (which include
a pivotal role for France), the equality of states would be in many ways
counter-productive. 'The whole conception is based on the assumption
that although the *status quo* is to be attacked, certain of its fundamental
aspects will nevertheless remain in being. . .'[9] It is therefore not a part
of Gaullist theory that the alternative to international monopoly (or
duopoly) is a system of perfect competition. Rather, the intention is to
escape from the strait-jacket of bipolar equilibrium with its rigid system
of roles for each country[10] by widening the duopoly to include a rather
broader leadership group based on a more flexible, quasi-hierarchical,
quasi-consultative, almost confederal principle. The key is to *add* the
principle of self-determination or national independence to the present
structure of international relations. This can be done by modifying the
hierarchical principle on which the present system rests.

The way to modify this hierarchical principle is to distinguish
between 'nations' and 'states', and to disassociate resource power somewhat from influence. For the first of these considerations, tradition and
history are variables. 'Endurance over time. . .is a distinguishing note of
a state.'[11] Remember, too, that for de Gaulle, the 'state', in terms of
decision-making, is the *active*, motor element in the nation-state. The
distinction, then, is between those legal entities which are usually called
states, and those states which have a capacity for action. Only the latter
are *true* states. These states, he believes, are 'the only effective entities
on the world stage', although it is often necessary to treat other
countries as if they were true states. True states are historical facts and
exercise real power. Although nationhood is important, it is secondary;
'France was a state before she was a nation.' But nationhood is important because the 'most viable states. . .are those that rest on the
support of a nation'. If such states, shorn of colonies and reduced in
relative power and independence by the advent of American and Soviet
economic and nuclear dominance, find themselves at a disadvantage,
then by all means, de Gaulle would say, they ought to cooperate by

building larger *ensembles* such as the European Community; however, such groupings of states cannot themselves be artificially made into states. They must remain at the service of their member states, which have a particular and enduring contribution to make.[12]

In addition to looking for specific ways of increasing material capabilities – through external economic cooperation or the development of a nuclear capacity – the moral role, so important to de Gaulle, can give the true state credibility as an arbiter or moral referee. As Tournoux paraphrases de Gaulle:

Rather than be classified on the lowest rung of the Great Power hierarchy, de Gaulle would prefer to occupy – vis-à-vis these two immense peoples [Russia and America] – the chair of a director of the world conscience. Thus France would again find a universal mission. And it was a matter of building up in the minds of the French a collective dream of strength, a dream superimposing its mirages over the real potential, of a France moving in the direction of the unexplored lands of the Third World! And thanks to which, our country would once again become – if only its herald uses his talents aright – the interlocutor of the superpowers.[13]

Thus we have identified the four key arenas of foreign policy activity within the Gaullist strategic image: the attack on the global *status quo*; the policy of *grands ensembles*; the potential reservoir of support from the Third World; and the significance of nuclear weapons as a symbol of the will to resist subordination. In this more specific context, the image of national independence and self-determination is only universal insofar as its propagation serves to increase support for Gaullist policies. But only the true nation-states, especially France, with her political–cultural tradition, can or even ought to expect to exercise a real influence in an effective manner.

It is interesting to note the analogy between de Gaulle's view of the international system and certain liberal-democratic views of society in which rights and votes are distributed equally, but actual power in the decision-making process is bestowed – by consensus, popular deference, or conspiracy (depending upon the interpretation at hand) – on those individuals and groups with the 'greatest stake' in the society, i.e. the concept of democratic elitism. De Gaulle's international vision of universal self-determination is, in effect, a plea for widening the recruitment of the elites, not only by admitting the middle classes to positions of responsibility, but also by allowing the newcomers to play a special episcopal role with the responsibility of pronouncing upon the moral worthiness of alternative choices. But unlike the American notion of the 'free world', which demands a narrower recruitment of leaders and a stricter ideological dogmatism, Gaullist self-determination is a general principle of global peace and stability, whereas the free world is the child of conflict and confrontation.

Furthermore, the wider international elite envisaged by de Gaulle is itself limited – in a world with approximately 150 sovereign states – to those four or five nation-states with a global role to play. Alfred Grosser sets out de Gaulle's definition of a 'great power' as 'one whose diplomatic objective is intervention anywhere in the international arena and not exclusively in her frontier areas'.[14] As André Fontaine points out, France is present on five continents through her alliances and friendship treaties, giving her not only global interests, but also an interest in the very stability of the international order itself. This role is consecrated in her presence as one of the five permanent members of the United Nations Security Council and her membership of the nuclear club. So instead of having the role of 'policeman of the world' limited to the two superpowers, de Gaulle wanted it broadened to include four or five states. There are two complications which present themselves at this point. Firstly, the smaller policemen would be limited much more to techniques of persuasion and cooperation rather than to the use (or threat) of force or economic muscle – a weakness which de Gaulle saw as having a hidden strength by bestowing greater moral credibility. And secondly, the four or five would have to come to agreements among themselves, presumably according to a United Nations-style veto principle, whenever or wherever either global problems or problems going beyond the interests of just one of the group were in question. For although de Gaulle did not use the phrase 'zones of influence', he believed in them.[15] Thus an essential feature of the widening of the international elite of states was the dividing up of certain problems among themselves, leading to greater self-restraint among all. In fact, France under de Gaulle applied just such a principle. As stated in an empirical study of nonconforming behaviour in alliance situations, comparing France and China, 'French nonconforming behaviour has remained confined to a few issue-areas, with little tendency for it to spill over into all issue-areas.'[16] French assertiveness remained circumscribed within well-defined areas within which French interests – the interests of France as a restricted but still a global power – were seen to be involved.

The agreement between writers on the issue-areas in which Gaullist policy took on an assertive posture is substantial. Edgar Faure identified six major points of the 'grand Gaullist design': (a) strenthening France's internal institutions; (b) military independence stemming from possession of nuclear weapons; (c) colonial disengagement; (d) reconciliation between France and Germany as the cornerstone of the new Europe; (e) the development of a European confederation with a minimum of supranationality led by France and Germany (the latter somewhat less than equal); and (f) 'an attempt at general "global" settlements together with the USA and the USSR, such settlements comprising the attainment of a *modus vivendi* with the East, and a world-wide organisation for dealing with the underdeveloped countries'.[17]

Certain issue-areas cut across these categories. The question of the Atlantic Alliance and the military organisation of NATO overlapped, for example, with the problem of nuclear weapons (integration of command, etc.), the principle of self-determination in the Third World (especially as regards American military intervention in Vietnam), the question of European integration (especially where the question of possible cooperation on foreign and defence policies was concerned), the relations between France and Germany (given Germany's closer alliance ties with the USA), and the question of relations with the Soviet Union (the question of whether or not detente reduced the value of the Alliance).[18] Often these cross-cutting issue-areas produced apparent contradictions. Hassner notes contradictions between: the division of Germany and Franco-German reconciliation (the 1963 Friendship Treaty); ending the cold war and preventing a detente (over the heads of the Europeans); 'at one moment the traditional great-power "Concert of Europe", and the next self-determination for all the smaller states'.[19]

Of course, such contradiction is not unique. The United States speaks of the 'free world' and until very recently has included Chile; the American Declaration of Independence declares the equality of all men yet enshrines private property. Such contradictions simply demonstrate the philosophical maxim that general principles do not admit of uniform application, and that inconsistencies in application do not necessarily invalidate the principle (though under certain conditions they may do so). Taken at the level of specific policy areas, this creates the apparent paradox of nationalism and internationalism not only coexisting, but becoming inextricably intertwined. Robert Gilpin's description of how this works in the area of science policy aptly demonstrates the point:

Contrary to the notion frequently expressed in the U.S. and elsewhere, that French science policy is totally chauvinistic, paradoxically her policy is the most internationalist, as well as the most nationalist, science policy pursued by any European state. Though no other nation in Europe equals France, for example, in the emphasis on national efforts in space and atomic energy the ultimate success of these undertakings is very much dependent on complementary international programmes (including Concorde, ELDO, ESRO, the International Centre for Cancer Research)...The logic of the French position is that while international programmes can supplement national programmes they cannot replace them.[20]

But despite the limitations and the apparent paradoxes, de Gaulle's grand design does form a whole of interrelated parts, which must be seen in a dynamic, diachronic relationship to each other and to the whole. As K. J. Holsti has written, 'Among the Western countries, only France under Charles de Gaulle has recently pursued a long-range foreign policy goal which compares in explicitness to the Soviet vision of the new order.'[21] De Gaulle re-emphasised two elements which have often been relegated to the historical past but which he saw as having a new relevance to the future: the role of the nation-state (with an emphasis on those states with a long historical experience of political development as well as a global vocation); and the particular role of France 'as a leading force in European civilisation'.

This long-range vision, while recognising the emergence of the United States, the Soviet Union and China as major powers, seeks to re-establish Europe, inspired by France, as an effective force in this new global alignment – basing Europe's strength and credibility on her solid achievements, represented in her nation-states, rather than on the shaky edifices of experimental supranationalism. It is Russia, a nation-state with a long but in some ways peripheral national tradition now consolidated in the Soviet Union, which is seen at the heart of the reality of Soviet international ambitions – not the chimera of international revolution but a great power interested in maintaining a continental balance of power. Communist doctrine he saw as increasingly irrelevant, both to the Soviet leaders who still used it to maintain their legitimacy but who more and more tended to pursue traditional Russian interests such as the search for access to warm-water ports, and to East European, Chinese and other foreign Communist leaders who, in the age of polycentrism, had more and more to justify themselves by reference to national interests and separate roads to socialism. The tendency of the international system, in de Gaulle's eyes, was more and more to reinvest the nation-state with its true legitimacy, whether in terms of looser alliances and ties of economic cooperation among the more developed nations, or the ambition of new Third World states to strengthen their *bona fides* and to become more like traditional nation-states (a process over which the developed states had a moral duty to preside in a beneficent manner).

In matters closest to the vital interests of France – the future of Europe and of France herself – de Gaulle's vision becomes more clearly delineated. France and Germany, the former through realising her world role and responsibilities and the latter bringing the contribution of her new-found political stability and economic strength, will lead a rejuvenated Western Europe into which Britain will be admitted when she has developed a clearer European vocation and limited her far-flung entanglements (as France has done). Russia and Eastern Europe, having turned more and more towards their national interests, will no longer reinforce such a clear-cut division of the continent but will accept a more flexible and fluid continental order. Europe will be independent of extra-continental powers where her own vital interests are at stake, although a common interest in liberal democracy, an expanding world economy and a stable global balance of power will strengthen the free and equal ties which will have developed with the United States and her sphere of influence; to some extent, Britain will always remain as a link between Europe and North America, providing a special relationship based on her own historical interests but complementing, rather than conflicting with, her European vocation. Supranational European integration will be limited, firstly, by using existing institutional means to maintain France's vital interests against the faceless Eurocrats, and secondly, by augmenting the more tightly integrated sphere of economic cooperation with a looser, but in political terms more important, sphere of cooperation on foreign and defence policies based on close intergovernmental cooperation. The separate identity of the European nation-states, which not only reflects a developed national identity and image of the national interest among the diverse peoples but also enables the active pursuit of the general interest through state structures, will be maintained, and the cooperation vital to those very national interests will be based on a 'Europe of the States'.

France, to de Gaulle, was the only European nation-state with the capacity to take a leadership role in this process, once it had solved the problem of its internal political stability and effectiveness. Germany was still preoccupied with its division and with its ties with America,

Britain saw herself as playing a marginal role (maintaining stronger external links) and Italy was a divided nation in a political and economic predicament; under French leadership, however, they would take their places and play constructive roles in the new Europe. But the malaise of the cold war and of dependency on the United States had to be reduced, especially in the minds of the peoples, for it had been sapping their will to take up their European responsibilities. This consciousness-raising operation depended upon the clear leadership of France, which must forge ahead despite the strong criticism evoked abroad. And of these countries, Germany – and thus Franco-German solidarity – was the most crucial to future development of a stable European order. De Gaulle devoted much time and energy to attempting to bring about this reconciliation, although it retrogressed seriously during the Chancellorship of Ludwig Erhard. And he was convinced that Britain, too, would eventually take up the role she was offered, once the loss of the two most important remnants of Empire – global military influence and the Commonwealth trading bloc – had been perceived and comprehended by her people and her leaders. Such an independent Europe of the European states, within a world in which Europe (and France) played an important *rôle moteur* in showing the way towards the necessary and proper changes, was his consistent and long-range objective, and the resources of the French state were marshalled in its pursuit.

He saw these changes as changes which were inherent in the nature of things. They were not to be brought about by force or pressure, but by moral leadership – by pointing out clearly to France and to the rest of the world where the future lay, and then by acting in accordance with that image. Insofar as the international system of the 1950s and early 1960s did not conform to this design, Gaullist France falls within Henry Kissinger's definition of a 'revolutionary power'.[22] On the other hand, de Gaulle's aspiration to change the international system rested not on a will to impose a new order, but on an interpretation of what was already there. De Gaulle saw his grand design as a potentiality of the *existing* system, which needed mainly a dose of prodding, coaxing and occasionally some open defiance in order to start a self-sustaining process of reappraisal, which would eventually lead to a general desire and will to escape the strait-jacket of cold war ideological rigidities and unstable bipolar balances.

There may be some evidence to support a view today that this process has to some extent taken place, mostly independently of de Gaulle –

but with de Gaulle as prompter if not as prophet. De Gaulle did not seek to 're-create the zero-sum conditions of mercantilism', as suggested by Edward L. Morse.[23] And the international system of the late 1970s has certainly not reached the level of smooth functioning, dependent upon stability and upon 'commensurate notions of what is just', that would have to be present if the Gaullist grand design were to have achieved fruition in a fully re-equilibrated international system.[24] But today's pattern of international relations, with its European Community summit meetings, its Groups of Ten, its European Security Conferences, its greater awareness of the need for international commodity regulation and so on, is a world which de Gaulle would have recognised as having more common sense and awareness of the real problems and limitations deriving from the dialectic of interdependence and independence than did the Western rhetoric which he incessantly confronted in the 1950s and the 1960s.

II. Sequences and categories of de Gaulle's foreign policy

It is worth briefly pointing out the ways in which de Gaulle's foreign policy, or the various aspects or elements which made up the fabric of that policy, can be distinguished. Three methods of classification are useful: operational formulae; systemic and sub-systemic arenas, primarily of a geo-political nature; and time sequences or historical phases.

A number of operational formulae can be distilled from the sort of analysis presented in Chapters 2 and 3. Like everyday proverbs, these formulae are not strictly speaking true in isolation, but only in a context. They have their own ambiguities and equally axiomatic negations.[25] Their simultaneous advocacy, however, does in fact help to define the predicaments which characterise de Gaulle's policies. For de Gaulle was ever the leader of *Le fil de l'épée*, seeking not to do away with principles, but to eschew dogma and to replace it with flexible principles which could be adjusted (in the Bergsonian manner) to the realities of events, to the ebb and flow of human experience, without forcing them into the static categories created by 'intelligence'. De Gaulle's principles define a problem in a certain way, but they rarely dictate a particular solution. The genius of the leader is to adapt the possible range of solutions to the necessities of both the problem as defined and the concrete historical circumstances. In the world of East–West relations, for example, the slogan of '*Détente, entente, coopération*' was not meant to prejudice the detailed nature of the unfolding of the process of *rapprochement,* but rather to identify the threefold nature of the task ahead. Other identifiable principles work in the same way.

Among the operational principles significant to the Gaullist ideological universe several particularly salient notions can be teased out. The first of these, and one which has already been considered in its broader ideological context, is that of *independence.* This involves, on the one hand, the traditional notion of national sovereignty – that within the territorial confines of an internationally recognised state, the power of the legitimate authorities is supreme – and, on the other, a much vaguer conception of freedom of action which claims that the state must be permitted a certain scope within which to pursue those objectives incumbent upon it as the repository of the 'national interest'. A second, and linked, operational principle is that of *non-interference.* This is a two-dimensional notion. On one level, it reflects the defensive reaction of states which see their independence as threatened by others; on another level, however, it reflects Wilsonian principles of international order and collective security, a kind of minimal threshold beyond which begins the grey area where domestic – i.e. legitimately protected and internally controlled – politics merges, imperceptibly at first but more and more distinctly, into international politics which require some sort of solution involving the interaction – and therefore *common* action – of more than one state. Such principles imply a further principle which, as we have already seen, has its limitations: *universal nationalism.* For although all nation-states cannot be equal in durability, stature, power and virtue, they all embody a vital minimum of status and legitimacy which defines the *sub-structure* of international politics. All political structures, in the Gaullist cosmos, aspire to become nation-states, for that is their *raison d'être*; their essential inequality, and the necessity for hierarchy for the sake of order in the system, do not invalidate their essential character as the fundamental building blocks or foundation stones of international relations *per se.*

The principles outlined so far represent a kind of horizontal photograph of international politics,[26] concerned with the base of the organisational pyramid of international decision-making. A second series of operative principles concern the vertical organisation of the international system. Two principles stand out. The first is that of *regional and international cooperation.* The liberal–democratic analogy recurs here; just as the polity is seen as the result of a social contract between naturally free individuals to pursue common interests (such as the protection of property), so the international system derives from the operation of the enlightened self-interest of its essential components, the nation-states. Rights imply corresponding duties; similarly, in today's dangerous and interdependent world, independence and non-interference demand a corresponding willingness to cooperate on a wide range of vital matters of common interest – economic, military and political. The implication is that supranationality and multilateralism represent a kind of international collectivism, to be resisted. Voluntary cooperation is de Gaulle's prescription. A second vertical principle adds the dynamic element, the motor element which crystallises the system as an active structure with functions to perform, which perceives, initiates and moulds action: the *international hierarchy of nation-states*. Thus international politics, in de Gaulle's view, requires leadership – the leadership of the big powers, a sort of 'natural *aristoi*' of nation-states charged, because of their very size and strength, with keeping international law and order. It is almost a kind of international *noblesse oblige*.

A number of further principles can be described as circumstantial. They derive from the application of the above principles, horizontal and vertical, to the concrete conditions characterising the longer-term development and the present conjuncture of the international system as we know it. They are merely general principles rather than universal principles. The first of these is *opposition to the bloc system* characteristic of the cold war. This highly integrated system, dominated by the juxtaposition of the two superpowers, was seen as unstable and even volatile: unstable because it denied the legitimate claims of other nation-states to their vital minimum of independence and non-interference; volatile because its balance of terror actually represented a worsening disequilibrium between base and superstructure. The greater the integration of the two blocs, the greater the disequilibrium, for the number of potential flashpoints of conflict would multiply as each far-flung outpost of the system became an essential commitment calling the overall strategic stalemate into question by the threat of escalation. To lower the temperature, the tight bloc structure needed to be relaxed and made flexible. The second circumstantial principle is the *development of more decentralised spheres of influence*. These spheres would exist at different levels and thus would necessarily overlap, making the big powers around which such spheres would revolve more dependent upon voluntary mutual cooperation; such cooperation would involve a different pattern of interaction at each level, thereby avoiding the crunch of escalation which the bloc system produces through its dangerous centralisation. Inter-bloc conflict would thus be defused by a diffusion of conflict points. At the same time, intra-bloc tensions and resentments would be lessened, because the independent sphere of the leading powers would be widened and their responsibilities enlarged within their own spheres – providing for a division of labour among the enlarged circle of 'big powers' which, like France, have an 'international vocation'. Thus a third circumstantial principle is less general than specific, deriving from the application of broader principles to the particular role and posture of one nation-state: the cultural and economic *rayonnement* of France. This is a twofold notion which subsumes both the particular moral contribution which de Gaulle felt to be the true vocation of France and the pivotal role which she could play in initiating and furthering the evolution of the international system towards the more flexible structure he envisaged by means of putting new life into France's traditional links abroad. France would thus develop a range of foreign policy instrumentalities ranging from the promotion of French language and culture, to the strengthening of trade and aid ties with former colonies, to the presentation of France as a safer partner in the developed industrial world for nations politically aiming to achieve some distance from the superpowers (the non-aligned states). While this last principle has been interpreted as a cover for French neo-colonialism, de Gaulle saw it as being fundamentally different from such domination, because it was based on voluntary bilateral cooperation and an explicit recognition by France of the legitimate national interests of her interlocutors in a world where such legitimacy was often still merely an objective and not an accomplished fact.

The thread which reconciles these different principles – principles which might be seen in practice potentially to conflict – is twofold: firstly, de Gaulle's own world view; and, secondly, the pivotal role of France. I would not go so far as to accept Kolodziej's view that de Gaulle had in mind the creation of an international system of permanently fluid and changeable relations between states. To adopt that model would almost be like suggesting that Thomas Jefferson's views on equality meant the abolition of status, privilege and property. On the contrary, de Gaulle, in asserting the need for independence and sovereignty, and in presenting this in a universalised fashion, was at the same time pursuing a more particular principle derived from the application of universal principles to the actual structure of international society – that of French culture, civilisation, maturity, seniority and fitness to provide needed leadership. Like the American Founding Fathers' defence of property, this meant the *independence of the best fitted to rule* – not the granting of popular power to the international *demos*. De Gaulle's support and initiation of various proposals based on a *directorate* structure, from NATO (1958) to the EEC (1961–2) to the solution of the Middle East crisis (especially 1967–9), are most indicative of the 'balance' which he sought to achieve in world politics between the various principles he espoused, a notion of balance not dissimilar in principle to that proposed by Aristotle between aristocracy and democracy in the domestic arena.

In this sense we can distinguish between two sorts of ideological assertion in de Gaulle's foreign policy: the *active* and the *reactive*. The 'reactive' form of assertion is presented in a context where French policy is reacting to existing rules or innovations and initiatives imposed from outside France – from outside the subsystem where Gaullism has already become the ruling set of operative ideals – and where such rules, innovations and initiatives are perceived as inimical to either French national interests or the French view of the world (i.e. the Gaullist perspective). In such cases the Gaullist principles are asserted in their full ideological splendour. It is in the context of 'reactive' assertion, too, where the relation between French national interests and the Gaullist world-view – the latter claiming universal validity to justify the former – can be turned on its head, the former in fact justifying the latter. It is a moot point whether the principles become a false consciousness or not in such cases. This form is exemplified by the resistance to American hegemony in Western Europe, to Soviet hegemony in Eastern Europe, to supranational encroachment on French sovereignty, and to superpower military interference in the Third World.

The 'active' form of assertion arises in the context of *French* initiatives – attempts to bend existing rules or to innovate new ones. In these cases empirical realities usually shape Gaullist actions and put greater emphasis on the flexibility of Gaullist principles while calling for little more than a diversification of responsibilities at the top of the international system. This form is represented by de Gaulle's proposal for a NATO triumvirate, by the negotiation of the Common Agricultural Policy, by support for the suggestion of a European Security Conference while other Western Powers were still emphatically opposed, and by the proposal for a four-power solution to the 1967 Middle East problem. The relationship between the active and the reactive forms of assertion can explain why de Gaulle wished to leave the NATO military organisation while remaining a full partner in the Atlantic Alliance; why he could reject the principle of supranationality for the EEC while vigorously supporting certain forms of common policy-making; and why he (twice) rejected Britain's application to join the Common Market while cautiously approving a wider customs union with a restricted directorate (the Soames Affair) Once again we see de Gaulle's belief in both the eternal quality of the nature of things and the need to adapt to circumstances – a paradox solved only by his belief in the existence of a quasi-ascriptive hierarchy of states which made French interests and the common global interest so inextricably intertwined. The apparent paradox of Gaullist principles is reconciled in the confluence of theory and practice.

Thus the interrelationship of principles only becomes concrete within the historical–empirical framework of international politics. Like most practitioners of international policy, de Gaulle also saw his concrete policy-making as being substantialised within the context of geopolitics, or, more precisely, within arenas formed by the interaction of geography and historical development. These arenas form our second set of categories for classifying Gaullist policy. These arenas can be conceived as four overlapping circles including France. The first is the *global* arena. This involves what international relations commentators would call the 'international system' as a whole, with a distinct structure of political, economic and strategic relations; it is characterised in overarching structural terms – bipolar, multipolar, balanced, transitional, unstable/stable, etc. This is the most structurally problematic arena for Gaullist policy, given France's lack of economic and strategic capabilities; she is much less powerful and influential than the superpowers, and so must effectively justify her right to a share in leadership. The next circle, squarely in the centre of the traditional East–West interface, is *Europe*. Like Germany before unification, her boundaries are fluid, her identity fragmented and multidimensional, her structure watched over by wary external powers, and her concrete role in the world yet to be determined. Here the French role is crucial, being economically the second and politically the first nation-state on the continent west of the Curzon Line. The third circle, historically peripheral, but promising to be ever more crucial to future world developments, is the *Third World* arena. Taking many shapes and cross-cut by many cleavages, the peoples, classes and nation-states of Latin America, Africa and Asia are in the process of attempting to define a new, post-colonial role in the changing world at the same time as they are trying to develop more effective political structures and more relevant socio-economic structures at home. France's role is based on three factors. Firstly, the historical, colonial relationship, which was brought to an end only in the first few years of de Gaulle's presidency, gives France undeniable ties with her former empire. Secondly, de Gaulle's view of the importance of national independence has a certain appeal to Third World leaders seeking a model for both domestic and foreign policy action. And thirdly, the Gaullist view of bloc politics accords with the desire of the non-aligned nations to avoid absorption into rigid bloc structures – a point of frequent convergence of French and Third World views on a variety of issues. The final arena is that of *national defence*, the circle around France herself. For the challenge of defence policy, given French objectives, is to build up a defence capacity which is suited to Alliance commitments, the simultaneous maintenance of both freedom of action and sufficient strength to be recognised by others as an independent threat, and the demands of budgetary restraint in the face of competing domestic priorities (all the more important in a period, after 1962, when France's direct involvement in war had ended and pressures for a de-emphasis on military spending had rapidly increased).

In each circle or arena, then, France, has a particular role to play, as both hinge and motor, linking the elements within each arena, but also linking the various arenas with each other. This pivotal role de Gaulle saw as crucial to the pursuit of French objectives. At one level, the arenas can be seen as the concentric circles of a Francocentric world, expressing the self-interested element in Gaullist policy. But at another level, they are simply those sub-systems of the international system in which France happens to be a major actor. In this case, French action within and across the four arenas reflects the ideological coherence and the practical diversity of the different elements of Gaullist policy. It thereby emphasises the broader structural links between the different levels of the international system itself.

Having attempted to classify the operative principles of Gaullist policy and to delineate the boundaries of its spatial categories, let us examine its development over time. In the years 1958–69 we can distinguish three clearly defined periods, although the chronological boundaries of each phase are blurred and overlapping. Indeed, the phases vary somewhat for each of the four arenas indicated above, and even within different sub-arenas. The main outlines can, however, be demonstrated.

The first phase consisted of the consolidation of the French position in the world and the laying of the ideological foundations of Gaullist policies. In defence policy, it involved the first development and elaboration of the nuclear deterrent. In European policy it meant successful entry into the EEC and the proposal of reforms leading up to the negotiation of the Common Agricultural Policy and the presentation of the Fouchet Plan. In Third World policy it consisted of the process of decolonisation, the winding down of the Algerian War, and the implementation of French aid programmes. And in Great Power policy it meant the suggestion of various avenues towards increasing the French role in the Atlantic Alliance and a policy of carrot-and-stick towards the Soviet Union, calling for detente but resisting encroachments in Berlin and supporting the American response to the Cuban missile crisis of 1962. The results of this first period were mixed. The independent deterrent was set in motion, the EEC take-off was cleared successfully, and Third World policy proved highly successful. However, American and British opposition slowed down the progress of the French nuclear force. Attempts to reform the European Community according to de Gaulle's political and ideological criteria failed. And the cold war system developed independently of the French pressure until well after the Cuban crisis had altered the international atmosphere.

The second phase began towards the end of 1962, and could be said to have finished finally in 1968, although in many ways the end of the second phase began in 1966. It was characterised by the vigorous assertion of the French viewpoint at all levels of foreign policy:

1963 was surely the year when, on a range of great and capital problems, like defence, NATO, nuclear weapons, a certain conception of European Europe, and projects for an Atlantic community, positions were taken which placed us squarely in opposition to the United States, if only for a time, and which, on the other hand, clearly fixed our policy within the Western world. Our posture towards the Eastern world was also clearly set out; everything became possible and everything would be desirable as soon as the language of threats was finally abandoned.

So the former Foreign Minister, Couve de Murville, described the beginning of the second phase within the global arena.[27]

The long-term plans for the nuclear striking force were set in motion, and the process of restructuring the armed forces was able to proceed in the wake of the Evian Agreements and Algerian independence. In Third World policy, the cooperation agreements were implemented with the recently decolonised states by the sending of large numbers of technicians and teachers; aid was maintained at a high level, the Yaoundé Agreements between the EEC and the associated states (ex-French colonies) were implemented in 1964; de Gaulle undertook an extensive voyage to Latin America and a number of trips to Africa and one to Asia, where he was welcomed in Cambodia by his protégé, Prince Sihanouk, and severely criticised US policy in Vietnam. In European policy, the Fouchet Plan was rejected but the Common Agricultural Policy was established, British entry was refused, the 1965 boycott of the Council of Ministers took place, and the Luxembourg Agreements enforced Gaullist demands upon the existing institutions. In Great Power policy, a series of trade and exchange agreements were negotiated with Eastern Europe and the Soviet Union – Couve called 1964 the 'year of the thaw' – China was recognised also in 1964, the French refused to support the United Nations Congo expedition, opposition to the American position in Vietnam hardened, the Multilateral Force proposals died, France withdrew from the NATO military organisation in 1966, de Gaulle also visited the Soviet Union in that year (along with several other East European nations in this period), a second veto on British entry to the EEC came in 1967, and French influence was extended in the Middle East to the detriment of both superpowers.

The results of this phase were also mixed, although the French posture as an opponent of the existing international order became an established legend, disquieting many, particularly in the West, and reinforcing the determination of de Gaulle's critics. French policies were occasionally successful, at a price. In particular, American willingness to compromise was reduced even further, and British reactions to French initiatives bordered on the paranoid. The hand of resurgent nationalism was diagnosed as the basis of Gaullist policy, destroying the balance of power which had maintained the precarious peace since 1945 and which had thus created the conditions within which Gaullist ambitions could rage with impunity – or so, at least, went the popular diagnosis (similar to the view that liberalism is its own worst enemy because it allows its enemies to proselytise). At the same time, however, the *rapprochement* between the United States and the Soviet Union progressed also, along with the Nuclear Test Ban Treaty (1963) and the increase of East–West trade. This de Gaulle also regarded as a threat – that the superpowers would no longer go to war with or without consultation, but would instead, without consultation, carve up the world between themselves, extending the bloc system further. The increasing weight of France and West Germany – indeed, of Western Europe as a whole – along with the recurring crises in the Third World, however, took the main arena of conflict out of the hands of the superpowers to a great extent, and gave the smaller nation-states much greater leverage.

It would be highly speculative to attempt to determine whether French policy *per se* had much impact, during this second phase, on what was in fact a general trend away from the bloc politics of the cold war. However, many of de Gaulle's initiatives indicated that he was fully aware of the trend even before he came to power, and that in this respect his analyses and predictions were more insightful than those of the superpowers themselves. By following de Gaulle's policies, France did increase her influence at all levels of policy and reinforce her credibility in the international system, although French influence was never a challenge to the superior status of the superpowers. 1965, however, as Couve has observed, marked the beginning of a real voice for France.

The emphasis of Gaullist foreign policy shifted considerably in the late 1960s, although the exact point at which the shift began is not self-evident. It is possible to suggest that the beginning of the shift came with the high water mark of French 'reactive' assertion – i.e. the aftermath of the withdrawal from NATO and de Gaulle's visit to the Soviet Union in 1966. After all, 1966 was the year when American policy towards the East began to change, too, with President Johnson's 'bridge-building' speech and the negotiation of a consular treaty between the USA and the USSR. The French withdrawal from NATO left defence gaps to be filled; French disruption from within NATO quietly turned into French cooperation from outside the integrated command structure. This cooperation was seen in such matters as the shared use of air defence warning systems, not to mention the problem of the stationing of French troops in West Germany and the issue of the possible degree of cooperation with NATO in case of an emergency; the problem of the troops in Germany might have been very tricky, but it was easily and quietly resolved after the fall of the Erhard Government and the accession of the Grand Coalition in late 1966. In addition, the signing of the Luxembourg Agreements in January 1966 began a process of *rapprochement* between France and the EEC. Nonetheless, the impact of the NATO withdrawal poisoned Franco-American relations and created an atmosphere in which France became a bogey to many groups, especially Atlanticists and 'Europeans' (i.e. supporters of supranationalism). Despite the beginnings of the German *Ostpolitik*, the attempt to use NATO as an instrument of detente, the UNCTAD meetings and similar things, French policy – which had anticipated many of these developments – was seen mainly as a maverick, disruptive force.

It is more usual to date the change in emphasis in French policy – the beginnings of the third phase – from 1968, as do Kolodziej, Tint and others.[28] It is widely believed that under domestic pressure from the Events of May 1968, and under external pressure from the Soviet invasion of Czechoslovakia shortly thereafter, de Gaulle decided that domestic policy would have to come first and that detente was still not feasible in the face of a belligerent Soviet Union. Whether these factors did, indeed, cause a fundamental shift in de Gaulle's perception of priorities – or whether they simply accelerated a change in *degree* which had already begun – is difficult to determine, and must be left to the study of official archives when these become available.[29] We shall argue, however, that these changes were already underway, but only became obvious to the world in 1968, although an increased emphasis on domestic policies was no doubt clearly linked with the Events of May and de Gaulle's subsequent attempt to fashion participatory reforms. 1968 saw France's first real economic and financial crisis, too, since the advent of the EEC. It marked a real change in defence policy, as a form of 'flexible response' was finally officially adopted and as defence spending had to be cut drastically. It marked the culmination of France's relatively unsuccessful attempt to impose four-power mediation on the Middle East, and heralded other later changes in French Mediterranean policy. It marked the end of the era when France could afford to continue to spend over 1 per cent of her Gross National Product (GNP) on foreign aid.

But all of these turning-points were developed over time, between 1966 or 1967 and 1969. The location of the causal factors in a sort of 'defeat' for de Gaulle at home by the Events of May – one must not forget the elections of June 1968 and the nomination of Couve de Murville as Prime Minister, which might have heralded new foreign policy initiatives – or abroad – where French policies were becoming grudgingly accepted in NATO and the EEC – is too simplistic and therefore fundamentally erroneous. An alternative argument will be developed here: that the main assertive objectives of Gaullist policies (mainly of the 'reactive' form) were *satisfied* by the end of 1966; and that France had reached a stage where her policies now reflected, rather than anticipated, the changing structure of the international system.

The period following the American withdrawal from France was characterised by a gradual process of normalisation of Franco-American relations culminating in a *rapprochement* with the newly elected President Nixon and his quasi-Gaullist foreign affairs adviser, Henry Kissinger,[30] in 1969. The French opening towards Eastern Europe could never be as straightforward again after Czechoslovakia, but other Western countries, especially West Germany, attempted to outdo France from stronger economic foundations. Relations with the Soviet Union continued to be significant, but the Soviet–American detente overshadowed France's earlier initiatives. Other countries began to court China. Third World policies lost their outward gloss as France's former colonies sought to escape from the economic pressures which stemmed from the structure of the French aid programme. The stalemating of the Vietnam peace talks, held in Paris, reduced the salience of French opposition to the war, and French relations with the Arab countries continued to improve. In Europe, the EEC's progress was slowed somewhat by the frustration of moves towards further integration and by the ill-feeling resulting from the second veto of British entry in 1967, but progress in most practical fields, such as the achievement of the customs union in 1968 and the harmonisation of a wide variety of less important policies, continued. Thus, while the achievements of the third phase of de Gaulle's foreign policy were complex and mixed, the period, beginning sometime in late 1966, marked a convergence between de Gaulle's objectives and the changing realities of the international system – due to the limited nature of the former and a number of indigenous changes in the latter.

Further changes in French policy under de Gaulle's successor as President of the Republic, Georges Pompidou, after June 1969, concerned primarily the reinforcement of the *rapprochement* with the United States, the reinforcement of France's position as a regional power in the Mediterranean, and several French initiatives on Europe. At the Hague summit conference in 1969, Pompidou gave the French *imprimatur* to a future enlargement of the European Community and to moves towards a strengthening of Community policy-making. However, moves towards a monetary union did not survive the changes in the world monetary system of 1971–3, and the idea of a political union did not survive British entry to the EEC and the energy crisis, both of which began in 1973. All of these changes in the European arena, however, took place within the framework of the post-Luxembourg relationship between Commission and Council of Ministers, the latter being identified by Pompidou in 1973 as an embryonic 'Senate' of a European 'confederation' – federalism and supranationalism having been successfully held in check since 1966.

In any case, the international system of 1968 and 1969 looked much more like the international system which de Gaulle had hoped to establish in 1958 – even in those areas where his policies had had little or no impact. France, having been the maverick, became the custodian of the new order – at least in her own eyes. The irritations and the idiosyncracies remained, but the context had changed, and France had become more or less like the others, or they like her.

III. French policy and the global order

The field of foreign policy in which French principles, French assertion and Gaullist idiosyncracy were most salient, and produced the most resistance and conflict, was the global arena. It was at this macro-systemic level that the Gaullist challenge to received notions (the necessity of integrated cold war alliance systems, in particular) produced the greatest sparks. De Gaulle's aims were to escape from the cold war ideological power structure and to replace it with a structure based upon 'national realities'. In this structure, the leading actors would perceive their relations in terms of national interests (in the broadest sense, including cooperation on interests held in common) rather than through a sort of false consciousness deriving from a perception of international relations as a clash between two ideologically incompatible types of social organisation.

The means which de Gaulle chose to pursue this goal centred upon an attempt to insert a more open bargaining–consultative framework into big power and alliance politics, involving more freedom of manoeuvre on the part of the superpowers themselves as well as drawing the second-rank big powers into the decision-making process. This framework was supposed to develop while at the same time maintaining alliances based on a community of interests (and values); such coalitions would be necessary in the more fluid situation which would result. Thus although the aim was to break down the rigid blocs, it was equally to maintain durable coalitions. At the time, such an aim was seen to be headed in the direction of international anarchy or an attempt to return to nineteenth-century nationalism, but it was in fact intended as a means of adjusting the balance of power to a more complex incipient post-cold war situation. In this matrix of goals, we see a dominance of 'reactive' assertion in de Gaulle's actual foreign policy behaviour. The active side developed with its own momentum from the course of international events in the 1960s and did not require aggressive assertion. De Gaulle's main specific proposals – the formation of a NATO *troika*, emphasis on bilateral rather than multilateral forms of cooperation, four-power consultation on major international problems and so on – failed in form but succeeded in substance.

De Gaulle's policy was founded on the conviction that the post-1945 international system was based on an imbalance – an imbalance created by the assumption by two individual nations, the United States and the Soviet Union, of responsibility for the defence and welfare of their respective blocs of nation-states, each however with its own personality and interests. This imbalance, in de Gaulle's view, was based from the start on a misconception – that transnational ideologies, based upon economic analyses of the world (i.e. both communism *and* capitalism), had superseded the political and psychological reality of the nation-states.

Criticising the hypocrisy of the early United Nations, de Gaulle wrote:

In short, we found occupying the comfortable chairs in the club of the great powers as many hallowed egotisms as there were charter members. On my visit to Washington, Roosevelt had disclosed the American ambitions, draped in idealism but actually quite practical. The London leaders had just demonstrated that they aimed at achieving specifically British goals. And now, the masters of the Kremlin were to show us that they served the interests of Soviet Russia alone.[31]

Draped in the idealism of the postwar period, these nations tended not only to lose their sense of their own limits – of balance and measure – but also to attempt to justify their expansion in terms of morality.[32] This self-justification, and the belief in their own universal righteousness, was, to de Gaulle, even more dangerous than outright hypocrisy, as it obscured the common sense basis of 'the nature of things'. And, in the final analysis, 'the ubiquity of riches, the intertwining of interests, the osmosis of ideas, have created among the peoples an interdependence which sets, by force, limits to their ambitions'.[33] His clear intention was to revitalise this sense of limitation and to restore the necessary balance of the international system. And because de Gaulle saw the international system of the 1950s and 1960s as fundamentally in *dis*equilibrium, it is not at all illogical to believe that in a re-equilibrated system France could play the pivotal role both of a sort of humanised great power and of the protector of the interests of the smaller nations *within* the great power framework.

This assumption lies behind de Gaulle's attitude to political coopera-tion on a world-wide scale. He was scornful of certain developments within the United Nations, of whose early development he approved:

I will add that [in 1945] the General Assembly then included only about forty states which had been in existence for a long time, which were endowed with cohesion and unity and which were used to international relations and to the traditions, obligations and responsibilities which these relations entail.[34]

Here his own views on the hierarchy of nations are clear. For de Gaulle, the United Nations would only work effectively again when the prestige and predominance of the permanent members of the Security Council were restored from the dysfunctional effects of the cold war (the exclusion of mainland China and the isolation of the USSR against the four permanent Western members). The possession of an independent deterrent was important, because the five permanent members of the Security Council (once China was admitted) were also the five nuclear powers, and any agreements which they might reach would therefore have that much greater impact on the world system as a whole. In practice, French attempts to stimulate such agreements had a limited effect. In 1960, the French-promoted summit conference of the 'Big Four' in Paris ended in total failure, despite de Gaulle's efforts as chairman to smooth over the conflict, because of the U-2 spy plane incident. In 1968 and 1969, some progress was made towards a four-power agreement (France, Britain, the United States and the Soviet Union) on the Middle East – at France's instigation – but the mistrust of France by Israel and the resolute opposition of the Palestinian guerrilla organisations made any concrete progress impossible.

Despite France's isolated and vulnerable position between the world of great power politics and the interests of the smaller nation-states, however, de Gaulle retained the hope of satisfying the latter by re-ducing the virulence of the former. Thus French global-arena politics, besides being the most salient field of French foreign policy, also had distinct priority over the other arenas:

The division of the peoples that inhabit Europe and North America is the main fact and the worst evil of our time. Two camps are set up, face to face, under conditions such that it depends solely on Moscow or Washington whether or not a large part of humanity is wiped out in a few hours. . .In the face of such a situation, France deems that there is no territorial or ideological dispute that has any importance in comparison with the necessity of exorcising this monstrous peril. In France's view, this situation implies three conditions.[35]

These conditions, repeated a great many times by de Gaulle in his public speeches, were *detente, disarmament* (or, even more often, *entente*) and *cooperation*. The progressive development of East–West relations based upon these three principles he saw as being indispensable to the peaceful resolution of international crises.

These crises, unlike previous types of international crisis which developed out of the balance of power in Europe, now tend to be located in peripheral 'hot points'; as the Gaullist commentator, Georges Broussine, has observed: 'Europe used to be the centre of great conflicts. Today the Continent, especially its western portion, seems like a protected harbour in a stormy sea.'[36] De Gaulle wished to accelerate the process of reducing the level of world conflict by reinforcing this European situation, but he saw the superpowers as anachronistic obstacles:

In a world atmosphere which had become that of cooperation between states and *rapprochement* between peoples, a problem like that of Germany would lose its acuteness and could, ultimately, at the appointed time, be considered objectively by the powers concerned. But as soon as a power, by making thunder in the wings, makes a show of dealing with Berlin as though three other great powers did not have their rights there, and as though the Berliners did not have the right to be their own masters, that power is taking upon itself in advance the responsibility for the grave consequences which may result.[37]

On the other hand, however, the great powers are seen by de Gaulle as having the potential to ameliorate this crisis situation: 'Of course we hope the day will come when common sense will again prevail and when reasonable nations, noting the results of experience, will wish to resume this great world undertaking on a new basis.'[38]

Paradoxically, in advancing the cause of such a reappraisal of the cold war system which had by 1958 become part of the normative expectations of both of the superpowers, the early effects of de Gaulle's policies were to create the impression that by loosening ties with the 'free world', de Gaulle was undermining the interests of the Western democracies and furthering the interests of the Soviet Union. Certainly, his positions concerning relations with Communist nations, although similar to those which he had expressed during the Second World War, were significantly different from those which he had later taken in the late 1940s and early 1950s and which had been fully compatible with cold war doctrines. Many of his more conservative followers were as alienated from his search for independence as were successive American administrations. On the other hand, the Gaullist *rapprochement* with the Soviet Union, Eastern Europe and China strengthened Gaullist support among neutralist and left-wing groups within France, and reinforced the credibility of Gaullist policies among the nations of the Third World as well.

The Gaullist opening to the East was in no way a one-dimensional phenomenon. Even French relations with the Soviet Union were conceived on several different levels. In the first place, de Gaulle, with his personal stress on history and geo-politics, felt that, with the exception of empty ideological quarrels, France and Russia could rationally have no fundamental quarrels among themselves. Historically, France and Russia have tended to ally themselves against Germany. And neither would have reason to threaten the other on a nation-to-nation basis today. Therefore their relations, although not necessarily involving agreement on a number of points, could be carried on in a full and frank manner. In the second place, Russian power – both economic and military – could not be ignored, and it seemed more sensible to de Gaulle to attempt to channel this power into less aggressive and more cooperative channels. And in the third place, de Gaulle sought to assure the Soviets that their own position was not being threatened, and that in consequence there was no reason for them to maintain as tight a grip on their satellites or as great a military threat in Europe as was the custom of the cold war.

The first of these levels was approached by de Gaulle mainly through the medium of personal diplomacy, particularly his attempts to keep the 1960 summit conference going, his invitations to Russian leaders to visit or stop over in Paris frequently, and his successful trip to the Soviet Union in 1966. The second level was approached through the means of expanding trade agreements, both with the Soviet Union herself and with Eastern Europe, although in the latter case the agreements were often counterproductive in the economic sense as they led to a growing unfavourable trade balance for the Eastern countries and their consequent disillusionment with the practice. But the growing involvement of French firms, particularly Renault, in trade and manufacturing cooperation with the East has been significant – Renault gradually replaced both Ford (USA) and Daimler-Benz (West

Germany) as the major Western contractor for the Kama lorry factory – and the adoption by the Communist states of the French colour television system (SECAM) over the German–American system (PAL) was a major step. The third level was approached by both of these methods, and also by the overall tone of French policy, especially in the West, where de Gaulle's emphasis on basing relations with the United States on a greater degree of equality was looked on with favour by the Soviet Union.

De Gaulle's approaches to Eastern Europe were more problematic. He sought to reassure the Russians, and yet simultaneously tried to wean the satellite nations away from the USSR. This was tolerated by the Soviet Union on an economic level, and the large series of trade agreements between Eastern European nations and France in the period 1964–6 (followed by French withdrawal from NATO) were looked on with favour by the Soviet leadership at the time. De Gaulle's attempts to add a political element to this *rapprochement*, however, met with less favour. Its most sympathetic and consistent advocates in Eastern Europe were also seen as threatening the political and military *status quo*. The economic impact of French trade on Czechoslovakia was small, but de Gaulle's policy of favouring the loosening of bloc ties and increasing political cooperation between Eastern and Western Europe was carefully listened to by reform-minded Communist leaders.

The invasion of Czechoslovakia following the 'Prague Spring' of 1968 brought a strong reprimand from de Gaulle. De Gaulle's close relations with Rumania throughout the period in question were not well received in the Soviet Union. France also maintained close relations with Poland, not the most acquiescent of the Soviet satellites. In his war memoirs, de Gaulle recalled his belief that although his opposition to the division of Europe consecrated in the Yalta Agreement of 1945 was futile at the time – the other Allied leaders did not even invite him to the conference – in the long run it would prove to have been wise.[39] The exposition of the Brezhnev Doctrine in 1968, however, seems to have been in part a reaction to French political attitudes and a reaffirmation of Yalta despite de Gaulle's explicit denunciation of its legacy again in 1968 after the Soviet invasion of Czechoslovakia. This disagreement has not, however, seemed to affect Franco-Soviet relations in general very much. Outside Eastern Europe, too, Soviet relations with France have often been seen as providing at least a partially acceptable counterweight to Soviet influence. Castro was accused in 1968 by a Moscow-oriented Cuban Communist leader,

Anibal Escalante, of 'planning to expand trade ties with France, thereby lessening Russian leverage'.[40] Thus Franco-Soviet relations, while continuing to be competitive in several sectors, nonetheless developed a certain amount of pragmatic common ground which emphasised the de-ideologisation of Soviet foreign policy but demanded a more conservative attitude towards the territorial *status quo* in Central Europe than de Gaulle would have liked.

French relations with China underwent a complete about-face between 1959 and 1964, as de Gaulle became convinced that the objectives of 'eternal China' were compatible with his own.[41] Certain parallels suggest themselves apart from that between the two countries' attitudes towards underdeveloped nations alluded to earlier. The desire of China to assert her independence from the Soviet Union – and her success in doing so – bore a striking resemblance to de Gaulle's objectives in the West, with the exception that the former conflict was much deeper and more intractable. The means were similar also, including the development of nuclear deterrents, the creation of links with the Third World and with the more independent nations of Eastern Europe, the *rapprochement* with the leader of the enemy camp (though Sino-American relations did not really begin to thaw until the early 1970s) and the gradual attempt to build an independent, self-reliant centre of power which could resist pressures from both East and West at the same time while constructing the basis for the predominance of each within its own regional sub-system. Indeed, Mao Tse-tung accorded rare honours and interviews to French officials when he was still inaccessible to most of the rest of the world, and gave official support to French positions on relations with the United States and Eastern Europe.

Through maintaining relations with the Communist nations on these various levels, de Gaulle managed to gain a rare diplomatic independence which gave him access to many conflicting groups. He was not, however, unaware of the conflicts involved, and was caught in the middle of the Czech crisis of 1968. His desire to build a 'Europe from the Atlantic to the Urals' was not, however, a hegemonic grand design, but, for him, simply the expression of not only a geographic but also a political and social reality which could flower only in a world where the cold war had been superseded. It also depended upon the reactions of the Soviet leadership, which has occasionally eulogised de Gaulle and his policies[42] and which gave tacit support to the Gaullists in certain election campaigns (particularly 1968 and 1969), thus affecting the allegiance of a number of Communist voters in France. He was, however, fully aware of the cold reality of Soviet power and policy, and the limits which these placed on his activities in Europe, with respect to the German problem in particular.

French policy towards the superpowers and the global order demonstrates both the inherent limitations of the Gaullist grand design and its strengths in practice. Its varied application did increase French influence far beyond her material capabilities, despite being faced with two massively superior powers determined to use the bipolar structure of the system to impose order upon the others. De Gaulle's grand design, then, was ahead of its time – but only by a few years. In those few years, however, France brought a number of latent issues to the forefront of world politics, and bobbed and weaved her way through the loopholes of the cold war power structure, always under great pressure, but with a certain flair and aplomb which made the rest of the world aware of the potentialities – not least the United States and the Soviet Union, who were forced to recognise the diversity of the world order which each had separately wished to lead to its own version of the promised land.

Many of the issues thus brought to the surface can be discerned and analysed in more detail by the choice of one salient set of relationships which seemed, most of the time, to dominate the others – the Atlantic Question. This aspect of de Gaulle's foreign policy will be examined in more detail in the next three chapters, but the conclusions which can be drawn from this more limited case study will have a wider validity for an understanding of the more general problems of the pursuit of *grandeur* and independence in practice. It reflects the overall structure of the grand design, the various strands and phases of policy which make up the broad fabric, and the strengths and weaknesses which it displayed. It has been a deliberate choice to provide such a case study, rather than a broad survey of the different arenas and strands of French policy.[43] This chapter will, I hope, stand as a means of relating what follows (and other parts which there is not space to study in detail here) to the whole.

Raising the Atlantic question, 1958–62

A semi-official French commentator wrote in 1966 that the problem of NATO, for France, 'is in a way a symbol both of a particular state of international society and of the policy which arose in response to that state of affairs'.[1] That particular state of world affairs involved a recrudescence of bloc intransigeance and opposition between East and West, and a resultant centralisation of the bloc system under the dominance of the two respective superpowers, with attendant consequences. Although both Soviet and American policy had undergone periods of 'thaw' in the years after the end of the Korean conflict, culminating in the Austrian State Treaty and the Geneva Summit Conference of 1955, there followed a 'period of conceptual and technological flux in strategic relationships which lasted from 1957', with the coming of the missile and space age, 'until at least 1963', with the post-Cuba Kennedy–Khrushchev dialogue and the Nuclear Test Ban Treaty. Superpower competition during this period 'not only revived the tensions of the earlier period of the Cold War, but also made each alliance system more hierarchical in character, for a mixture of political and strategic reasons'.[2]

Fixing the responsibility for the origins of the cold war is itself a complex and highly charged issue. However, whatever the causes of the overall conflict situation, each power defined its own policies in terms of its own perceptions of the purposes of the other.[3] Thus, in operational terms, 'the United States has advanced the Soviet military threat as the principal motivation for the Western Alliance'.[4] Such factors were readily assimilated into the opponent's ideological framework. In the American ideological framework, typified by the perspective of Eisenhower's Secretary of State, John Foster Dulles, the combination of the American role in the two world wars and the American perception of the dangers of Communism, the result was a moralistic undertaking to guarantee the 'free world' – a duty which many Americans felt should have been shouldered with regard to both

Communism and Fascism after the First World War. America assuaged her guilt by becoming the conscience of liberal democracy, assuming a posture based on philanthropic, ethical and legalistic rationalisations.[5] Penitence for earlier isolationism was felt through a new dedication to its supposed opposite, interventionism.

As a result, this period was characterised by the tightening of alliances, a context in which each superpower *held the other responsible for its allies' behaviour*. Khrushchev was said to fear that independent Chinese action would entangle the Soviet Union in an unwanted war with the United States, and US Secretary of State Herter, Dulles's successor, asserted that the USSR would be held responsible for Chinese aggression. This response reflected an essential characteristic of this 'period of extreme bipolarity'.[6] As far as French foreign policy is concerned, the broad framework of the Atlantic Alliance was accepted and its limitations respected. Continued Soviet pressures in Western Europe, Soviet advances in weaponry, especially missiles, the continuing strength of Soviet forces in Central Europe, Soviet encroachments in other parts of the world, like Cuba, and the need to direct French military policy towards the demands of fighting in Algeria, which was both expensive in men and *matériel* and socially and politically divisive at home, were all factors which kept France in the Atlantic camp.[7] Other countries' attempts, in this atmosphere, to loosen the ties of American leadership proved counter-productive: the Diefenbaker Government in Canada lost an election partially because of its anti-American stand on control of nuclear weapons on Canadian soil; and the successor Pearson Government accepted the American 'double-key' system, which was a form of compromise. The French understood the lesson.[8]

In the American alliance system, pressure for centralisation stemmed from a series of factors which Buchan lists. The Suez Crisis of 1956 indicated that America's major allies were not reliable. Continuing colonial wars meant that her allies' power and prestige were diminishing in global terms as conflict came to centre on China and the Soviet Union. The introduction of tactical nuclear weapons into the European theatre under the double-key system – under which either the USA or the government of the country in which they were stationed could veto their use – made the United States the sole arbiter of any effective *European* response to a crisis. Missile and space technology, after the first impact of the Sputnik in 1957, gave the Soviet Union unmatchable prestige on the European continent. The Berlin Crisis of 1958–61 led to the institutionalisation of *crisis management methods* which required centralisation to be effective. And, paradoxically, the Americans and the British took a softer line on the making of new agreements with the Soviet Union than did France and West Germany, who at that time, particularly given the closeness of Adenauer and de Gaulle, saw any such agreements as threats to the *status quo* and therefore took a harder line. In fact, during this period, it was the United States, among the Western allies, which was most afraid of being dragged into an unwanted war caused by the independent action of her European allies. Thus interventionism came to mean a potential for intervention against allies to keep the Atlantic Alliance solidly behind American leadership, and any amelioration or relaxation of the 'balance of terror' would therefore have to be derived from action at the apex of the alliance pyramid, in order to prevent destabilisation. The last phase of this process was the end of the threat to Berlin, with the building of the Berlin Wall in 1961 becoming the symbol of the need for intra-alliance discipline in the Warsaw Pact, the Cuban Missile Crisis of 1962, which demonstrated the successful working of the centralised alliance systems in 'crisis management', and the setting up of the 'hot line' telephone link between Washington and Moscow, which symbolised the institutionalisation of this system.

The outcome was a recognition of the common interests of both the USA and the USSR in the stability of the bipolar system, a stability which seemed to depend upon the maintenance, and not the loosening, of alliance ties. Thus there developed a conflict between Kennedy's 'grand design', based upon the notion of US–European 'partnership' within a more egalitarian Atlantic Community, and the integral imperatives of the new defence system which the USA proposed, and which insisted on the centralised strategic control of crises leading to the use of force. The main proponent of the latter was Defence Secretary Robert McNamara, whose technocratic reforms of the Department of Defence were meant to improve the efficiency of the American military system at all levels, nuclear and conventional. In both cases, American policy was propelled forward by the inspiration of the '*mission civilisatrice*' of the New Frontier.[9] The logical force of the system was that the goal – effective strategic response to the Soviet threat – requires centralisation of decision-making; effective centralisation creates a vested interest by both superpowers in a bipolar system in the maintenance of that system; the existence of stability creates a sense of common interest in combating destabilising factors; 'in a bipolar system, any local conflict threatens the system';[10] and therefore the real enemy of the super-powers becomes *not* the other superpower, but whichever of its own allies threatens to undermine the stability of the system by asserting the primacy of its own interests and therefore its right to independence.

For the superpowers, and for those of their allies who perceive their own interests as inextricably intertwined with those of the superpowers, the answer is to construct a form of integration, a system which sub-ordinates the interests of each member to a hierarchical structure pursuing the interests of the whole system. This sort of integration has been taken by some writers to be something new, based on a principle superior to national sovereignty, and thus representing the common interests of the whole. Johannes Gross, in contrast, develops a more sceptical argument, and his description is worth quoting in full for its conciseness and clarity:

The principle of integration, which German writers in particular are prone to take as the touchstone of the new, superior nature of NATO, can no more support the theory that NATO is a unique type of association, than ideology can support the same theory with respect to the Warsaw Pact. In the case of NATO, the principle of integration means neither more nor less than that its structure takes the form of supra-national hegemony. 'Integration' means that when the emergency for which the alliance was formed arises, national military sovereign-ties are suspended; that the *casus foederis* is not declarable by individual members of the alliance; that military strategy to deal with the emergency is not decided in accordance with the interests of the individual members; that equipment and logistic systems are as far as possible standardised; and that in practice the multi-national staffs use only one working language. The language used is English. Thanks to technological superiority and political pressure, weapons systems and their development are under predominantly American influence; planning and decision remain in the hands of those who are in possession of a credible nuclear deterrent; and control of this deterrent remains with the Chiefs of Staff of the United States of America. Thus integration as an organisational principle of the alliance secures and reinforces the hegemony of one partner, due to the political, military and economic relationships between the U.S.A. on the one hand and all the other member states on the other...This role of NATO as merely a part, although an important part, of an American political presence reaching right round the globe, means that its value in American eyes is judged not in isolation, but as part of a global political concept...As a power committed to intervene in any part of the world, the U.S.A. cannot allow itself to become bound by any of its associates in a political community (as many Germans wanted) and thereby admit an overriding higher priority and limit its world-wide freedom of action.[11]

Thus NATO, having been a whole of which the United States was but one part, appears to Gross and like-minded critics, including de Gaulle, as but one part of the global American posture in its competition – leading inexorably, for survival's sake, to a *tête-à-tête* – with the USSR.

The tensions inherent in such a situation are obvious. As Raymond Aron has written:

Either the great power [in an alliance] will not tolerate equals, and then must proceed to the last degree of empire, or else it consents to stand first among sovereign units, and must win acceptance for such pre-eminence. Whatever the choice, it will live in danger, never having won all the victories necessary, always suspected of aspiring to domination.[12]

And any aspirations to change the overarching structure of power come up against obstacles inherent in that structure. Naturally, each superpower, as well as the smaller countries, will wish to reduce the overall level of tension in the international arena. But conflicts over both the means and channels most appropriate to achieve this, and the implications for the shape of the structure itself once change has occurred, are built into any process of change. In the context which has been described by Gross, we can see that any moves which were not the result of centralised (i.e. American) decision-making would threaten the whole structure of the alliance (and of America's global alliance system), and thereby threaten international stability in the American perspective. As Gross points out, both the Soviet Union and the United States, within their respective alliances, want a reduction of tension, but they want it to come about in distinct stages, step by step, in a process 'under their political control, and not as a series of wildcat moves towards relaxation undertaken independently by their allies. Their interests require that any such independent moves made in the opposing camp are welcomed, but viewed with mistrust if made in their own camp.'[13] Thus American public opinion sees Rumania's independent initiatives within the Warsaw Pact as a positive sign of relaxation and change, but comparable moves in France are thought virtually treasonable. Russia reacts the same way, in reverse.

The problem is increased greatly when, for whatever reason, a reduction of tension *does* occur. For it is the threat of war or of irresistible outside pressure which causes a smaller nation to join an alliance in the first place – not a desire to give up sovereignty. It is true that an alliance of relative equals with strong transnational political, economic and cultural ties may consider a mutual pooling of sovereignty on a number of levels, in the way that the six signatories to the European Defence Community Treaty did in 1952, but the EDC was exceptional; furthermore, it was defeated in the French National Assembly in 1954 precisely because of widespread domestic opposition to the pooling of military sovereignty. Normally, a perceived external threat is the primary cause of alliance cohesion. Now once that perceived external threat is removed, or even reduced by a critical minimum, then all but the dominant member of an alliance will *expect* to see their independence increased, their options widened and their manoeuvrability enhanced. Indeed, whereas the alliance was joined because of the belief that the opposing superpower (with its allies) was the main threat to independence, it now appears that its own main alliance partner has become the primary custodian of alliance constraints. Whether or not the motives of the superpower in question are self-interested, or merely dominated by its own, perhaps even idealistic, notion of the common interest, a conflict of interest naturally arises which then develops a momentum of its own, threatening the cohesion of the alliance itself unless a political compromise can be reached.

In the cold war, and after, Germany has made the Atlantic Alliance a cornerstone of national policy, for various reasons. Her defeat and division meant that the Federal Republic's entire existence and political form depended upon the policies of the occupying powers. Her long border with the East heightened the perception of threat from that quarter. And her very national identity was somehow incomplete, with the Democratic Republic to contend with. France, in contrast, played an ambivalent role in the development of the bipolar structure of international politics. De Gaulle brought together people from all political persuasions when he defended French honour during the war, and attempted to re-establish sovereignty and national cohesion afterwards. Full French acceptance of the logic of the cold war situation – and its implications for postwar occupation policy in Germany, when France held out for a decentralising, deindustrialising approach until 1947 – only developed slowly even after de Gaulle's resignation. Even when the pro-Western *Mouvement Républicain populaire* (MRP), the French Christian Democrats, controlled the Ministry of Foreign Affairs in the Quai d'Orsay from 1947 to 1953, France did not accept American leadership in the same way that Britain did. The wartime Churchillian perspective, the still-extant Empire, and the relatively strong economic position of Britain (which suffered little wartime damage relative to much of the Continent) as compared with dependence of the latter on Marshall Plan aid for reconstruction[14] – all combined to keep Britain from desiring to change NATO once it had been established. The development of her small nuclear deterrent in the 1950s – abetted by the USA – was sufficient to maintain British status and prestige, while her long-internalised 'special relationship' was sufficient to maintain her loyalty once Roosevelt's wartime policy of trying to shrink the British Empire had been replaced by a more pragmatic sharing of 'free world' responsibilties in Africa, the Indian Ocean and so on.

France, whose memories of the wartime alliance were much more discordant, whose position on the reconstruction of Germany was diametrically opposed to the American position, whose attempt to develop her nuclear potential had been opposed all along by the Americans,[15] whose embroilment in drawn-out colonial wars was met either by American opposition or by an American attempt to replace the French as the anti-Communist protector (as in Indo-China), whose attitude towards NATO was ambivalent from the start and emphasised her role in entangling the United States in the defence of Western Europe – and not the reverse[16] – and whose combined polar oppositions of Communists and Gaullists went against French integration in *any* supranational organisation while at the same time questioning the legitimacy of the Fourth Republic itself, had no such organic bond with the Western Alliance.[17] Faced with a United States attempting to consolidate its 'leadership' role, a Britain interested primarily in domestic or extra-European problems and sentimentally closer to the United States, and a reviving West Germany whose peculiar position made it interested in *increasing* the integrated nature of her 'free world' linkages, the French response was, in the Fourth Republic, to seek to create a European pillar which would be both closely bound to the Atlantic Alliance *and* a potentially independent economic and political force in its own right. Only such an arrangement would ensure that an 'integrated' alliance would serve French (and European) interests as well as those of the United States.

In many ways, this policy was opposed, in essence, to the recrudescence of German power, and German support for the policy of European consolidation derived partially from her desire to be *more closely* integrated with the West as a means of solving the double 'German problem' of democratic development at home and legitimation of her frontiers, which had never been truly fixed since her unification in the nineteenth century (a problem profoundly complicated by the division between East and West Germany).[18] Defeat of the European Defence Community Treaty in 1954 highlighted all of these problems, as it signalled the defeat of the French initiatives in the arena of Atlantic relationships. The diversion of energies into economic integration within the European Economic Community (which came into being in 1958) did not affect these *strategic* issues until the 1963–5 period, when de Gaulle clashed with Atlanticists and 'Europeanists' over both NATO and the EEC – over the essential principle of integration – at the same time. Furthermore, the inability of the French regime to develop a strategic policy initiative to replace EDC – due to the requirements of the coalition-building process which characterised the Fourth Republic[19] – played a major role in reinforcing the view held by French public opinion that French interests were being neglected abroad and that the regime was not doing its duty in this area. This perception was reinforced by American opposition to the Suez expedition of 1956 and to the lack of American support for the French position in the worsening Algerian liberation struggle which had broken out in 1954.[20]

It was in this context of the recrudescence of cold war conflict, the centralisation of blocs involving American pressures for further 'integration', and the widespread perception that the Fourth Republic's foreign policy was not effectively pursuing French interests, that the accession to power of General de Gaulle – long known for his emphasis on foreign policy matters as one of the essential characteristics of statecraft (and stagecraft) – introduced a new element into the Atlantic complex. This was a demand for *consultation* – in a specific form which will be described below – and the veiled threat of non-compliance if such consultation was not forthcoming. The development of the Strategic Nuclear Force (FNS) – the *'force de frappe'* (literally, 'striking force') – was the symbolic declaration of intended independence.

The formal – though secret – notification of intent on the part of the de Gaulle Government (the last government of the Fourth Republic, though granted exceptional powers) was the famous memorandum to President Eisenhower and Prime Minister Macmillan of 24 September 1958. This initiative, however, was no bolt from the blue. It was the result not only of the conditions described above combined with de Gaulle's desire symbolically to restore French independence and *grandeur* – for remember that the memorandum was kept officially secret for a long time, indicating that the negotiated *result*, and not the memorandum itself, was meant to provide the symbolic reference point. But it was also the consequence of the failure of various soundings made by de Gaulle after his return to power. *At that time*, de Gaulle did not seek to confront the United States nor the Atlantic Alliance. American leadership was, on the whole, accepted as a matter of course. As Michel Debré pointed out, and as de Gaulle has pointed out privately at other times, 'there can be no question but that political and military capabilities [of the USA] confer upon it certain rights'; but such rights are *limited*, according to Debré, by the fact that the European physical risk (in any war with the Soviet Union) is so much greater than the American risk (Europe being vulnerable to conventional and tactical nuclear weapons as well as strategic weapons) – evening out the balance of responsibilities and therefore of rights.[21]

The beginnings of the nuclear clash can be traced back to the Fourth Republic, to 1957 at the very least. In that year, two things happened. In the first place, the nuclear partnership between Britain and America developed rapidly from the Defence White Paper of 4 April, the Sandys Declaration (16 April) on the rundown of conventional forces, the explosion of the first British thermonuclear device on Christmas Island (15 May) and the Eisenhower–Macmillan 'declaration of common goals' (25 October) which stated that: 'As far as we are concerned, we consider that the possession by both of our countries of the strength of nuclear weapons is a guarantee for the defence of the free world.' Thus was established an Anglo-American '*directoire à deux*' in nuclear matters within the Western Alliance. These events were followed in 1958 by the passing of a new Atomic Energy Act in the United States, revising the MacMahon Act, originally passed in 1954. This new act stipulated that only nations having already made substantial progress in developing nuclear weapons would get American nuclear assistance; it seemed aimed against France, which had had a small nuclear weapons programme in embryo since 1952. In line with the new American criteria, an Anglo-American agreement was signed on 3 July 1958 calling for an exchange of confidential information and for the sale to Britain of nuclear submarine motors, plans and sufficient uranium 235 for ten years.[22]

In the same period, NATO had accepted the emplacement of American intermediate-range strategic missiles (IRBMs) in Europe while awaiting the time (projected for the end of 1959) when Atlas intercontinental missiles (ICBMs) would become operational; France did not permit the emplacement of IRBMs on her soil, for the same reasons as Norway and Denmark, who also refused. It was, in fact, the day after the completion of the Anglo-American agreement that Secretary of State Dulles arrived in Paris to meet with the month-old government of General de Gaulle (4–5 July 1958). As one commentator, Wilfrid Kohl, remarks, this meeting 'marks a major turning point towards deterioration in Franco-American relations. It is probably the only time when the General personally raised the question of American nuclear assistance to France with an American official.'[23] Dulles linked nuclear aid to France with the establishment of IRBM sites, which de Gaulle is said to have refused point-blank. At the same time, American intervention in the Lebanon – formerly an area of French influence – along with British intervention in Jordan were set up without France, and Dulles, on his visit to Paris, attempted to pacify de Gaulle, who sent a cruiser symbolically to mark the French presence.[24]

The refusal to aid the development of the French nuclear force was the beginning of an American policy which, although it often bitterly divided various factions in Washington – including dividing Eisenhower, favourable to helping France, from his own Secretary of State – prevented the United States from offering anything but palliatives which would further alienate de Gaulle in the early 1960s. A well-known Harvard political science professor and theorist of strategic nuclear policy of the time, Henry A. Kissinger, wrote to the effect that the American refusal to help France 'threatens to turn an erroneous French doctrine into an obsession', and that the failure of the FNS (the *Force Nucléaire Stratégique*) policy would not lead to a greater French conventional contribution to NATO (which America wished) but to impotence and neutralism, preventing not proliferation but any build-up of local defence forces.[25] There seemed to be an attitude in Washington that the FNS was somehow illogical and that the French, if ignored long enough, would abandon it. Hopes were occasionally raised by domestic French opposition to the *force de frappe*, but these proved to be illusory.

The contents of the memorandum of 24 September 1958 are well known. It called for the institutionalisation of a political directorate of the North Atlantic Alliance consisting of the United States, Britain and France. In practice, this would most likely have meant the raising of the military Standing Group in Washington from its subordinate status and instituting a more regular form of consultation among the Alliance's Big Three. This consultation procedure would lead to the elaboration of a military *and political* strategy for the entire free world and would jointly control the Alliance's nuclear weapons. Atomic secrets would be held in common, and combined commands would be instituted in the different theatres of the world in which the Alliance members had interests – thus somewhat extending the *range* and *scope* of the Alliance as well as flattening the top of the hierarchical pyramid.[26] A quasi-official French commentator has suggested that de

Gaulle was mainly interested in gaining *equality with Britain*, as well as consultation on such things as coordination of objectives, joint targeting, etc.[27] In contrast, American and British (and even some French) commentators have suggested that de Gaulle wanted no less than full equality with the United States, and that this was his constant objective.[28]

Indeed it is still a matter of controversy among scholars as to whether the 1958 memorandum was a serious effort to reform the organisation or a tactical ploy – with de Gaulle expecting Britain and the USA to reject it – to cover a later French withdrawal from NATO.[29] Professor Kolodziej, writing in 1968, saw an inexorable trend on the part of de Gaulle to withdraw France completely from the Alliance when the North Atlantic Treaty itself came up for renewal in 1969,[30] whereas he later accepted,[31] along with Herbert Tint,[32] the proposition that de Gaulle's real objection was merely to the military organisation and not to the Alliance *per se*. In 1969, France reaffirmed – well before de Gaulle's resignation at the end of April – her support of the Alliance.[33] There is also a controversy over just how far de Gaulle really wished to go in 1958. The rejection of de Gaulle's memorandum by Eisenhower on 20 October 1958 was outright, on the grounds that:

(a) US interests were too extensive and its responsibilities too much greater than France's to permit their reduction to a tripartite arrangement; (b) other NATO allies would object to being excluded from the group, which would be making decisions affecting their interests; and (c) the US saw too many difficulties in extending the NATO Treaty to other areas of the globe.[34]

De Gaulle, however, has been quoted as saying 'I asked for the moon',[35] implying that he expected immediate rejection but was using the memorandum as a basis either for future negotiations on *parts* of the package, i.e. using standard techniques for initiating a bargaining process, or in case such negotiations were not forthcoming, to provide a *rationale* for the development of future independent initiatives.

Paul-Marie de la Gorce considers that too much has been made of the military–strategic implications of the memorandum, and that the Anglo-Saxons could not understand the symbolic importance to de Gaulle of the political nature of his demands. Commenting on the whole panoply of French decisions as regards NATO in the 1958–62 period, he writes: 'These decisions did not bring the Alliance into question, but its functioning. Besides, they had only limited practical consequences. The only thing that mattered was their political objective.'[36] Kolodziej, indeed, emphasises the fact that de Gaulle did not call in 1958 for a formal Atlantic Directorate, but rather for close cooperation and coordination in all areas, in order that France might benefit more from the Atlantic Alliance and might therefore be more willing to cooperate wholeheatedly with it.[37] Kohl points out that: 'Had the tripartite scheme been accepted, the result would have been the consolidation of a system of East–West bloc politics. France, however, would have achieved special status within the Western bloc.'[38] There is also controversy as to how profound the issues really were. According to C. L. Sulzberger, Douglas Dillon, then the American Ambassador to France, 'said that the trouble with de Gaulle was that he always returned to his September, 1958, letter on the *directoire*. On this, de Gaulle really wanted the form and not the substance, while his government – such as Couve de Murville – wanted the substance, not the form.'[39]

Couve himself has defined the essential issues – which remained unsolved – as 'the participation in the various high commands and the presence on our territory of foreign troops which were not placed under French authority'.[40] In any case, given the context of developments within the Alliance and the Gaullists' long-established desire for equality with NATO and abhorrence of the idea of France being forced to become 'the infantry of the alliance',[41] given the American refusal to give fundamental assistance to the development of the French deterrent, and given de Gaulle's objective – whether limited or extensive, material or symbolic – of modifying the essential decision-making structure of NATO, the 1958 memorandum and its aftermath created a situation of fundamental opposition of viewpoints on a major set of issues: the roles which both the United States and France would in future play in the Atlantic Alliance. De Gaulle would seem to have been consistent in his rejection of integration in principle *along with* his acceptance of the validity of the Alliance itself on the levels of both theory and practice; this line was symbolised, as Gross has noted, by 'his denial of the effective authority of the USA to determine the *casus foederis*'.[42]

The next three years or so were taken up with jockeying for position between the USA and France on a series of levels. De Gaulle used the Berlin Crisis to get closer to Adenauer, with whom he had already established a bond, and this led to a series of joint initiatives in Europe including the Fouchet Plan for intergovernmental political cooperation among the six member-states of the EEC, and, ultimately, the disappointing Franco-German Friendship Treaty of 1963.[43] A number of minor skirmishes occurred between France and the United States. On 11 March 1959 de Gaulle withdrew the French Mediterranean fleet from the NATO command. France refused the United States permission to stockpile nuclear weapons on French soil unless they came under French control, which was naturally refused, and in December 1959 General Norstad's command transferred the American fighter-bombers stationed in France, at Toul, to Germany, where acceptable arrangements had been agreed for the depositing of nuclear weapons. 'The French government considered the move final and gave no sign of revising its position.'[44] The IRBM dispute continued. An agreement on the coordination of air defences was finally reached after complex negotiations in February 1960, and the French consented to Norstad's insistence on 30 NATO-controlled divisions. The French atomic bomb was pushed ahead, and the second test of the bomb coincided with Khrushchev's visit to Paris in March, 1960, indicating the symbolic significance of this development.[45] During this period, then, new developments were taking place, which the United States expected to be treated within the framework of the NATO *status quo*, but which France saw as essentially affecting that *status quo* – strengthening it and reinforcing its integrated character on the qualitatively higher plane of nuclear weapons – and which therefore raised questions of principle which she viewed in a quite different light.[46]

And finally, a number of abortive approaches were made to the United States for aid with the development of the FNS, approaches which met with a mixed reception in Washington due both to the differences within the Eisenhower and Kennedy Administrations and to the content of the requests themselves and the economic context in which they occurred – the worsening American balance of payments from 1958 and the beginning of a chronic trade deficit in 1959.[47] One of the effects of this development was that the Kennedy Administration sought to conclude offset agreements in Europe to help pay for her contribution to NATO. These offset agreements usually meant either direct payments by a European country to cover some day-to-day maintenance costs of American troops stationed on its territory, i.e. those costs which involved payment of dollars into the European country's economy (purchases of goods and services in Europe), or agreements to buy certain goods, usually military hardware, from the United States, thus helping American exports. On this latter ground, de Gaulle's independent line on nuclear development ran directly counter to American aims. As John Newhouse has pointed out: 'France was the last of the big markets. Contact between McNamara and Pierre Messmer, France's Defence Minister, had been established;

Messmer, in fact, had agreed at the end of 1961 to buy $50,000,000 worth of American hardware that would normally have been procured elsewhere.'[48] The problem was that the kind of goods France really wanted to buy – goods which would further her nuclear development – were not forthcoming.

In fact, French nuclear development did not fit in with a major evolution of strategic thinking in Washington. This new doctrine, called 'flexible response', meant more than merely a change from dependence on massive nuclear retaliation to more graded forms of conventional-to-nuclear escalation. It also meant a division of labour within the Alliance. The United States would be the nuclear sword, Europe the conventional shield. As Newhouse describes it:

> Its thrust in Europe, where the balance of power was centred, was to be on qualitative and quantitative improvements in non-nuclear forces, so as to give the United States the broadest possible range of military options. France's battle-hardened Algerian army would admirably fit this strategic design; it was, by any military measure, an important asset; in NATO, it would reduce the pressure on American forces as well as the growing dependence on West German units. Numerous elements in the Pentagon, civilian and uniformed, were determined to find some means of overcoming de Gaulle's reluctance to assign these units to NATO.[49]

France was determined to resist this change. The Indo-China and Algerian wars had drained her economically and emotionally and the maintenance of a large standing army such as this – accustomed to fighting in colonial conditions – was not politically acceptable in peacetime to many groups spread across the political spectrum. Furthermore, to become the infantry of the alliance, something which France had sought to resist well before de Gaulle's arrival in power in 1958, was to accept a *reduction* in status, prestige and global vocation just at a time when these were considered symbolically indispensable to the development of a strong national spirit, a stable regime and healthy social and economic development. Such changes – they again involved new elements and a modification of NATO's *status quo* according to America's self-perceived 'enlightened' self-interest – were politically and symbolically unacceptable to de Gaulle and to many others in France of all political colours.

Points of friction continued to grow and to deepen. An offer by Eisenhower and Dulles to provide France with a propulsion system for nuclear submarines was continually delayed and obstructed in Washington, and the issue of which country should sell advanced weapons to Germany was a related bone of contention. This was particularly true of the matter of combat aircraft, where the West Germans purchased large quantities of the Lockheed F-104 Starfighter which later proved to be unsatisfactory as they crashed at an alarmingly high rate; in the mid-1970s, the Lockheed bribery scandals in other parts of the world aroused speculation about other aspects of this sale. In March 1962, the Lavaud mission finally presented the United States with the French $50,000,000 shopping list, which again highlighted the different perspectives of the two governments:

'They wanted samples of this and samples of that – samples which in effect embodied hundreds of millions of dollars in research and development,' one Pentagon official said. Broadly speaking, the French wanted items of a highly specialised and advanced nature in naval, aircraft and missile technology. They wanted star-tracker systems, long-range sonar, valve-control technology for nuclear submarines, inertial-guidance parts and data, avionics, and so on. They showed no interest in buying complete weapons systems, only parts and data that simplify and shorten their own programmes.[50]

The list included nuclear submarine data, equipment for a gaseous diffusion plant, guidance systems, missile parts and propellants.[51] Thus, the American initiative to draw France back into the Alliance structure proved counterproductive; it simply widened the gap between the two countries' views on the necessary steps to bring about a reconciliation. The United States did offer to supply France with KC-135 jet tankers for refuelling her Mirage-IV bombers, which gave the FNS the only real credibility it possessed during the 1960s, before the later development of nuclear submarines, silo-based missiles and tactical nuclear weapons; these did not come into full operation until the 1970s.

The split became complete with the official American adoption of the doctrine of flexible response to replace the official American – and NATO – doctrine of massive nuclear retaliation in the event of a Soviet invasion of Western Europe. Not only did this raise the bogey of the role of French forces within the Alliance – infantry or nuclear partners – but it also raised the question of the credibility of an effective Western response to invasion. The fear that America, behind her nuclear defences, would use flexible response as an excuse not to use nuclear weapons and thereby to abandon Western Europe to its fate exercised the French considerably. The American alternative, a Multilateral Force, was seen as just another attempt to reintegrate France under American command. And the aftermath of the Skybolt Affair, in which the United States unilaterally cancelled production of the missile on which Britain had been almost totally relying for maintaining the credibility of her small deterrent, and the Nassau talks of December 1962 which substituted Polaris for Skybolt and extended the offer to France (subjects dealt with at great length by all of the major commentators on Gaullist foreign policy)[52] finally seem to have determined the lines of conflict which were to characterise intra-Alliance relationships over the next four years.

At the same time, however, an event occurred which provided the French with a more obvious rationale for their action: the Cuban missile crisis of October 1962. Government officials returned to this theme again and again during the 1960s, that the real solidarity of the Alliance lay with the concrete common interests of the members, and that the pursuit of these common interests could be ensured only by their independence of will and their strength of purpose and not by integration and division of labour, which sapped their sense of solidarity and purpose.[53] To Couve de Murville, the dissensions in the Alliance were secondary compared to its underlying solidarity and strength.[54] And the outcome of the Cuban crisis, along with the defusing of the Berlin crisis, meant that the immediacy of the Soviet threat, which had been the real cement of that solidarity and a brake on reform in the 1958–62 period, was no longer so primordial. The Alliance, by demonstrating its solidarity in these situations, had reduced the proportion of the Soviet threat and thus the international context which we have previously described was no longer such an all-embracing constraint on furthering the process desired by de Gaulle and explicated in the 1958 memorandum: the development of a *de facto* directorate of the three NATO nuclear powers.[55] The process is well described in Couve de Murville's memoirs:

A very different approach was required. Everything had to begin with a profound transformation of the psychological conditions of the situation, starting with those created by the Soviet Union herself. This transformation had become possible since the nuclear *grande peur* which the two giants experienced in October 1962, and which seemingly had not been fully taken into account in Europe. It was further facilitated by the situation of Russia herself, confronted with serious economic problems, especially in the agricultural sector, and now in open conflict with China, which signalled a radical change in the balance of forces in the communist world, hence in the world as a whole. Under these conditions, as I stated before the National Assembly on 29 October 1963, 'if threats to Berlin really stop, and if, over a reasonable number of months, no incident arises regarding our communications with the former capital, then detente will no doubt begin to manifest itself by itself, and the real problems can be approached and then tackled'.

Then the doors would open and dialogue would become possible. Not a bloc-to-bloc dialogue, but a dialogue between all those involved on both sides of the old iron curtain and particularly between the European countries, in such a way that one day truly normal relations might be established between them from the Atlantic to the Urals. The discussions which were required in our view were envisaged firstly within the framework of practical relations, in the economic, technical and scientific, cultural and tourist sectors. If these relations, once agreed to, were to consolidate and grow, and if contacts were established, then a new climate could appear and talks could start and continue in a truly renewed context. Thus one might see Europe reappearing, led once again to make its voice heard and to shoulder its responsibilities in the discussion of matters directly concerning it – even if, on the part of the Western states on the continent, nothing had yet been possible to arrange insofar as organising the beginnings of political cooperation was concerned.[56]

The Cuban crisis, however, had exactly the opposite impact on the United States. American foreign policy-makers became even more convinced that in a bipolar world, characterised by the kind of face-to-face confrontation bargaining and conflict management manifested in the resolution of the October missile crisis, the superiority of superpower supremacy in keeping the peace was proven, and that attempting to loosen alliance ties from within would make the world a more dangerous place. This state of mind was well described by George W. Ball, a leading figure in the foreign policy-making structure of the Kennedy and Johnson Administrations:

Living in political structures that were out of date a hundred years ago, man is still so bedevilled by greed and passion that force and authority must be ever at hand if he is not to blow the world up. So, unhappy as may be the policeman's lot, if we do not walk this thankless beat, who will?[57]

The nation-state, then, was out of date – though the United States, in its best nineteenth-century tradition, was not a nation-state like the others, and could be trusted to lead the way out of the impasse caused by the recrudescence of parochial nationalism. To these American policy-makers, the answer was clear. The Europeans were neither willing nor able to take up the burden (through regional integration in partnership with the USA), and their reluctance to accept American leadership in these matters on trust was dangerous to the peace and stability of the world order. And that world order was seen as self-evident. There could be no conflict of interest between *American* power and superpower hegemony, and so it was that European assertions that such conflicts of interests did exist – seeing superpower hegemony as a restriction on independence whereas the Americans saw it as an essential guarantee of independence from the other bloc – were interpreted in Washington as so much narrow and self-centred nineteenth-century-style nationalism.

The American preoccupation was not to allow France (as the only really troublesome European nation-state) more freedom of manoeuvre, but less. At the same time, French criticisms of the Alliance structure were mounting. American policy in general was being criticised 'on the basis that it tended to freeze the East–West split by concentrating on ideological questions instead of promoting a *rapprochement* through the use of the traditional diplomatic methods'.[58] To the United States, the European problem could be solved only by increasing the integration of Western Europe and by tying this 'New Europe' to the USA in an Atlantic community. To de Gaulle, the European problem could be solved only by breaking down the barriers between the two halves of the divided continent, and that could best be done by bilateral relations among the nation-states of that continent themselves, not by allowing themselves to become the periphery of a system based on an extra-European centre. The split in perspectives was complete. From the Gaullist perspective, the whole basis of national sovereignty was at stake, and with it, the entire foundation of political legitimacy. Indeed, for de Gaulle, the very justification of foreign policy, as such, was not to be found in stability of the international system, *as an end in itself*. Of course, such stability was a necessary prerequisite for the achievement of more important ends, and such stability had, in his view, been achieved with the superpower stalemates in Berlin and Cuba. But stability was essentially an instrumental goal, necessary for creating the conditions in which states would be able to pursue their national interests, on which their internal legitimacy and *raison d'être* were based, within reasonable limits. This conflict of political paradigms was to dominate the Atlantic question for the next four or five years.

8

Atlantic divergences:
the phase of reactive assertion, 1963–6

The period of reactive assertion which developed out of the Atlantic disagreements described in the last chapter was characterised by the coordination of different elements of French policy in an attempt to escape from the strait-jacket of Atlantic integration. French policy crystallised in three ways, ways which were highly symbolic, but which, we shall argue, did not threaten the basic coalition of interests which characterised and justified, in de Gaulle's eyes, the Atlantic Alliance itself. In the first place, de Gaulle's special brand of personal diplomacy, especially given the nature of the so-called 'reserved domain' of the President within the French executive branch, highlighted and emphasised the role of the charismatic leader in asserting the national interest in a salient and symbolic fashion. Secondly, France asserted and underlined her political distance from the United States in a variety of arenas and settings, thus emphasising the singular nature of the French national interest, its distinction from the American national interest, and the links of political legitimacy and responsibility which made the assertion of the national interest the highest duty of the leader. And thirdly, there was the focusing of the conflict itself upon the most important symbolic point, the NATO military organisation, and the culmination of this conflict in a highly stylised breaking of these ties in 1966.

The completion of this symbolic manoeuvre, combined with other changes in the international context, made possible the gradual normalisation of Franco-American relations over the subsequent three years, as it eliminated the major bone of contention between the two states insofar as the *form* of their relationship was concerned. Needless to say, differences of policy *content* have remained until the present day. But we argue that the major conflict between de Gaulle and the United States was around an issue of form, particularly the issue of integration, and that other policy differences, though no less real, only became salient in the difficult environment created by the integration issue. Many of these differences of content remained unresolved long after the atmosphere of Franco-American relations had returned to normal consequent upon the resolution of the integration question. Furthermore, as Kulski suggests, de Gaulle's severest disagreements with the USA were on issues where he was not consulted; one wonders whether consultation, or a collaborative form of independence, was not more important to de Gaulle than any total independence in an atmosphere of conflict.[1] In any case, however, refused the kind of collaborative independence he sought *within* NATO, de Gaulle turned to the pursuit of independence against American wishes by withdrawing from NATO, thereby changing the nature of the problem itself and permitting the normalisation of relations in a bilateral context.

Following the stabilisation of the superpower balance after Cuba and Berlin, and after the end of French military entanglement in Algeria in 1962, the conditions existed for a concerted French approach to global questions to develop. Kolodziej suggests three strands of policy which we will adopt in a somewhat modified form. Firstly, France wished to prevent the superpowers from turning their own relations into norms of the system, by preventing both a confrontation between the USA and the USSR and the conclusion of a superpower condominium detrimental to the assertion of European and French interests and aspirations. Secondly, de Gaulle saw the superpower balance as tilted in favour of the United States, and wished to offset this military superiority (and the consequent Soviet fear of 'capitalist encirclement', which was leading to a worsening of the arms race) through diplomatic action which would draw the Soviet Union into a normalised world of nation-states. Finally, de Gaulle wished to re-equilibrate the international system itself in the way described in Chapter 6, retaining the advantages of stability but allowing greater political autonomy and manoeuvrability, especially for the broadened elite of nation-states represented by the nuclear club.[2]

A basic element of this approach was to reaffirm loyalty to the United States, insisting on the great 'moral capital' that had been built up,[3] and to the Atlantic Alliance.[4] Secondly, however, he sought to warn of the consequences of 'infinitely serious and infinitely long dissension', and noted the need to put 'political divergences' and the 'journalistic ill-will of the moment' into perspective.[5] But at the same time, he sought to play what Hoffmann has called an 'exacerbating' role, in order to create *consciousness of distance* from the United States.[6] Indeed, he used personal diplomacy to heighten this effect; his visits to

Russia and to Cambodia in 1966 highlighted his approach at a time when French (and indeed world) public opinion was becoming more and more worried by the growing American intervention in Vietnam.[7]

In this highly symbolic arena, de Gaulle tended to rely on two characteristic methods of diplomacy. The first was to attack the strongest ally, the United States. This course involved minimum cost and low risk, for there could be little risk of direct retaliation. Indeed, any such retaliation would involve a self-fulfilling prophecy for de Gaulle. In fact, American reactions were ambivalent and tended to try to bypass de Gaulle rather than confronting his demands head-on. However, this line of action highlights the existence of an independence of will and purpose which, even if it does not extract concessions, creates what Kolodziej calls 'psychic income'[8] – i.e. it creates a feeling of what political psychologists call 'political efficacy'. The second method was the tactic of the 'empty chair'. This course, while drawing fire upon France, made whatever proceedings were involved seem somehow less legitimate, as whatever decisions were reached could be said not to be binding on France. It allowed France to assert her traditional interests in a more direct way, gave the impression of a special role for France, undermined the superpowers' domination of certain bodies, created new opportunities for alignment, and allowed France to avoid the role of *demandeur* or suppliant.[9]

Within this overall approach, as it developed after 1962, French policy tended to emphasise the differences between France and the United States over a number of specific issues relating to the structural form of their relationship. We shall now turn to these specific issue conflicts, from relations with the East to the NATO crisis of 1966, through the perspective of their connection with the Atlantic question. In fact, each of the areas dealt with can be seen to have a rationale and dynamic of its own. But each was also significant to French policy differences with the USA, and this is how we shall treat them.

I. The opening to the East

De Gaulle's policy towards the Communist bloc – the Soviet Union and Eastern Europe – was two-pronged: an opening towards the Soviet Union; and an opening towards the satellite nations of Eastern Europe. These two prongs could never be fully compatible with each other; support for the Eastern European states in developing their national interests tended to make them more conscious of differences with the

USSR and dovetailed with endogenous pressures within the 'iron curtain' countries towards polycentrism.[10] These pressures had been built in to the relations between national Communist parties and the Soviet Union from the mid-1940s, and had reached a climax in the Hungarian rebellion and the accession to power of Wladyslaw Gomulka in Poland in 1956; they involved the intersection of two processes – destalinisation and 'desatellisation' – which resulted in somewhat different patterns of political change in each of the satellite countries.[11] But in the context of alliance structure and cohesion in the cold war, both prongs challenged cold war orthodoxy.

In seeking to strengthen bilateral relations with the Soviet Union, de Gaulle was challenging America's right to speak for her allies in their relations with the other superpower. At the same time, he was encouraging direct bilateral relations between the states at the lower levels of the two alliance hierarchies; this strengthened the legitimacy of the East European regimes, in the hope of encouraging them to assert their own national interests. France thus challenged not only 'rollback', but 'containment' itself. Seeing the development of polycentrism, and the Sino-Soviet split (long before American policy-makers were fully conscious of its repercussions), de Gaulle believed that the independence of the various Communist countries could best be reinforced by traditional diplomatic methods. He also believed that the Soviet Union would seek good relations with Western Europe in opposition to China – provided that Western Europe was not itself a satellite of the United States.[12]

The Soviet Union was in the same dilemma about her own allies as the USA was about France. The difference was that she had the geographical position, the military strength and the will to crush opposition, as she showed in Hungary in 1956 and Czechoslovakia in 1968. However, if France could convince the Soviet leadership that she had no desire to undermine their position of predominance *per se*, but just to loosen the bonds within a context of generally relaxed tensions in both West and East, then it might even be in the Soviet interest to accept such an easing of ties, in terms of facing the Chinese problem and internal Soviet economic weakness, which would push her towards greater cooperation with the West.[13] In this sense de Gaulle did not attempt to attack the *status quo* as such, but rather sought, in both the strands of his Eastern policy, to show that greater long-term stability would result for all concerned if intra-bloc linkages were relaxed somewhat and 'national realities' permitted greater expression. The attractiveness of this proposition was not altogether missed in the Soviet Union and the United States – Zbigniew Brzezinski considered de Gaulle's approach as the formula most likely to appeal to both Eastern Europe and the USSR because it would recognise the existing territorial *status quo* and balance of power in Europe, but he feared that such a situation would be unstable, which always proved to be a major objection of American policy-makers.[14]

The French approach to the Soviet Union emphasised 'practical' areas of cooperation between the two countries. The diplomatic offensive began in early 1964, at about the same time as France was preparing to recognise China (a policy which the USSR still strongly supported at that time despite the growing Sino-Soviet split). Reciprocal visits were the highlight of this period. The French Finance Minister, Valéry Giscard d'Estaing, visited Moscow in January 1964, and the next month the Soviet Vice-Premier in charge of scientific questions visited Paris. A Soviet parliamentary delegation came to France from 25 February to 5 March, and a convergence of French and Soviet views became clear on the application of the 1954 Geneva agreements as a way to end the Vietnam War, on the neutralisation of Cambodia and Laos, and on the need to adjust the United Nations to reflect the interests of Security Council members more clearly. The first concrete result was a five-year commercial agreement signed in October 1964, while 1965 saw agreements on scientific cooperation, SECAM and cultural cooperation.[15] The visit of Soviet Foreign Minister Andrei Gromyko to Paris (26–30 April) was followed by a joint communiqué which emphasised the cordiality of relations and outlined the general areas of agreement and disagreement on a range of issues: Vietnam (agreement); European security (vague agreement); disarmament (a mixture of the Soviet proposal to convene a UN committee and the French proposal for a five-power conference, which came to receive Soviet backing); the distribution of power at the UN; and cultural and technical cooperation.[16]

A revealing indicator of Soviet attitudes is found in an article in *Pravda* commenting on de Gaulle's press conference of 4 February 1965, and it is worth quoting at length, following Kulski's translation:

The straightforward and realistic manner of formulating the most important matters, such as the fate of the United Nations, the tidying up of currency accounts, European security and the related German question, pleases an objective observer...The President of France rightly remarked that the Charter, which had been calculated to ensure the balance of power between, and the security of, the United Nations, was grossly violated in 1950 when the General Assembly (under the pressure of the USA), ignoring the prerogatives of the Security Council, appropriated for itself the right to decide the question of the use of force and consequently transformed itself immediately into the field of 'verbal battles'. . .

The Soviet society entirely shares the French President's view that 'the serious changes, which have taken place in the United Nations following those violations of legality, have indeed undermined its unity, prestige and functioning. . .'

The French President equally realistically treated the problem of international currency accounts which had ripened a long time ago. He rightly pointed out that the system established as far back as 1922 which had bestowed on the dollar and the pound sterling the privilege of being considered equivalents of gold in external inter-state trade has become obsolete. . .Not one man of common sense may disagree with de Gaulle's thesis that 'it is difficult to imagine that there might be any other standard but gold. . .'

How may one deny that European problems are, first of all, the concern of Europeans?. . .The French President was absolutely right when he declared that any solution of the German problem must include the settlement of the questions of German frontiers and German armaments through the agreement of all neighbours of the former Hitlerite Reich, both Eastern and Western neighbours . . .Any solution of the German problem is inconceivable without due consideration of vital interests and security requirements of those countries which were victims of the aggression by Hitlerite Germany. De Gaulle's formulation of the problem of cooperation between the Western European and the Eastern European states for peace and security is fully correct and comes at an appropriate time.

However, one cannot refrain from observing that the author of this correct conception was, at a certain moment, deserted by his sense of reality. He seemed not to notice the principal factor in the German problem of the sixties, the existence on the territory of the former German Reich of two independent German states, which have different economic and social foundations and which have developed in two diametrically opposed directions. To think that some external forces, but not they themselves, should settle the problem of their future fate, means to lose sight of the reality. In this respect one must stress that the problem of European security may and should be solved by all the European countries without any exceptions, including the two existing German states. There is no way to escape this elementary reality.

. . .In passing, one may not avoid remarking that the solution of ripe international problems would not be promoted by the President's observation that an effective settlement of the problem of European security within the framework of 'Big' Europe would become possible only at a time when the social regime of the USSR and the other Socialist countries of Europe have undergone a certain evolution according to Western taste.

The French President correctly pointed out that John Foster Dulles, who had conceived of the reckless plans 'for pushing back communism in Europe', was finally compelled to abandon them. General de Gaulle said that 'this was only a dream'. Absolutely true! This justifies even less the unrealistic dreams of a somewhat different kind. . .

On the whole, the French President's press conference, which was concerned with several ripe international problems and during which he brought forward a number of important and constructive ideas, had a not unimportant significance. It has, without doubt, opened interesting perspectives.[17]

The culmination of this opening to the Soviet Union was de Gaulle's visit to Moscow in June 1966, which was highly successful in personal terms and which has given rise to a certain folklore, as Alexander Werth observes:

> Stressing that he was neither pro-Russian, nor pro-American, he even remarked on one occasion: 'I am very pleased that the existence of the Soviet Union should cancel out the danger of the American hegemony, just as I am pleased that the United States should be there to cancel out the danger of the Soviet hegemony.' The Russians thought that this was a nice way of putting it, and laughed heartily, as though it were meant to be a joke.[18]

The trip, however, did not signal a new era of Franco-Soviet *rapprochement*, but rather was the high-water mark of this *rapprochement*, highlighting its limits and constraints as well as its achievements. De Gaulle refused to make any concessions on issues such as German reunification, which were still major bones of contention then. A Paris–Moscow 'hot line' was set up, and the Soviet leaders paid much attention to France, but this did not fundamentally alter their own perception that their conception of intra-alliance relationships was much closer to the American viewpoint than to the French, and that the future of her international policy was far more closely bound up with the United States.[19] Despite this ambivalence, however, the USSR did recognise the relevance of French claims that nation-states were still – and increasingly – a force to be reckoned with in world affairs. It is this recognition of existing reality, rather than great consensus on issues, which characterises Premier Alexei Kosygin's observation during a visit to Paris in December 1966:

> We attach great importance to France's place and role in international life and in European affairs, for France is a great State whose people have surprised the world more than once by their firmness and wisdom in defending her legitimate interests.

In this context, French relations with the Eastern European states, although highly innovative at the time, could not aspire to establishing a new pan-European order, but merely to loosening existing structures. French leaders assured the Soviet Union that their new relations with the satellite nations were not directed against the USSR, but were part of a wider attempt to improve relations with the Communist states in

general and the USSR in particular. As Kulski points out, this French
approach holds certain advantages for the Soviet Union:

Her cultural influence was dominant prior to the last war in almost all Eastern
European countries. At that time France was an ally of Poland, Czechoslovakia,
Yugoslavia and Rumania. No Communist government fears France, and all of
them welcome the new course of French policy towards West Germany. The
cultural exchanges between France and the Soviet Union as well as Eastern
Europe are reviving old contacts which have not been forgotten. The French
Ministers and deputies travel to Eastern European capitals, and the high dig-
nitaries of Communist governments repay these visits. The agreements for
mutual trade and for cultural cooperation have been concluded. The warm
reception given to official and non-official French representatives is not limited
to the governments; the people, who do not feel happy under the Soviet pro-
tectorate, are glad to renew contacts with a Western power which is not suspected
of evil intentions either by the local Communist parties or by Moscow. France
has the merit of helping to build bridges towards Communist Europe, a venture
which is easier for her than for the United States and even Britain.[20]

In fact, these relations were essentially symbolic. They consisted for the
most part of diplomatic exchanges, which were, of course, new and
quite extensive given the previous cold war context. A number of visits
by East European ministers were returned by Couve de Murville in
1966. The actual agreements concluded between France and the
various countries differed from state to state, and are noteworthy for
their extent and their capacity to break the ice in a way that was
obvious to the world. Bilateral committees were set up. The agenda was
dominated by technical, scientific and economic concerns. Trade agreements, usually for five years, were signed with all of the states except
East Germany (which had not yet been officially recognised). The
French SECAM colour television process was adopted by all. Bulgaria
and Czechoslovakia signed agreements for cooperation over nuclear
energy. Hungary and Rumania favoured industrial exchanges, including assistance from Renault (following the Soviet lead); Poland
signed similar agreements. And lower-level industrial contacts, through
Chambers of Commerce, were multiplied.[21]

The results were ambiguous. Although France had taken the all-
important symbolic initiative, French trade with the East lagged well
behind West German trade. In fact, although French political and
cultural contacts with Eastern Europe had a long tradition, commercial
relations did not.[22] The gloss had worn off the trading agreements
within a short time, too. While favourable for France, they had certain
disadvantages for the Eastern European countries; not only did they
create huge deficits in trade with France, but they had structural

disadvantages too, consisting for the most part of the export of agricultural products to France and the import of manufactured goods.[23] Cultural relations, which were of some importance to the French, did not interest the Eastern European countries to the same extent, and exchanges languished.[24]

The most spectacular French successes in Eastern Europe occurred in relations with Rumania, where the ideological nature of the ties were most obvious. Certain parallels existed between Rumania's position in the East and the French position in the West. They both sought greater independence within the structure of their respective alliances. And they both were relatively disfavoured within the economic context of their respective blocs. France, industrially overshadowed by West Germany, was faced with the problem of defending her agricultural position within the EEC; Rumania, overshadowed by East Germany and Czechoslovakia, sought to industrialise and to avoid the 'bread-basket' role attributed to it by Comecon (Council for Mutual Economic Assistance). They both sought to emphasise national identity as the source of political legitimacy rather than supranational ideology.[25] It was in this political arena that de Gaulle's foreign policy was most clearly successful, and de Gaulle himself placed great symbolic emphasis on his openings to the East. On the economic side, France was always overshadowed by West Germany, and after 1966 came to be overshadowed on the political side as well with the beginnings of the *Ostpolitik*.[26] At a time when American foreign policy depended more than ever on the strengthening of alliance bonds, with the lessons of Cuba in mind and the growing conflict in Vietnam to contend with, de Gaulle's contrary initiatives drew only suspicion and a fear that he was thereby weakening the structure of world peace as well as giving the Soviet Union greater influence in the West.

II. The structure of NATO

The basic contours of de Gaulle's disagreement with the United States over alliance integration developed prior to 1963. In the crucial period which followed, French policy unfolded only gradually; in the earlier period, Soviet belligerency (especially over Berlin), as well as the direct constraints on France caused by her Algerian quagmire, had to be taken into account. Thus, although the goal was never in doubt, only a 'slow and measured progression towards the *dénouement*', in Couve's words, could take place. The French saw a need for discussions to 'prepare the way' and to 'try and get them [the Americans] to understand our preoccupations, and to see whether an agreement was possible', but this merely degenerated into a *'véritable dialogue des sourds'.*[27] One of the sources of this dialogue of the deaf was the confusion which existed about the meanings of key terms. While de Gaulle asked for 'consultation', meaning an institutionalised procedure giving symbolic status to France in equality with Britain and a 'special relationship' with the USA, the American government replied that a wide range of consultative mechanisms already existed within NATO; besides, they said, giving any special status to France would arouse demands from other allies for compensating forms of influence. And, as Alastair Buchan has pointed out, a further confusion complicated both alliance relationships and disarmament negotiations, 'between the French concept of *contrôle*, which means examination, verification, the right to criticise, and the English word *control* which in this context means the physical grasp of buttons and levers'.[28] The Americans wanted forms of 'consultation' and 'control' which did not weaken, but rather enhanced, the military and administrative efficiency of the crisis management procedures explicit in the post-Cuba international system – based implicitly on the controlled and graduated escalation procedures of 'flexible response'. They took the structure for granted, and wished to control its stress points efficiently. The French, in contrast, wanted some institutionalised means of influencing American strategic policy, and 'the context of peace and war'.[29] As the eminent French strategist, General André Beaufre, wrote at the time:

The sharing of nuclear responsibilities, which formerly always envisioned war, is now directed primarily towards *a foreseen and concerted coordination of national strategies in peacetime*, making use of every available means – including nuclear threat – to avoid possible crises.[30]

Many Europeans, not just de Gaulle, viewed the 'flexible response' strategy as unsuited to the French interest. According to Beaufre, Kennedy's strategic reforms included: centralisation of all decision-making in the hands of the President, including the withdrawal of weaponry (such as the Davy Crockett mobile missile) capable of being unleashed by field commanders or weapons too near the front and in danger of capture; 'flexible response' itself, the brainchild of General Maxwell Taylor (its ramifications will be discussed below), which increased the dependence of Europeans on policy decisions of the American President just at the moment when Europe was becoming more independent in other ways (e.g. nuclear capability); closing the missile gap (development of the Polaris and Minuteman), thereby reducing American dependence on the European conventional shield; and primary dependence on conventional forces in Europe itself.[31] In this context, as Kolodziej stresses, 'the spectre of United States liberation of a devastated Europe loomed large in allied thinking'.[32] These potential costs were highlighted and emphasised by the French, but even some of de Gaulle's most outspoken critics, including Dirk Stikker, the former Secretary General of NATO, agreed about the dangers for Europe in America's new policies. And Germany, in NATO's conventional front line, was also loath to surrender the territorial guarantee built into the massive retaliation doctrine. Thus France appeared to be the only power able to defend European interests. In addition, the French argued, the division of labour inherent in the new American policies would keep Europe in a condition of 'economic vassalage' and 'mortgage their future irremediably to American economic and technological prowess'.[33]

It is a matter of dispute whether the French were in fact willing to come to a compromise solution on the matter of participation in the NATO military structure, or sought a pretext and justification for eventual withdrawal. One prominent participant in these debates at the time, and a virulent anti-Gaullist on these as well as European policy matters, former Belgian Prime Minister Paul-Henri Spaak (also former Foreign Minister and ex-Secretary General of NATO), confirms Couve de Murville's analysis that a 'dialogue of the deaf' took place, but suggests that every time the Americans asked for *constructive* criticism, it was the French who turned a deaf ear.[34] On the other hand, the American conception of what was constructive criticism seemed to presume a few minor modifications of their strategic formulae but not their integral rejection. At the meeting of the NATO Ministers in spring 1963, all governments but the French eventually accepted flexible response. John Newhouse, however, suggests that the French veto, far from being resented by the European allies, 'was probably applauded silently by most of the other European members, few (if any) of whom felt comfortable about the new strategy'. This feeling, however, did not affect the Americans: 'Rhetoric aside, the doctrine of controlled response had somewhat less to do with NATO than with the Pentagon; it was one of a number of devices to concentrate control of weapons in the office of the Secretary of Defence.'[35] The all-pervasive reorganisation of Pentagon structures and procedures undertaken by McNamara since 1961 with a view to making American defence and military administration more efficient and technologically advanced had more relevance than the political views of America's allies.

Structural conflict was exacerbated by the inability of the Americans and the French to reach a compromise agreement. The area which exercised the French most as regards lack of consultation was that of defence planning. Beaufre describes the French (or European) view of the situation:

Planning begins with political directives from the Council [of Ministers of NATO]. These are translated by the Standing Group into military directives, which are approved by the Military Committee. On these generally very broad bases, the Supreme Commands work out detailed plans which must go back for approval first to the Standing Group, then to the Military Committee, and finally to the Council. On the basis of these plans, national and infrastructure programmes are worked out. That is how the procedure operates in theory. In practice, it has generally been the powerful Supreme Commands that have taken the initiative in proposing measures that seemed necessary to them. These measures have then been approved or modified by the Council, on the basis of the reactions of the various countries. Even when the Council has appeared to take the initiative, it has generally been under the influence of the Supreme Command in Europe. Here again, the superior weight of the American chain of command, acting of course in accordance with the Pentagon, has contributed in large measure to depriving Alliance strategy of a truly collective character.[36]

The cause of this *de facto* situation is the dominance of American participation in the command structure as well as the dominance of its overall military – especially nuclear – contribution; the result is a very lopsided picture: 'in the whole of this complex, overstaffed organisation, the United States holds the most important commands (seven out of thirteen), Great Britain has five subordinate commands, and France has *only one* subordinate command'.[37]

One authoritative French politician stated that the withdrawal of French Mediterranean naval forces from NATO command was due to the retention of a British commander for the region, despite French naval predominance in NATO's Mediterranean theatres.[38] French exclusion, in fact, reinforced the American position, resulting in American over-representation in subordinate commands which 'have tended to become independent of the interallied hierarchy while depending directly on the Pentagon in their capacity as commanders of American forces'. This very situation, which France in the 1950s allowed to develop by her own lack of pressure, 'has altogether falsified the original plan of NATO and placed practically the entire defence organisation under the close control of the American general staff', Beaufre observes. Indeed, the cooperation of American commanders with other American commanders *rather than with NATO as such* was made inevitable by the fact that the United States herself only committed certain of her operational units to NATO command, while other units directly relevant to European defence were kept under American national command:

among the troops that are 'assigned' to NATO, America places only those of her forces stationed on European soil. The Sixth Fleet in the Mediterranean is not 'assigned' but merely 'earmarked'. The most important factor of all, however, results from the MacMahon Act, which prescribes that everything nuclear must remain strictly American. Thus the American chain of command and the atomic stockpiles are closely 'national' in character, as is everything that relates to the nature and use of American strategic nuclear force, including the strategic bombing force, strategic missiles and Polaris submarines. The result is that the entire nuclear area of war planning, which forms the backbone of Alliance strategy, is not only outside NATO but is kept strictly secret from non-Americans. For this reason, Alliance strategy cannot be properly studied by inter-allied organisations.[39]

This situation was unimportant when European conventional forces were backed up by the massive retaliation strategy, although its inconveniences have already been seen in de Gaulle's attempt to get American assistance with the development of the FNS; however, it became so when flexible response *and* the development of tactical nuclear weapons came more or less simultaneously to the fore after 1960. Thus attention came to be focused on nuclear sharing and consultation.[40] Indeed, Couve de Murville has called the NATO command structure 'in the effect a regime of extra-territoriality', with three sorts of consequent problems.[41] Firstly, a foreign command which is acceptable in times of crisis would not be acceptable in perpetuity. This problem is not as clear-cut as it might at first seem, however, for as General Beaufre points out, 'contrary to all too general belief, forces "assigned" to NATO remain subject to their national headquarters during peacetime and. . .measures for an alert may vary considerably from one country to another';[42] although this makes Couve's charge of 'foreign command' less credible in certain aspects (the problem being more directly related to the command of American forces in the European theatre and their relationship to NATO), nevertheless it actually exacerbates the problems of alliance planning and consultation, especially on nuclear matters, both between and within periods of tension and crisis.

Secondly, Couve felt that the French armed forces had lost their sense of mission:

Our resources, integrated into those of others, were merged into a larger entity [*ensemble*] and consequently were without responsibilities of their own. France could only feel that her defence was no longer her own business, that she had somehow been relieved of it. Therefore she could only lose interest in it, while at the same time her army risked to lose any sense of its essential mission, which was rooted in the soil of the nation.

Indeed, in his view, the attitude of the army during the later stages of the Algerian conflict, when some of its leaders, believing that they were fighting a universal war for Western civilisation against Communist barbarism, showed the danger of this development, for it led to the disregarding of orders, extreme brutality and attempts at a military *coup d'état* in 1958 and 1961. Thirdly, there was the risk of being involved in a conflict which concerned America but not France. The Vietnam situation was very much in the foreground of world events, and in the background of French policy-makers' minds, according to Couve, 'during the period when the major decisions were taken in 1965–6'.[43] De Gaulle made much of the second point right from the beginning of his period in office, and his well-known speech of 3 November 1959 at the *Ecole militaire* underlined this emphasis:

The defence of France must be a French defence. This is a necessity which has not been very familiar over the course of the last few years. I am well aware of it. It is indispensable that this become a reality again. A country like France, if it should happen to make war, must make its own war. Its effort must be its own effort. If it were otherwise, our country would be contradicting everything that has characterised it since its origins, its role, its self-esteem and its soul. Naturally, French defence would, should the occasion arise, be combined with that of other countries. That is in the nature of things. But it is indispensable that our defence be our own, that France defend herself by herself, for herself and in her own way.

If it were otherwise, if it was admitted over a long period that the defence of France ceased to be within the national framework and that it was jumbled together, or blended, with something else, it would not be possible to maintain a State here. The Government has as its *raison d'être*, in any epoch, the defence of the independence and of the integrity of the territory. It proceeds from this task. In France, in particular, all our regimes have come from this source.

The symbolic content of national control of defence extended even to the question of the formal command structure on foreign bases, where France was comparatively worse off than some other countries:

According to the French formula, the national ensign flies side by side with that (or those) of the users, but French authority is represented only by an officer who merely fulfils a liaison role.

According to the Spanish formula (cited for the purposes of comparison since Spain is not a member of NATO and since only the Americans use bases constructed there at their own expense [unlike the American–NATO bases which are joint ventures]), the Spanish flag flies alone over the bases and command is nominally assured by a Spanish officer.

In England, the bases are placed under a double command, British and allied. On nuclear bases, the British officer exercises jointly with his American counterpart control of atomic weapons placed under the double-key system.[44]

Of course, this last arrangement was made impossible in France, as a result of the French refusal to accept the double-key system. Thus the conflict over the form of the NATO command structure worsened over the period concerned, with neither side willing to make serious concessions, even, or especially, on the symbolic level, where the French concern for defence as an integral element in national identity and the legitimation of the authority of the state itself comes through clearly – and where American concessions would not only bring the entire set of Kennedy–McNamara reforms into question but also diminish American authority and prestige at home as well as abroad with the consequent *loss of face* as well as of power.

One of the main aspects of this conflict was the continuing question, significant in different ways for each side, of American–Soviet collaboration at the expense of their own allies' immediate interests, but ostensibly in the interest of the stability of the international system as a whole. Such liberal stalwarts as George W. Ball favoured the gradual establishment of joint US–Soviet hegemony in world affairs. Ball, an influential State Department official (he had been Under-Secretary of State for both Kennedy and Johnson, and was later named Ambassador to the United Nations despite his resignation from the State Department over Vietnam in 1966), was something of a liberal hero because of his early opposition to the escalation of the Vietnam War from within the Johnson Administration. But he was the State Department's most outspoken anti-Gaullist as well. Arthur M. Schlesinger Jr has written of him 'uncharacteristically letting his rhetoric run away with him' as he 'discoursed publicly about unspecified European leaders dominated "by a nostalgic longing for a world that never was" and seeking to revive the "vanquished symbols of beglamoured centuries" '.[45] Although this position never dominated either Kennedy or Johnson fully – Kennedy in his American University speech in 1963 and Johnson in his reaction to the French withdrawal from NATO in 1966 clearly did not accept its full consequences – it was the dominant view of the State Department and had great impact on day-to-day relations and mutual perceptions of hostility.

De Gaulle's rejection of this viewpoint was based firstly on his conviction that 'international condominium' was an unstable situation, a zero-sum game which would draw in other states as 'the objects, not the subjects, of the competition'.[46] If a small state had claims or grievances against a local opponent, Kolodziej points out, then the absence of any alternative (e.g. regional) sources of support would be likely to lead it to appeal to a superpower. Indeed, as two American critics of NATO policy have pointed out:

Both in Europe and in South Viet Nam, the situation has been over-Americanised, fostering a psychology in which our allies can pressure us into doing more, under the threat of 'collapsing' if we don't. American actions have encouraged our allies to believe that their security is our responsibility, not theirs.[47]

But, as well as sapping the strength of the allies of the United States, American leadership, according to de Gaulle, could not be totally relied upon to be completely disinterested – despite the protestations permeating cold war ideology about the 'free world'. As André Fontaine observes, de Gaulle's fundamental 'difference with the other NATO members is that he considers that its very power creates a temptation for the United States to dominate'.[48] Whether at the level of an American president's broad policy views, or at the level of the military or diplomatic bureaucracy in Washington, or at the level of the American field commanders in Europe (both inside and outside NATO itself), America's *de facto* hegemony meant that, however honourable and good the intentions, American perceptions of strategic situations, American expectations of others' behaviour, and American views of what was politically – as well as militarily – necessary would prevail. Alternative perspectives and attitudes could not possibly be taken properly into account at all levels, because they were never meaningfully canvassed on a day-to-day operational basis; the Europeans still remained structurally on the outside, looking in.

The ramifications of such an assertion were extensive. The most salient of these was the belief that America might not come to the aid of Europe in the event of a Soviet invasion – that the USA would hide behind the shield of 'flexible response'. Indeed, in 1959, Secretary of State Christian Herter, in the hearing before the Senate Committee on Foreign Relations to confirm his nomination, stated that he could not 'conceive of the President involving us in an all-out nuclear war unless the facts showed clearly that we are in danger of devastation ourselves, or that actual moves have been made towards devastation'.[49] This statement was, significantly, made when massive retaliation was still the official American strategic doctrine, even before 'flexible response'. As Kissinger wrote in 1962: 'A general war is certain to be more destructive to our European allies than to the United States.'[50] This prospect was stressed again and again by Gaullist observers, who tended not to question American intentions, but rather the dynamic of the situation itself: the 'partial character of American engagement';[51] the determining role of technology (especially military technology) in 'conditioning political manoeuvres';[52] and the contradictions inherent in the combination of both the commitment of the American nuclear umbrella and the *de facto* requirements of flexible response.[53]

The Americans could, therefore, expect only negative responses to such suggestions as setting up the 1965 McNamara Committee to examine nuclear policy in the Alliance; the committee would only 'study, not share, nuclear-decision responsibility with the US'.[54] The French did not, in fact, turn down the McNamara proposal immediately, but indicated that it might be willing to negotiate a more far-reaching proposal; the matter, however, went no further.[55] Shortly thereafter, an American aircraft was forced down by the French after photographing the Pierrelatte uranium enrichment plant.[56] The conflict could only worsen, and the conditions developed for the eventual French withdrawal from the NATO military organisation, which we shall describe later. The seriousness of such a step is quickly evident. France's geographical location, in the centre of the Alliance, is pivotal, especially if a limited war is to be fought in Europe; it would be vital for supply lines, for placing *matériel* out of the reach of invading forces, for building up reinforcements and back-up while Germany became a battlefield, and for providing room for manoeuvre should tactical or strategic withdrawals or large-scale displacements of troops and/or supplies be necessary. As Kulski points out, in a limited war, 'in which tactical nuclear weapons would probably be used by both belligerents, . . .any prolonged concentration of troops' would be very dangerous.[57] Germany, Belgium and Holland would be insufficient.

But with the Algerian situation resolved, the nuclear 'balance of terror' settled into a stalemate, Soviet intentions in Western Europe seen in a less aggressive light, and relations developing with both the USSR and her European satellites – at the same time that conflict *within* the Atlantic Alliance was turning into a 'dialogue of the deaf' –

French policy-makers were presented with an environment which was in transition. The international system, at the global strategic level, was emerging from the cold war. And yet no discernible alternative developmental construct had begun to crystallise to replace bipolar confrontation. De Gaulle's objective, primarily symbolic and political in nature, focused on the point at which potential leverage seemed the greatest – the military structure of NATO. Because any constructive impact upon the Americans was precluded by attitudes and reinforced by fears of destabilisation, both sides were led to overstate their case and overestimate the weaknesses of the other in public. As Kolodziej writes:

NATO never achieved the hopes of its public pronouncements in integrating the military capabilities of the member states within a single command structure. The French were not unaware of the difference, but preferred, often solely for reasons of domestic and foreign diplomatic consumption, to beat the NATO horse when political opportunity beckoned.[58]

Yet the lines of conflict went deeper than the public battle or even than the mutual perception of threat, whether from integration or from destabilisation. The real difference, and the one which could not go away, was wrapped up in the changing nature of the cold war, and the different paths which the French and the Americans envisaged leading to a more peaceful post-cold war world.

III. Weapons and technology

Enmeshed in these differences over the direction to take in the future were the problems of nuclear weapons and nuclear technology. The need for the most modern weapons, and the adoption of the most modern strategy for their use, had been a central feature of de Gaulle's thinking since his fight over tanks in the 1930s.[59] Combined with his views on the need for defence to be national and not integrated, de Gaulle's conclusion was that 'so long as others have the means to destroy her, it is necessary for her [France] to have the means to defend herself'.[60] In the contemporary world, moreover, nuclear weapons have taken on not merely a symbolic quality, representing real potential power, but a more dramatic quality, allowing statesmen and national actors to appear at the centre of the world stage where day-to-day events develop into complex public scenarios. To de Gaulle, therefore, nuclear weapons were more a factor leading to the decomposition of blocs rather than to their integration. Their possession was a highly concrete symbol of the will of states to survive and to defend themselves, even for small countries,[61] and one which gave small countries not only a greater influence than their traditional resources and capabilities might have otherwise permitted[62] but also provided an *entrée* into the exclusive club of the Great Powers.[63] The importance of atomic questions increased greatly in the atmosphere of Franco-American conflict which developed under the Kennedy and Johnson Administrations, as France put more and more emphasis on nuclear weapons as the core of her national defence system.

Nuclear questions should not be taken in isolation. Wilfrid Kohl suggests the opposite, that they had a primarily political role: 'nuclear arms do not in themselves cause the disintegration or the integration of alliances; instead they tend to play the role of a multiplier of existing integrative or disintegrative forces...'.[64] The political significance of nuclear weapons has been usefully summarised by a semi-official French study group. (1) They consecrate the French position as one of the five permanent members of the UN Security Council. (2) They associate medium powers with the great decisions of war and peace. (3) They reinforce the important regional roles which France and Great Britain are called upon to play, leading to a more real sharing of responsibilities in the Atlantic Alliance insofar as it grants a wider freedom of action; such effects are, of course, only indirect, as nuclear weapons would not be used in local affairs to support claims or interests. (4) They permit more freedom in, and give more weight to, initiatives towards the East on matters of cooperation and development. (5) However, it must be remembered that Britain and France are unique cases – with *both* global interests *and* significant regional roles – and do not reflect any universalisable rule as regards the relationship between nuclear weapons and political influence.[65] 'The effect is meant less to make France a world giant than to give her a key role in certain situations where her vital interests are involved.'[66] The wider implications for the Atlantic Alliance are clear: 'independent national nuclear forces, whatever their military effectiveness, will have the practical consequences of impelling the coordination of policies which President de Gaulle first proposed in his scheme for a directorate'.[67]

The material development of the FNS has been treated at length elsewhere,[68] and a detailed description will not be offered here. However, there is one aspect which is significant for the political argument: the strategic and political *credibility* of the FNS. The arguments which posit that the French force is not a credible strategic instrument revolve around two specific points. The first of these is the vulnerability of the force itself and the overwhelming superiority of Soviet nuclear forces if arrayed against France alone. The use of the FNS is seen as nuclear suicide, since no matter how large or 'unacceptable' the damage which could be caused to the USSR, the latter would totally destroy France.[69] 'Soviet retaliation capacity may be measured by the French air force commanders' admission that "five 100–megaton bombs would suffice to erase France from the map of the world." '[70] The second point is the weakness of the force itself. Its dependence on medium-range, low altitude Mirage-IV bombers, themselves dependent on American-supplied KC-135 jet tankers to refuel sufficiently to reach the USSR in the first place, limited its effectiveness throughout the 1960s (before the development of submarine-based missiles, silo-based missiles and Pluton tactical nuclear missiles at the end of the 1960s and into the 1970s).

It was too expensive to keep the Mirages airborne, and they were vulnerable to destruction even before taking off; the warning time was 15 minutes in the case of incoming planes, but just 2–3 minutes in the case of incoming missiles. If they got off the ground, they were vulnerable to SAM-3 (Soviet surface-to-air) missiles and, as Armed Forces Minister Pierre Messmer pointed out to the Finance Committee of the National Assembly in 1964, they would not be able to pass through Soviet air defences after 1967. As Kulski concludes: 'the most pessimistic estimate is that only three out of the fifty Mirages would attain their targets'.[71] On the other hand, a semi-official French commentator has claimed that Soviet air defences were vulnerable to low-altitude planes which could fly below effective radar height, and that there were serious gaps in the Soviet peripheral radar line, with its relatively short range limiting the earliness of its warning.[72] The lack of a French second-strike capacity was also seen as a severe weakness, although this was to be modified later with the coming into service of the submarine fleet.[73]

But the seriousness of these weaknesses was questioned on two bases. Firstly, it was suggested by supporters of the FNS that the penetration of even *one* Mirage would be enough to make Soviet leaders 'think twice' about risking an attack on France when – given the French insistence (in opposition to the Americans) on a countercity rather than a counterforce targeting strategy – a city like Leningrad might be 'taken out'. Secondly, it was questionable whether the use of the French force was even conceivable except in relation to its ability to 'trigger' use of American nuclear forces by a combination of its 'trip-wire' and 'massive retaliation' features.[74] This point is argued concisely by Kissinger:

It is easy enough to demonstrate that national nuclear forces in Europe are ineffective because they cannot withstand a determined surprise attack and to use them independently against the Soviet Union would be to commit suicide. However, the key question is whether these forces are intended to be used separately. Could the Soviet Union ever conduct a surprise attack against the strategic forces of Great Britain or France without running an unacceptable risk of a counterblow from the United States or from the other European ally, temporarily spared? Alternatively, if the strategic forces of one of our European allies were to attack the USSR without our consent or perhaps against our wishes, it is of course possible to say petulantly that we would then leave our ally to his fate. However, in the real world, such a course would be extremely unlikely. It is not only that the Soviets might retaliate against us in any case. More important, to 'punish' a recalcitrant ally by leaving him at the mercy of a Soviet counterblow would be scarcely less serious for us than for the offender.[75]

Even if a counterforce theory is accepted, European nuclear forces are not without significance. While these forces could not be decisive against the USSR, they might substantially weaken it relative to the United States and thereby exercise a deterrent effect beyond their actual strength. Second, the Soviet Union could not unleash the full force of its retaliatory power against a European ally without running an unacceptable risk of a counterblow by the United States. This triggering effect is one of the incentives for the acquisition of a nuclear arsenal and one of our reasons for opposing the spread of nuclear weapons within the alliance. In short, European national forces are not designed for independent action.[76]

These points were fully supported by the 'father of the FNS', General Beaufre, in his book on deterrence and strategy,[77] where he argues that 'French deterrence plays only a complementary role in the Allied deterrence system, though a useful one because it intrudes on a balance that is at present too stable and because its very existence introduces a germ of instability and doubt that helps to re-establish in part the deterrent strength of the entire system.'[78] Indeed, Beaufre offers the rule of action that independent nuclear forces 'contribute to general stability *always provided that the threat of these forces is not used in an irresponsible manner and without regard for the very strict rules governing the nuclear game*'.[79]

Thus the real significance of the FNS is not a general usability; it is intended to 'cover the 5 per cent of hypothetical cases when the United States might not retaliate. . .'.[80] Furthermore, if Soviet leaders *believed* that they could undertake a limited action in Europe without American intervention, they might (so the theory goes) be tempted to try. In such a case, independent European deterrent forces would be vital to the viability of the entire Western deterrent.[81] Despite all of these arguments and counter-arguments, the main lines of divergence between American and French views on the FNS were based on much more political criteria. The Americans feared accidental or frivolous nuclear escalation and proliferation; and the French felt that defence could only be effective if it reflected national realities. Raoul Girardet has turned the question around, and asked whether any nuclear force is credible *outside* of a national framework.[82] The examination of public opinion is of little help, as supporters of a national nuclear force in France were rarely in a majority, and the debate took place at elite level.[83] Indeed, the ramifications of the domestic debate were significant, given the environment of interservice rivalry[84] and the reform of the entire structure of the armed forces in the period following the end of the Algerian conflict; both of these factors led to the ascendancy of the air force and the nuclear-armed components of each service.[85]

However, the consequences, in terms of the Franco-American conflict, were far-reaching. Neither side was willing to admit that there was some truth in the views of the other. Raymond Aron summarises the position:

The American experts are correct in asserting that France will be incapable of possessing an independent retaliatory force, hence a deterrent, for another ten years. They are wrong to forget that the possession of even a minor atomic or thermonuclear apparatus confers some authority within the context of the Alliance, some prestige on the world stage, some diplomatic autonomy. The French are not alone in thinking that there will be no great power tomorrow without thermonuclear weapons, as there was no great power yesterday without heavy industry and armoured divisions. Even if this thermonuclear force is not utilisable diplomatically against either a great power or a small power, it establishes the status of states, their rank in the hierarchy of the actors on the diplomatic-strategic stage. Henceforth, if it wants to coordinate military programmes, the United States will be led to grant concessions to France, with regard to atomic secrets, delivery means, or the leadership of the Alliance.[86]

In fact, however, the United States did not make the concessions which Aron envisaged as necessary, and France withdrew from NATO.

The conflict over nuclear questions between France and the United States went much further than just the role of the FNS in the Atlantic Alliance. It also included differences on the 1963 Nuclear Test Ban Treaty, which France refused to sign, both because of her own need for continued testing in order to develop the FNS autonomously, and because of the implications of the treaty for the alliance system and the global order. The effects were the same in the East; Khrushchev's signing of the treaty – with the enemy – consecrated the Sino-Soviet split. Both China and France saw the treaty as an attempt to make the acquisition of nuclear weapons more difficult for each superpower's own allies.[87] French refusal to sign was the pretext for Washington's further refusal to aid France's nuclear force or to make any further attempts at consultation and coordination.[88] Even the requirement of 'substantial progress' written into the MacMahon Act, a demand which had originally stimulated French nuclear development in order to qualify for American assistance, was conveniently forgotten (or revised upwards) because of Kennedy's determined opposition to proliferation. Even existing assistance was withdrawn, such as the supplying of enriched uranium for the Cadarrache plant which was developing a prototype nuclear submarine reactor.[89] The flat French rejection of Kennedy's proposals for a 'mixed-manned' Multilateral Force, which were revived time and time again by a determined American government (and which were favoured by West Germany), was another bone of contention relating to nuclear issues.[90]

Indeed, the combination of the French determination to become independent in nuclear forces, and American reluctance to assist, led to a broad French effort to become more independent of the United States not only in nuclear technology and related areas of defence technology, but in government-supported scientific research in general. Government aid and guarantees were channelled to private companies, not only to the armament and aircraft industries, but also into advanced sectors of the economy such as electronics, molecular chemistry, engineering and nuclear research.[91] As Robert Gilpin points out in his useful study, 'nearly 80 percent of the total French R and D effort is being devoted to four industrial sectors – aeronautics, energy, electronics and chemicals'. 89 per cent of these funds went to aerospace industries (which were 73 per cent state-financed), nuclear energy (81 per cent state-financed) and electronics (36.5 per cent state-financed). In fact, ten firms received three-quarters of state funds to the 'competitive sector' despite weaknesses in these fields.[92] The French government had not failed to notice the fact that, as Kolodziej points out, 'three quarters of the research and development effort in the United States, both public and private, was financed by the federal government...The most capitalistic nation in the world, concluded the French, rested on a socialised science.'[93]

Of course, such arguments were not new. Analyses of the development of nuclear capacity in the Fourth Republic had asserted the interlocking nature of industrial and military development.[94] But according to Gilpin, the Fifth Republic developed a more coordinated approach:

The budget envelope, the programmes of concerted action and the *conjoncture scientifique* of the CNRS [the National Centre for Scientific Research] were innovations intended to expand and channel the national scientific effort along more socially 'productive' lines. Of greatest long-term significance, however, has been the attempt of the Fifth Republic to utilise scientific research in the pursuit of its two major but interrelated political goals: the social and economic modernisation of France; and the development of capabilities in advanced military weaponry (especially nuclear weapons) and space technology.[95]

The results of French programmes were never spectacular, and, particularly in the weapons field, much time was lost in duplicating developments already at a highly advanced level in the United States but unavailable to the French for political reasons (although American cooperation was not totally nonexistent and what there was of it was very useful in the early years).[96] Similar comments can be made about the space programme.[97] The economic effectiveness of 'spill-over' from military to industrial uses of the results of research and development has been questioned.[98] The economic cost of the programme has been criticised as channelling resources away from domestically significant sectors,[99] and the effects of the level of French spending on the balance between the different French armed services has involved not only interservice rivalry but also a significant internal debate on the effectiveness of and the requirements for the remaining conventional forces.[100] Nonetheless, the 5- to 8-year technology gap with the USA which was estimated for 1959 was halved by 1963 insofar as the missile programme was concerned.[101] But on the whole the results were very mixed. Costs mounted, and the technological development needed for real credibility was slow, despite the fact that on average over a quarter of the entire defence budget went into nuclear weapons in 1965–71, and about half of French spending on heavy military equipment went on the nuclear programme.[102]

Following high levels of defence expenditure on conventional capabilities in the 1950s and until 1962, in order to cover NATO commitments as well as the colonial wars in Indo-China and Algeria, French defence spending was steadily declining as a percentage of Gross National Product. But at the same time, more resources were going to the nuclear programme. Not only were conventional forces suffering, but the relative French contribution to Alliance defence spending as a whole continued to decline. This factor did not ameliorate relations with the United States, plagued with a growing balance-of-payments deficit (which led them to seek offset agreements) and an escalating war in Vietnam. Thus US policy-makers were highly sensitive to the French (and European) tendency to de-emphasise defence spending as a whole, along with French overtures to the East, while still remaining ostensibly under the indispensable protection of the American nuclear umbrella.[103]

The internal impact, however, was not negligible despite results which are difficult to measure. The main benefit was symbolic. Gilpin stresses the significance of the psychological impact of the French military and space programmes, which represent the French commitment 'to become a modern scientific–technological society'. As had already happened in America, these goals, 'by making great demands on French managerial and technical skills', lead to efforts which force 'society to set a higher standard of performance and expectation for itself'. The ambitious and prestigious nature of the programmes 'have indeed undermined the psychology of dependence on American science and technology which had dominated French thinking for the past several decades'.[104] In this way, the impact was a social and economic rather than merely a military one, and it reinforced other changes which have characterised France's postwar transition from a state of uneven and arrested socio-economic development into that of an advanced industrial society:

More concretely, the military R and D programme provides reformers with a much needed lever for overturning the power structure and the attitudes which have held back the advancement of French science and technology for a century and a half. New organisations have been created and new fields of study have been launched, which will increase the pace of change in French science and industry. In this connection it is instructive to note that when the accelerator was constructed at Saclay in the early postwar period, France had few theoretical or experimental physicists and many argued that it was folly for France to undertake such a project. The success of Saclay in changing the attitude of Frenchmen towards modern physics and the traditional pattern of scientific institutions is being repeated by the Directorate of Research and Testing and the National Centre for Space Studies.[105]

But the costs were high, both in the financial sense, and in the sense that in many ways military priorities have been at the expense of civilian technological development.

The symbolic significance of the FNS, however, goes well beyond its impact on science, technology or even defence *per se*. It also symbolises a new authority structure. Strategic failures by the French Army had led to near-defeat in both world wars; its modernisation was seen as a way of revitalising its essential *raison d'être* and reconciling army and nation following the estrangement of Indo-China and Algeria. Shedding its imperial role, and becoming a national defence force closely controlled by the President of the Republic, the military received a new identity, and helped to restore the psychological confidence in national purpose and national survival which was so important for de Gaulle's 'certain idea of France'. Political and military criteria for reform were inextricably linked. The move to a technically advanced military structure also heralded the advancement of a new generation of officers, more strongly imbued with a 'modernised' conception of society and of the army itself. As Couve de Murville pointed out, nuclear weapons gave France a defence capability which was politically the most effective possible, relatively inexpensive compared with the increased firepower as well as the increased status which resulted, integrally linked with the social and economic developments which the Fifth Republic felt necessary to French progress, and a reinforcement of the national basis of political legitimacy.[106] Such a policy could only further reinforce the lines along which conflict between France and the United States was developing.

IV. Some other areas of disagreement

The differences between de Gaulle and the American government did not only concern those areas where direct Franco-American relations or related cold war relationships were involved. They extended all over the globe. They involved issues such as foreign aid, US–EEC relationships, UN attitudes to Rhodesian sanctions and the management of the international monetary system. All of these areas have been treated in detail by various writers, and here we will deal with only those aspects which were linked to Atlantic questions.

French policy towards the Third World was closely linked to de Gaulle's desire to escape from the logic of the bipolar international system. As Raymond Aron has written: 'The rivalry of the two blocs causes the world to become an object of permanent competition, the stake of which is a choice, both diplomatic and moral, which the non-aligned nations cannot elude.'[107] De Gaulle's greater stress on national development meant that he did not see the Third World as a kind of battleground in which the superpowers could continue to confront each other as if trying to extend the Iron Curtain beyond Europe. But to the United States, the lack of superpower control over the Third World countries, like the growth of nationalism in Europe, left a sphere of instability, a point of access by which the equilibrium of the overarching system, the 'balance of terror', could first be tipped, and therefore destabilised, and then be undermined in principle, in the latter case through the creation of an entire sphere of world politics where the *logic* of the bipolar international system might be replaced by a different one. They feared that a North–South instead of an East–West conflict would develop, creating a sphere where the writ of the developed nations, and the superpowers in particular, would no longer run.

American policy saw any attempt to alter the balance in the Third World as both tipping the bipolar balance and undermining the system. Soviet policy had a similar perspective; however, it saw in such changes a potential to exploit the situation to its own advantage, given Soviet desire to escape capitalist encirclement and American strategic predominance as well as Soviet expectations that national–revolutionary movements would be favourable to increased Soviet influence. Gaullist national ideology, combined with French efforts to introduce more autonomous intermediate strata into a re-equilibrated international system, led France to support certain tendencies in Third World countries which emphasised their position *outside* the blocs. In addition, France's good relations with most of her ex-colonies after 1960–2 gave Gaullist policies a resonance which made her a real force to contend with in this arena.

De Gaulle combined a 'little France' view of Third World entanglements[108] with the *expansion* of French influence there. Tint identifies four ways in which de Gaulle attempted the latter: cultural linkages; economic and technical aid; decolonisation; and diplomatic courting of the Third World.[109] As with other arenas of French policy, the approach to the Third World was couched in the rhetoric of *grandeur*:

> We have always had a humane mission, and we still have it, and it is necessary that our policy conform to our spirit...In other words, France's policy with regard to these countries is to respect and to recognise their free disposal of themselves and, at the same time, to offer them an opportunity to form with her a whole in which they will have her support and in which she will have their participation in her world-wide activity.[110]

De Gaulle then sought to create the image that France's interest in the area was no longer imperial exploitation but a kind of fraternal nationalism which would benefit both France and the embryonic Third World nation-states which were striving to establish themselves as viable and autonomous entities in the world context.

Decolonisation was the first method of attempting to establish this *rapport*, and it was such a momentous ideological and symbolic upheaval that it required themes which would be acceptable at home as well as abroad. The emancipation of the colonies had to be linked with the national interest of France herself and must appear, as la Gorce argues, 'as a free decision of the country and of its government'. Indeed, the process must seem devoid of force or violence; 'on the contrary, France must herself make those gestures of liberation called for by the spirit of the age and by consciousness of her own interests. . .Independence ought to seem. . .the very accomplishment of the colonial task itself, the final manifestation of the liberating genius of the nation.'[111] Beyond the actual granting of independence, one can identify three main aspects of the Gaullist approach. Firstly, the presentation of France as an alternative to the superpowers emphasised French external support and bilateral links; these ties, based ostensibly upon a universal aspiration to national independence and the lack of French ambition to dominate, would thus permit the countries concerned to maintain their integrity, whereas superpower linkages were more invidious. Secondly, the superpowers themselves were presented with a slightly more differentiated 'spheres of influence' conception of alliance relationships outside the immediate North Atlantic theatre; this ensured that the pursuit of the first point established France in a *de facto* sphere of influence which could be used as a bargaining resource in global relationships. And thirdly, France developed an aid programme which, though plagued by contradictions and assailed by charges of a new style of neo-imperialism, did involve a conceptual shift from direct aid for friendly allies to a more 'infra-structural' form of assistance based on the sending of teachers, technical advisers and so on, whose job was supposed to help the Third World country to achieve its own developmental base.

French recognition of China was closely linked to the first aspect. The attempt to establish a visible French presence in many areas of the Third World was aimed at symbolising both the French desire to play some sort of world role and not to retreat into isolationism[112] and her wish that the bipolar system be loosened and that areas of the world be kept at least partially free from the East–West conflict.[113] The second aspect was formally enshrined in the 1958 NATO memorandum. It also appeared explicitly in French postures on South-East Asia – a factor tacitly recognised both by Sihanouk, at the time of de Gaulle's 1966 Phnom-Penh speech attacking America's Vietnam policy, and by Ho Chi Minh, when he sought French diplomatic assistance in ending the war in January 1966[114] – and on the Middle East. The *rapprochement* with the Arab states, involving the symbolic visit to Paris of

General Aref, President of Iraq, and the emphasising of French economic and cultural interests in the area (including access to oil), was also an attempt to provide the Arabs with an alternative to both superpowers in the Mediterranean region.[115] On the other hand, de Gaulle was reluctant to condemn the United States too harshly in 1965 for its action in Santo Domingo,[116] just as he had not hesitated in 1962 to support the position of the United States in the Cuban missile crisis.

The third aspect, aid and development, is altogether more complex, as it ostensibly involves both moral considerations[117] and questions of French interest. French aid policies involved not only a comparatively high level of foreign aid compared with most developed countries, although this level, measured in terms of percentage of GNP, tended to drop towards the end of the 1960s and into the 1970s, but also distinct structural features.[118] In addition, France formally supported extensive reforms in the structures of commodity trade between the Third World and the developed world which would have reduced the dependence of raw material-producing countries upon the fluctuations of world price levels.[119] Given the ideological context of French aid programmes in the 1960s and the desire of political elites of all shades of opinion to concentrate on the task of 'nation-building', and to reduce simultaneously their political and economic dependence on the superpowers, the response of the Third World was highly favourable to the French approach.[120] This fact was interpreted by the United States as a hostile posture, but was greeted by sceptical support in the Soviet Union.

French policy towards the Third World was a mixture of the three styles and approaches discussed above. But tensions and conflicts existed within the overall structure. These tensions were between the ostensible French championing of universal nationalism, on the one hand, and, on the other, both French pretensions to sharing the role of world policeman with the rest of the Big Five, a desire demonstrated by French policy in the Middle East[121] and towards the United Nations[122] as well as on nuclear questions, and specifically French interests, such as maintaining supplies of raw materials, including oil, continuing French political influence and the desire for markets. De Gaulle managed to walk this tightrope for several reasons. In the first place, the speed and efficiency of decolonisation, and the 'cooperation agreements' which were a major aspect of this process, created a great deal of moral capital in the Third World.[123] Secondly, French assertiveness in the rigid environment of the cold war gave France not only a high degree of credibility in the Third World, but also the appearance of a less damaging alternative for countries which both economically and politically were still not merely dependent upon the industrialised world, but becoming more so as the illusion of political independence and economic take-off faded into the reality of the vicious circle of under-development. France for a long time seemed to escape the label of neo-colonialism which has finally caught up with her in the 1970s.[124]

Finally, de Gaulle's own brand of personal diplomacy and his identification for many Third World leaders with the struggle for national integration – which meant everything from the revolutionary sort of nation-building by the regime in Congo (Brazzaville), whose budget was subsidised by French aid funds, to the maintenance of a crude and cruel dictatorship by General Bokassa in the Central African Republic (a source of uranium for the French nuclear effort) – provided a symbolic linkage which can be traced back to the rallying of the Empire to Free France in the Second World War, but which has scarcely survived de Gaulle's departure from the presidency. Through-out the period with which we are concerned, French policy diverged further and further from American policy and fed into the revival of American cold war fears – especially in the context of the Vietnam conflict which engulfed public opinion and which is said to have been an important motivation in de Gaulle's decision to withdraw from NATO in 1966.[125]

In addition to differences over the Third World, Gaullist policy diverged from American policy on the question of the organisation of Western Europe. As has been shown earlier, Franco-American differ-ences over East–West relations in Europe crystallised quickly, and several writers feel that following the failure of the 1958 memorandum on NATO, de Gaulle turned to the EEC as a possible arena for extend-ing and consolidating French influence.[126] The Gaullist conception of Europe was different not only from the widespread federalist and functionalist views,[127] but also from the view taken up and at times vigorously championed by US policy-makers. The French view con-sidered that any unified Europe would have to be independent of the superpowers[128] as well as based on the free cooperation of independent governments, and that only when a *European* national identity had been formed through practice could there be anything like a European state, federal or otherwise. As Couve stated: 'As far as nationalism goes, I would be quite satisfied to rally myself to European nationalism.'[129]

American policy was based on a quite different set of assumptions. It was originally a product of the American debate on 'containment' and 'rollback' of Communism in Europe. Once the cold war split between the United States and the Soviet Union had crystallised into full confrontation in the period between the Berlin municipal elections of 1946 and the consolidation of Western Germany into a partially sovereign state in 1949, American policy-makers had already decided that some sort of unification of Western Europe on a political and economic level, within the framework of an Atlantic military pact, was necessary. The American pressure exerted through the Marshall Plan and its offspring, the Organisation for European Economic Cooperation (OEEC), evidenced a clear desire for establishing such regional integration, in order to accomplish three things: to prevent the development of nationalist rivalries, which were blamed for two world wars; to prevent the recrudescence of autarchic economic policies, blamed for the economic crises of the 1930s and seen as a serious obstacle to the restructuring of the world economy which lay behind US war aims but which had not been realised on a global level; and to allow the United States to pursue cold war policies while not having to pay the full economic cost, a major motivation behind all of America's interdependent defence and alliance policies.[130] Thus the American debate was clearly structured by the middle of 1949:

A critical discussion of the American viewpoint was, it would seem, set out by George Kennan in a paper of that time. Apparently he suggested a form of organisation under which a continental axis based on France and Germany, and more or less identical with what came to be the 'Six' of little Europe, should co-exist with a United Kingdom–United States–Canadian axis which might also include countries on the Atlantic periphery of Europe such as Norway, Iceland and Portugal. The main advantage of this alternative, as Kennan said it at the time, was that the continental European grouping might still have had an attraction for the countries of central and east-central Europe, while it was out of the question that they would be permitted by the Russians to engage themselves in any organisation which included the United States and Britain. In this sense it marked something of a return to the original plans put forward by Rostow in the early part of 1946.[131]

Much of the European debate between 1952 and 1954 on the European Defence Community Treaty took place in the context of American reactions. These were sceptical at first, but then, under Dulles, so strongly favourable to the EDC that the spectre of its rejection by the French National Assembly caused him to threaten an 'agonising reappraisal' of American policy towards France in such an eventuality.[132] Such a reappraisal did not, in fact, take place, because in the context of the Paris and London Agreements of 1954 (which admitted West Germany to the Brussels Treaty, now the Western European Union, and to NATO) and the development of proposals for a European common market – along with the rapid development of the American nuclear umbrella under the massive retaliation doctrine[133] – the essential principles of American defence policy were sufficiently catered for. European and Atlantic integration were parts of a fabric, as an establishment view of the period makes clear:

It is noteworthy that these two principles of Western unification are complementary and interdependent. The progressive organisation of the West depends on the exercise of American economic and political power. But if that power is to be acceptable to the European nations – if it is to be leadership rather than domination – it must be counter-balanced by strengthening the institutions of European unity and creating – as soon as possible – a supranational European union. Conversely, European unification depends upon progress in the unification of the Atlantic community as a whole.[134]

Thus American policy was concerned to use European unity as a way of making American 'leadership' palatable to the European nations, not of making Europe independent of that leadership. Although American enthusiasm waned in the later Eisenhower years because of hostility to real and potential European commercial competition, the view described above continued to influence certain sections of the American foreign policy establishment right through the 1960s – especially the 'liberal' sections, who were convinced that the American *mission civilisatrice* not only justified such a position but would make it desired by the Europeans themselves.[135] It also came to dominate President Kennedy's views on 'Atlantic partnership',[136] which, analogous with the integration of the Atlantic Alliance on a strategic level, sought, through such instruments as the 1962 Trade Expansion Act and the general policy of tariff reduction, later embodied in the 'Kennedy Round' negotiations, to bring Western Europe and the United States into a general free-trade area – to link the prospering developed industrial economies in such a way that it would be compatible with the American notion of the 'free world'. As Couve de Murville describes Kennedy's viewpoint:

The success of the Common Market struck him forcibly [in contrast to America's growing balance-of-payments problems]. . . , and he attributed to it the prosperity, which was then running at an unprecedented level, of the six partners. In the minds of Kennedy and his advisors, the only solution was for America to take the direction of operations in hand. As Christian Herter wrote in a report commissioned by the State Department and published in November 1961: 'The United States must form a commercial association with the Common Market and assert its leadership in the expansion of an economic community of the free world.' This was the grand design of President Kennedy.[137]

In the view of the Kennedy Administration, the necessary precondition for such a development was the admission of the United Kingdom to the EEC. America's potential for applying pressure in these circumstances was enormous. Despite the fact that the Six had since 1958 become the world's first commercial power, they were far from being the first economic power.[138] The United States dominates not only Europe, but the world as a whole.[139] In search of economic returns, American business expanded into Western Europe itself, taking advantage of the facilities offered by this huge market with its free-trade area and developing customs union. As one well-known critic of the era wrote: 'The Common Market has become a new Far West for American businessmen.'[140] The problem of American investment did not bypass France, where it was welcomed at first for its expansionist effects, but where in the atmosphere of conflict between de Gaulle and the United States in the period we are discussing, certain restrictive measures were taken. In the view of the French government, the problem was not only the mass of American investment, but also the structure of American scientific and technological superiority.[141] This problem was linked, furthermore, to the Franco-American disagreement over the functioning of the international monetary system, a problem fascinating in its details and ramifications.[142]

In the French perspective, then, a whole series of problems linked with the development of the EEC were inextricably intertwined with Atlantic relationships. Perhaps the ramifications of these problems would not have been so virulent had there not been, so to speak, a conflict of paradigms. The French were not the only ones to see the problem of the EEC as one which closely involved the whole structure of Atlantic relations. So did the American government, and so did de Gaulle's European critics, whom it will be useful to quote directly: firstly Joseph Luns, a leading Dutch politician, and former Foreign Minister as well as Secretary General of NATO; secondly Paul-Henri Spaak of Belgium:

For the Netherlands, there certainly can be no question of a choice between European and Atlantic collaboration; we should be quite unable to make it without disowning our history and shrinking from what we are convinced is our responsibility. Ever since the emergence of the Netherlands as a nation, we have derived our strength from being open to the movement of men, ideas and goods to and from all parts of the world. The brief periods in our history when we linked our fate predominantly to the continent alone were not happy ones, and we soon turned our eyes seawards again. Living in a country to which land and sea are equally important, the very idea of locking ourselves up in an inward-looking group of continental nations is alien to us.[143]

Thus Luns, writing for a British audience, emphasises how the national interest of the Netherlands propels her towards the sort of Europe in which Britain would be at home; Spaak, writing for an American audience, castigates the revival of nationalism:

There was [in 1948] no contradiction or conflict between the concept of the Atlantic Alliance and of the European alliance. Rising from its ruins, Europe rallied to both ideas, and – let it never be forgotten – found peace and prosperity.

How is it possible that a system which brought peace and prosperity can now be in danger? The answer is perfectly clear. The enemy we thought we had defeated raises his head once more, not yet strong enough to win but vigorous enough to cause serious trouble. The enemy is nationalism.[144]

In this perspective, de Gaulle became, to Spaak and his followers, the 'grave-digger' of both the Atlantic Alliance and European unity.[145]

De Gaulle's position always involved a choice between Alliance and European priorities; consider his conflict with Churchill during the Second World War, particularly the famous exchange in which Churchill states: 'This is something you ought to know: each time we must choose between Europe and the open sea, we shall always choose the open sea.'[146] At a different level, however, de Gaulle's Europe was quite different from the Europe of the Atlanticists. Only in the late 1960s did the conflict structure which linked Atlantic and European questions in this way shift significantly – when the constitutional problem of relations between the Commission and the Council of Ministers of the EEC had been resolved by the 1966 Luxembourg Agreements, and Europe itself had developed a non-Atlantic rationale through the efforts of revisionists like Jean-Jacques Servan-Schreiber (as regards economic objectives) or Viscount Etienne Davignon (as regards decision-making structures).

The overarching conflict of paradigms is reflected in the specific disagreements which arose in Europe in this period. The traditional view is typified by Newhouse, whose very title – De Gaulle and the Anglo-Saxons – sets the boundaries of his analytical framework. In fact, the very supranational nature of EEC institutions – especially the association of those institutions with men such as Jean Monnet, Walter Hallstein (then President of the Commission), Robert Schuman and Paul-Henri Spaak – seemed to show that the officials most likely to be involved in supranational policy-making were also fervent Atlanticists and cold warriors. On the question of the enlargement of the EEC, a clear contradiction appeared between supranationality and the admission of the UK; however, these were presented as 'either/or' alternatives after the collapse of the Fouchet Plan (by the Netherlands in particular).[147] The logic of their interchangeability, clear enough in the Atlanticist perspective, seemed to the Gaullists to indicate both the fundamental insincerity of the Benelux leaders and the fact that the Atlanticist–Europeanist perspective, behind the rhetoric of a grand vision of the European 'general interest', was based firmly on the national self-interest of the Benelux countries themselves. From this standpoint France was led to reaffirm her intention of seeking to resist further integration on either level. In this context, too, the refusal of the Benelux countries to agree to the Fouchet Plan appeared to be opportunism of the worst sort, cloaking national ambitions in rhetoric of the highest international principle, which was just what they were accusing de Gaulle of doing.

In the Gaullist view, opportunities to extend the *scope* of European cooperation to political and defence questions were much more important than the creation of supranational institutions. The modalities of political cooperation, however, were recognised as more complex, as Couve de Murville makes explicit:

General de Gaulle's government, when in 1958 it resolved to apply the Common Market effectively, of course had as its primary concern to find the means therein of accelerating the economic development of France and of leading its industry, its agriculture and its trade to adapt to the requirements of the contemporary world. But he also saw as being just as important its role as an appropriate instrument for creating a solidarity among its members which would lead them more or less naturally to seek to extend their enterprise into the political arena. No-one was under the illusion that this would be easy. It was only to be predicted that it would be only too quickly apparent that there was a difference in kind between economic action and political action. In the first case, it was primarily a matter of creating conditions which would allow the multiplication of exchanges and the harmonisation of the conditions of production. The means were technical, and if often, as in agriculture, governments conflicted and politics intervened, this was only to find honourable compromises between the interests of their countries. On political questions, if it was really a question of politics, something totally different was called into question, perhaps the very existence of a nation, often enough its position in the world, and always its security and its future. This did not involve reaching compromise positions between friends on more or less vague or equivocal formulas, but rather tackling questions in such a way as to reach agreement on a firm position. It was a question of deciding and of acting.[148]

Indeed, de Gaulle himself treated the lines of Franco-American conflict as a passing phase which detracted from, rather than expressed, the underlying significance of the changes which characterised this period. In a private letter to Paul-Marie de la Gorce, for example, he chides the author

...for having painted too pessimistic a picture of the rejection of the Fouchet Plan in 1962 and of the growing quarrel between France and the United States and its West European partners. He explained that these conflicts were but means to larger ends. Since these alignments had lost some of their usefulness, others would have to be sought.[149]

For example, a number of causes and justifications may be adduced for the rejection of British entry into the EEC in the famous press conference of 14 January 1963. For the Atlanticist–Europeanists, such as Spaak, it was an explicit attack on sacred symbols:

It becomes clearer and clearer that January 14, 1963, is fated to go down in history as the 'black Monday' of both European policy and Atlantic policy. What occurred that day was something much more significant than the mere dooming of negotiations between Great Britain and the European Community. It was, in plain fact, an attack on the Atlantic Alliance and the European Community – an attack, that is, on the two most significant achievements of the free world since the end of the Second World War.[150]

And for the Gaullists, it symbolised a rejection of the *conjunction* of these symbolic structures. The development of the EEC itself provides further examples. The test did not come right away, for the successful completion of the Common Agricultural Policy in 1962 indicated that there was sufficient room within the EEC for compromise. However, the serious and prolonged clash over agricultural financing, the financial powers of the Commission and majority voting in the Council of Ministers – which occurred simultaneously in 1965 and were resolved simultaneously in the Luxembourg Agreements following the six-month French boycott of the Council – indicated the depth of divergence on matters of principle.[151]

At the same time, the retirement of Chancellor Adenauer in 1963 brought to an end an era of close personal collaboration which occasionally transcended differences of principle, especially on this very question of the linkage of Atlantic and European relations, to culminate in the Franco-German Friendship Treaty of 1963, which was meant to provide a narrower substitute for the failed Fouchet Plan. De Gaulle saw the disjunction of Atlantic and European relations as a precondition of the settlement of the German problem itself, as Couve explains:

The only road open was an evolution of Europe itself, which would permit a preparation of the paths leading to a general agreement; this naturally supposed that the Russians would consider their interests to have been taken satisfactorily into account as to frontiers and weapons. For this to occur it was necessary to establish a form of cooperation within the continent as a whole, particularly as regards the economic order.[152]

Of course, the United States felt that the question of the division of Europe and Germany had to be solved within the framework of the Atlantic Alliance. As the conflict between Gaullist and Atlanticist conceptions of Europe widened in 1962–3, the retirement of Adenauer and the succession of Ludwig Erhard as Chancellor destroyed the symbolic and sentimental links. Franco-German opposition appeared on a number of levels.

In what the French interpreted as a direct attack on the Franco-German Treaty, the Germans and the Americans in the summer of 1963 concluded the Von Hassel–McNamara Agreements on logistics and the common manufacture of arms.[153] Erhard, in contrast to Adenauer's soft-pedalling of Franco-German disagreements on NATO and American protection, agreed to take part in the Multilateral Force which had been revived by Kennedy; the issue of German access to nuclear weapons thereby became tied up with this dispute.[154] French recognition of the Oder–Neisse line in 1959 as the definitive border of East Germany and Poland (at a time when West Germany still considered the area as Soviet and Polish 'occupation zones') was underplayed when Adenauer was Chancellor, but foreshadowed a more profound symbolic debate over German reunification. As one Gaullist commentator wrote in 1967, German reunification was in the interest of neither Paris nor Moscow – without 'unusually stringent guarantees' – and the fact that France officially supported reunification had a rather different rationale, that 'the division of Germany symbolises the division of Europe and perpetuates the continuance of opposing power blocs'.[155] But in a wider sense, as Jacques Vernant observes, de Gaulle believed that the only sure means of achieving the progressive reunification of both Germany and divided Europe was to seek 'political solutions to European political problems through a dialogue with the East, rather than in limiting oneself to consolidating the Western citadel militarily and politically'.[156] With Adenauer, it had been possible to continue the overall posture which had been consecrated in the EDC – i.e. German integration into Western Europe and the Atlantic Alliance – while balancing this with a longer-term political vision closer to de Gaulle's. Under Erhard, the two approaches were seen to be contradictory, and American protection was seen to be more important to Germany's survival and development.

A series of other policy disagreements further reinforced the break. They clashed over British admission to the EEC, the financing of the CAP, the development of EEC institutions, German participation in Western nuclear policy-making, in particular the 1965 McNamara proposals, colour television systems (the German PAL system, derived from the American system, was the main rival to SECAM, whose successes were in the East and the Third World), and other less important issues.[157] Indeed, Franco-German relations were coloured by the sour personal note between the two leaders themselves.[158] Here again, the conflict of paradigms dominated. Issues were conceived on both sides as involving the very survival of each nation. In German policy, a revival of pro-Western dogmatism under the particular influence of Foreign Minister Gerhard Schroeder and Defence Minister Kai-Üwe von Hassel[159] had been one of the consequences of the 1961–2 Berlin crisis,[160] and in the period 1962–6 the conflict between France and the United States was reflected in miniature in Franco-German relationships, which were in turn characteristic of the atmosphere generated in this period.

The Franco-American conflict was the accumulation of a series of divergences which were not so significant in themselves, but which became crucial when set in the context of the conflict of paradigmatic perspectives described in this chapter. It dominated the policy disagreements over the structure of the international monetary system which highlighted the difficulties of the dollar and led to the abandonment of the Gold Exchange Standard and dollar parity in 1971. It dominated North–South relations, where the EEC, in many cases taking over French economic relationships with her former colonies, was thought to be developing a new mercantilism which threatened cherished American notions of freedom of trade.[161] It spread to the Middle East, where French efforts (coming at a slightly later period) to introduce the concept of an arms embargo on both sides after the June 1967 war did not at first lead to any wider attempts at defusing the situation until the advent of Secretary of State William Rogers's attempt at a more 'even-handed' policy in 1969 (which laid the groundwork for Egypt's recent shift from the Soviet sphere of influence to the American). Positive Arab reactions to the earlier French initiatives aroused only suspicion and rejection from the United States at first.[162]

It affected French attitudes to British entry into the EEC – again, a problem which lingered on into the late 1960s – and it dominated the early stages of the process of detente in Europe itself, *vis-à-vis* both the USSR and the East European states. It must be remembered that the USSR looked on French diplomatic expansion into Eastern Europe with a certain tolerance, while, until the advent of the new Eastern policy (*Ostpolitik*) under the Brandt Government in the Federal Republic in 1969, its attitude towards German economic expansion was decidedly suspicious and provided at least the overt Soviet rationale for the invasion of Czechoslovakia in August 1968.

As the lines of the conflict hardened and were seen to affect a wide range of international issues, the possibility of some sort of explosive reaction increased. The NATO crisis of 1966, in fact, was just such a reaction. However, in the longer term, the results of the crisis removed the source of the major structural bone of contention between the allies and profoundly altered the relationship between France and the United States.

V. The NATO crisis of 1966

The final French decision to leave the military organisation (NATO) of the Atlantic Alliance was presented in a dramatic manner characteristic of Gaullist politics when significant symbolic issues were at stake. Kolodziej summarises the memorandum sent to all allied powers on 10–11 March 1966:

It outlined France's plans to withdraw its units from NATO, to expel all foreign troops from French territory, and to void certain bilateral accords with the United States, Canada and West Germany that largely dealt with their installations on French soil. The French justified their actions on previously articulated grounds: (1) the diminution of the Soviet threat; (2) the depreciation of the United States nuclear guarantee; (3) the unwillingness of the de Gaulle government to integrate France's nuclear forces into NATO; (4) the resurgence of a politically and economically strong Europe; (5) the reconstitution of France's sovereignty that had been impaired not only by the presence of foreign bases on French territory but also by dependence upon the United States for its defence; (6) the need to thaw East–West relations frozen by monolithic blocs under the control of the superpowers; and (7) the increasing influence of the Third World, especially of China, in world politics which occasioned the reevaluation of alliance ties. France also countered American criticism that it had unilaterally changed its alliance obligations by asserting that the NATO organisation was never meant to be an indispensable condition for the operation of the 1949 alliance. Indeed, the United States was said to have been the more serious offender in having revamped its strategic policies and posture without having first consulted its European allies.[163]

The conflict of standpoints was thus consummated, even though the mutual adjustments needed for compromise were said by *both* sides to be small, and the conclusions each side drew about the other's intentions was similarly exaggerated. The American perspective was the mirror image of the French, as we can see from Newhouse's view:

In return for very little – an occasional bow to NATO, a commitment to remain an active partner – de Gaulle at various moments could have had almost anything he wanted from the Americans and British. But even a gesture towards NATO was unthinkable. France 'with free hands' was the eternal and supreme goal.[164]

Indeed, it was characteristic of de Gaulle's dramaturgical style that he should consider that the only solution in such cases – as with his veto of the first British EEC application in January 1963 or the use of the 'empty chair' in the EEC crisis of 1965–6[165] – would be *a crisis which would force the resolution of the key stalemated issues.* 'After all', he said, 'from time to time it is necessary to upset the flower pot.'[166]

The crisis, however, was not merely a dramatic rabbit-from-a-hat. It was also the culmination of a long incremental process. We have already discussed some of the earlier tentative French reactions to the American rejection of the 1958 memorandum, as well as American reactions to early French requests for assistance with the FNS, the French refusal to allow stockpiling of nuclear weapons on French soil, and the like, which foreshadowed the 'gradual, yet systematic withdrawal or nonparticipation of France in the NATO organisation in the period 1963–66'.[167] The process began with the rejection of the MLF, which had been proposed at the Nassau meeting as part of the American package of proposals to replace Skybolt with Polaris for the British and bring de Gaulle back into the NATO fold by offering him (but without negotiating with him directly) what had already been offered to the British. French pilots had in fact been trained under the auspices of NATO in the use of nuclear weapons, and the French had even agreed to a double-key system for some of their more than 400 combat fighter planes in Germany.[168] But they stayed clear of the MLF, the proposals for which at that time included the integration of existing strategic and tactical units under direct NATO command. The two French divisions returning from Algeria were not assigned to NATO, nor did France try to meet her quota of the fifty-division overall level of alliance strength on the continent which she had previously agreed to. The Atlantic fleet was withdrawn from NATO in June 1963, following the withdrawal of the Mediterranean fleet four years earlier. In April 1964 French naval staff officers were withdrawn from NATO service as a result of their changed duties. French naval units were withdrawn at the last minute from the NATO naval war games of September 1964, and the French publicised the deliberate nature of the decision to underline the fact that it was meant as a way of putting pressure for NATO reform; the only part of the French navy still assigned to NATO consisted of five submarines.

As Kolodziej observes: 'It is interesting to note that the French initially challenged integration by withdrawal of their naval forces, which, although important to NATO, were less central to its planning than ground and air units.'[169] However, as French pressure continued to be treated by the USA as idiosyncratic deviance, these too were included. Her army units did not participate in the 'Fallex' exercise in June 1965. The army also decided not to adopt a rifle calibre compatible with the American. Reports indicated that France did not fulfil her agreement of 1960 to provide full coverage in a coordinated air defence system, NADGE (NATO Air Defence and Ground Environment System). And throughout this period, the French strenuously resisted anything it saw as an extension of the principle of integration – the MLF, the establishment of American missile launching sites or the stocking of nuclear weapons on French soil. And guidelines for the use of atomic weapons which had been adopted in Athens in 1963 were rejected by France. Indeed, within NATO institutions themselves, the French insisted on maintaining their independent stance, whether through split communiqués after ministerial meetings or, as Dirk Stikker emphasised, by her 'hostile attitudes towards the International Secretariat and the Secretary General on basic questions of procedure and administration'.[170]

In fact, the process, though systematic, may not have been as monolithic as it might appear at first glance. Naval units were withdrawn first to impress the United States with both the seriousness of French intentions and French reluctance to act too hastily if some convergence of *principle* were to be discerned. Indeed, the French reaction to the McNamara proposals for a special nuclear committee was not immediate rejection, but rather the presentation of counterproposals, in the spirit of the 1958 memorandum (but watered down).[171] The fact that Germany was to be included in the committee annoyed not only the French, and rejection of permanent status for the committee by NATO Ministers was seen as a defeat for Germany;[172] and refusal to participate in Fallex highlighted both the practical consequences of strategic differences between France and the United States and the fact that

France acted only after long attempts to change the basic assumptions around which Fallex had been designed. The exercise was conceived in the context of the American strategic switch to flexible response. As *L'Année politique* wrote:

The French government advocated an immediate nuclear reply to any recognised aggression; it reminded the NATO Defence Ministers that such was the strategy defined by the Atlantic Organisation in 1956, but which the latter had replaced with one of graduated response, such as had been practised by the American government at the time of the Cuban affair in October 1962. It seemed politically difficult for Washington to declare officially that the threat of immediate nuclear response had been fully effective when the United States alone possessed the atomic bomb or possessed a large nuclear superiority, but that it was no longer suitable, since two powers, the United States and the Soviet Union, had achieved the balance of terror. However, it is doubtful whether French public opinion was fully aware that in adopting the doctrine of massive reprisals, the French government implicitly confirmed that it was ready to take on eventual responsibility for being the first to use this most destructive weapon.[173]

A German attempt to reconcile the two positions by means of adopting a low nuclear threshold was said to have received some French response, which left the definition of 'recognised aggression' up to the Alliance, but this did not prove fruitful. At the same time, the French, although not participating in Fallex, did allow all preparations and so on to operate smoothly even when French elements were involved.[174]

Nonetheless, Gaullist threats in October to leave the Alliance if it was not transformed led not to new American moves, but to a vigorous counter-attack by the US State Department and American newspapers.[175] Creating a smoke screen for his final move, de Gaulle declared in his press conference in February 1966 that French withdrawal from NATO would continue until the pact came up for renewal in 1969, but promised that 'the changes will take place gradually so that her allies do not suddenly find themselves inconvenienced by her action'.[176] The swiftness and completeness of his action a fortnight later was thus unexpected – withdrawal of all French units from integrated NATO commands and the demand that all foreign bases on French soil be responsible only to French authorities.[177] Although certain bilateral accords were declared null and void, the French government declared itself ready to discuss the consequences of this action and to negotiate new bilateral agreements covering the use of French facilities by the United States and Canada in case of a conflict involving the Alliance, the arrangements for the maintenance of French forces in Germany under the Paris Agreements of 23 October 1964, and arrangements for German installations in France.[178] In addition, memoranda issued on 29 and 30 March set the timetables for this process, denounced the protocol which had established the Supreme Headquarters Allied Powers in Europe (SHAPE) and the headquarters of Allied Forces Central Europe in Paris, made special provisions for the NATO pipeline, and offered to set up French liaison missions with the NATO commands.[179]

With the flower pot thus upset, it became crucial to see how the two governments would act in the aftermath of the crisis. Given the extent and complexity of Franco-American disagreement over NATO, it might have been expected that French withdrawal signalled the arrival at a total impasse – a situation in which France would gradually dissolve her remaining Alliance ties over the period leading up to the expiration of the original 20-year treaty period in 1969, the United States would consolidate the integration of the rest of the NATO structure, and France would adopt a neutralist stance in world affairs. De Gaulle's impending state visit to the Soviet Union in June 1966, growing French disapproval of the American role in Vietnam, and growing contacts with Eastern Europe and the Third World seemed to make this outcome at least plausible; in fact, as we have already noted, it is usual for observers to assume that such was actually the general drift of French policy until the multiple upheavals of 1968 caused both a reappraisal of foreign policy and a new priority for domestic affairs to develop simultaneously. NATO's formal reply to the French memoranda, on 18 March, seemed to leave little room for compromise, pointing out that 'no system of bilateral arrangements can be a substitute' for NATO arrangements on collective security. The double-key arrangements on French supply of nuclear weapons were terminated, there were calls in the United States for the recovery of old First World War debts from France and demands that French payment be forthcoming for the infrastructure and facilities of the bases which would be left behind, and, so the French claimed, the delivery of atomic fuel for French submarines was stopped by the US in violation of an agreement of 1959 (the Americans disagreed on the interpretation of the agreement). On the French side, the government began to require monthly instead of annual) notification of allied overflights from 5 May.[180]

American action, however, was notably mild, in contrast to the chilliness of the atmosphere. Johnson's reply stated that: 'Every advance in the technology of war makes more unacceptable the old and narrow concepts of sovereignty.'[181] The Americans made no concessions, but the President resisted pressures for reprisals. Louis Heren's sketch of Johnson's reaction is instructive:

Johnson was generally impatient with the niceties of diplomacy. He accepted existing trucial arrangements, such as NATO, as a politician would accept a coalition of local and state political forces. He regarded other heads of government as fellow politicians, to be helped whenever necessary as he had helped senators when he was the Senate majority leader. This had its drawbacks when, acting as if he were still in the Senate, he tried to call in a few political IOUs... He refused to go along, at least publicly, with the shrill condemnation of President Charles de Gaulle of France. If the European enthusiasts in the State Department and grand old men such as Dean Acheson, who ought to have known better, had had their way he would have contested de Gaulle's demand for the withdrawal of American troops from France. The legalisms of the draft notes drawn up for him to sign delighted diplomats of the old school, but he would have none of them. Naturally he regretted the French withdrawal from NATO, and the removal of American troops in France was shaming and costly. Nevertheless, he recognised an adamant statesman when he saw one, and his own tactical helplessness. Accordingly, striking the right note of regret, he withdrew gracefully. In so doing, the essential unity of NATO was preserved, and a sensitive situation was not exacerbated. Perhaps one of his successors will collect that IOU in Paris as a consequence of this shrewd statesmanship.[182]

Nevertheless, American judgment was severe. The United States had come to have a certain image of the role which it played in the Atlantic Alliance, an image based on the presupposition that the American contribution was to some extent the response to a call above and beyond the needs of national self-interest alone – an image which resulted from the global role played by the United States combined with the massive relative weight of American military forces and American economic strength within NATO.[183] Although some American commentators could call for fundamental reforms within NATO, giving a larger share of decision-making to Europeans,[184] this was generally viewed as a kind of overcompensating disproportionality, perhaps to be grudgingly granted, but somehow felt to be unjust to America, with her commitments and responsibilities. Secondly, many Americans feared that NATO had been emasculated, that its ability to meet crisis situations had been diminished, and that the fundamental problem for the future was to adjust to France's departure.[185]

Indeed, in geo-political terms, the total absence of France from the Alliance would be a grave blow. Much would therefore depend upon the quality of the bilateral agreements France was seeking and upon the cooperation in practice which would be forthcoming between France and the other allies in the future. In addition, there were fears in the United States that France would be an unreliable ally, especially as she now seemed to be redefining the terms on which her entry into a conflict would depend. De Gaulle wrote to Johnson on 7 March 1966, and indicated that French assistance to a NATO ally would be limited to cases of 'unprovoked aggression'. When Pompidou addressed the National Assembly on 13 April, he made the same point: 'We wish to maintain the Alliance concluded in 1949 that makes us united in the face of possible unprovoked aggression.' The following week, Couve de Murville, in a radio interview, returned to the theme: 'The alliance is a treaty that joins all the member countries – there are fifteen at present – and that binds us to go to the aid of any one of our allies who is the object of an attack, of an unprovoked attack.'[186] Thus France stressed the need for provocation for the alliance provisions to come into force, and the thought that an ally might think the United States even capable of unprovoked aggression was badly received in the United States, as *L'Année politique* describes:

When the French note of 22 April had been published by the press on 25 April, the State Department spokesman, Mr McCloskey, declared: 'In their *aide-mémoire* of 12 April, the United States had asked questions concerning the legitimacy [of the French decisions] and the timetable for their application. The French note provides no response whatsoever to some of the most important among these questions. We must take this factor into account and we will do so in consultation with our allies. After these consultations, we will decide the form which our response must take.' One of these questions was no doubt that envisaged by the evidence given by Mr Dean Acheson to a Senate sub-committee in the following terms: the French promise to come to the aid of her allies in case of an unprovoked attack comes down to saying that France will herself decide if an attack has been provoked or not. This position, confirmed by General de Gaulle at the beginning of his personal letter addressed to President Johnson on 7 March, effectively constituted the essential political problem; it determined the character which the Alliance was taking on.[187]

This highly charged and typically symbolic disagreement has remained hypothetical, rooted as it was in the context of French fears of being drawn into an escalating conflict in South-East Asia. And as Heren has written of LBJ: 'The refusal of the Western European allies to become involved in Vietnam genuinely hurt and bewildered him, but with the possible exception of Harold Wilson he was willing to accept that they too had their problems.'[188] The only comparable example, Cuba, gave rise to different interpretations. Both were stressed by the French as complementary – that de Gaulle's immediate and thorough support of the American action proved his reliability, but that at the same time the French had reservations about having been presented with a *fait accompli* (the old bugbear of consultation). Pompidou made this point on 13 April:

Facing the threat weighing on the United States, President Kennedy took immediate measures. He did not consult us, but rather informed us, quickly, to be sure, but *a posteriori*. I specify this because you [M. Pleven] have spoken of *our* policy of the *fait accompli*. We approved President Kennedy's actions. However, before we had even made known our position, when NATO forces were not yet involved in the conflict, when even though precautionary measures had been recommended, no coded alert procedure had been set in place, American forces in Europe, including France, had been put in a state of alert by themselves – and, I must add, to the highest degree of alert.[189]

Thus, in practice, Pompidou added, France would have been involved in any US action if only because she would be the target for bombs aimed at American troops stationed there. The Czechoslovak crisis of 1968 provided no test at all, for there was no aggression against any member of the Alliance; however, diplomatic solidarity within the Alliance did prevail.[190]

On the whole, then, American reactions on the practical level were mixed. American attitudes towards France, however, hardened generally. Public opinion came to see France as hostile, with widespread but ineffective moves to boycott certain French products. In an opinion survey taken in early 1968, favourable opinion of France, which had been equal to that towards Britain in 1957 (68 per cent each), fell to 49 per cent (Britain having risen to 85 per cent), putting France behind Argentina, Uruguay, South Vietnam and Iran, and ahead only of Egypt, Russia, North Vietnam, Cuba and the People's Republic of China in public esteem.[191] On another level, however, convergence was already beginning to appear in US policies towards the Soviet Union and Eastern Europe.

French reaction was also hostile, though more divided. Fairly complete and wide-ranging attempts to restate the bases of Gaullist policy were made by Pompidou and Couve de Murville. Running throughout was the standard Gaullist theme, in Pompidou's words: 'Good allies are not the most docile. Only free and sovereign people accept to fight.'[192] Couve said in a radio interview:

Defence has become something a bit anonymous which we don't have the feeling of really participating in. And from the moment a country is no longer interested in its defence, it is not far – it must be said – from losing its independence. . . What the Americans must understand – and I am sure they will come to understand – is that what we are doing, what the government is doing, is not intended in the slightest to put them out. Once again, we are doing it because we think it in the country's interest and also because we think it in no way contrary to the considered interest of our allies.[193]

Nevertheless, Couve notes 'the volume of reactions of stupor, indignation and, sometimes, of fury':

First of all, of course, in France. Such reactions were certainly not found in public opinion, to which it seemed that national independence was an elementary and normal notion, and which was not afraid for a minute that the security of the country had been called into question. The explanations and details which I myself offered on television and radio, particularly to emphasise the fundamental distinction made by the government between the Alliance and the Organisation, were, according to opinion surveys and commentaries, widely understood and well received.

Things developed in a very different fashion in those circles – especially political circles – which had trouble detaching themselves from the past and which remained penetrated by the Atlantic tradition. They had a chance to express themselves during a debate in the National Assembly in the middle of April. They did not fail to make use of the occasion, but I did not get the impression that the dramatic presentation which they delivered found any great resonance in public opinion. The censure motion which was tabled – not without problems – by certain groups within the opposition received only 137 votes. The question was settled in the internal context.[194]

Of course, the question was not so simple, but the general mildness of the American reaction did not lead to any overt conflict, and domestic French conflict over the Atlantic issue soon centred on two derivative issues, which we shall deal with in the next chapter: these were the question of whether General de Gaulle intended to take his break with the Alliance further in the period leading up to the 1969 expiry/renewal date; and that of areas in which practical cooperation could be both maintained and initiated in the Atlantic arena.

Conclusions

French policy in the period 1962–6 stemmed from a series of factors which proved to be mutually reinforcing: the institutionalisation of the nuclear balance of terror and the resulting desire on the part of both superpowers to iron out possible destabilising factors in each alliance system in the wake of the Cuban missile crisis; the demystification of the cold war itself, due both to the growing situation of relative calm (which showed more clearly the spheres of influence of the two superpowers) and to the sense after Cuba that the era of confrontation was over; the sense that with the cold war thawing it might be possible for states to begin to pursue their own national interests to a greater extent, a sense which was reinforced by the establishment of a large number of new nation-states in the process of decolonisation and which in turn strengthened the reviving belief that pursuit of national interest was the *normal* and respectable course of action for sovereign governments in the age of the 'end of ideology' (at least in the sense of the end of the mystification of the 'free world' and its communist counterpart);[195] and a series of *specific* policy disagreements between France and the United States over Atlantic and global questions. In addition, as Kolodziej points out, publicising her differences with America had certain advantages for France: it increased her credibility with the USSR as an interlocutor; it could attract other states in America's shadow by showing that France was actually doing something to resist American hegemony and pursue an independent line; it created the aura of policies which were somehow 'European', thus giving an example to the other European states; and it strengthened French credibility and sentimental ties in Latin America (Santo Domingo), South-East Asia (proving attractive to communist and neutralist elements), the Arab states (after June 1967), etc. And finally, as a balance-of-power policy, French policy tended to provide a counterweight to shifts which had previously tipped the balance, whether the global nuclear balance (where it added an extra element of instability to American superiority in the arms race) or in the Mediterranean.[196]

Throughout all of these contextual factors and specific issues, however, runs the conflict of paradigms which linked the separate components into an overall structure of Franco-American conflict, from Suez and Cuba (for the American paradigm), and from the 1958 NATO memorandum (for the French paradigm). Each of these overarching conceptual frameworks contained more that was symbolic than material, each involving fundamental assumptions about the necessities for survival of state and society in the contemporary world, and each was expressed in a way which made it more difficult to retreat from without entailing complex changes of perspective and perception – changes which would have meant not only the abandonment of cherished principles which had received the highest official sanction and reaffirmation[197] (like the American 'commitment' in Vietnam), but also loss of face.[198] To have altered the principles would have meant throwing doubt on the very fabric of French or American credibility in international relationships. This was the dialogue of the deaf, and it is a familiar feature of human communities, political or academic.

To be sure, this argument may be circular: the conflict was irresolvable within the existing framework of relations because it was a conflict of paradigms; and it was a conflict of paradigms because it was irresolvable within the existing framework. However, 'not all circularities are vicious',[199] and the test of an analysis is not always its logical structure, but its fruitfulness for discovering ways of identifying and describing the clues most relevant to examining a range of hypotheses. In de Gaulle's case, we have argued that broad ideological and symbolic frameworks are the most significant clues for understanding foreign policy. The development of the Atlantic crisis came from a 'dialogue of the deaf' in which both sides spoke at cross-purposes. But de Gaulle's actions fit with his broad ideological purposes and are best explained by them. As Couve de Murville has said:

people are always astonished when someone does what he said he would do, and this applies in particular to the French government, which, unlike many other governments, seeks to have a policy and to do what it says.[200]

9

Convergence and reconciliation, 1966–9

The French withdrawal from NATO altered the fundamental circumstances of the Atlantic relationship. At a stroke, the French would *have* to be consulted over Western coordination, whether the United States liked it or not. De Gaulle's introduction of the notion of 'unprovoked aggression', which summed up the essence of the consultation issue, could not be ignored by American policy-makers. Otherwise, it was difficult to tell who had benefited more from the crisis, France or NATO. Indeed, the resulting shakeup did have beneficial (though unanticipated) side-effects. The US Ambassador to NATO during the French withdrawal assesses how the changes affected NATO's response during the 1968 Soviet invasion of Czechoslovakia:

When the Russians struck, NATO was readier for round-the-clock crisis management than it had ever been before. For one thing, when NATO's political headquarters was moved from Paris to Brussels in October 1967, the Council decided to build into the new headquarters a modern Situation Room, complete with up-to-date visual aids and serviced by a new NATO-wide communication system. And the Council's Committee of Political Advisers, in earlier times a once-a-week mutual information society, had been converted to an every-day 'watch committee' producing overnight political assessments to guide NATO's military commanders. These facilities proved their value as the allies turned immediately to consulting together about what had happened, and what it meant for Western security.[1]

But the crisis did not settle points in dispute smoothly, quickly or evenly. What it did was to remove the central and all-subsuming symbolic dispute, leaving a series of specific areas of disagreement on significant but circumscribed policy issues. Seen over time and in a different structural perspective, these issues either came to be more or less resolved, or *ceased to be seen as issues* by the two policy-making establishments. This chapter will outline the general *rapprochement* of French and American views on global issues, treat the development of certain specific issue-areas, and then look at the evolution of the international system itself and the place of Franco-American relations within it at the end of this period.

As we have seen to some extent already, the anti-Gaullist position of the Kennedy Administration (before mid-1963), which had become entrenched in the State Department, had already run into serious opposition from no less than President Johnson. After de Gaulle's ultimatum to the USA to remove her military installations and various NATO headquarters from France in February–March 1966, leading figures in the State Department – former Secretary of State Acheson, Secretary of State Rusk and Under-Secretary Ball – all urged the President to take retributive action against France. Ball's outspoken attitude, expressed in a public speech, led Johnson to order a stop to such public criticisms in the future. From 1965 onwards, Johnson was at various times advised to seek a confrontation with France over strategic or fiscal issues, and in the spring of 1965 he was asked whether the Administration might reclassify France as no longer a 'friend' or 'ally'. Johnson turned down such advice and stated that he did not feel that just because France was doing certain things that the USA preferred not to be done – her privilege as a sovereign state – that the United States should start feuding with a proud and independent leader like de Gaulle. He was supported on this issue by the American Ambassador in Paris, Charles Bohlen, who had developed a relationship of mutual respect with de Gaulle. Johnson's attitude, reported by Cyrus L. Sulzberger, who provided an important informal link between the American Administration and de Gaulle (Sulzberger was an important source of inside information on de Gaulle's foreign policy attitudes, as they had many off-the-record talks which then appeared in Sulzberger's paper, *The New York Times*, as analyses), in fact went further than a mere low profile:

He [Johnson] was grateful that France had recovered its pride and sense of nationalism. Despite any inconveniences, a stable France was a more valuable asset to the Western community than a France in which governments changed every few months.

Johnson made a point of reminding his advisers that de Gaulle stood fast beside the United States during the great Cuban showdown with Russia. He would sometimes conclude discussions by telling anti-Gaullists around that if the general 'threw his fast ball' (a simile difficult to imagine), he [Johnson] would simply 'step aside'.

Even after the NATO crisis caused by de Gaulle's expulsion order, the President insisted that the United States loved France and looked upon developments with sorrow, not with anger. He philosophically hoped that the French people would not always feel about the United States the way their government seemed to feel and that the general would find there were some burning problems he could work out with Washington.

As a matter of fact, this calm approach had already paid off prior to the current French crisis [the May Events of 1968]. Had it not been for Johnson's unflappability it is unlikely that France could have been persuaded to help initiate Vietnamese peace negotiations or that talks would have started in this city [Paris].[2]

Thus Johnson picked up his IOU.

It is interesting to note the differences between the old Democratic foreign policy establishment in Washington, all leftovers from the Kennedy era (and, in Acheson's case, of course, from the Truman era) – Rusk, Ball and Acheson – on the one hand, and the American Ambassadors in the field – Bohlen and Cleveland. Indeed, Bohlen was given an unusually cordial farewell in January 1968 by de Gaulle himself, who stated that despite 'certain feelings of friction, the capital of mutual interest, attraction and admiration between our two peoples which weighed decisively in the world's destiny on several occasions should not be impaired'.[3] And in Cleveland's view, 'the whole highly publicised affair was an elaborate charade designed for domestic political effect'. Cleveland's interpretation of de Gaulle's objectives was that NATO protection was irreplaceable, and that it should remain essentially intact; Cleveland agreed with the remark of a NATO colleague that French 'withdrawal' was a symbolic anti-American gesture 'which changed almost nothing militarily, certainly did not harm French security, yet enabled the General to crow that he had "withdrawn from NATO" – for home consumption'.[4] Thus while serious disagreement remained between the United States and France on NATO, divergences within the American policy-making establishment had already arisen as to what the *consequences* of this disagreement should be. Intra-bureaucratic rivalries had surfaced in the past, especially as regards aid to the embryonic French nuclear programme in the 1958–62 period, and they did so again in 1966. In May, the US government refused export licences for high-performance computers to France (Control Data 6600) because they might be used in the weapons programme; this was strongly resented in France, and reinforced the government's view that France ought to pursue technological independence. In the USA, however, bureaucratic skirmishing followed: 'Somebody then suggested to the French government that it disavow any intention to use the computers in weapons-connected research. This was done, and the first decision reversed.'[5]

But the changes in American foreign policy were not merely the result of the victory of a bureaucratic faction. They represented a much wider debate in the government and in American society on the American role in the world. The impetus behind this debate did not come from changes in the European arena, but, of course, in relations with the Communist nations generally, and concerning the Vietnam War in particular. The arrival of 'detente' (as even American policy-makers had already begun to call the thawing of the cold war, following the French lead) in Europe, the development of the Sino-Soviet split and the concomitant development of 'polycentrism' within the Soviet bloc system in Europe,[6] Soviet cooperation in settling the 1965 Indo-Pakistani conflict in the Tashkent agreement of January 1966, the suspension of the bombing in Vietnam in early 1966 while attempts were made to begin negotiations with the North (including the attempts of Soviet leaders, while on a visit to Britain, to facilitate communication between the two sides), the opening of negotiations for a USA–USSR Consular Treaty (completed in 1967), and the like, were all indications that detente diplomacy required an atmosphere and a style in marked contrast to cold war diplomacy. Both Couve de Murville[7] and a highly placed anonymous French commentator[8] put strong emphasis upon the importance of President Johnson's speech of 7 October 1966 in New York, in which he called for 'bridge-building' towards Eastern Europe. Couve interpreted this as ratifying the French policy of bilateral ex-changes with the East rather than bloc-to-bloc diplomacy. A factor which is said to have entered this debate, a factor which we shall meet shortly in other contexts, was the change in government in West Germany. The replacement of Erhard, mainly for internal reasons, and the accession of the 'Grand Coalition' of Christian Democrats and Social Democrats under Kiesinger (as Chancellor) and Brandt (Deputy Chancellor and Foreign Minister) led to a cautious opening to the East which presaged the full-blown post-1969 *Ostpolitik*, again a factor considered highly significant by Couve de Murville.[9]

Thus the conditions of the cold war, in which 'self-interest and inter-national do-goodism are not easily distinguishable',[10] were changing. Significant debates took place concerning the nature and consequences of these changes. These debates, however, tended to result less in solutions than in agreements to disagree. The urgency of the cold war was lacking. Professor Alastair Buchan, writing in 1974, sums up the effect of different member-states' priorities and attitudes on the post-1966 development of NATO. In the first place, the Eurogroup, an attempt by the European members to develop a forum for the working out of common postures, remains merely embryonic. NATO has thus not become the framework for an effective European–American dialogue on security questions. At the same time, the evolution of member-states' attitudes has increased resistance to the dominance of the strongest members and largest contributors; American leadership has not been effective either. Seven years passed between the American adoption of flexible response in 1962 and the Alliance's reluctant acceptance of the doctrine in 1969. And the inevitable consequence of detente, 'in which pressure or threats from the East have both diminished and become more diffused', thus reducing the priority that the USA gives to Alliance questions, and of the inability of the Alliance structure to handle the divergences of national viewpoints which have been more strongly expressed as the territorial *status quo* has crystallised and the intra-NATO balance of power has altered, has been a reinforcement of conflicting attitudes and perspectives on the part of the members:

It is not even possible to get a coherent decision on what the principal security problem in Europe now really consists of: whether it is still to deter the possibility of attack by the Soviet Union or the Warsaw Pact by maintaining a comprehensive war-fighting capability; whether it is to prevent a European crisis from acquiring a military dimension; whether it is to deter unfriendly actions outside Europe; or whether it is primarily to provide a politico-military system that by its solidarity and capacity for rapid and clear decision-making discourages adventurism wherever the interests of the NATO powers are clearly involved. The Americans in NATO tend to be preoccupied with the problems of strategic deterrence; the British with extending its interests to new areas and retaining American involvement in European security; the Germans with the danger of politico-military blackmail; the Turks and other delegations with the dangers of civil disorder or civil war; the Canadians and the Danes with domestic neutralist pressures; and so on.[11]

Thus the Atlantic Alliance, though retaining NATO with its formally integrated military structure, has, over time, reflected more and more its character as a traditional alliance or coalition of member-states, each having reasons of national interest for accepting constraints on its independent action; its originality is less and less evident.

Thus the period since 1966 has seen a separation of *strategic–political* issues, which since the 1963 Nuclear Test Ban Treaty had been limited more and more to direct Soviet–American relations – a pattern which would continue to develop until 1973–4, with Watergate, the Jackson Amendment, the Middle East and Angola slowing down the process which had reached its peak in Brezhnev's visit to Washington in 1972 – from foreign policy issues generally, in which all but some military integration slowly faded and the *norm* became the pursuit of 'national interests' so long as they did not tilt or seriously destabilise the super-power balance. The seal was set on this development in 1967–8, with the reactions to the Six-Day War and the Middle East problem generally; these were exemplified by the Johnson–Kosygin meeting in Glassboro (following which Kosygin symbolically stopped over in Paris) and the famous compromise Resolution 242, which France helped to draft, in the UN. Even before the full impact of the 1968 May Events upon France, a former high-level adviser to President Kennedy, Arthur M. Schlesinger Jr, could stress that: 'Nationalism has changed the relations between America and the Western world and Russia and the Communist world, and it has defeated both Russian and American influence in the Third World. It has emerged as the most powerful political emotion of our time.'[12] And in his short-lived attempt to obtain the 1968 Democratic presidential nomination, Robert Kennedy could call nationalism 'the most potent force in the world today', which could be either America's strong ally or her nemesis 'if we continue to ignore it'.[13]

This growing awareness within higher political circles was mirrored in the academic debate of the era, which saw the development of a 'limitationist' school of American foreign policy. Its substantive perspective involved the following: acceptance in practice, though not in principle, of the division of the world for political purposes into spheres of influence; the need for multilateral involvement (possibly under UN auspices) in both economic assistance and peacekeeping actions; and 'the expectation of a diverse and pluralist world order'.[14] Public opinion, influenced mainly by Vietnam, also reflected this changing mood. Survey researcher Louis Harris, in an article setting out 'the limits of commitment' as seen by his respondents, wrote:

The mood of the American people is to take a hard look at the limits of US military power in the world. Only a small 8 per cent want to see a larger role in the world for American military power, on the assumption that 'this is the only way in which Communism can be stopped' and 'this is the only way respect for the US can be maintained'. But more than four times this number, 34 per cent, say they would like to reduce the US military role in the world, reasoning that 'we are overextended now', 'it is too expensive to become too involved', 'others ought to solve their own problems', and 'we have suffered too many casualties already'. A majority of 51 per cent feel our present stance is as far as we ought to go.[15]

Indeed, despite many decades of socialisation into the view that the concept of the 'balance of power' was the wicked legacy of the corrupt old world, this very notion came in through the back door – through such terms as 'balance of terror', 'nuclear parity', 'sufficiency', 'deterrence', 'strategic equilibrium', and the like – to dominate the thinking of the American foreign policy establishment in the 1970s. This atmosphere became dominant in the Nixon Administration, in which Henry Kissinger, long an advocate of American accommodation with de Gaulle – at least in the European theatre – became the principal architect of foreign policy,[16] and Nixon himself, who maintained cordial relations with both de Gaulle and his successor, Pompidou,[17] explicitly recognised and approved of the broad lines of General de Gaulle's foreign policy. As Nixon stated following his European tour in February–March 1969:

I would not be betraying a confidence if I pointed out that President de Gaulle has completely set aside any anti-American position in the views which he expressed to us in great detail on the European Alliance and France's relations with it.

He believes that Europe ought to have an independent position. Frankly, so do I. I think that most Europeans believe the same thing. I think that the time is past when it was in our interest for the United States to be the predominant partner in the Alliance.

We will still be dominant because of our immense nuclear power and also because of our economic wealth. But, on the other hand, the world would be a much safer place, and from our standpoint, a much healthier place economically, militarily and politically, if there were a strong European community, to be a balance basically, a balance between the United States and the Soviet Union, rather than to have this polarisation of forces in one part of the world and another.

As for President de Gaulle, insofar as I have understood his position, he spoke very eloquently of his desire to see established a united Europe and a distinct European entity. But he disagreed with the propositions generally put forward by most of the other countries of Europe. He thinks that European unity will come about more easily, as he has stated publicly and as he told me in private, through an agreement among the big powers rather than through an assembly or a meeting of all the European powers.[18]

This shift in American policy, emphasised during Nixon's European tour, was clearly noted by French policy-makers. By 1970, under Pompidou, the French and Americans had 'agreed to disagree' on some matters, but relations were at their high point,[19] after which they would decline for a number of reasons. 1970, of course, was the year of the 'Nixon Doctrine', a time when a high-powered group of foreign policy academics could write that in future the United States would have to take into account three sorts of factors in assessing any possible case for intervention: the American sense of commitment, the American sense of interest, and the estimated possibility of success. Of course, the most significant new element was the 'sense of interest': 'Since this interest is no longer a function primarily of trading opportunities, territorial ambitions or imperialist pretensions, it is to be measured largely in terms of the sense of danger to the delicate equilibrium between the major world powers.'[20] In fact, the policy of the Nixon Administration was generally tolerant of greater latitude on the part of its allies, and did not confine this to France.[21] Thus although the main symbolic shift in American policy came with the inauguration of the Nixon Administration, the spirit of foreign policy had been undergoing a long-term change, adjusting to the new situation created by the lack of a major European conflict; this had been going on since the Berlin blockade of 1948–9, through the establishment of the nuclear balance, and in the context of America's own success (through the Marshall Plan, etc.) in helping to get the Western European nations on their own feet economically and politically in the two decades after the end of the Second World War. The Atlantic dream, that extension of the American dream, died a natural death. General de Gaulle did not cause this death. However, in the context of the 1960s, he did discern the broad lines of development which were emerging, gave NATO a nudge, and waited for the world to come round to a Gaullist perspective, mainly of its own accord.

Couve de Murville asserts that, over the long term, American policy changed most significantly – not French policy.[22] The business in hand, for the French government, was to take French withdrawal from NATO as given, and to get on with the task of making Alliance relationships run as smoothly as possible on a mixed basis of bilateral negotiations, continuing *de facto* military liaisons, and an affirmation of the underlying strength of Alliance (as distinct from NATO) ties. Later, in 1971, Michel Debré, as Minister of National Defence in the Chaban-Delmas Government, would refer to this as a policy of 'selective co-operation'.[23] The first issue was that of overflights, which were subjected to monthly scrutiny from May 1966. These new regulations did produce a 'mountain of red tape', but did not significantly affect overflight patterns; annual clearance was in fact restored in January 1968.[24] American observers attribute this change to a combination of pressures from European allies who were directly affected and the un-expected speed of American withdrawal.[25] Secondly, in his announce-ment of the French withdrawal, de Gaulle had offered to negotiate a bilateral agreement with West Germany to allow the French troops there to remain. Air units and ground-launching rocket and missile forces had to be withdrawn, because the withdrawal of American nuclear warheads, previously held by French forces under the 'two-key' system, made them redundant; their NATO role depended upon a well-developed system of 'automatic response' and could not easily be 'coordinated', but, even more fundamentally, the conditions set by the USA for their original loan 'clearly stipulated. . .that they would only be assigned to an integrated NATO mission'. Thus the French forces lost firepower several times greater than the *force de frappe* of the period.[26]

Negotiations on the status of French ground forces in Germany were delayed by the atmosphere subsequent to the French announcement, by the symbolic commitment of the Erhard Government to NATO as the only framework for German defence, and by the growing unsteadiness of that government. The fall of Erhard and the construction of the Grand Coalition was shortly followed by the signing of an agreement;[27] Couve attributes this rapid progress directly to the change in government.[28] Although the terms of the continued French presence did not entirely satisfy the Germans, it did involve a tangible French commitment to defend Germany. Negotiations between the French and SACEUR (Supreme Allied Command Europe) took place on the co-ordination of French forces in Germany with NATO in a crisis, but NATO planners did not feel that French assurances were sufficient. Thus the agreement of 21 December 1966 was purely bilateral giving French troops a 'privileged' status 'with no defined NATO role'.[29] It is a moot point as to whether the French troops are less valuable or more valuable in their independent role in Germany. If we are to believe George Ball, with the exception of the air units, the new status of French troops changed little, for even under the pre-withdrawal arrangements 'no French soldier can be given an order to make the slightest move by anyone but the French command'.

Even in case of war, troops would be placed under the operational command of SHAPE only if the French government 'deemed it necessary', under Article 5 of the North Atlantic Treaty. Consequently, for the NATO command to be able to dispose of French forces, a national decision, made by the French government, would be necessary.[30]

Indeed, it has been pointed out by a British pro-Gaullist commentator that the French commitment to maintain forces in Germany has been better kept than the British commitment, given British defence cutbacks (even as far back as 1967).[31] And direct cooperation between France and NATO continued in a number of significant areas.[32]

Despite Pompidou's claim that the French air defence system was of more immediate value than the NATO system, the French government immediately opted for participation in NADGE. 'French companies built radar components for the network, and a French general assisted in installing the warning system in Turkey. Progress was recorded, too, in coordinating French–NATO air defences.'[33] France never gave up its seat on NATO's highest political body, the North Atlantic Council, which simply adopted the practice of considering defence questions in France's absence as the Defence Planning Committee. Since 1969, France has maintained close liaison with the Eurogroup, and always maintained a high-level liaison with NATO's Military Committee, though formally a member of neither. Liaison arrangements were kept up through contacts with another member state, 'which was charged with the mission of keeping the French informed and even of reporting back French views for consideration'. Membership of several NATO organisations has been maintained, especially where research and development of military technology, useful for the French themselves, were concerned:

France has continued to participate in the following NATO agencies: the Central Europe Operating Agency, which controls a NATO oil pipeline and storage system, with headquarters in Versailles; the NATO Maintenance and Spare Parts Agency in Luxembourg; the NATO Hawk Production and Logistics Organisation, established for the Hawk antiaircraft missile, located at Rueil-Malmaison, France; the Military Agency for Standardisation in Brussels; the Advisory Group for Aerospace Research and Development in Neuilly, outside Paris; the Allied Naval Communications Agency in London; the SACLANT Anti-Submarine Warfare Research Centre in La Spezia, Italy; the Conference of National Armament Directors in Brussels; and three small organisations, the Allied Radio Frequency Agency, the Allied Long Lines Agency and the Allied Communications Security Agency, whose personnel are drawn from the NATO International Military Staff in Brussels. France also displayed great interest in the NATO Integrated Communications System, but finally did not accept membership.[34]

Finally, French cooperation extended to various NATO military and naval exercises well before the 1968 invasion of Czechoslovakia, although prior to that time, such cooperation tended to remain 'discreet and unpublished, since the French officers did not want to present an open challenge to Gaullist theory', writes Goodman, 'while NATO commanders were pleased to get French cooperation on any terms that, in practice, were often surprisingly good'. Later, this cooperation became more open. Close liaison between the two French divisions in Germany and the NATO forces in Central Europe developed rapidly in this key sector. 'When MARAIRMED, a NATO command to improve air surveillance of Soviet activity in the Mediterranean, was activated in November 1968, French air reconnaissance squadrons informed NATO of their flight plans and of results obtained.'[35] In the autumn of 1968, French admirals actually commanded joint NATO exercises in the Mediterranean in which French naval and air units participated and took responsibility for surveillance over Soviet movements in the area. The French air force took on the defensive role against other NATO countries in exercises in 1971, and French troops in Germany conducted joint exercises with American troops.[36] Indeed, the commander of the US Sixth Fleet could remark that, although the French navy was not committed to an integrated NATO command in time of war, French withdrawal 'had brought little change in close cooperation between French and NATO naval operations in the Mediterranean'.[37]

Certainly, French non-cooperation continued in key symbolic areas – the areas which characterised the period leading up to the 1966 crisis: control of the military nuclear programme; silence on the French commitment to join NATO in a European war; and silence on willingness to use French troops to strengthen NATO's front-line defences. It is highly significant that these areas were those which remained under sole *presidential* control,[38] reflecting the central role the presidency had come to play as the locus of accountability for decisions which would actually engage the French defence machine in any real conflict, a point which lay at the heart of Gaullist ideology. Indeed, in late 1968, the French put out feelers to the American government about restoring French access to US nuclear warheads in Germany (about which the actual NATO response and the French counter-response are in doubt because of the sensitivity of the French government to the issue).[39] And two important Gaullist personalities, Pierre Messmer and Alexandre Sanguinetti (a former minister), reaffirmed France's loyalty to the Alliance in late 1968, Sanguinetti claiming that despite France's reducing defence budget over the 1960s, France was contributing the greatest number of effectives, both in absolute numbers and in proportion to the population, of any Western European ally.[40] In 1970, Debré reaffirmed France's position:

At a time when struggles take the form of conflicts of civilisations, it is normal that a country like ours should need alliances. . .that should be prized.

These alliances can lead to close understandings. They can justify in certain circumstances unified commands in certain theatres of operation. But from this necessity one should never conclude as to the value of permanent integrations which have no other object than to impose on France the strategy of dominant powers.

The Army remains solely at the disposal of the national government, which must retain the mastery of strategy – otherwise there is no longer any nation.[41]

This position is, then, as clear as it can be under the circumstances. And it is becoming clearer as more specific examples of its functioning become discernible. It is now accepted that to all intents and purposes French forces, though not integrated into NATO, can be included in measurements of the strength of the Alliance. In de Gaulle's words of 1963, the underlying danger inherent in the atomic age 'justifies both alliance and independence'.[42]

The balance which de Gaulle saw developing between the Soviet Union and the United States in the 1960s was not one which required a reversal of alliances. It merely required, for France and for Europe, 'shifting the centre of influence of the alliance blocs on European policy', an objective in which a stronger France with a minimal nuclear deterrent would be sufficient.[43] And the various subtle balances necessary to achieve the overall objective – the various elements of French foreign policy – had all crystallised by the late 1960s; France became less and less interested in shifting the overall equilibrium of East–West relations in Europe, 'however much it pressed for greater diplomatic, cultural, economic, scientific and technical exchanges between all European states'.[44] It was the very overall balance which, in the French view, should make such exchanges possible. Indeed, significant domestic pressures, not linked with the May Events of 1968, reinforced this view. One of the main undercurrents of justification for the strategic changes characterising the switch to the FNS had always been the need to reintegrate the French Army into society after the incredibly alienating Algerian experience. Military techniques were changing, and, despite sacrifices, it was seen as necessary to adapt to 'modern times', consistent with and relevant to 'the preoccupations of the age. . . Thus it will contribute to the development of the sense of collective values.'[45] The FNS had its internal ideological rationale as well as its external technological rationale. The mood of the army, pleased at first with its new toy, the FNS, was in flux in the late 1960s, disillusioned with the breadth of the government's nuclear ambitions when measured against practical problems like delays, shortages, and budget cuts, and looking for an answer in closer practical cooperation with NATO, though not a return to full integration.[46] In addition, public opinion was opposed to withdrawal from the Atlantic Alliance, and that opposition grew from 54 per cent in October 1967 to 74 per cent in April–May 1969.[47] Therefore, by the late 1960s, the momentum behind the more innovative aspects of French policy had declined.

The withdrawal from NATO in 1966 and the subsequent readjustments thus marked the apogee of Gaullist 'maverick' behaviour over the Atlantic question, and did not mark the first stages of a longer process designed to give France totally 'free hands' in the world. Indeed, it is not clear just how committed de Gaulle was to the radical policy of multi-directional defence (*défense tous azimuts*) officially adopted in 1968 and apparently aimed at the USA as well as the USSR. This doctrine, developed by General Ailleret in his official capacity as Chief of the French General Staff,[48] was the logical outcome of the philosophy which Ailleret had been propounding since the early 1960s, when this 'father of the *force de frappe*' – known as '*le général presse-bouton*' (General Pushbutton)[49] – was involved in the interservice rivalries which characterised the post-Algerian reintegration epoch. He won out in this competition because of his strong championing of the nuclear solution. Although de Gaulle officially set his seal on the new doctrine in early 1968, up to that point official French spokesmen 'had been maintaining that Général Ailleret was only speaking for himself' in his famous article.[50] It has been claimed, further, that although the doctrine may have been approved in principle, no decision was taken to carry out the necessary measures to make it effective.[51] The actual infighting which took place will remain obscure,[52] but it is a fact that following Ailleret's death in an air crash in March 1968, his successor as Chief of Staff was not committed to the *tous-azimuts* strategy, and it was officially replaced in early 1969.[53] Indeed, an official study group noted a *rapprochement* of strategic concepts between France and the USA – both a nuclearisation of the McNamara doctrine, due partly to European reservations about the wider implications of 'flexible response' (which was not officially adopted by NATO until 1969), and the introduction of various degrees of flexible response into official French doctrine.[54] Thus the main difference was no longer one of kind, but one of degree – the identification of the nuclear 'threshold' when various kinds of nuclear weapons could be brought into use. The main impact of the FNS in this context was still seen as psychological deterrence, rather than total independence or equality with the superpowers.

This *rapprochement* between France and the United States over the

NATO issue mirrored their overall *rapprochement* which has already been described and which extended into various other areas where US policy was changing. As a result of lack of military success and the force of domestic public opinion, President Johnson, in his 'abdication' speech of 31 March 1968, called a partial halt to the bombing of North Vietnam and began the process which later led to the long, drawn-out peace talks in Paris. Couve de Murville cites this as a major factor in immediately improving Franco-American relations.[55] American monetary policy also underwent some change in the period, and French policy moved closer to a compromise on this highly sensitive symbolic issue.[56] In fact, it has been suggested that although de Gaulle stressed the role of gold in his public pronouncements on the monetary system, he had always been more flexible in practice.[57] It might be inferred that these policies should be seen in the context of overall Franco-American relationships, insofar as they progressed from being symbolic positions of principle to becoming specific disagreements over the means of reforming a system under great pressure, once the broad structure of Franco-American relations had been clarified after the 1966 crisis.[58] Franco-German relations, which had been soured primarily by differences over the proper relationship between France and Germany (and Europe), on the one hand, and the United States on the other, improved considerably after the change of government in Germany in late 1966 combined with the changing of American policy over relations between the West and Eastern Europe.[59] American policy towards China, which the French saw as aggravating China's fears for her own security,[60] began, especially under the Nixon Administration, to come closer to the French view, which saw China's intentions as 'more nationalist than ideological', marked by 'the ambition to return China to an eminent role within her traditional sphere' combined with her 'fear of encirclement'.[61] In fact, Franco-Chinese relations, while cordial on several basic points, were never idyllic,[62] and came to be overshadowed by the Kissinger–Nixon opening to the Far East. On the question of relations with the Soviet Union, French awareness of Soviet military strength underlay her prudent policy which paralleled the political detente. De Gaulle regularly pressured the Soviet leadership, even during his 1966 visit as well as on more normal diplomatic occasions, to moderate its hard line on the German question, especially after the Grand Coalition made its first small steps towards an *Ostpolitik*. One American journalist, writing on the limits of de Gaulle's overtures to the USSR, wrote in March 1968 that 'his behaviour shows that he knows that the cold reality of Soviet power and policy places definite limits on his activities in Europe, the only place that truly matters to Gaullist France'.[63]

The Middle East problem was complicated by the impact of domestic pro-Israeli response to de Gaulle's arms embargo policy adopted at the time of the June 1967 war and to some remarks which de Gaulle made shortly thereafter which were interpreted as anti-Semitic.[64] In this area, French and American policies have gone through periods of *rapprochement* and further divergence since 1967, along with the political flux of the region itself. The French call for a four-power settlement did make some ground on all sides, but especially with the Arab states and the Soviet Union, and the American search in the late 1960s for a more 'even-handed' Middle East policy reduced their conflict with the French. In the 1970s, the changed balance of power in the region altered the situation. Not only did the oil crisis accompanying the Yom Kippur War in 1973 lead to a more pro-Arab stance by all the West European powers (through the EEC), but, para-doxically, French policy in the region was aimed more at containing Soviet power than American at a time when the former was more firmly implanted in the Arab countries than the latter. The French ambition to become a recognised *regional* power, with important Mediterranean political and economic interests, made much headway.[65] Regional interests and international standing – the latter symbolised by French membership of the UN Security Council – combined in a circular French diplomatic perspective in which each role reinforced the other.[66]

An area in which French and American policies continued to diverge, but which was defused and did not remain such a bone of contention, was arms control and disarmament. The 1963 Test Ban Treaty had been at the centre of a major storm between Kennedy and de Gaulle. France's refusal to sign the 1968 Nuclear Non-Proliferation Treaty (NPT), however, was received in Washington with regret but resignation. Couve de Murville has set out the official reasons for France's refusal to sign, when she had only just signed the treaty on the peaceful utilisation of space in January 1967:

France did not oppose either of these two treaties [in fact, she announced publicly her intention to abide by the terms of the non-proliferation treaty]. She signed the first [on space] because it imposed the same obligations on all signa-tories, nuclear or not. She refused to sign the second obligation because the situation was different...What our country did not accept was that the Giants could claim that the others had recognised their monopoly without having to offer anything from their side in the way of a will to disarm. Neither did we accept that such decisions should be taken à deux, just to be virtually imposed on third parties for their signatures – including France.[67]

This was consistent with the perennial French insistence that disarmament talks demanded a 'big power' – rather than merely a superpower – framework. The French view was that nuclear arms control treaties reduced the potential influence of the smaller states without really affecting the balance of terror and leading towards real peace. Thus superpower disarmament was seen as a *precondition* of the acceptance of self-denying ordinances (like the NPT) by the smaller states. And any such disarmament was inextricably intertwined with detente – with the achieving of progress in the solution of the pressing political problems facing states, like the division of Europe or the German question. As Kolodziej writes: 'For France, disarmament proceeded first through detente; for the superpowers, detente developed initially through arms control followed perhaps at some distant period by disarmament.'[68]

In the two cases of Middle East policy and arms control policy, the French approached the possibility of a solution through the framework of a 'directorate' of the major powers involved – much broader than any superpower 'condominium', but much narrower than any system which would be representative of the range of states in the international system. This recalls the 1958 NATO memorandum and its sequels, as well as de Gaulle's proposals for neutralising South-East Asia and controlling conflict there in the mid-1960s.[69]

Other areas which had been symbolically prominent in the mid-1960s were also defused, though not always settled – e.g. the collapse shortly after de Gaulle's resignation in 1969 of the policy of producing electricity from natural uranium and basing the entire nuclear programme on natural or home-enriched uranium,[70] or the policy of restricting American investments in France. This latter policy, which had only started in 1962 (and limped through such setbacks as the Machines Bull Affair, where a leading French computer firm was refused permission to be taken over by one American firm only to be taken over by another when financial difficulties worsened three years later) was reversed, though formally on only a selective basis, upon Debré's return to the government as Finance Minister in 1966.[71] One area in which conflict actually worsened was that of the Common Market, where American solidarity with the Five against France on a range of issues often connected with Atlantic ties was replaced with French solidarity within the Six (and later the Nine) over a series of questions. America feared European economic and commercial competition generally, felt that the CAP was protectionist and discriminated against US farm products, believed that the extension of Europe's preferential trading agreements with the Third World undermined the principle of free trade, and resented Europe's reluctance to fall in line with American reactions to the Yom Kippur War and oil and energy policy in general. Dr Kissinger's 'Year of Europe' (1973) tended primarily to highlight US–European differences, although it did push France into closer cooperation with her European partners at the time. Therefore, with the growing exception of the EEC, Franco-American divergences over a wide range of specific policy issues tended to become 'normalised' and to some extent defused in the late 1960s and early 1970s.

In the longer perspective, there is some evidence that the symbolic nature of the Franco-American conflict over Atlantic questions disguised the fact that, under the surface, relations had never deviated very far from the 'normal'. According to a study of France and China as 'alliance mavericks', little change is found in French actions over different issue-areas between the Fourth and Fifth Republics; the authors found 'some deterioration in cordiality in the security issue-area', but overall stability in French ties with her allies (including the United States). Ties with Communist countries increased, with only a brief gap in 1968 (following the Soviet invasion of Czechoslovakia), but these ties were in addition to, not in place of, ties with the West. In fact, 'during the Fifth Republic the number of French agreements with the United States has shown an increase in proportion to those with other partners, and in no issue-area has there been a significant decline in agreements between Paris and Washington'. This normalcy can be partially explained by the very fact that Franco-American conflict took place in the ethereal regions of high policy rhetoric. Although high-level communication was not good, other formal and informal channels of communication remained:

One significant barrier against a complete French break from its alliance exists in the many national and international organisations – governmental, semi-governmental and private – through which French elites can communicate with their top counterparts in allied nations...Such organisations tend to generate multiple interests and loyalties which cut across national boundaries, as well as across issues.[72]

Furthermore, de Gaulle's 'anti-Americanism' was no pathological hatred, but simply a logical deduction from his view of the 'nature of things':

In truth, de Gaulle did not accuse the United States, *a priori*, of having an ideological will to power. He considered that the dynamism of the USA, her power of industrial expansion, her physical strength, and her richness, provided the vehicle for a *de facto* imperialism, because that was the nature of things. The logic of that conjuncture led the Americans, pushed by a missionary sentiment, animated by the consciousness of their responsibilities, to exercise a *de facto* domination over the world, contrary to their own philosophy.[73]

His immediate goal was to give the Americans a jolt, to force them to take account of and to comprehend non-American yet Western and liberal ways of seeing the contemporary world – to get them out of the strait-jacket of the 'free world' in which nations, states and governments are good or bad insofar as they support an anti-Communist foreign policy, and into a situation of awareness of a plurality of standpoints. In this task, de Gaulle was aided by wider changes in the structure of international relations, as Professor Buchan observes:

Some of the great objectives of Gaullist policy, the loosening of the bipolar world, increasing contact with Eastern Europe and with China, have been largely achieved, though as much by the actions of other powers as by France, and the value of a special French relationship with the Soviet Union now looks more dubious than five years ago, especially as it is overtaken by Soviet–American intimacy.[74]

In fact, in pushing the United States to see the world more in terms of 'national interests', de Gaulle in some ways heightened American perception of its *own* power and its need to serve its *own* interests rather than those of the 'free world'. Before the advent of President Carter's Human Rights offensive, which has made Soviet–American relations far more problematic again, an even closer condominium at the highest strategic level seemed to be in the making. Other negotiations could be broadened to include the European allies (the MBFR force-reduction talks), or even the whole gamut of European states (the European Conference on Security and Cooperation), but the Strategic Arms Limitation Talks (SALT) are strictly superpower business. Thus there is little sign of the five permanent UN Security Council members taking on a general brief to sort out world problems. And there is also little sign that cooperation among West European states can provide a strong and independent foreign policy voice in the world, as hoped for by such Gaullist spokesmen as Chaban-Delmas and Couve de Murville.

If, as Galtung suggests, a 'new superpower' is emerging in Western Europe,[75] it is not a political superpower with a unified diplomatic voice, but an economic giant, whose voice reflects the deepening division between the developed world in general and the huge, under-developed 'periphery'.

Yet the blocs *have* been eroded, by economic processes as well as strategic–diplomatic (including nuclear) developments. Power centres have emerged 'of different strengths and interests, and in which ideo-logical differences can, within limits, be overridden by other considera-tions'.[76] Power itself has become more complex, eliminating the possi-bility of a return to traditional balance of power politics, because there are quite different balances to take into account at different levels. As Buchan writes:

Only the Soviet Union and the United States are both great military and great industrial powers; China can exert influence on both of them and in certain other areas as well, but in economic terms is still a developing country; Japan is the world's third most powerful economic state but has only the military capacity to defend her home islands from conventional attack; Europe, though both economically powerful and heavily armed, has yet to acquire the institutions to take political, strategic or even major economic decisions centrally.[77]

And although war is no longer acceptable as a regulator of the system – thus reducing one of the central traditional forms of upholding order in an international system – ideological differences are still alive and generating perceptions of threat and, indeed, real conflicts. Therefore the bloc system has been replaced by various triangular relationships on different levels – economic power, political influence, strategic power. These levels overlap and interact, producing a cross-cutting inter-national system of unprecedented complexity, in which stability depends upon the development of general rules, accepted roles, recog-nised symbols and rituals, and a range of adjustment mechanisms which can resolve conflicts.[78] The system is becoming a society in which the wisdom of earlier periods – as recent as the cold war – has become inappropriate.

The postwar vision, which kept the peace, to some extent at least, has turned out to be insufficient. As Raymond Aron has said of the men who created this vision: 'Walking backward into the future, statesmen were inclined to believe that the North Atlantic Pact would prevent the next war since, had it existed, it would have prevented the previous one.'[79] De Gaulle perceived and exploited most of the major weaknesses of the postwar system, and developed a vision of his own of the future, in which the great nation-states, combining diplomatic, strategic and economic strength, but not narrowly confined to rigid bipolarism nor ideological strait-jackets – and aware of a plurality of forces and interests – would together reconcile their interests in an enlightened and rational manner. But he did not foresee the multidimensional nature of the plurality which would succeed the bloc system, and which would require a wider range of *ad hoc* responses and solutions than he envisioned, even within NATO itself, the centre of the storm. It is unfortunate that the critical response to de Gaulle has generally missed the mark. To one school, he tried to destroy the free world with his delusions of grandeur; to another, grandeur was merely the outward disguise of advanced capitalism and neo-colonialism. Both are partly right, but de Gaulle's grand design went further, based on the resurgence of a more responsible and extensive form of national legitimacy than the world had known before, and he tried to influence the evolution of structures to take this force into account – and to harness it to his supreme task, the stabilisation of the French polity and the construction of a French state capable of effectively pursuing the general interest of the French nation and people.

10

The impact of Gaullist policy on political change in France: consensus-building and the routinisation of authority

The foreign policy goals pursued by General de Gaulle during his eleven years of power in France (1958–69) were important not merely for their ideological content, nor for their impact upon the world of international relations alone, but also for the role they played as potent and flexible symbols in deepening the receptiveness of the French public to national-identity stimuli and associating the consciousness of membership in the national community with the establishment of new political institutions based on the 1958 Constitution. This chapter will consider the hypothesis that there occurred a spill-over of affect from the salient and charismatic Gaullist pursuit of *grandeur* to the then embryonic (and today still developing) political system of the Fifth Republic.

The most significant test of such an hypothesis may be found in the reaction of the various components of the domestic political system to the intentions and practices of de Gaulle's foreign policy. However, the search for relevant evidence encounters certain difficulties. In the first place, any political leader's control over goal-formulation or policy-making practice does not necessarily imply that he can control the reactions of mass or elite publics. Attempts at manipulation are often self-defeating, and attempts to follow rather than to lead public opinion often merely recreate the atmosphere of earlier times or focus on problems which are transparently contrived. In the second place, the range of evidence which might potentially be called upon is enormous. Any minor speech, party dispute, voting shift and so on might involve implications deriving from images and beliefs about the nature of the national community, while at the same time *overt* questions of foreign policy do not receive a high priority as far as the mass public is concerned. Therefore, while a great mass of material may be potentially relevant, its relevance will normally be marginal or peripheral, and its interpretation will have to be based upon the reading of implications and nuances. Given these limitations, the most that can be expected from an enquiry of this sort will be an explanatory structure which is mainly suggestive, nebulous, and the coherence of which may exist more in the mind of the analyst than in any self-evident tendencies in the evidence.

Despite these necessary qualifications, it would seem that a fairly plausible case can be constructed that de Gaulle's foreign policy has played a significant, if not primordial, role in creating the conditions for change in the French political system and in maintaining the main thrust of that change in the ongoing politics of the Fifth Republic. The French public has been extraordinarily responsive to the ideas of *grandeur* and independence as manifested in the public image and actions of General de Gaulle himself. Such response would seem to have spilled over into the processes of institutional socialisation and authority legitimation. And French political elites, which fought de Gaulle on the battleground of both institutions and foreign policy in the early years of the Fifth Republic, have been led by pressure from below as well as from above to accept both of these phenomena as integral parts of a working political consensus in France in more recent years. These, taken together, seem to point to a fairly plausible case. Indeed, such a situation is not without precedent in contemporary French history; observers have asserted that foreign policy was a significant factor in maintaining the 'Republican synthesis' of the Third Republic.[1] In this chapter we shall first look at the bases of Gaullist foreign policy consensus and the way in which it developed, and then turn to the implications of this consensus for the 'routinised' political processes of the Fifth Republic.

I. Foreign Policy, Authority and the Changing Context of French Politics

Kissinger has identified two levels of support which a foreign policy must achieve in the domestic arena: 'the problem of legitimising a policy *within* the governmental apparatus, which is a problem of bureaucratic rationality; and that of harmonising it with the national experience, which is a problem of historical development'.[2] For de Gaulle the first level of support was less of a problem. The increased power of the executive branch in the Fifth Republic, combined with the political circumstances which made de Gaulle not only President of the Republic but also, especially after 1962, leader of a plebiscitary majority, an electoral plurality and a parliamentary majority, had a particular significance in the field of foreign affairs – the cornerstone of the 'presidential sector' or 'reserved domain' within which presidential primacy was explicitly recognised by Gaullists and many others. This is not to say that there was a uniform process of bureaucratic steamrolling, as resistances persisted and differences of opinion arose – especially in those areas where tangible resources had to be committed in order to pursue presidential options (as with defence or foreign aid) or in those areas where domestic opposition took more concrete forms (e.g. the opposition of agricultural pressure groups to the 1965 French boycott of the EEC). On the whole, however, the broad presidential options prevailed, and were often internalised by bureaucratic actors, if only because they increased the influence and prestige of those actors both at home and abroad.

The problem of harmonising Gaullist foreign policy with the national experience was more complex. Many areas of ideological continuity with pre-existing foreign policies and national self-images could be pointed to. But the aspect of the problem which is most significant for this analysis concerns the influence of foreign policy and foreign policy symbolism on the legitimation of presidential authority. On the one hand, the President of the Republic has always been credited with greater power and influence in the diplomatic sphere than in domestic affairs.[3] However, this influence existed somehow in *isolation* from power or authority in general. It was a particular exception which was a residue of the power of the monarch. And indeed, previous attempts at widening the scope of presidential powers had been regarded, for historically arguable reasons, as counter-revolutionary (in the context of 1789, of course) and therefore anti-Republican. The literature on the structural–functional significance of crisis authority – as an occasional resource in the face of the fragility of "routine authority" [4] – is large, and is one of the best-known parts of the conventional wisdom on French political history.[5]

As far as foreign policy was concerned, national unity was for the most part associated with either the rhetoric and practice of 'heroic leaders', whether in power (the Bonapartes, Clemenceau) or out of power (Boulanger),[6] or the extreme nationalism of (often anti-system) oppositions.[7] Thus it was a part of the accepted wisdom of French political culture that a strong political authority with a nationalist message was bound to be either dictatorial (if in power) or sufficiently anti-democratic to be kept out of power by its inherent unpopularity. The exception, as we have said, was crisis authority, which was seen as functional:

In part, the way in which change is thereby introduced is often still in conformity with the basic values of France's style of authority: the avoidance of face-to-face relations and the preference for homeorhetic change, as if the authorities to whom power had been given by and for the crisis understood exactly the nature, conditions and limits of the power delegated. In part, the structure and values of French authority relations are so firm that a crisis leader's attempt to change the style of authority away from the model described by (Michel) Crozier or to produce non-homeorhetic social change would end in fiasco.[8]

It was this vicious circle – which, in de Gaulle's view, prevented France from having a true state and a real policy-making capacity (or actual *politique*) – which the General saw himself as being historically required to break. He believed that the defects in French political life resulted from the combination of underlying cleavages with unique historical events – the dissolution of the Chamber of Deputies by the President of the Republic, Marshal MacMahon in 1877, for example – and that this very fact provided the key to change as well as the origins of immobility. To break the circle required a critical realignment of *existing* forces.

Whether the leader's role is determining in such a change may be more a function of image and perspective than a true reflection of the complexity of the real world, but its symbolic function is no less significant. It is the glass through which the world comes to be perceived. According to Edelman, the key symbolic function of the leader is 'the creation of law and regularity and personal planning where accident, chaos and impersonality are feared'. However much we speak about a 'government of laws and not of men', historians must focus on 'culture heroes' who 'established the laws and sustained them'. He goes on to suggest that leadership symbols may be even more powerful a factor in the re-creation and inculcation of historical meaning than in explaining contemporary political behaviour: Franklin Roosevelt's introduction of the Lend–Lease programme in 1940 was not merely a factor which automatically increased his personal authority, though it did have that effect, but its controversial nature was widely perceived. (Arbitrary and unconstitutional? A sellout of the national interest?) However, 'As time passes, the lend–lease agreement grows less controversial, coming to stand for effective leadership and correct judgment, for we read our knowledge of Pearl Harbour and a successful war back into it.'[9] It is the *image* of the leader's action which develops and becomes accepted wisdom over time which is important in understanding his symbolic function. Such an image can be manipulated by the construction of symbolic 'scenarios' which tell a story that can be quite different from the story as understood by critics who concentrate on 'information' rather than on symbolic meaning.[10] General de Gaulle's comment is relevant here: 'De Gaulle interests me only as an historical personality.' In looking at the meaning of this role, and the perception of that meaning by the public, the test is whether the role (or the image which has come to be held of this role) symbolises the resolution of the well-known cleavages between authority and democracy, and between the nation and the state, which are usually seen to characterise French political historiography.

In this sense, we have gone beyond the question of asking whether de Gaulle was a 'charismatic' leader as such, for the concept of charisma is one which is essentially romantic. De Gaulle's 'historical personality' was not just there as if by magic; it was, as we have already pointed out, manufactured. Its scenarios were meticulously constructed. And the dividing line between charisma and a manufactured personality cult is a fine one to draw. The key to leadership lies not in charisma, or even something called 'leadership' if this is understood as a characteristic or quality of the individual – something he possesses or does not possess at all times and places. Rather, leadership is situational: 'It is always defined by a specific situation and is recognised in the response of followers to individual acts and speeches. *If they respond favourably and follow, there is leadership; if they do not, there is not*' (my italics).[11]

This is particularly true of de Gaulle's leadership. Jean Charlot describes explanations based on charisma as 'vulgar', and open to a major objection: 'the periods when General de Gaulle's popularity was in eclipse'.[12] Tucker stresses the importance of looking at a leader's charismatic qualities *before* he achieves power;[13] in de Gaulle's case, his popularity prior to his return to power 'varied according to the political circumstances of the day'. These circumstances came to favour him at the beginning of 1958, but this was 'due much less to the grace of his charisma than to the insufficiencies and the failures of the Fourth Republic'.[14] As Charlot goes on to demonstrate, de Gaulle's popularity continued to vary with political circumstances throughout his presidency. Its regularly high level – for France – was not dissimilar to normal levels of popularity achieved by British Prime Ministers and American Presidents. Charlot notes that the popularity of British and American executives sometimes falls lower – between 30 and 40 per cent – than de Gaulle's ever did; but he explains this, in the British case at least, by the Prime Minister's 'constant competition with the leader of the Opposition, which is not the case in France, given the lack of a dominant figure and the lack of unity among the opposition',[15] in the 1960s.

Rather than being (as Schweitzer has asserted) 'the outstanding example of a Caesarist leader in our time',[16] de Gaulle's position in public opinion would seem to exhibit the characteristics normal in a modern liberal–democratic system with a strong and salient executive. Indeed, what extraordinary popularity de Gaulle received was rather rapidly 'routinised'. According to Charlot, various quantitative indicators converge in establishing a distinction between two different 'epochs' in de Gaulle's resonance in public opinion: the 'Algerian' period, lasting from 1958 to April 1962, 'during which General de Gaulle, as the leader of national union, was regularly supported by 6 or 7 Frenchmen out of 10 and opposed by 2 out of 10'; and the subsequent period, leading up to his resignation after defeat in the April 1969 referendum, 'during which de Gaulle appeared more and more as a leader of a majority'. In this latter period, Gaullist support dropped by about 10 per cent overall, while opposition to him grew as much. 'The two curves approached each other while keeping a characteristic symmetrical shape – which leads one to think that "satisfied" respondents were not prompted by motives essentially different from those of "dissatisfied" ones.'[17] It was this process which de Gaulle was most probably referring to in his well-known conversation with Malraux after the 1969 defeat, when the former President told his long-time collaborator that he had had a 'contract' with the French people, a contract which was broken (he did not specifiy just when) thus leading him to appoint Pompidou as Prime Minister – and thus leading Malraux to wonder why de Gaulle considered this contract broken as early as 1962![18]

After 1962, furthermore, the relative curves of de Gaulle's popularity and the popularity of the Government come to move in tandem – with presidential popularity normally 10–15 per cent higher than that of the Government, but the difference varying according to the issues of the day. According to Charlot, the President's distance from daily economic and social problems gave him an advantage over the Government;

'on the other hand, his popularity was more sensitive to the international situation and to crises, internal or external, which called into
question the authority of the state and the stability of the regime'.[19]
In fact, in terms of academic images of political rationality, the public's
judgment of de Gaulle was highly political. The members of a sample
surveyed by Philip Converse and Georges Dupeux replied to the
question 'What pleases you, and what displeases you, about General
de Gaulle?' in a way which supports Charlot's analysis.[20] While 47.5
per cent of Gaullist sympathisers referred primarily to the General's
personal qualities, '60 per cent of the references to personality dealt
with "public" qualities (attributed to de Gaulle)'. Charlot elaborates
upon these findings:

[These public references mentioned] his patriotism, his disinterest, his honesty –
while American voters favourable to Eisenhower, for example, put the accent on
his 'private' qualities – intelligence, physique, education, religious beliefs – or
were content with vague declarations of sympathy. Thus, confidence in de Gaulle,
although personal in nature, was nonetheless political. Neither was it blind: in
August 1958, according to IFOP [the French Institute of Public Opinion], 83 per
cent of the French had confidence in him to make the Army obey; 70 per cent to
reform the constitution; 68 per cent to settle the Algerian question; 67 per cent
to improve the international position of France; 61 per cent to restore national
unity; and only 44 per cent to resolve economic questions. This already shows
the range of Gaullism in public opinion: its peaks – institutions, colonial policy,
foreign policy – but also its troughs – economic and social policy.[21]

Thus the specific areas in which support for de Gaulle was firmest were
those most closely linked with the 'presidential domain' – those areas in
which de Gaulle himself sought to set his action apart and infuse it with
the prestige and mystique of the 'supreme authority', guiding the
national destiny, and furthest removed from the day-to-day politics of
resource allocation. Indeed, as we shall see, support for de Gaulle's
foreign policy actually rises during his later years in office, going against
the broad but gradual downward trend of his overall popularity over
the years.

The significant aspect of de Gaulle's support, then, is not that it
reflected personal charisma of a romantic kind, nor did it represent
merely a kind of extraordinary support for the traditional French
practitioner of 'crisis authority' (the latter having faded by the middle
of 1962). Rather, it represented a fairly clear appreciation of the issues
– and, particularly, of the issues which were considered central and
salient by de Gaulle himself. His popularity was not a transient
phenomenon, but the beginnings of a changing perception of what was

'normal' in French politics, towards a focus on the normality – and thus the legitimation and routinisation – of a kind of differentiated authority exercised by de Gaulle, as President of the Republic, in a regular, more or less constitutional manner. He no longer represented just another exception, just another lone figure seeking to change the entire context of French political life by himself (though he may have projected himself into such a role at times), but rather the development of a new context.

That new context had deep roots. It had deep roots, especially, in public opinion about institutions. In 1945, a majority of respondents to an opinion survey favoured the election of the President of the Republic by universal suffrage, and respondents to a survey in Paris in 1944 strongly supported the reinforcement of the executive power.[22] Thus despite the preference of postwar voters for the Communist Party (PCF), the Socialist Party (SFIO) and the MRP – support which rested mainly on considerations of social and economic policy and which *coexisted* with the preference that de Gaulle remain as head of the executive[23] – and despite the defeat for Gaullist opposition to the Fourth Republic constitution in the October 1946 referendum, a large reservoir of latent support for institutional change already existed. On the eve of the 1965 presidential elections, 78 per cent of respondents supported direct election of the President by universal suffrage, and this proportion rose to 81 per cent in May–June 1969.[24]

There were deep roots in party politics, too. The basis of support for a pro-Gaullist bloc was laid in the late 1940s. In November 1947, 35 per cent of voters were prepared to vote for the RPF should general elections have taken place. The combined Socialist and Communist bases of support (remember that the two parties were mutually antagonistic at the time because of the cold war) totalled only 42 per cent of the electorate. Charlot's description is incisive:

Only MRP leaders and voters blocked the return of General de Gaulle to power. If the anticipated legislative elections had taken place in November or December 1947, after the Gaullist surge in the municipal elections (earlier in that year), then the process which got underway in May–June 1958 (when de Gaulle did return to power) would quite certainly have begun eleven years earlier. Public opinion – if not the political elites – was ready; IFOP asked 'If there were only two blocs in France, one made up of the supporters of General de Gaulle and the other of his opponents, for which of these two blocs would you feel most sympathy?' In June 1947 the Gaullists reached 40 per cent, and by September 1948 they had risen to 43 per cent; the anti-Gaullists stayed at the same level, 33–34 per cent, and the undecideds fell from 27 to 23 per cent. These are astonishing figures, which seem to foreshadow the balance of political forces in the Fifth Republic: 40–44 per cent for the majority, 32–33 per cent for the hard-core anti-Gaullist left, and the rest for the centre which does not want to have to choose and the '*marais*' which is not interested in the debate. This analysis is confirmed by the survey taken by IFOP on the voting support for the various parties in February–March 1952, after the elections of June 1951.[25]

This situation was also reflected in a survey taken in September 1958. When asked: 'If General de Gaulle took up the leadership of a political party, would you vote for that party?', 46 per cent replied 'probably' or 'certainly' yes, 30 per cent 'probably' or 'certainly' no, and 24 per cent did not reply. Charlot's thesis is, of course, that 'the end of the regime of parties which was sought by General de Gaulle came about through the creation and maintenance of a Gaullist party, which he did not want'.[26] But whether he wanted it or not, he recognised its impor-tance as early as 1947 – when he founded the *Rassemblement du peuple français* (RPF) – although it was not until he came to power in 1958 (and indeed until he had resolved the Algerian crisis in 1962) that the process of 'routinisation' could really get underway. This process involved a threefold strategy of institutional structuring (the 1958 constitution), the creation of a majority party, and the spreading of a national ideology – *grandeur* and independence.

This new context of French political life was also characterised by social change, which is too complex a subject to go into in any depth here. Several elements combined to link this process with the consoli-dation of the new regime.[27] The triumph of the Gaullist party in 1958 was not merely a change in office-holders, but the coming to power of a 'counter-elite' which was the culmination of a process of *embourgeoise-ment* among French social and political elites generally.[28] At the same time, the Converse–Dupeux model of low partisanship among French voters combined with high issue-orientation[29] gave way in the 1960s to a surge in partisan identification, particularly among the Gaullists and the more ideological (usually called 'extreme') left-wing groups.[30] The Gaullist party (called the UNR from 1958–67, and the UDR until 1977) rapidly developed into a 'catch-all' party,[31] weighted, to be sure, towards traditional right-wing bases of support (e.g. women, the middle classes, etc.). but gaining significant levels of support in all social strata.[32] In particular, although the Gaullists reinforced their support in traditionally right-wing areas characterised by economic decline, they also gained strength in traditionally left-wing areas characterised by economic modernisation,[33] drawing much support from the newer strata of industrial society, the technicians and the *cadres*.[34] And although the industrial working class remained more hesitant than most strata (excluding intellectuals) to the appeals of Gaullism, nevertheless significant working-class support did go to the Gaullists at certain times, such as the referendum and elections of 1958, and the presidential election of 1965.[35] Indeed, it has been suggested that a Gaullist appeal merely to right-wing and centrist support would have been insufficient to give the Gaullists a majority in any election, and that significant shifts in support from the pre-1958 left to the Gaullists was a fundamental underpinning of Gaullist dominance in the 1960s.[36]

This is not to assert that the UNR was not '*un grand parti de droite*', as Charlot shows it to have been;[37] it is merely to say that the bases of party politics had changed along with the changes in the system of rewards and penalties in the coalition-building process – deriving from the constitutional changes of 1958 and 1962.[38] In a system based on the formation of *pre-electoral* coalitions – as the Fifth Republic came to be in October 1962 (as distinct from the normal multi-party–parliamentarist practice of *post*-electoral coalitions) – parties need to seek as broad a base as possible for majoritarian support, i.e. to win the votes of at least a significant minority within a wide spectrum of different social strata as well as a majority in some. In this context, parties in the Fifth Republic became rather different behavioural structures from what they were prior to 1958 (or 1962). Furthermore, within this context, the Gaullist phenomenon itself had to take on a mutually reinforcing dual dimension.

To borrow Nettl's terms, Gaullism – and here I am deliberately lumping together so-called 'presidential' ('*gaullien*') Gaullism *and* 'legislative' Gaullism – had to fulfil *both* of the major functions of *interest articulation* and *authority legitimation*, though not without a partial division of labour. The interest-articulation function manifests itself primarily in party and parliamentary politics, while the authority-legitimation function is found primarily in presidential and 'constitutional–national' politics. Nettl's description of French politics is still relevant (though not without qualification) today:

The French Fifth Republic has attempted to embody an even 'purer' functional specificity and structural differentiation than the American model. Instead of dual-function parties we have here parties confined as far as possible to interest-articulation only – and the National Assembly reduced from an authority-building forum to one of interest articulation. According to de Gaulle, political parties should not participate in presidential elections or referenda. . .Instead of

the parties carrying out a dual function, as in America, which de Gaulle believes
to be impossible in the well-entrenched French multi-party system, the duality
reverts to its basic, theoretically 'proper' level – to the individual voter mobilised
by party for his interests, but 'unattached' for the purpose of authority legitimation. Not quite unattached, however; de Gaulle's identification of himself as the
unique personification of the national interest enables him to justify constitutional-
national symbols of mobilisation...on behalf of himself in the roles both of
candidate and president.[39]

This formula needs qualification, however, as its over-simple clarity
is compelling. We must not be too eager to accept its full implications
without refinement. For both presidential *and* legislative Gaullism in
large part acted as – and were perceived as – fulfilling both functions at
the same time, though certainly to different degrees, and varying
according to the circumstances of the day. Thus the major shift in
presidential Gaullism occurred with the assumption by de Gaulle of the
role of party leader in October–November 1962 and the resulting
demystification of the presidency which was consecrated in the 1965
ballotage,[40] and which marked the period of 'routinisation' of previously exceptional presidential authority. Similarly, the Gaullist party
has been said to attempt to fulfil an authority-legitimating 'constituent
function', which submerged the 'programmatic function' traditional to
French parties and which thus made every election into a global
process which even today calls into question 'not only a policy, but an
entire regime'.[41] Thus the then Prime Minister, Jacques Chaban-
Delmas, speaking at the conference of the UDR parliamentary party on
18 September 1970, could say:

we have opponents, of course, who attack us and who fight amongst themselves;
but we have no true opposition...Consequently, we have responsibilities towards
France and towards the French people: not only the French who vote for us, and
those social categories who vote for us most heavily, but also towards those
people and those categories which have not yet given us their votes but which
are beginning to consider doing so.[42]

There would appear to have been, then, until 1973–4 at least, a
symbiosis between presidential and legislative Gaullism, a symbiosis
which is not unreminiscent of the relationship between the presidential
and the congressional parties in the United States prior to Watergate,
and not unconnected with the different constituencies of the Presidency
and the Congress – the former having a 'national' constituency and the
latter local constituencies (with the twain meeting only in the presidential nominating conventions).[43] Therefore it would seem that in the
context of a changing socio-political environment Gaullism in the 1960s

and 1970s lasted as an effective majority movement only so long as the presidential and legislative aspects of the movement maintained their essential complementarity.[44]

Indeed, two factors have heralded the end of Gaullist dominance. The first is the development of an effective left-wing opposition organised, like the Gaullists in the 1960s, effectively on both legislative and presidential levels for fighting elections.[45] The second is the disappearance, with Pompidou's death, of the last vestiges of presidential Gaullism, splitting the Gaullist movement in the presidential election of 1974 and creating conditions where an alternative right-wing presidential strategy could emerge under Giscard d'Estaing.[46] As was said of the 1973 parliamentary elections, 'the masquerade of nationalist and étatiste unanimism is over'.[47]

But in developing a differentiated bipolar system, with broadly based presidential blocs emerging from the 1974 first ballot and looser governmental coalitions emerging from the parliamentary balance of forces,[48] perhaps it might be thought that the problem of authority legitimation has now been absorbed into the normal functioning of the institutions. It has not disappeared. Indeed, fundamental Gaullist orientations in foreign policy have not disappeared as part of the cement holding the various forces in the system together. They have, however, come to be taken for granted to a large extent; so much so that when, in mid-1976, President Giscard d'Estaing sought to modify France's stance towards military cooperation within the framework of the North Atlantic Treaty, a raw nerve indeed was exposed.[49] Of course, constitutional questions and problems of foreign policy are not as salient today as they were in de Gaulle's time – and, in fact, such problems are rarely salient to the public except in periods when shifts in posture and objectives conflict with previously internalised symbolic images. But they still lurk beneath the surface. Indeed, the problems most central to authority legitimation are those about which the greatest degree of public acceptance or consensus developed during the presidencies of de Gaulle and Pompidou. Foreign policy was an especially significant factor.

II. The Development of the Foreign Policy Consensus

One of the factors which makes foreign policy susceptible to symbolic manipulation by political elites is the fact that it tends to concern areas not involving large amounts of expenditure, and therefore rarely draws into the circle of potential disagreement and conflict those groups whose primary activity is interest articulation and resource allocation. The most obvious exceptions to this rule – defence spending and foreign aid – merely confirm the rule; the need for an 'adequate' defence budget is widely accepted, though controversies over what is 'adequate' (the actual content of spending) are frequent, and the debate tends to be carried on in rhetorical terms more closely related to the duties of the legitimate authorities than to the competitive language of interest-group politics. Decision-makers dealing with foreign policy – particularly in diplomatic arenas where 'intangible means' are more important than tangible resources – are freed from having to pay attention to the demands of local opinion-makers and are permitted to develop what Rosenau has called 'continental orientations'.[50] Furthermore, because it deals with attitudes towards non-members of the national community and not towards other groups of fellow citizens, it enhances feelings of solidarity and belonging:

Foreign policy goes beyond the normal boundaries of party conflict, and in moments of crisis brings out a common feeling of belonging to the national group, a feeling which may seem to be in a state of suspended animation in the ordinary course of day-to-day affairs. . .Public opinion does not shift from black to white when affected by just any impulsion; nor is it made up of the pure and simple addition of individual choices of a more or less discordant nature. Rather it is a collective body which is penetrated a bit at a time by the wider repercussions of the circumstances. This process is more or less rapid depending upon the sudden or slow pace of events. No doubt public opinion does not dominate events, but it is imbued with them and considers them with realism.[51]

The stress on foreign affairs in de Gaulle's France was intended to maximise this feeling of collective belonging in a way which cut across the political boundaries which had become so deeply entrenched within French society. Its intangibility[52] made it more manipulable, and its salience was intended to allow elites as well as public opinion to 'develop continental orientations'. According to Shils, habits of compliance with macro-social norms developed concerning 'those components of culture which do not refer directly to macro-social allocative problems' are likely to spill over, presumably in *analogical* fashion, into other areas of political culture where once tangible resource-allocation problems are involved, because the consensus developed in the former instance 'fortifies the sense of affinity within the consensual community and thus renders dissensual *beliefs* less divisive and less significant in generating conflict'.[53] De Gaulle's foreign policy orientations were intended symbolically to modify certain salient characteristics of the belief system of French mass and elite publics and to channel beliefs in such a way that they should reinforce public compliance with the norms of the Fifth Republic itself – with an emphasis on general institutional stability and on the role of the state as the active, policy-making agent and expression of the collectivity.

In Third Republic France, not only were political beliefs socially divisive in themselves,[54] but also the ideological consciousness – the structures of condensation symbolism – of entire socio-political 'subcultures' were – and were seen to be – divided from each other along multiple dimensions.[55] On the whole, de Gaulle's political appeal was designed to reach across traditional subcultural boundaries and achieve a broad base of support. American social anthropologist Laurence Wylie has described how the various traditional 'families' were included in the Gaullist circle:

De Gaulle has appealed to each of the spiritual families without seeming to favour any one over the others. Like a good head of the household, playing favourites with no child – but satisfying no one completely – he seemed to be motivated primarily by a desire to preserve the identity and to work for the welfare of the national family as a whole. He addressed his appeal to all the political families in ways which were significant and meaningful for their particular sets of symbols. De Gaulle was himself a member of the Traditionalist family and spoke easily in its terms. His rejection of extremists of both the right and the left gave reassurance to the Liberal family. To the state planners of the Industrialist family that sought to renovate economic France, he gave full rein. His religious devotion appealed to the Christian family. His direct appeal to the people in 1940, 1944, 1958 and 1961 related him to the Jacobin family. His preoccupation with building a better future made him acceptable to many within the Socialist family.[56]

In order for foreign policy to play a key role in this process, it had to appeal to pre-existing attitudes across the ideological spectrum. The ideas of national *grandeur* and independence, as formulated by de Gaulle and applied in a wide range of symbolic scenarios across the foreign policy spectrum, did just that. This symbolic structure was specific enough to be recognisable to the various subcultural categories, yet vague enough not to be limited to any of the pre-existing – and divisive – categories of nationalism which characterised the various French families. As Michelat and Thomas, in their study of a student sample, have shown, nationalism, in a vague sense, is characteristic of the entire spectrum of French politics, but the very idea of nationalism means something different to each group. There is a distinct nationalism of the left, which is presented as a 'nationalism of belonging, admitting the determining character of the *fait national*'. There is also a nationalism of the centre, which, as with the nationalism of the left is grounded in the feeling of membership of a national society, but which 'adds to this consciousness of belonging to a nation the feeling – if not quite the claim – of the superiority of this nation over the others'. Finally, the strongest and most ideologically explicit form of nationalism is of course the nationalism of the right, which 'combines feeling and doctrine, affective nationalism and ideological nationalism'; in other words, the *fait national* becomes for the right the origin and justification of the social bond itself, which is expressed in the formal sovereignty of the nation-state and involves the maintenance of the social structure which has developed within the national unit and the maintenance of that society's rights against both external and internal enemies.[57]

Indeed, the affective nationalism characteristic of the left did not emerge from the formal questions of the closed interviews, which treated nationalism more in terms of specific ideological propositions, but from a related set of open-ended interviews.[58] The response of French public opinion on foreign policy *issues*, and the gradual but reluctant compliance of the opposition groups to the new Gaullist foreign policy norms, indicate that de Gaulle's appeal on foreign policy issues provided effective integrative symbols on two complementary levels. It effectively crossed left/right boundaries; and it also maintained the crucial symbolic links between presidential and legislative Gaullism. In the first instance, it provided those groups socially and ideologically opposed to 'personal power', to the Gaullist Fifth Republic, and to the right-wing character of much of the Gaullist movement itself (especially the attitudes of its militants), with a channel to the new regime, an image with which such groups could identify, and a sense of belonging to a national unit which was being effectively represented in world affairs by the state. Foreign policy gave the regime legitimacy in the eyes of its opponents. In the second instance, it strengthened the implantation of the political system through allowing those groups in the 'majority' to exercise – and to be seen to exercise – effective decision-making power. It gave Gaullist supporters, and, more importantly, potential Gaullist sympathisers (floating voters and other forms of ephemeral support) a sense of personal political efficacy, thus multiplying the impact of the Gaullist movement as the 'party of the system', the legitimate exerciser of majority rule.

The potential influence of such a symbolic strategy was strengthened by pre-existing attitudes. French public opinion did not need to be convinced that France was still a 'great power'. In May 1945, after a war in which France did not play a particularly significant military role, 80 per cent of respondents to an IFOP survey said that they considered France a 'great power', 10 per cent a 'small power', and 10 per cent did not reply.[59] This attitude was coupled, in the last years of the Fourth Republic, with a sense that American influence in France was too great and that American bases ought to be removed.[60] Indeed, a strong neutralist current, which was already well established in the mid-1950s, gained the support of an absolute majority of respondents on every IFOP poll from 1954 to 1969.[61] Charlot shows how this tended to work out in practice on specific issues.

For example, public attitudes towards Franco-American relations seem to correspond quite closely with de Gaulle's carefully orchestrated balancing act on NATO, in which he sought to act as the midwife of a new world balance of power based on detente, but nevertheless retaining the cover of the Atlantic Treaty, on the one hand, and the integrated NATO military organisation, on the other – reaffirming loyalty to the former, while, in an apparent paradox, denouncing and withdrawing from the latter. In a survey taken in May 1966 (only weeks after de Gaulle's dramatic and symbolic master scenario), French respondents approved de Gaulle's NATO policy by a ratio of 4:3, 'while at the same time remaining convinced that the security of France demanded that she stay in the Atlantic Alliance and consequently preparing to vote "no" in the referendum which certain ultra-Gaullists wanted to organise in order to obtain French withdrawal' from the Atlantic Treaty itself.[62] Defence policy elicited a more cautious response, involving, as it did, large amounts of expenditure on the FNS. Supporters were in a minority in 1963–4, although they had been in the majority in 1957–63 and again took the lead in April 1966. Support for a united Europe remained a constant factor, but the perception of Europe by public opinion – the image which respondents tended to have of that Europe – was closer to the image elaborated by de Gaulle than to that of his pro-'European' opponents (mainly of the centre); not only do surveys make it clear that a united Europe ought to be independent of, rather than closely associated with, the United States (while most prominent 'Europeans' were Atlanticists), but they also show opinion clearly to consider de Gaulle to be a 'decided supporter' of European unification.[63] The other partners in the EEC were held to blame for the 1965 'empty chair' crisis, and the French position was strongly approved.[64] Opposition to de Gaulle's EEC policies did come, however, from a major sector – farmers – who switched their votes heavily away from de Gaulle in the 1965 presidential elections.[65]

The significance of this support is well summarised by Charlot:

To conclude, the strength of the broad options of General de Gaulle's foreign policy is that they find support beyond the partisan limits of the majority; they express and reinforce a certain national consensus. Furthermore, de Gaulle, on this level, is even sometimes rather more willingly followed by the opposition than by the majority. The idea of an independent Europe, in particular, is acceptable to seven out of ten Communist voters, that of an Atlantic Europe is accepted by only one out of ten, while 2–3 Socialist, Gaullist or Centrist voters against five support a close association between Europe and the United States. The anti-Gaullists, paradoxically, are more *gaullien* than the Gaullists.

In addition, the more left-leaning sectors of the Gaullist movement itself were attracted by de Gaulle's foreign policy, as was made explicit in the case of the Group of 29. And the inroads made by de Gaulle himself into the bases of working-class support normally expected to go to more left-wing parties were also linked to the impact of foreign policy issues.[66]

For example, Charlot establishes a category of 'cumulative' groups – groups sharing more than one characteristic which can be linked with a Gaullism–anti-Gaullism scale. In contrasting the reactions of two cumulative anti-Gaullist groups – young workers and young intellectuals (youth, working-class membership and intellectual status being broadly anti-Gaullist indicators) – he points out that young workers reacted favourably to de Gaulle's foreign policy at its apex in 1966, with their overall anti-Gaullism falling to a relatively low level. On the other hand, the reactions of young intellectuals were relatively unaffected. '*Gaullien* Gaullism sometimes made an impression on young people in the factories, but it seemed to have provoked a sort of repulsion in the younger French intelligentsia.'[67]

Indeed, in the 1965 presidential election 15 per cent of all voters invoked reasons of foreign policy to justify their choice, while a minimum of 14 per cent of Gaullist voters supported de Gaulle *primarily* for reasons of foreign policy (a percentage which was higher among younger voters).[68] Given the relative inattention of public opinion to foreign affairs in general, this figure is highly significant; such voters would have to be retained at a very high level if Gaullist candidates were to maintain their plurality over the combined opposition.

Thus despite a clear drop in support over such issues as the Six-Day War and de Gaulle's controversial visit to Canada (both in 1967), and despite considerable scepticism about the real chances for French political, economic and military 'independence' and divisions over the more tangible resource-allocation problem of the nuclear force,[69] general satisfaction with France's role in the world increased between 1965 and 1968 as shown by two surveys which asked: Are you satisfied with the role played today by France on the international plane?[70]

	satisfied %	dissatisfied %	no reply %
February 1965	44	16	40
March 1968	56	25	19

Indeed, de Gaulle's main period of strength (after the Algerian settlement) in terms of respondents' satisfaction with his overall performance in office, was in 1966. In contrast to the periods of social crisis in 1963 and 1968, when de Gaulle's popularity was at its lowest points, surveys in June, July and August 1966, and again in September, showed his popularity rising to the highest level of the entire period between the end of the Algerian crisis and his departure from office in April 1969; approximately two-thirds of the sample were 'satisfied', while only one quarter were actively 'dissatisfied'. Charlot's 'Gaullism index' stood at 44.[71]

The lack of domestic problems in this period was notable. The opposition was reflecting on the 1965 presidential election and preparing its strategy for the legislative elections of 1967. This was the era which represented the culmination of de Gaulle's foreign policy initiatives. In three months in early 1966 he made several speeches in which France's foreign policy was explained 'to the world and to the French, de Gaulle's grand design taking concrete shape under the arc-lights of immediate events'. In this setting, salience of foreign policy for public opinion increased dramatically; normally regarded as 'important' by only 10–20 per cent of the public, nearly 30 per cent of respondents now regarded foreign policy problems in this way. Only at the time of the Cuban missile crisis of 1962 did interest reach such a high level. And respondents who thought de Gaulle's overall performance satisfactory were in a majority among both sexes, all age cohorts, all levels of educational attainment, and all occupational categories 'without exception'.[72] Only during the Algerian crisis, at the time of the 1960 barricades, had there been such a spread of 'satisfied' responses.

A highly significant characteristic of this widespread popular support for de Gaulle during this period was the response of the working class.

Unlike the other extreme point of his popularity (1960) and his two most unpopular periods (1963 and 1968), summer 1966 was the only critical period 'where the working class was not the least approving and the most critical of his performance'. Higher management and the liberal professions not only contained 6 per cent fewer 'satisfieds', but also 7 per cent more 'dissatisfieds' came 'from the social elite relative to the workers. . .'. And respondents with higher education 'were distinguished by a very much above-average hostility and reserve'.[73] At this time, the base of de Gaulle's support broadened significantly, and his appeal was received and understood on a cross-cutting, national level.

Thus 1966 was not only the year of the culmination of de Gaulle's grand design at a practical level of policy-making, but was also the year in which foreign policy really took its place alongside the desire for stable institutions as the second pillar of the emerging French consensus.[74] Indeed, if these two phenomena are taken alongside the development of a differentiated bipolar party system around the dominance in the 1960s of the Gaullist party, they become the three legacies of de Gaulle's presidency.

By 1967, in fact, foreign policy had overtaken other general areas of favourable reaction to de Gaulle's performance to become that aspect of Gaullist policy-making which was most favourably received.[75] Its significance grew with time, and its appeal was widespread over different social categories – at the same time as the Gaullist *party* was beginning to shed its nationalitarian image and become, in terms of its electorate, more and more a party of the right. As the Gaullist party became more and more involved with interest articulation, then, the '*gaullien*' image of the presidency came to be associated even more with foreign policy and the legitimation of national authority. Indeed, de Gaulle's foreign policy would seem to be a paradigm case of the use of foreign policy as an instrument for consensus-building – the consensus here being quite clearly on the acceptability of the political system as a whole and its relation in the public mind with belonging to a wider national community which has its own norms. Here we have the legitimation of authority and the growth of system affect, features missing from the French political scene for most of the period since 1789.

That this mass public consensus had developed was not immediately recognised by the other actors and elites within the French political system – another area, like that of institutions, where de Gaulle's *rapport* with public opinion completely broke the traditional boundaries of established patterns of political behaviour and the practice of power and influence. Attacks on de Gaulle's foreign policy actually increased, but 'it emerges very clearly from these overall evaluations and these images of Gaullism in public opinion that the oppositions, by attacking ceaselessly, whether over institutions, or Europe, or foreign policy, chose their terrain badly, because these are precisely its strong points'.[76] It had appeared to de Gaulle since the Liberation that:

> More than ever, then, I had to seek support from the French people rather than from the 'elite' groups which tended to come between us. My popularity was a kind of capital with which I could pay off the disappointments that were inevitable among the ruins.[77]

This view seemed to be reinforced. However, the conditions of the time ruled out 'heroic' leadership (except over Algeria), and de Gaulle was well aware of the changes of twenty years:

> Certainly, in contrast with the task which was conferred upon me eighteen years earlier, my new one [in 1958] would be divested of the exalting imperatives of an heroic period. The peoples [of the world], particularly our own, no longer experienced that need to rise above themselves which is imposed by danger. For almost everyone – including ourselves – the immediate question was no longer victory or defeat, but a more or less easy way of life.[78]

Any legitimation of authority therefore had to take place within a context characterised by norms of interest articulation.

Rosenau has pointed out that in the United States, legislators, who are primarily concerned with interest articulation, tend to be isolated from movements of opinion in the foreign policy field: 'whenever an issue separates the national and local opinion-making publics, two mutually exclusive communications systems come into being, one culminating in the segmentally oriented legislative branch and the other in the continentally oriented executive branch'.[79] In France in the 1960s, the first reaction of all non-Gaullist groups (especially on the right) was to reject the new foreign policy consensus concluded over their heads. Charlot's book on legislative Gaullism is vague as to how the anti-Gaullism of the traditional right flavoured opposition to de Gaulle with an 'all-party' image, which was at its height in the *Cartel des Non* in 1962 and again in the 1969 referendum. As René Rémond has written: 'If General de Gaulle did not encounter so much opposition on the left, one could make anti-Gaullism one of the contemporary criteria of the right.'[80] Such would indeed seem to have been partially the case in 1966, when de Gaulle's foreign policy offended right-wing groups and pleased left-wing groups! French local elections, for example, have been highly significant arenas in the past for legitimating the authority of particular political *notables* and leaders. On the second ballot of the 1965 municipal elections, cases were observed of Communist voters voting for Gaullist lists against SFIO–Centrist coalitions, 'the PCF leaders playing the Gaullist card for reasons of foreign policy'.[81] Of course, not only was Gaullist foreign policy characterised by moves towards a Franco-Soviet *rapprochement*, but the Communist Party was attempting to prove its nationalitarian *bona fides* in the quest for respectability. A month later, the same source had this to say about the reaction to a major foreign policy speech by de Gaulle:

It is necessary to read *La Nation* [the Gaullist party paper] and *L'Humanité* [the PCF paper] to find the most favourable commentaries. The UNR organ paraphrased the Head of State's speech; the Communist paper 'took note of the changes' in General de Gaulle's attitude and found in his speech 'views more in conformity with the nature of things'.[82]

Indeed, de Gaulle's foreign policy partially had the effect of helping to assimilate the PCF into French political life, as it reflected traditional Communist themes.[83] Independence from the United States and selective acceptance of the Common Market were prominent Communist themes which overlapped with de Gaulle's concerns. Thus it was the parties which after 1947 had been classed together as the 'anti-system opposition' in the Fourth Republic – the Gaullists and the Communists (the latter really only after the beginnings of Franco-Soviet *rapprochement* in 1963–4) – which sought national legitimacy in the Fifth.

The dilemma of the opposition groups, which were divided against each other on foreign policy issues, reached a crisis point in 1966. Prior to that time, symbolic opposition in the National Assembly had concentrated its censure motions on issues of foreign policy and the budget for the FNS. The centrist leader Jean Lecanuet was prominent in the Senate's refusal to discuss the Government's *force de frappe* proposals in 1960 which led to a formal question of confidence; all told, three censure motions on this subject failed in the National Assembly.[84] Foreign policy issues also played a significant role in the government crises of 1962. De Gaulle's European policy led to the resignation of MRP ministers after the press conference of 15 May 1962; had only 40 more votes been cast for the censure motion on credits for the construction of the nuclear facilities at Pierrelatte, the Government would have fallen; and the question of the aftermath of the Algerian situation, as well as the problem of military credits in the next budget, were both central features of the political debate of that crucial year.[85]

Indeed, as Karl Deutsch's analysis shows, the opposition of French elite groups to de Gaulle's foreign policy, and particularly his defence policy, was thoroughgoing.[86] But the internal contradictions of this opposition have been well documented by Lawrence Scheinman, who suggests that their arguments often hid the real sources of their opposition:

> The Gaullist regime pursues policies which the opposition itself has pursued in the past or in many respects is sympathetic to in the present. But the opposition's antipathy to 'le pouvoir' forced it to adopt positions which radicalised the differences between itself and de Gaulle in order to avoid falling into the trap of acquiescing in Gaullism.

Traditionally, Scheinman states, the nationalist foreign policy posture in French politics had been professed by the parties out of power, 'while the Gaullist regime has appropriated the politics of nationalism to itself and forged it into official policy'. Thus the 'oft-professed anti-nationalism' of the oppositions 'is more a function of anti-Gaullism and anti-regimism than it is a function of a conviction of the fundamentally unethical character of nationalism and nation-statism'.[87] Whereas the appeal to nationalism had often been the basis of attacks on the system (e.g., the right in the Third Republic), it was now the main bulwark of a pro-system consensus: opposition to it was an attack on authority.

For example, Morse identifies four types of opposition to the FNS: 'those for whom the institutions of the Fifth Republic were illegitimate' (thus 8 of a total of 14 censure motions in 1959–62 concerned the FNS in some way as a tangible symbol of Gaullist policy); those opposed to French strategic autonomy (mainly Europeanists); those who criticised its strategic efficacy; and 'those, including many from the scientific and technological elite, who opposed the Government's defence policies for economic reasons and who sought other uses of national resources'.[88]

By the time that de Gaulle's grand design began to take more shape, in the period 1965–6 in particular, a gap had developed between the opposition groups and public opinion on how to react to de Gaulle's foreign policy, and the PCF were quicker to climb on the bandwagon than were the other groups. The crunch came on a censure motion, presented on 15 April 1966, over the French withdrawal from NATO. The major proponents of censure were Lecanuet's Centre Democrats, a group which was described by a writer in L'Humanité (Etienne Fajon) as 'fieffés réactionnaires' and 'pro-American ultras'.[89] The Socialists

(SFIO), seeking alliances following the Popular Front experiment in the 1965 presidential elections, were divided, but eventually supported the motion. In fact, the motion received only 137 votes (the necessary majority being 242 votes). During the preparation of the motion, the Communists wrote that: 'A part of the Left has fallen into the trap prepared by the Gaullists.' Thus the difficulties facing the left-wing forces, so recently united, were highlighted, their divisions emphasised, although on virtually all issues *except* the regime's Atlantic policy the PCF and the SFIO were far closer to each other than they were to the Gaullists.[90] And despite their joint support of this motion, the Centrist–SFIO anti-regime alliance – that tattered remnant of the governing coalition which had dominated the Fourth Republic – gave way within a year to the necessities of the new electoral politics of the Fifth. By that time it had become obvious that de Gaulle's foreign policy was a fact of life, and no longer a rallying point for the opposition. The last bone of contention between government and the oppositions – the EEC – was defused in 1969 by de Gaulle's successor, Pompidou, with the result that it was said in 1970: 'For the first time in more than twenty years, France's foreign policy no longer seems to divide the parties.'[91]

Thus foreign policy issues, in this critical period, had a significant impact upon a broad cross-section of the electorate, going well beyond the boundaries of the right and the Gaullists and developing a consensus in public opinion, a consensus which was eventually recognised by the opposition parties, and which, once recognised, enabled political disagreements to polarise along a domestically oriented left–right dimension instead of the pro-regime–anti-regime dimension which had previously been symbolised by conflicts over foreign policy. In this process, foreign policy salience gave an aura to the institution of the presidency which helped to create the basis for its development into a significant socialising agent, a factor which also appears in American studies on political socialisation. Furthermore, given the fact that general levels of political information have not been high in the French electorate,[92] and considering the findings of the Grenoble political socialisation study – which showed among schoolchildren a widespread perception of the President as a political figure, alongside a very hazy knowledge of other political figures[93] – it might seem that, via the institution of the presidency and the personage of the incumbent President, issues of a 'presidential' or authority-legitimating character may prove to have a significant impact upon the political perceptions of future generations. If this should be the case, then we may expect the significance of foreign policy as a mechanism of consensus-building to continue to be strong, and perhaps even to grow relative to other authority-legitimating issues, for example, as the stability of the institutions of the Fifth Republic comes to be more and more accepted as a fact of political life.

In conclusion, then, it would not seem implausible to suggest that de Gaulle's foreign policy fulfilled a vital function of normative integration in the French polity in the crucial developmental years of the mid-1960s. According to Ole R. Holsti and his co-authors, this phenomenon is not unique to France; it has been suggested that 'cold war competition has been instrumental in maintaining the American and Soviet "establishment" in power...[and] that the symbols of intra-alliance competition have similarly been used by French and Chinese leaders'.[94] And now that this pattern has been established, it is unlikely to change. As Frankel has pointed out: 'It is a basically sound economic principle that change is not even considered as long as no distinct danger signals have arisen indicating that the original choice is wrong and has unwelcome effects.' Even when one actively desires change, a strong pull of inertia still favours existing orientations, 'as, in order to prevail, the benefits of a change which are, by their nature, speculative, must appear to be clearly greater than the cost of their disturbance'.[95]

It was symptomatic that de Gaulle was removed from power on an issue which had nothing to do with foreign policy. His speech of 25 April 1969, just before the referendum of 28 April, did not refer to foreign policy; it was less well received by his audience than previous speeches during the Fifth Republic.[96] Indeed, after the trauma of the Events of May 1968, working-class support for Gaullism declined significantly and stabilised at a lower level than it had reached in the mid-1960s. But then, de Gaulle's foreign policy – because of its presidential character – had not been intended to be a vote-getter for legislative Gaullism, as Pompidou found to his cost in the 1972 referendum on the enlargement of the European Community. Rather, it had been intended to create and to reinforce macro-systemic norms. In a sense, this is the continuing legacy of 'gaullien' Gaullism – a strong state and an 'independent' foreign policy.

Indeed, from the perspective of late 1978, it seems that pressure from coalition politics on the RPR (the new successor to the UDR, led by former Prime Minister Jacques Chirac) has called into question the heritage of 'legislative Gaullism', based on Gaullist predominance within a cohesive parliamentary majority. The results of the parliamentary elections have established a rough electoral balance between the Gaullists, the Giscardian UDF (an Independent Republican–Centrist alliance), the Socialists and the Communists. The role of the President of the Republic has become more problematic; in this context, a more *gaullien* style of politics – whether practised by a 'Gaullist' like Chirac, a liberal conservative like Giscard d'Estaing, or a social democrat like Mitterand, both before and after the next presidential elections scheduled for 1981 – must be one of the most compelling options of a President of the Republic. And any such re-emphasis of foreign policy issues by the President would certainly provide an acid test for the hypothesis that foreign policy is an indispensable element of the French political consensus – in the same way that solidity or fragility of the American institutional consensus can often be measured by the strength or weakness of bipartisanship in foreign policy.[97] How a French President deals with foreign affairs in the future may, like de Gaulle's foreign policy, have ramifications for the functioning of the political system which go far beyond the ostensible intrinsic significance of the issues in themselves, and may affect the future of French politics in general. The pursuit of a little bit of *grandeur*, at least, will have come to be expected of him.

Conclusions

The legacy of grandeur

We have now come full circle. General de Gaulle was the first major Western leader consistently to attempt to break the vicious circle of cold war politics, and clearly to demonstrate that, in a world characterised by thaw and detente, the role of nation-states, and the concept of national interest, would become more, rather than less, important and that superpower hegemony rationalised in universal ideologies would decline.

In pursuing this policy, however, his first priority was not that of making France a new superpower equal to the United States and the Soviet Union. Nor was it to level all states down to a fictional equality based on the legal notion of sovereignty, but which would ignore the vast differences in resource power and political efficacity between them. Rather, it was to permit France, and certain other nations, to play a role more commensurate with what he saw as her political potential, her historical contribution and her world-wide network of interests and influence, and to revalue the role of voluntary cooperation of nations and states – rather than blocs or international institutions – in the solution of world problems. Indeed, while de Gaulle wished France to be autonomous and capable of asserting her independence in matters most crucial to her, this independence was seen to be part of a wider, cooperative interdependence, symbolising French autonomy and the accountability of authority within France, not a permanent threat of disruption.

But in being symbolic, it was not merely a case of pious wishes or lip service. Independence was an operative ideal meant to serve a specific purpose – or, to be more exact, a specific constellation of interconnected purposes. It was meant to link foreign policy and national identity in such a way as to maximise the political efficacity of the French state both at home and abroad. The internal instability of French politics immobilised governments and made consistent policy-making and authoritative decision-making extremely difficult, and de Gaulle was not alone in attributing France's uneven social and economic development to this factor. The international weakness of France at crucial periods since the latter half of the nineteenth century was also seen to stem from her ideological and partisan divisions, her lack of capacity to make and implement collective decisions, and the consequent gap between the *pays réel* and the *pays légal*. To close this gap, in de Gaulle's view, required the formation of a new and stronger sense of national consciousness, a consciousness which would identify legitimate authority with strong and effective political institutions capable of meeting crises and of planning for future development.

In order to impress this consciousness upon the body politic, de Gaulle continually emphasised the one issue-area which highlighted common and exclusive social membership and which could be invested with a high level of ideational content because of its specific cultural and psychological structure – foreign policy. To give foreign policy the appropriate level of cultural and emotional significance to its audience, he emphasised terms like *grandeur, independence* and the *national interest* – terms which underlined and reinforced the sense of autonomy, moral authority and political efficacy of the French public. And he did it in such a way that his very actions demonstrated his *prouesse* and thus legitimated them in a deeper cultural sense.

Furthermore, his use of the term 'grandeur' gave it – and French foreign policy – a particular and specific substantive content, a content which emphasised qualitative and symbolic goals, which acknowledged French weaknesses in resource power but stressed her cultural maturity and moral authority in the world, and which avoided adventurism. While French initiatives and objectives were strenuously resisted in the United States and in certain other countries such as Britain and the Netherlands – an opposition which actually increased de Gaulle's credibility at home – they were cautiously welcomed in Russia, and wholeheartedly embraced in Rumania, China and a number of post-colonial nations of the Third World.

Whether reactions were negative or positive, however, they were often based on expectations out of proportion to the aspirations of de Gaulle himself as well as of other French policy-makers. For, just as he was not acting to attack America or Britain purely because of war-time grudges, neither could he hope to provide a formula which would end superpower hegemony or solve the economic and political problems of the new states, although the French pattern of development aid proved popular in its heyday in the mid-sixties. Rather, his objectives were necessarily attuned to the problems, as he saw them, of France – of the French political system and of the French national interest.

In this way, de Gaulle had much in common with the American 'founding fathers', or leaders of Third World independence/inheritance movements, seeking to create the basis for legitimating a new style of authority and routinising a new set of institutionalised patterns and practices in politics. And his methods had much in common with those of an actor or a lecturer using dramaturgical styles and techniques to bring points home to his audience – in this case, the French public. Once this fundamental duality is perceived, it becomes possible to read between the lines of Gaullist rhetoric, and to judge the relevance of what has so often been dismissed as anachronism, in a way which explains the strengths and weaknesses of his appeal more accurately.

In domestic French politics, de Gaulle represented more than the traditional 'heroic leader'. His appeal cut across social categories and party labels. His cultural appeal was a consciously constructed attempt to achieve a working synthesis of trends in French society. He combined traditionalism with modernism. He industralised France while arguing the evils of the machine civilisation. He presided over an era which effectively fitted France for participation in the interdependent world of advanced industrial societies, while calling for national pride and consciousness – independence and grandeur. He was ahead of his time in seeing some of the characteristics of the post-cold war era, and led France dramatically towards what he thought were its heights, while supporting a new *status quo* which achieved far less than rhetoric would have had it. He symbolised a set of political institutions which changed the organisational behaviour patterns of French political and social elites, yet he eventually succumbed to the development of a new elite which claimed his name and heritage.

In international politics, he was a 'maverick', but one who did not really destroy the essence of the ties which bound France to her various partners. He saw international relations partly – and most significantly – as a set of rites for legitimating authority, so long as the risks were not unacceptable. In this way, he was representative of a major trend in contemporary world politics, well described by Edelman:

Whatever its other political functions are, the whole nation-state system, including its negotiating mechanisms, international organisations and accompanying rhetoric, serves also as an intensely publicised rite. It is an acting out of the message, absorbed by mass publics all over the world, that nation-states are the units in contention in international conflict: that the president, ambassador, foreign minister or United Nations delegate somehow transcends the conflicting interests of domestic politics and speaks for the whole nation, which, in turn, negotiates, resists or fights other nations in defence of transcendent national interests. In this ever present, continuously publicised and deeply threatening drama of nations in temporary alliance, in cold war and in hot war, the myth finds its strongest bulwark.[1]

The nation-state has become the most salient cultural reference point in the contemporary world, more important even than class, and its symbols have become more thoroughly implanted in the popular consciousness than other symbols.[2]

Couve de Murville, in concluding his memoirs, emphasises the importance of all this for France today. For him, as for de Gaulle, independence and grandeur are seen both as a necessity and as a heuristic device – a way towards a better society as well as the improvement of the present one.[3] Ideology and dramaturgy come together; what is important is that the consciousness of unity and potentiality become understood and internalised. Such a world may not produce nations which can effectively become 'the custodian of cultural diversity among groups mutually granting each other their peculiar worth',[4] but it may preserve some of that diversity in the face of technological conformity.

What is more difficult to determine, however, is whether such a state of affairs, no matter how intensely wished, is a viable ideal. Not only is the state – de Gaulle's cherished active element in the political reality of the nation – increasingly ineffective in certain areas, like the redistribution of wealth and the spreading of economic development, but its existence often provides the cover for a series of forces which it cannot control. As the state has become more and more involved in social and economic structures and processes, more and more private elements have carved out and defined their own spheres of influence within the state itself. We may be entering an era in which that structure which is meant to pursue the general interest is becoming ever more privatised from within, and thus in which political culture and popular accountability are becoming ever more divorced from real political effectiveness. And no political unit will be able to undertake effective policy-making unless it is susceptible of becoming the object of system affect – of achieving and retaining democratic legitimacy. At the same time, the development of ever more sophisticated international and transnational networks of forces threatens the accountability of the nation-state from without and makes democratic accountability and political efficacity seem even more difficult to achieve.

However, in the absence of a wider form of international community, the nation-state is still the all-important intermediary structure through which all these processes must pass, and there is much slack which remains to be taken up in the name of the national interest. And, in such a context, the creation and awakening of national consciousness, as exemplified in the foreign policy of General de Gaulle, will continue to be an essential element of political activity and aspiration. Within this framework, Gaullist foreign policy was particularly effective. It has become part of the French national myth, and its impact upon the political process within France is a continuing one. This is the substance of de Gaulle's historical personality and the legacy of his politics of grandeur.

Notes

Introduction: politics and grandeur

1. Kenneth E. Boulding, 'National Images and International Systems', in James N. Rosenau (ed.), *International Politics and Foreign Policy* (New York: Free Press, 1969), p. 423.
2. Murray Edelman, *The Symbolic Uses of Politics* (Urbana: University of Illinois Press, 1964), p. 130.
3. Jean-Baptiste Duroselle, in Pierre Renouvin and J.-B. Duroselle, *Introduction to the History of International Relations* (London: Pall Mall Press, 1968), p. 267. Cf. also Maurice Couve de Murville, *Une politique étrangère1958–1969* (Paris: Plon, 1971), p. 15.
4. Michael K. O'Leary, 'Linkages between Domestic and International Politics in Underdeveloped Nations', in J. N. Rosenau (ed.), *Linkage Politics* (New York: Free Press, 1969), p. 330.
5. David Thomson, 'General de Gaulle and the Anglo-Saxons', *International Affairs*, 41, 1 (January 1965), 21.
6. Jean Lacouture (ed.), *Citations du Président de Gaulle* (Paris: Editions du Seuil, 1968), p. 42.

Chapter 1
The personal equation: psychology, socialisation and culture

1. *L'Express*, 12–18 October 1970, pp. 18–19.
2. J. N. Rosenau (ed.), *Domestic Sources of Foreign Policy* (New York: Free Press, 1967), Introduction, p. 2.
3. The main periods of exception being *revanchisme* after 1871 and the *Union sacrée* of the First World War. Consider Duverger's distinction between 'pure' and 'impure' nationalism, cited in W. W. Kulski, *De Gaulle and the World: The Foreign Policy of the Fifth French Republic* (Syracuse, N.Y.: Syracuse University Press, 1966), pp. 76–7.
4. Charles de Gaulle, *The Complete War Memoirs* (New York: Simon and Schuster, 1967), p. 335.
5. Nathan Leites, *Médiocrité et grandeur: Essai sur Charles de Gaulle* (unpublished manuscript, no date).
6. Kulski, *De Gaulle and the World*, pp. 1–2 and 76–7.
7. Cf. discussion in Elie Kedourie, *Nationalism* (London: Hutchinson, 1966).
8. Professor Harold Kaplan, quoted in *Time*, 15 January 1968, p. 21.
9. It is usually taken for granted, when studying French foreign policy under de Gaulle, that the most significant variable to be explained is the 'individual' or

'idiosyncratic', one of Rosenau's five sets of major variables – the others are 'role', 'governmental', 'societal' and 'systemic': J. N. Rosenau, 'Pre-Theories and Theories of Foreign Policy', in Rosenau (ed.), *The Scientific Study of Foreign Policy* (New York: Free Press, 1971), p. 108.

10. Brian Chapman, 'Prince and Player', *The Guardian*, 8 May 1969.

11. From *The Second World War*, vol. IV, quoted in Alexander Werth, *De Gaulle* (Harmondsworth: Penguin, 1967), p. 101.

12. 'The psychological environment determines the limits of possible decisions whereas the operational environment determines the limits of possible actions. The two environments do not necessarily coincide.' Joseph Frankel, *Contemporary International Theory and the Behaviour of States* (London: Oxford University Press, 1973), p. 66; cf. also Frankel, *The Making of Foreign Policy: An Analysis of Decision-Making* (London: Oxford University Press, 1963), p. 4.

13. Quoted in Jean-Raymond Tournoux, *Jamais dit* (Paris: Plon, 1971), pp. 71–2.

14. This theme continually recurs in the perceptive works of Tournoux, especially: *La tragédie du Général* (1967); *Le mois de Mai du Général* (1969); *Le tourment et la fatalité* (1974) (all published in Paris by Plon); and *Pétain and de Gaulle* (London: Heinemann, 1966).

15. Quoted in Jacques Fauvet, *La IVᵉ République* (Paris: Fayard, 1959), p. 64n. On the subject of de Gaulle's continuing tergiversation on the subject of retirement, see the various works of Tournoux.

16. Tournoux, *Tragédie du Général*, p. 164.

17. Pierre Viansson-Ponté, *The King and His Court* (Boston: Houghton Mifflin, 1965), original title *Les gaullistes*.

18. David Schoenbrun, *The Three Lives of Charles de Gaulle* (London: Hamish Hamilton, 1965), pp. 94–5.

19. See Charles de Gaulle, *Mémoires d'espoir*, vol. I, '*Le renouveau 1958–1962*' (Paris: Plon, 1970), p. 34.

20. See Aidan Crawley, *De Gaulle* (London: Collins, 1969), pp. 17ff.

21. For example, see the epigraph to ch. I, de Gaulle, *Le fil de l'épée* (Paris: Berger–Levrault, 1932), p. 13.

22. Cf. Lucien Nachin, Introduction, in Charles de Gaulle, *Trois études* (Paris: Berger–Levrault, 1945), p. x; the various works of Tournoux; and de Gaulle, *Fil de l'épée*.

23. Stanley Hoffmann and Inge Hoffmann, 'The Will to Grandeur: De Gaulle as Political Artist', *Daedalus*, 97, 3 (Summer 1968), 832–3.

24. De Gaulle, *Complete War Memoirs*, p. 3.

25. Hoffmann and Hoffmann, *Daedalus*, 97, p. 834.

26. Tournoux, *Jamais dit*, p. 363.

27. Crawley, *De Gaulle*, p. 21.

28. Hoffmann and Hoffmann, *Daedalus*, 97, p. 834.

29. Tournoux, *Pétain and de Gaulle*, p. 7.

30. *Complete War Memoirs*, p. 656.

31. Tournoux, *Tourment et fatalité*, p. 157. From the context, this would seem to be a direct quotation of de Gaulle's own résumé of Burckhardt's ideas, though Tournoux is not explicit.

32. Godfried van Benthem van den Bergh, 'Contemporary Nationalism in the Western World', *Daedalus*, 95, 3 (Summer 1966), 833.

33. Tournoux, *Tourment et fatalité*, p. 180.

34. Robert Aron, 'The Political Methods of General de Gaulle', *International Affairs*, 37, 1 (January 1961), 21.

35. Charles Morazé, 'La politique du Général de Gaulle d'après le Tome III de ses Mémoires', *Revue française de science politique*, 10, 1 (March 1960), 13.

36. Speech to the French colony in Warsaw, 11 September 1967.

37. I.e. perceptual selection criteria constructed from experience and socialisation at a diffuse, pre-rational level; see Rosenau, 'Pre-Theories. . .'.

38. *La discorde chez l'ennemi* (Paris: Berger–Levrault, 1924).

39. *Fil de l'épée.*

40. *La France et son Armée* (Paris: Berger–Levrault, 1938).

41. *Vers l'Armée de métier* (Paris: Berger–Levrault, 1934).

42. Douglas Johnson, 'The Political Principles of General de Gaulle', *International Affairs*, 41, 4 (October 1965), 651.

43. *Complete War Memoirs*, p. 576.

44. Pierre Billotte, 'La France et la puissance mondiale', *Revue des deux mondes*, 1 September 1966, p. 12. The words 'grandeur' and 'greatness' will be used more or less interchangeably in this book: the first when it is a question of evoking the overarching Gaullist *symbol*; and the second when certain characteristics of its ideological *content* are to be emphasised.

45. Tournoux, *Jamais dit*, ch. 1.

46. Joseph Frankel, *National Interest* (London: Macmillan, 1970), pp. 24–6 and 31–4.

47. Raymond Aron, *Peace and War: A Theory of International Relations* (London: Weidenfeld and Nicolson, 1966), p. 75.

48. Murray Edelman, *The Symbolic Uses of Politics*, p. 124.

49. Arnold Wolfers, 'The Goals of Foreign Policy', in *Discord and Collaboration: Essays in International Politics* (Baltimore: Johns Hopkins University Press, 1962), ch. 5.

50. Jacques Vernant, 'L'O.T.A.N.: Les raisons des décisions françaises', *Revue de défense nationale*, 22, 5 (May 1966), 898.

51. Machiavelli, quoted in Frankel, *The Making of Foreign Policy*, p. 156.

52. Henry A. Kissinger, *A World Restored: Metternich, Castlereagh and the Problems of Peace 1812–22* (Boston: Houghton Mifflin, 1957), p. 325.

53. Jean Touchard, *Le mouvement des idées politiques dans la France contemporaine* (Paris: Institut d'Études Politiques, 1965), p. 3.

54. Speech, 8 May 1961.

55. Stanley Hoffmann, 'De Gaulle's Memoirs: The Hero as History', *World Politics*, 13, 1 (October 1960), 154.

56. De Gaulle, *Mémoires d'espoir*, vol. I, p. 7.

57. Kolodziej, 'Patterns of French Policy, 1958–1967' (McLean, Virginia: Research Analysis Corporation, 1968), p. 10.

58. *L'Armée de métier*, p. 18.

59. See his description of France in *ibid.*, pp. 9–18.

60. See the various works of Tournoux.

61. *Fil de l'épée*, p. 27.

62. *L'Armée de métier*, p. 19.

63. André Malraux, *Les chênes qu'on abat...* (Paris: Gallimard, 1971), p. 43.

64. André Fontaine, 'What is French Policy?', *Foreign Affairs*, 45, 1 (October 1966), 61–2.

65. *Ce que veut l'U.N.R.–U.D.T.*, quoted in Pierre Avril, *U.D.R. et gaullistes* (Paris: Presses Universitaires de France, 1971), p. 48.

66. Ernst Robert Curtius, *The Civilisation of France: An Introduction* (New York: Vintage Books, 1962), p. 219 (originally pub. 1929).

67. Douglas Johnson, *France* (London: Thames and Hudson, 1969), p. 199.

68. Rhoda Métraux and Margaret Mead, *Themes in French Culture* (Stanford, California: Stanford University Press, 1954), p. 36.

69. Laurence Wylie, 'Social Change at the Grass Roots', in Stanley Hoffmann, *et al.*, *In Search of France* (Cambridge, Mass.: Harvard University Press, 1963), p. 205.

70. *Ibid.*, pp. 227–8.

71. Jesse R. Pitts, 'Continuity and Change in Bourgeois France', in Hoffmann, *et al.*, *In Search of France*, p. 244.

72. *Ibid.*, pp. 241–3.

73. *Ibid.*, p. 244.

74. Curtius, *Civilisation of France*, p. 215.

75. Hans Kohn, *Nationalism: Its Meaning and History* (Princeton, New Jersey: Van Nostrand, 1965), p. 11.

76. Curtius, *Civilisation of France*, p. 236; de Gaulle, *Complete War Memoirs*, p. 3.

77. Johnson, *France*, pp. 20–1.

78. See François Goguel and Alfred Grosser, *La politique en France* (Paris: Armand Colin, 1964); and, for a more detailed analysis of this aspect of the Fourth Republic, cf. Duncan MacRae Jr, *Parliament, Parties and Society in France 1946–1958* (London: Macmillan, 1968).

79. Kulski, *De Gaulle and the World*, pp. 72–4.

80. Alfred Grosser, *La politique extérieure de la Ve République* (Paris: Editions du Seuil, 1965), pp. 79, 167.

81. Florian Znaniecki, *Modern Nationalities: A Sociological Study* (Westport, Connecticut: Greenwood Press, 1973), p. 41 (originally pub. 1952).

82. Cf. R. P. Calvez, 'Les raisons spirituelles de l'aide des pays plus développés aux pays moins développés', *Revue de défense nationale*, 24, 8 (October 1968), 1438.

83. Kohn, *Nationalism*, pp. 20–2.

84. Pitts, *Continuity and Change*, pp. 259–60. This reflects Pitts's wider theories about the nature of authority and delinquency in the bourgeois family; cf. also Métraux and Mead, *French Culture*.

85. Fred I. Greenstein and Sidney G. Tarrow, 'The Study of French Political Socialisation: Toward the Revocation of Paradox', *World Politics*, 22, 1 (October 1969), 105.

86. Stanley Hoffmann, 'Paradoxes of the French Political Community', in Hoffmann, *et al.*, *In Search of France*, p. 19.

87. Roy C. Macridis, 'French Foreign Policy', in Macridis (ed.), *Foreign Policy in World Politics* (Englewood Cliffs, New Jersey: Prentice-Hall, 1962), p. 63.

88. François Mauriac, *De Gaulle* (Paris: Grasset, 1964), p. 285.

89. Manuela Semidei, 'De l'Empire à la décolonisation à travers les manuels scolaires français', *Revue française de science politique*, 16, 1 (Feb 1966), 85n.

90. Robert Bloes, *Le 'Plan Fouchet' et le problème de l'Europe politique* (Bruges: Collège d'Europe, 1970), pp. 205–6.

91. See Karl W. Deutsch, *Nationalism and Social Communication: An Inquiry*

into the Foundations of Nationality (Cambridge, Mass.: M.I.T. Press, 2nd edn, 1966).

92. Renouvin and Duroselle, *Introduction to the History of International Relations*, p. 173; Touchard, *Mouvement des idées politiques*, p. 16; cf. also Raoul Girardet, 'Autour de l'idéologie nationaliste', *Revue française de science politique*, 15, 3 (June 1965), 426–8.

93. Touchard, *Mouvement des idées politiques*, pp. 123–4; René Rémond, *The Right Wing in France from 1815 to de Gaulle* (Philadelphia: University of Pennsylvania Press, 1966), p. 214.

94. Touchard, *Mouvement des idées politiques*, pp. 227–8; Louis Dollot, *La France dans le monde actuel* (Paris: Presses Universitaires de France, 1964), pp. 119–20.

95. Dollot, *France dans le monde actuel*.

96. Renouvin and Duroselle, *History of International Relations*, p. 180; cf. J.-B. Duroselle, 'Changes in French Foreign Policy since 1945', in Hoffmann, et al., *In Search of France*, pp. 305–58.

97. Dorothy Pickles, *The Uneasy Entente: French Foreign Policy and Franco-British Misunderstandings* (London: Oxford University Press, 1966), p. 82; Touchard, *Mouvement des idées politiques*, pp. 272–2.

98. Grosser, *La politique extérieure*, p. 37.

99. Couve de Murville, *Une politique étrangère*, pp. 431–2.

100. Tournoux, *Jamais dit*, p. 143.

101. Mauriac, *De Gaulle*, pp. 344–5.

Chapter 2
The philosophical roots of Gaullism

1. *Vers l'Armée de métier*, p. 69.
2. Speech at Algiers, 18 June 1943.
3. *L'Armée de métier*, p. 175.
4. Address, 31 May 1960.
5. *Le fil de l'épée*, p. 13.
6. Address, 31 May 1960.
7. Speech at the luncheon of the Royal African Society, London, 23 October 1941; see Aristotle, *Politics*, pp. 1333a–b.
8. Tournoux, *Jamais dit*, p. 143.
9. Press conference, London, 9 February 1943.
10. Press conference, Paris, 5 September 1960
11. *La France et son Armée*, p. 9.
12. Broadcast on the BBC, 20 April 1943.
13. *The Complete War Memoirs*, p. 773.
14. Goethe, *Faust*, Part I, tr. by Philip Wayne (Harmondsworth: Penguin, 1949), p. 71.
15. *Faust*, Part II, tr. P. Wayne (Harmondsworth: Penguin, 1959), p. 267.
16. Press conference, 21 February 1965.
17. Broadcast on the BBC, 8 August 1940.
18. Press conference, 29 July 1963.
19. Speech closing RPF Congress, 17 April 1948.
20. Broadcast speech, 13 April 1963.

21. *L'Armée de métier*, pp. 76–7.
22. Press conference, 9 September 1965.
23. *War Memoirs*, p. 3.
24. Broadcast speech, 31 December 1960.
25. *Fil de l'épée*, pp. 92, 126.
26. Speech to the Consultative Assembly, Algiers, 22 November 1944.
27. Speech at Oxford, 25 November 1941.
28. Speech at the University of Mexico, 18 March 1964.
29. Broadcast on Algiers radio, 27 July 1943.
30. *France et son Armée*, p. 270.
31. Speech to the 'French of Great Britain', London, 1 March 1941.
32. Speech to the Consultative Assembly, Algiers, 25 November 1943.
33. Speech at Toulouse, 6 May 1951.
34. See Tournoux's discussion of his period of captivity, in *Pétain and de Gaulle*.
35. *La discorde chez l'ennemi*, p. viii.
36. *Ibid.*, p. x.
37. See Curtius's contrast between French 'civilisation' and German 'culture', *The Civilisation of France*.
38. Maurice Duverger, *La Ve République* (Paris: Presses Universitaires de France, 1963).
39. BBC broadcast, 22 August 1940.
40. Press conference, 5 September 1960.
41. *Mémoires d'espoir*, vol. 1, p. 7.
42. Speech at Saint-Maur, 6 July 1952.
43. Speech at Clemenceau's tomb, 12 May 1946.
44. Speech at Tananarive, Madagascar, 22 August 1958.
45. Speech at Neuilly-sur-Seine, 12 October 1952.
46. Declaration to the press, 27 August 1946.
47. Speech at Saint-Étienne, 4 January 1948.
48. *Ibid.*
49. Speech at the Albert Hall, London, 11 November 1942.
50. Speech at Bayeux, 16 June 1946.
51. Press conference, 11 April 1961.
52. Speech at the Palais de Chaillot, 12 September 1944.
53. Broadcast on the BBC, 20 April 1943.
54. Press conference, 17 November 1948.
55. Press conference, 10 March 1952. This generalisation has been partially supported by opinion polls: see Institut Français d'Opinion Publique, *Les Français et de Gaulle*, ed. Jean Charlot (Paris: Plon, 1971), p. 22.
56. Speech at Tananarive, Madagascar, 22 August 1958.
57. Press conference, 15 May 1962.
58. *L'Armée de métier*, p. 116.
59. Speech at Dakar, 26 August 1958.
60. Broadcast, 16 April 1964.
61. Press conference, 9 September 1965.
62. Speech at Casablanca, 8 August 1943.
63. Press conference, 12 November 1947.
64. Speech to the Provisional Consultative Assembly, Algiers, 18 March 1944.
65. Press conference, 25 February 1953.

66. Press conference, 12 November 1953; see similar remarks in press conference, 15 May 1962.
67. Press conference, 1 October 1948.
68. Speech at Beirut, 28 August 1942.
69. Speech to the Federal Assembly of Mali, 13 December 1959.
70. Address, 31 May 1960.
71. Anthony Hartley, *Gaullism: The Rise and Fall of a Political Movement* (London: Routledge and Kegan Paul, 1972), p. 196.
72. See Henry A. Kissinger, 'Strains on the Alliance', *Foreign Affairs*, 41, 2 (January 1963), 261.
73. Speech at Casablanca, 8 August 1943.
74. Broadcast, 17 November 1945.
75. Interview with *Réalités–Entreprises*, 18 October 1966.
76. Press conference, 31 January 1964.
77. See Tournoux, *La tragédie du Général*, annex.
78. See Bloes, *Le 'Plan Fouchet' et le problème de l'Europe politique*.
79. Press conference, 23 October 1958.
80. Message to Latin America on the BBC, 19 April 1943.
81. Broadcast on the BBC and CBS, 8 July 1942.
82. Speech at Oran, 12 September 1943.
83. Address, 31 May 1960.
84. Press conference, 10 November 1959.
85. Address, 3 October 1958.
86. Press conference, 5 September 1961.
87. *Mémoires d'espoir*, vol. I, p. 159; speech at opening session of Provisional Consultative Assembly, Algiers, 3 November 1943.
88. Message to the National Assembly, 11 December 1962.
89. *Mémoires d'espoir*, vol. I, p. 171.
90. *Ibid.*, pp. 144–5; cf. also broadcast on the BBC, 20 April 1943; speech at Saint-Étienne, 4 January 1948; press conference, 1 October 1943; and several statements in the 1968–9 period.
91. Speech to the Provisional Consultative Assembly, Algiers, 18 March 1944.
92. Declaration, 18 August 1947.
93. Broadcast on the BBC, 20 April 1943.
94. Reply to Papal Nuncio, 22 January 1959.

Chapter 3
The dynamics of Gaullist ideology

1. Robert Aron, 'The Political Methods of General de Gaulle', *International Affairs*, 37, 1 (January 1961), 22.
2. *Vers l'Armée de métier*, pp. 169–70.
3. *Mémoires d'espoir*, vol. I, p. 40.
4. Schoenbrun, *The Three Lives of Charles de Gaulle*, p. 95.
5. *The Complete War Memoirs*, pp. 82–3.
6. *L'Armée de métier*, p. 160.
7. Grosser, *La politique extérieure de la Ve République*, p. 39.
8. Consider the title and theme of J. E. S. Hayward, 'Presidential Suicide by

Plebiscite: De Gaulle's Exit, April 1969', *Parliamentary Affairs*, 22, 4 (Autumn 1969), 289–319.
9. *Mémoires d'espoir*, vol. I, p. 34.
10. His poetry was the centre of his adolescence; and in *Who's Who* he listed his books, not his honorary degrees.
11. See Tournoux, *La tragédie du Général*.
12. Press conference, 5 September 1960.
13. For a detailed first-hand report of the event, see Schoenbrun, *Three Lives*.
14. *Le fil de l'épée*, p. 9.
15. *Mémoires d'espoir*, vol. I, p. 51.
16. *Ibid.*, pp. 49ff.
17. Jean-Marie Cotteret and René Moreau, *Le vocabulaire du général de Gaulle: Analyse statistique des allocations radiodiffusées 1958–1965* (Paris: Armand Colin, 1969).
18. Note that certain words, particularly 'France', occur in both types of speech; *ibid.*, p. 27n.
19. See Jean Charlot, *Le phénomène gaulliste* (Paris: Fayard, 1970); cf. also de Gaulle's relations with collaborators during these periods as related in Tournoux, *Le tourment et la fatalité*, and Edgard Pisani, *Le général indivis* (Paris: Albin Michel, 1974).
20. See Hartley, *Gaullism*, ch. 1.
21. Strictly speaking, it is a book about military leadership, and the ends which are taken for granted are the standard ones of relative military advantage and victory, which are difficult to equate with the more complex goals of political action.
22. *Fil de l'épée*, pp. 66–7.
23. *L'Armée de métier*, p. 174.
24. *Fil de l'épée*, pp. 69–71.
25. *Ibid.*, pp. 72–3.
26. *Ibid.*, pp. 73–5.
27. *Ibid.*, pp. 76–7.
28. Murray Edelman, *The Symbolic Uses of Politics*, p. 138; and Edelman, *Politics as Symbolic Action: Mass Arousal and Quiescence* (Chicago: Markham, 1971), p. 81.
29. Edelman, *Symbolic Uses of Politics*, pp. 96–7.
30. *Ibid.*, p. 137.
31. *Fil de l'épée*, pp. 89–90.
32. *Ibid.*, p. 95.
33. *Complete War Memoirs*, p. 499.
34. *Fil de l'épée*, pp. 76–7.
35. *Ibid.*, p. 54.
36. *Ibid.*, pp. 13–14.
37. *Ibid.*, pp. 14–15.
38. *Ibid.*
39. *Ibid.*, pp. 15–19.
40. *Ibid.*, pp. 22–8.
41. *Ibid.*, pp. 28–30.

Chapter 4
National consciousness and the role of France in world politics

1. Voltaire's phrase is useful here in indicating the ambivalence of the French tradition – its duality in seeking to create a particular kind of cultural milieu (and here our previous reference to the cultural significance of the French garden is important) alongside the tendency of the cultural environment itself to prescribe norms expressed in the form of universalised values – a tradition which culturally attempted to transcend cultural limitations, thus turning outwards again.

2. Raymond Aron, *Peace and War*, p. 189.

3. Cf. Charles P. Kindleberger, *Economic Growth in France and Britain 1851– 1950* (Cambridge, Mass.: Harvard University Press, 1964); and Barrington Moore Jr, *Social Origins of Dictatorship and Democracy: Lord and Peasant in the Making of the Modern World* (Harmondsworth: Penguin, 1967), ch. 2.

4. Stanley Hoffmann, 'Paradoxes of the French Political Community', in Hoffmann, *et al.*, *In Search of France*, pp. 19–20.

5. See Edmond Jouve, *Le général de Gaulle et la construction de l'Europe (1940–66)* (Paris: Librairie Générale de Droit et de Jurisprudence, 1967), 2 vols.

6. Jean-Baptiste Duroselle, 'Changes in French Foreign Policy since 1958', in Hoffmann, *et al.*, *In Search of France*, pp. 310–17.

7. Dorothy Pickles, 'French Foreign Policy', in F. S. Northedge (ed.), *The Foreign Policies of the Powers* (London: Faber and Faber, 1967), pp. 187–8.

8. *The Complete War Memoirs*, p. 80; cf. Tournoux, *Pétain and de Gaulle*; W. L. Shirer, *The Collapse of the Third Republic* (London: Heinemann, 1969); and J. Néré, *The Foreign Policy of France from 1941 to 1945* (London: Routledge and Kegan Paul, 1975).

9. Duroselle, 'Changes in French Foreign Policy', p. 319.

10. *Ibid.*, p. 316.

11. Alfred Grosser, *La IVe République et sa politique extérieure* (Paris: Armand Colin, 1964), p. 9.

12. Roy C. Macridis, 'French Foreign Policy', p. 73.

13. Grosser, *La IVe République*, p. 399.

14. Henry Tudor, *Political Myth* (London: Macmillan, 1972), p. 73.

15. Tournoux, *La tragédie du Général*, p. 93.

16. *Ibid.*, pp. 267–8.

17. *Ibid.*, p. 310.

18. Znaniecki, *Modern Nationalities: A Sociological Study*, p. 4.

19. Erik Erikson, *Young Man Luther* (New York: Norton, 1958), p. 111, quoted in Edelman, *Politics as Symbolic Action*, p. 54.

20. Herbert C. Kelman, 'Patterns of Personal Involvement in the National System: A Social Psychological Analysis of Political Legitimacy', in Rosenau (ed.), *International Politics and Foreign Policy*, p. 285.

21. Elie Kedourie, *Nationalism* (London: Hutchinson, 1966), p. 101.

22. Kelman, 'Patterns of Personal Involvement in National System'.

23. Giovanni Sartori, *Democratic Theory* (New York: Praeger, 1965), p. 20.

24. According to Edelman's usage, referential symbols are symbols with associations with specific and limited points of reference, which they stand for or

represent; condensation symbols, in contrast, are associated with a far more complex and variegated range of phenomena, which they condense into a single linking image; see *The Symbolic Uses of Politics*, p. 6.

25. Kelman, 'Patterns of Personal Involvement in National System', p. 284.
26. Edelman, *Symbolic Uses of Politics*, p. 34.
27. George Herbert Mead, *Mind, Self and Society* (Chicago: 1934), p. 78, quoted in Edelman, *Symbolic Uses of Politics*, p. 35.
28. Ferdinand de Saussure, *Course in General Linguistics* (New York: McGraw-Hill, 1966), p. 68, quoted in Tudor, *Political Myth*, p. 58.
29. Edelman, *Symbolic Uses of Politics*, p. 134; C. J. Bartlett, *The Rise and Fall of the Pax Americana* (London: Elek, 1974), p. 6.
30. Edelman, *Symbolic Uses of Politics*, p. 102.
31. *Ibid.*, p. 107.
32. Hoffmann, 'De Gaulle's Memoirs', p. 145.
33. Gabriel A. Almond and Sidney Verba, *The Civic Culture: Political Attitudes in Five Nations* (Boston: Little, Brown, 1965), p. 242.
34. Quoted in Ralph Miliband, *The State in Capitalist Society* (London: Weidenfeld and Nicolson, 1969), p. 208.
35. P. G. Cerny, 'The Role of the Military in Socio-Political Value Systems', *The British Army Review*, 34 (April 1970), 54–60.
36. J. P. Nettl, *Political Mobilisation* (London: Faber and Faber, 1967), p. 254.
37. Bloes, *Le 'Plan Fouchet' et le problème de l'Europe politique*, pp. 466–7.
38. Pisani, *Le général indivis*, p. 21; see also his description of de Gaulle's distinction between the *national* and the *politique*, ch. 5, pp. 38–48.
39. Pompidou claimed, to a luncheon meeting of UNR and Independent Republican members of the bureau of the National Assembly, that de Gaulle's speech of 27 April 1965 was meant to open the 1965 presidential campaign: *L'Année politique 1965* (Paris: Presses Universitaires de France, 1966), pp. 33–4.
40. See Cotteret and Moreau, *Le vocabulaire du général de Gaulle: analyse statistique des allocations radiodiffusées 1958–1965*.
41. In 1965. Tournoux, *Le tourment et la fatalité*, p. 164.
42. Tudor, *Political Myth*, p. 52.
43. *Ibid.*
44. Harold D. Lasswell, 'Key Symbols, Signs and Icons', in Lyman Bryson, *et al.*, *Symbols and Values: An Initial Study* (New York: 1954), p. 201, quoted in Edelman, *Symbolic Uses of Politics*, p. 128.
45. Tudor, *Political Myth*, p. 127.
46. Edward Shils, 'Consensus', Paper delivered at the Seventh World Congress of the International Political Science Association, Brussels, 18–23 September 1967, mimeo.
47. Johnson, *France*, pp. 117–18.
48. For a discussion of the term 'level of aspirations', cf. Frankel, *The Making of Foreign Policy*, p. 136.
49. Hoffmann, 'De Gaulle's Memoirs', p. 145.
50. *Ibid.*
51. Several writers have devoted books to this theme of the gap between presumed Gaullist objectives and the mediocre nature of Gaullist successes. By far the most methodical and complete of these, and therefore the least

polemical and most convincing, is Edward L. Morse, *Foreign Policy and Interdependence in Gaullist France* (Princeton, N.J.: Princeton University Press, 1973).

52. Renouvin and Duroselle, *Introduction to the History of International Relations*, p. 348.

53. Cf. Tournoux, *Tragédie du Général*; also Cyrus L. Sulzberger, *The Last of the Giants* (New York: Macmillan, 1970).

54. Edward A. Kolodziej, *French International Policy under de Gaulle and Pompidou* (Ithaca, N.Y.: Cornell University Press, 1974); the conclusions here are more nuanced than in Kolodziej, 'Patterns of French Policy'.

55. Lawrence Scheinman, 'French Foreign Policy', in John Ambler, *The Government and Politics of France* (Boston: Houghton Mifflin, 1971), p. 214.

56. Pierre Hassner, 'Nationalisme et relations internationales', *Revue française de science politique*, 15, 3 (June 1965), 518.

57. 'Nationalism, wherever it occurs, draws on certain universal psychological dispositions, and on a set of norms established in the contemporary international system, in order to promote a particular set of goals shared by an identifiable population or segment of such a population. What is common to all cases of nationalism is the attempt to promote these goals by maintaining or establishing a nation-state as an effective political unit. The nature of the goals involved, however, may vary widely from country to country, from period to period, and from group to group within a given country. Nationalism may be mobilised, for example, in the service of economic development, or of military expansion, or of internal democratisation; and in each of these cases a different segment of the population is likely to provide the impetus and the leadership for this effort.' Kelman, 'Patterns of Personal Involvement in National System', pp. 276–7.

58. Cf. Kedourie, *Nationalism*; Hassner, 'Nationalisme et relations internationales', and Johan Galtung, *The European Community: A Superpower in the Making* (London: Allen and Unwin, 1973), ch. 3, 'On Power in General'.

59. 'Extroversive goals result in the priority of foreign policy – power, security, glory and *grandeur*, the sense of a civilising mission. Introversive goals result in the priority of internal matters with foreign policy serving as an instrument only. Where this type prevails, foreign policy must avoid risks that would interfere with the achievement of domestic goals. Wealth, peace, social cohesion or the domination of a particular class are goals of the introversive type.' Duroselle, 'Changes in French Foreign Policy', p. 306. Compare Arnold Wolfers's 'goals of national self-extension', 'goals of national self-preservation' and 'goals of self-abnegation', in Wolfers, 'The Pole of Power and the Pole of Indifference', in Rosenau, ed., *International Politics and Foreign Policy*, p. 177.

60. André Malraux, 'Une présence humaine et généreuse', *Nouvelle frontière* (January 1964), pp. 3–4, quoted in Hassner, 'Nationalisme', pp. 516–17.

61. Georges Pompidou, Speech to the Institut des Hautes Études de Défense Nationale, 3 November 1967, in La Documentation Française, *La politique étrangère de la France*, 1967, no. 2, pp. 127–9.

62. Couve de Murville, *Une politique étrangère*, pp. 481–2.

63. Couve de Murville, Speech to the National Assembly, 14 April 1966 (London: Ambassade de France, Press and Information Service, document A/38/5/6).

64. Gustavo Lagos, *International Stratification and Underdeveloped Countries*

(Chapel Hill, N.C.: University of North Carolina Press, 1963), quoted in K. J. Holsti, *International Relations: A Framework for Analysis* (Englewood Cliffs, N.J.: Prentice-Hall, 1967), p. 73.

65. See Galtung, *The European Community*, pp. 34–47.

66. This point is extensively and convincingly argued in Robert Gilpin, *France in the Age of the Scientific State* (Princeton, N.J.: Princeton University Press, 1968).

67. Tournoux, *Tragédie du Général*, p. 199.

68. Tournoux, *Tourment et fatalité*, p. 163.

69. Harold D. Lasswell, *World Politics and Personal Insecurity* (New York: Free Press, 1965), p. 82 (originally published 1935); consider, however, the comment attributed to Jan Masaryk, that the problem with being a bridge is that the bullocks are always walking across and defecating on one. Cf. also Frankel, *National Interest*, pp. 79–80.

70. Tournoux, *Le tourment et la fatalité*, p. 163.

71. Cf. Billotte, 'La France et la puissance mondiale', pp. 14, 47.

72. J.-P. Derriennic, 'Relations interétatiques inégales et conflits', *Revue française de science politique*, 19, 4 (1969), 848.

Chapter 5
Foreign policy leadership and national integration

1. I.e. the change from 'status' to 'contract', from a diffuse socio-economic structure to one based on a complex division of labour, from decision-making structures based on 'right reason' or natural law to ones based on formal economic rationality, from authority based on traditional or charismatic legitimation to authority based on legal-rational norms: cf. Max Weber, *The Theory of Social and Economic Organisation*, ed. Talcott Parsons (New York: Oxford University Press, 1947); Amitai Etzioni and Eva Etzioni (eds), *Social Change: Sources, Patterns and Consequences* (New York: Basic Books, 1964); M. J. Levy Jr, *Modernisation and the Structure of Societies: A Setting for International Affairs* (Princeton, N.J.: Princeton University Press, 1966), 2 vols.; and Barrington Moore Jr, *Social Origins of Dictatorship and Democracy*.

2. Direct economic exploitation, administrative decision-making divorced from the local socio-cultural context, lack of 'national' consciousness or political expertise on the part of both elites and masses, etc.

3. Contrast: from the Western perspective, see Reinhard Bendix, *Nation-building and Citizenship* (Garden City, N.Y.: Anchor Books, 1969), and S. N. Eisenstadt and Stein Rokkan, *Building States and Nations* (Beverly Hills: Sage, 1973), 2 vols.; from the Third World perspective, further contrast Helio Jaguaribe, *Political Development: A General Theory and a Case Study* (New York: Harper and Row, 1973), and Samir Amin, *Accumulation on a World Scale: A Critique of the Theory of Underdevelopment* (New York: Monthly Review Press, 1974), 2 vols.

4. Moore, *Social Origins*, ch. 2.

5. Hoffmann, 'Paradoxes of the French Political Community'.

6. Barbara Ward, *Nationalism and Ideology* (London: Hamish Hamilton, 1966), pp. 17–19.

7. In effect, the concept of a 'legitimate order' can (but does not necessarily) imply a 'reciprocity of expectations' (which Weber identifies as that basis of social relations distinct from those based on an 'exercise of authority': Bendix, *Nation-building*, p. 19) between the governors and the governed in the manner of a social contract; ideology in this sense provides the specific *content* of such a relationship.

8. Although the potentialities – and dangers – of the manipulation of kinship structures for the purpose of creating national solidarity can be seen in the history of German unification.

9. 'Because the meaning of the [political] act in these cases depends only partly or not at all upon its objective consequences, which the mass public cannot know, the meaning can only come from the psychological needs of the respondents; and it can only be known from their responses.' Edelman, *The Symbolic Uses of Politics*, p. 7.

10. Henry A. Kissinger, *A World Restored*, p. 331.

11. See Dennis Kavanagh, *Political Culture* (London: Macmillan, 1972), pp. 10–11.

12. Almond and Verba, p. 305.

13. Znaniecki, *Modern Nationalities: A Sociological Study*, pp. 114–15.

14. Nettl, *Political Mobilisation*, pp. 174–5.

15. A claim for such convergence is made in Harry Eckstein, *Division and Cohesion in Democracy: A Study of Norway* (Princeton, N.J.: Princeton University Press, 1966); for a comparative perspective, cf. Hans Daalder, 'Parties, Elites and Political Developments in Western Europe', in Giuseppe di Palma (ed.), *Mass Politics in Industrial Societies: A Reader in Comparative Politics* (Chicago: Markham, 1972), pp. 4–36.

16. Edelman, *The Symbolic Uses of Politics*, p. 4.

17. Norman L. Stamps, *Why Democracies Fail* (Notre Dame, Indiana: Notre Dame University Press, 1957), p. 47.

18. Almond and Verba, *The Civic Culture: Political Attitudes in Five Nations*, p. 192; also Sidney Verba, 'Comparative Political Culture', in Lucian W. Pye and S. Verba (eds.), *Political Culture and Political Development* (Princeton, N.J.: Princeton University Press, 1965), p. 529.

19. Kelman, 'Patterns of Personal Involvement in the National System', pp. 280–3.

20. Talcott Parsons, 'A Functional Theory of Change', in Etzioni and Etzioni, *Social Change*, p. 87.

21. John H. Herz, 'The Territorial State Revisited: Reflections on the Future of the Nation-State', in Rosenau, *International Politics and Foreign Policy*, p. 83.

22. Verba, 'Comparative Political Culture', p. 530.

23. Lasswell, *World Politics and Personal Insecurity*, p. 77.

24. Claude Ake, 'Charismatic Legitimation and Political Integration', *Comparative Studies in Society and History*, 9, 1 (1966–7), 1–13. I prefer Ake's term 'political integration' (which he distinguishes from the meaning of the term used by Haas and others in referring to international integration) to 'nation-building', 'authority legitimation', etc. because it indicates a more overarching process which subsumes the others. Nettl distinguishes between ideology – the active ingredient in this symbolic process – and culture – which is created and moulded by ideology; *Political Mobilisation*, p. 27.

25. Almond and Verba, *The Civic Culture*, pp. 105–6.

26. Edelman, *Politics as Symbolic Action*, pp. 31–2.

27. Deutsch, *Nationalism and Social Communication*, p. 97.

28. See Bernard E. Brown, 'The French Experience of Modernisation', *World Politics*, 21, 3 (April 1969), 376.

29. Deutsch, *Nationalism*, p. 172; also see Kelman, 'Patterns of Personal Involvement in National System', p. 278.

30. Nettl, *Political Mobilisation*, p. 111.

31. *Ibid.*, p. 199.

32. Edelman, *Symbolic Uses of Politics*, p. 138.

33. Nettl, *Political Mobilisation*, p. 144.

34. *Ibid.*, p. 115.

35. *Ibid.*, p. 247.

36. *Ibid.*, p. 300.

37. *Ibid.*, p. 143.

38. *Ibid.*, p. 219.

39. Edelman, *Symbolic Uses of Politics*, p. 19.

40. Verba reminds readers of the significance of 'salient crises' in this regard; 'Comparative Political Culture', pp. 555ff.

41. J. N. Rosenau, 'The National Interest', in *The Scientific Study of Foreign Policy*, p. 239.

42. See Gunnar Myrdal, *et al.*, 'The Principle of Cumulation', in Etzioni and Etzioni, *Social Change*, pp. 457–8.

43. Neil J. Smelser, 'Mechanisms of Change and Adjustment to Change', in Bert F. Hoselitz and Wilbert E. Moore (eds.), *Industrialisation and Society* (The Hague: UNESCO–Mouton, 1963), p. 45.

44. Frankel, *National Interest*, p. 43.

45. Edelman, *Politics as Symbolic Action*, p. 101.

46. See Marcel Merle, *Sociologie des relations internationales* (Paris: Dalloz, 1974), ch. 1.

47. J. N. Rosenau, 'Foreign Policy as an Issue-Area', in Rosenau (ed.), *Domestic Sources of Foreign Policy*, p. 24.

48. *Ibid.*

49. Lasswell, *World Politics and Personal Insecurity*, p. 55.

50. Rosenau, 'Foreign Policy as an Issue-Area', p. 45.

51. Stability is, of course, by definition a 'conservative' objective; in this sense we do not see it as an inherent property of functional general systems in the structural–functional sense so much as the logical goal of a dominant group or structure (whether newly established or long established, traditional or revolutionary). It is possible, of course, to posit that the right or correct goal of any system worth the name is the maintenance of stability because peace and lack of violent conflict is good in itself; this is the Hobbesian principle which political scientists and sociologists have been dealing with throughout the modern and contemporary periods. But to treat stability as somehow above issues is to miss the fact that stability itself is a central issue. See pertinent remarks in *ibid.*, p. 13n., and Merle, *Sociologie*, pp. 273–5.

52. See David E. Apter, *The Politics of Modernisation* (Chicago: Chicago University Press, 1965), pp. 138–44.

53. Weber, *The Theory of Social and Economic Organisation*.

54. Johnson, *France*, p. 108.
55. Dankwart A. Rustow, 'Atatürk as Founder of a State', *Daedalus*, 97, 3 (Summer 1968), 794.
56. Robert C. Tucker, 'The Theory of Charismatic Leadership', *Daedalus*, 97, 3 (Summer 1968), 744.
57. David E. Apter, 'Nkrumah, Charisma and the Coup', *Daedalus*, 97, 3 (Summer 1968), 760.
58. Quoted in Tucker, 'Theory of Charismatic Leadership', p. 745.
59. Edelman, *Symbolic Uses of Politics*, p. 76.
60. Tucker, 'Theory of Charismatic Leadership', p. 745.
61. Lasswell, *World Politics and Personal Insecurity*, p. 19.
62. Edelman, *Politics as Symbolic Action*, p. 81, and *Symbolic Uses of Politics*, pp. 96–7.
63. Arthur Schweitzer, 'Theory and Political Charisma', *Comparative Studies in Society and History*, 16, 2 (March 1974), 153–4.
64. *Ibid.*, pp. 154–65, 179.
65. Apter, 'Nkrumah, Charisma and the Coup', p. 766.
66. Tucker, 'Theory of Charismatic Leadership', p. 737.
67. Max Weber, 'The Routinisation of Charisma', in Etzioni and Etzioni, *Social Change*, ch. 9.
68. Rustow, 'Atatürk as a Founder of a State', p. 797.
69. Weber, 'Routinisation of Charisma', p. 54.
70. Ake, 'Charismatic Legitimation and Political Integration', p. 2.
71. Apter, 'Nkrumah, Charisma and the Coup', p. 770.
72. Indeed, if the leader has no new norms to impose, and if his charisma simply masks a petty and stupid tyranny, then any 'normative exemption' may be followed by a period of *normative collapse* characterised by lack of value direction or authority along with widespread criminal activity on the part of the lower echelons of the army, the police, the bureaucracy, etc. This was the case in Idi Amin's Uganda; I am indebted to Professor Ali Mazrui for this observation.
73. Raymond Aron, *Peace and War*, p. 49.
74. Nettl, *Political Mobilisation*, p. 142.
75. *Ibid.*
76. Lasswell, *World Politics and Personal Insecurity*, p. 35.
77. Edelman, *Symbolic Uses of Politics*, pp. 32–3.
78. Smelser, 'Mechanisms of Change', p. 47.
79. Edward L. Morse, 'The Transformation of Foreign Policies: Modernisation, Interdependence and Externalisation', *World Politics*, 22, 3 (April 1970), 389.
80. See P. G. Cerny, 'The Fall of Two Presidents and Extraparliamentary Opposition: France and the United States in 1968', *Government and Opposition*, 5, 3 (Summer 1970), 297. The controversy surrounding Nixon even before the Watergate revelations is also an archetypal example; for a good analysis of the symbolic process involved, see W. Lance Bennett, *The Political Mind and the Political Environment: An Investigation of Public Opinion and Political Consciousness* (Lexington, Mass.: D. C. Heath, 1975), chs. 3 and 4.

Chapter 6
Structure and development of the grand design

1. Couve de Murville, *Une politique étrangère*, p. 448.
2. Press conference, 10 November 1959.
3. Frankel, *Contemporary International Theory*, pp. 71–4.
4. Georges Pompidou, Declaration to the National Assembly and Senate, 13 April 1966, in La Documentation Française, *Notes et études documentaires*, nos. 3384–7 (29 April 1967), p. 66.
5. Fontaine, 'What is French Policy?', p. 68; cf. also Frankel, *The Making of Foreign Policy*, p. 199.
6. Kulski, *De Gaulle and the World*, pp. 153–5; Kolodziej, *French International Policy*, pp. 40–1; Kolodziej, 'Patterns of French Policy', p. 14.
7. P. Maillard, 'La défense nationale de nos jours', *Revue de défense nationale*, 22, 5 (May 1966), 778–9.
8. As Galtung uses the term; 'The European Community', p. 34–47.
9. Pierre Hassner, 'Détente à la française', *Modern World*, vol. 6 (1968), p. 42.
10. Aron identifies three classes of actors in the bipolar system – leaders, allies and neutrals; *Peace and War*, p. 136.
11. Kolodziej, 'Patterns of French Policy', p. 11.
12. William Pickles, 'Making Sense of de Gaulle', *International Affairs*, 42, 3 (July 1966), 412–13.
13. Tournoux, *La tragédie du Général*, pp. 310–11.
14. Grosser, *La politique extérieure de la Ve République*, p. 120.
15. Fontaine, 'What is French Policy?', pp. 68, 70–1.
16. See Ole R. Holsti, P. Terrence Hopmann and John D. Sullivan, *Unity and Disintegration in International Alliances: Comparative Studies* (London: Wiley, 1973), p. 160.
17. Quoted in Alexander Werth, *De Gaulle: A Political Biography* (Harmondsworth: Penguin, 1967), p. 312.
18. See John Newhouse's interview with C. L. Suzberger, 27 December 1964, in Newhouse, *De Gaulle and the Anglo-Saxons* (New York: Viking, 1970), p. 277.
19. Hassner, 'Détente à la française', p. 41; see also Kolodziej's list of conflicting policies, *French International Policy*, p. 21.
20. Gilpin, *France in the Age of the Scientific State*, p. 382.
21. K. J. Holsti, *International Politics*, pp. 143–4. Holsti's skeletal outline of the Gaullist grand design provided a useful reference point for the more elaborate treatment which follows in the next three paragraphs.
22. Kissinger, *A World Restored*, p. 2.
23. Morse, *Foreign Policy and Interdependence*, p. 29.
24. Henry A. Kissinger, 'Domestic Structure and Foreign Policy', *Daedalus*, 95, 2 (Spring 1966), 503–4.
25. For every maxim, there is an equal and opposite counter-maxim: 'Too many cooks spoil the broth' versus 'Many hands make light work'; 'Absence makes the heart grow fonder' versus 'Out of sight, out of mind'; etc.
26. Referring again to the analogy with democratic theory, consider Sartori's distinction between *horizontal* versus *vertical* organisational characteristics (the former concerning equality and participation – the sub-structure – and the

latter concerning the problem of leadership and decision-making – the super-structure): Sartori, 'Anti-elitism Revisited', *Government and Opposition*, 13, 1 (Winter 1978), 60.

27. Couve de Murville, *Une politique étrangère*, pp. 196, 198–9, 460.

28. Kolodziej, *French International Policy*, pp. 70–1, 140–1, 393–4; also Herbert Tint, *French Foreign Policy since the Second World War* (London: Weidenfeld and Nicolson, 1972).

29. French official archives are released only after fifty years, as compared with thirty in Britain.

30. Kissinger's 'Gaullism' consisted of an acceptance of Bismarckian *Realpolitik*, entailing an acceptance of the 'reality' of national sentiments and politics; however, it was firmly anchored in an American context and thus did not accept any fundamental re-equilibration of the international system of super-power dominance. He simply wanted to be less doctrinaire and more subtle about the organisation of the structure on which American hegemony was built (the bloc system).

31. *The Complete War Memoirs*, p. 729. Cf. also Gabriel Kolko, *The Politics of War: The World and United States Foreign Policy, 1943–1945* (New York: Vintage, 1968), chs. 11–13 and 18.

32. Stephen Ambrose, *Rise to Globalism: American Foreign Policy 1938–1970* (Harmondsworth: Penguin, 1971).

33. *Vers l'Armée de métier*, pp. 72–3.

34. Press conference, 11 April 1961; cf. also 'France and the United Nations' (London: Ambassade de France, Press and Information Service, documents B/20/7/5 and B/60/11/70).

35. Address, 31 May 1960.

36. Georges Broussine, 'World in Revolt: A Gaullist Viewpoint', *International Herald Tribune*, 23–4 March 1968.

37. Broadcast speech (during Berlin crisis), 8 May 1961.

38. Press conference, 11 April 1961.

39. *The Complete War Memoirs*, p. 750.

40. *Time*, 9 February 1968.

41. Press conference, 31 January 1964; also R. Cléry, 'Les objectifs extérieurs de la Chine', *Revue de défense nationale*, 22, 5 (May 1966), 881.

42. Consider Kosygin's reply at a dinner during his visit to France, 1 December 1966.

43. Other topics which could have been covered in detail include: the conflict between France and the USA on monetary questions; the German problem *per se*; trade relations with the East; the recognition of China; de Gaulle's personal diplomacy; the United Nations; etc. For greater detail on these and other topics, see particularly Kolodziej, *French International Policy*, which is the best of the large number of secondary surveys which exist.

Chapter 7
Raising the Atlantic question, 1958–62

1. Jacques Vernant, 'L'O.T.A.N.', p. 899.

2. Alastair Buchan, *The End of the Postwar Era: A New Balance of World Power* (London: Weidenfeld and Nicolson, 1974), p. 21.

3. Even when the other's purposes had domestic sources, like the Republicans' exploitation of 'roll-back' in 1952: 'the policy of liberation seems to have been devised primarily to roll back the Democrats in the United States; not the Red Army in Eastern Europe. And for this purpose, liberation was a highly effective strategy.' J. W. Spanier, *American Foreign Policy since World War II* (New York: Praeger, 1968), p. 111.

4. Marshall D. Shulman, ' "Europe" versus "Detente" ', *Foreign Affairs*, 45, 3 (April 1967), 390.

5. C. M. Woodhouse, 'Attitudes of the NATO Countries Toward the United States', *World Politics*, 10, 2 (January 1958), 209.

6. Buchan, *The End of the Postwar Era*, p. 22.

7. See Kolodziej, *French International Policy*, pp. 70–1.

8. Couve de Murville, *Une politique étrangère*, p. 66.

9. Buchan, *The End of the Postwar Era*, pp. 23–7.

10. Aron, *Peace and War*, p. 139.

11. Johannes Gross, 'Towards a Definition of Alliances', *Modern World*, vol. 6 (1968), pp. 32–4.

12. Aron, *Peace and War*, p. 70.

13. Gross, 'Towards a Definition of Alliances', p. 34.

14. Tint, *French Foreign Policy since the Second World War*, pp. 12–27.

15. Wolf Mendl, 'The Debate over Defence Policy in France, with Special Reference to Nuclear Armament, 1945–1960' (unpublished Ph.D. thesis, University of London, 1966).

16. See comments of Robert Schuman and René Mayer in debates in the National Assembly, 22 and 25 July 1949, cited in Simon Serfaty, *France, de Gaulle and Europe: The Policy of the Fourth and Fifth Republics toward the Continent* (Baltimore: Johns Hopkins University Press, 1968), pp. 34–5.

17. Cf. Daniel Lerner and Raymond Aron (eds.), *France Defeats E.D.C.* (New York: Praeger, 1957); and Grosser, *La IVe République et sa politique extérieure*, which is the best overall survey of the period.

18. Philip Windsor, 'West German Foreign Policy', in F. S. Northedge (ed.), *The Foreign Policies of the Powers*, pp. 221–52; also Ralf Dahrendorf, *Society and Democracy in Germany* (London: Weidenfeld and Nicolson, 1968).

19. See Philip M. Williams, *Crisis and Compromise: Politics in the Fourth Republic* (London: Longman, 1964), p. 434.

20. Alain Girard, 'Sondages d'opinion et politique étrangère', in Léo Hamon (ed.), *L'élaboration de la politique étrangère* (Paris: Presses Universitaires de France, 1969), pp. 21–41.

21. Quoted in Serfaty, *France, de Gaulle and Europe*, p. 122.

22. Descriptions of this period can be found in several of the general surveys, although I depend particularly upon Dimitri Kitsikis, 'L'attitude des Etats-Unis à l'égard de la France de 1958 à 1960', *Revue française de science politique*, 16, 4 (August 1966), 685ff.

23. Wilfrid L. Kohl, *French Nuclear Diplomacy* (Princeton, N.J.: Princeton University Press, 1971), p. 66.

24. Kitsikis, 'L'attitude des Etats-Unis', p. 703–5.

25. 'The Unsolved Problems of European Defence', *Foreign Affairs*, 40, 4 (July 1962), 538–9. See also Newhouse, *De Gaulle and the Anglo-Saxons*, pp. 21–2, 113, and Kitsikis, 'L'attitude des Etats-Unis', pp. 695–9.

26. *Ibid.*, p. 707. Kitsikis, 'L'attitude des Etats-Unis', p. 707.

27. XXX, 'La politique européenne des Etats-Unis', *Revue de défense nationale*, 23, 3 (March 1967), p. 386.

28. Kohl, *French Nuclear Diplomacy*, p. 92.

29. Such is Kohl's view, *ibid.*, pp. 74–7.

30. Kolodziej, 'Patterns of French Policy', p. 44.

31. Kolodziej, *French International Policy*, pp. 82–6.

32. Tint, *French Foreign Policy since the Second World War*, pp. 138–9.

33. See Debré's remarks to the National Press Club in Washington, 10 April 1969, *Le Monde*, 11 April 1969.

34. As outlined by Kolodziej, 'Patterns of French Policy', p. 27.

35. Tournoux, *La tragédie du Général*, p. 321.

36. Paul-Marie de la Gorce, *De Gaulle entre deux mondes* (Paris: Fayard, 1964), p. 712.

37. Kolodziej, 'Patterns of French Policy', pp. 23–6.

38. Kohl, *French Nuclear Diplomacy*, p. 133.

39. Conversation reported by C. L. Sulzberger in *The Last of the Giants*, pp. 707–8.

40. Couve de Murville, *Une politique étrangère*, p. 76.

41. Serfaty, *France, de Gaulle and Europe*, p. 39.

42. Gross, 'Towards a Definition of Alliances', p. 33.

43. See Jouve, *Le général de Gaulle et la construction de l'Europe (1940–1966)*, vol. 1, 129–36, 277–367.

44. Kolodziej, 'Patterns of French Policy', pp. 29–30.

45. 'In effect, the hierarchy of peoples is determined more and more as a function of the nuclear factor. The "modern" weapon confers a predominant rank on whoever possesses it...whatever we undertake in our policy also takes place in an international context. In this context, the existence of a national French force exercises an influence on each of the Great Powers in turn.' Raymond Bousquet, 'La Force Nucléaire Stratégique française', *Revue de défense nationale*, 22, 5 (May 1966), 795, 799.

46. Kitsikis, 'L'attitude des Etats-Unis', pp. 706–9; Kolodziej, 'Patterns of French Policy', pp. 29–30; and *French International Policy*, p. 269.

47. Kitsikis, 'L'attitude des Etats-Unis', pp. 693–5.

48. Newhouse, *De Gaulle and the Anglo-Saxons*, p. 153.

49. *Ibid.*

50. *Ibid.*, p. 156.

51. *Ibid.*, p. 157.

52. Cf. Kolodziej, *French International Policy*, pp. 115ff.; also Newhouse, *De Gaulle and the Anglo-Saxons*, pp. 189ff.

53. See Pompidou's speech to the National Assembly and Senate of 13 April 1966.

54. Couve de Murville, *Une politique étrangère*, p. 108.

55. The United States had, in effect, recognised France's nuclear status at the time of Secretary of State Rusk's visit to Paris (19 June 1962 – three days after McNamara's flexible response speech at the University of Michigan), when Washington sought unsuccessfully an agreement on joint targeting; Newhouse, *De Gaulle and the Anglo-Saxons*, pp. 189ff.

56. Couve de Murville, *Une politique étrangère*, p. 194.

57. George W. Ball, 'Slogans and Realities', *Foreign Affairs*, 47, 4 (July 1969), 623.
58. Serfaty, *France, de Gaulle and Europe*, p. 43.

Chapter 8
Atlantic divergences

1. Kulski, *De Gaulle and the World*, pp. 164–73.
2. Cf. Kolodziej, *French International Policy*, p. 123; we emphasise a rather different interpretation of these strands.
3. Press conference, 29 August 1963.
4. Press conference, 15 May 1962; cf. also Vernant, 'L'O.T.A.N.', p. 902.
5. Press conference, 29 August 1963.
6. Quoted in Jouve, *Le général de Gaulle et la construction de l'Europe (1940–1966)*, vol. I, pp. 601–2.
7. Werth, *De Gaulle: A Political Biography*, p. 405.
8. Kolodziej, *French International Policy*, pp. 52–3.
9. *Ibid.*, pp. 53–4.
10. Cf. Adam Bromke (ed.), *The Communist States at the Crossroads: Between Moscow and Peking* (New York: Praeger, 1965); and Ghiţa Ionescu, *The Break-up of the Soviet Empire in Eastern Europe* (Harmondsworth: Penguin, 1965).
11. Pierre Hassner, 'L'Europe de l'est entre l'est et l'Europe', *Revue française de science politique*, 19, 1 (February 1969), 102–3.
12. Tournoux, *Le tourment et la fatalité*, p. 127: see de Gaulle's report of Khrushchev's remarks in 1963.
13. J. Brest, 'L'U.R.S.S. face à la guerre nucléaire', *Revue de défense nationale*, 22, 5 (May 1966), 826.
14. Zbigniew Brzezinski, 'The Framework of East–West Reconciliation', *Foreign Affairs*, 46, 2 (January 1968), 256. Cf. also Pierre Hassner, 'Change and Security in Europe', Adelphi Papers nos. 45 and 49 (London: Institute for Strategic Studies, February and July 1968).
15. See Tint, *French Foreign Policy since the Second World War*, pp. 149–52.
16. *L'Année politique 1965*, pp. 242–3.
17. Quoted in Kulski, *De Gaulle and the World*, pp. 307–9.
18. Werth, *De Gaulle: A Political Biography*, p. 407.
19. See Malcolm Mackintosh, 'The Evolution of the Warsaw Pact', Adelphi Paper no. 58 (London: Institute for Strategic Studies, June 1969), and Institute for Strategic Studies, 'Soviet–American Relations and the World Order', Adelphi Paper no. 66 (London: Institute for Strategic Studies, March 1970).
20. Kulski, *De Gaulle and the World*, pp. 306–7.
21. Kolodziej, *French International Policy*, pp. 367–9; Couve de Murville, *Une politique étrangère*, pp. 202ff. and 213–14.
22. Kolodziej, *French International Policy*, pp. 367–9.
23. *Moniteur officiel de commerce et industrie*, nos. 753, 791, 802, 805 and 809 (1968).
24. Kolodziej, *French International Policy*, pp. 367–9.

25. It was fitting that de Gaulle was on an important state visit to Rumania during a crucial period of the Events of May 1968, as it symbolised both the strengths and the weaknesses of his policy. See Corneliu Mânescu, 'Rumania in the Concert of Nations', *International Affairs*, 45, 1 (January 1969), 1.

26. France's leverage in Eastern Europe always lagged behind that of West Germany, although in the earlier period the West Germans did not possess France's *political* credibility; one of the rationalisations of the Czechoslovak invasion was German aggressive intentions. See Alfred Grosser, 'France and Germany: Less Divergent Outlooks?', *Foreign Affairs*, 48, 2 (January 1970), 235–44.

27. Couve de Murville, *Une politique étrangère*, pp. 76–7.

28. Alastair Buchan, 'The Reform of NATO', *Foreign Affairs*, 40, 2 (January 1962), 180.

29. *Ibid.*

30. André Beaufre, *NATO and Europe* (New York: Vintage, 1966), p. 90.

31. *Ibid.*, pp. 62–5.

32. Kolodziej, *French International Policy*, p. 114.

33. *Ibid.*

34. Paul-Henri Spaak, *The Continuing Battle: Memoirs of a European 1936–1966* (London: Weidenfeld and Nicolson, 1969), pp. 464–6.

35. Newhouse, *De Gaulle and the Anglo-Saxons*, pp. 243–4.

36. Beaufre, *NATO and Europe*, p. 41.

37. *Ibid.*, p. 37.

38. René Pleven, 'France in the Atlantic Community', *Foreign Affairs*, 38, 1 (October 1959), 28–9.

39. Beaufre, *NATO and Europe*, pp. 34, 42.

40. *Ibid.*, pp. 42–3.

41. Couve de Murville, *Une politique étrangère*, pp. 74–5; cf. also Philippe Devillers, 'La politique française et la seconde guerre du Vietnam', *Politique étrangère*, 32, 6 (1967), 569.

42. Beaufre, *NATO and Europe*, p. 45. Although this makes the charge of 'foreign command' less credible, it actually exacerbates the problems of alliance planning and consultation, especially on nuclear matters.

43. Couve de Murville, *Une politique étrangère*, p. 75; Devillers, 'La politique française et la seconde guerre du Vietnam'. On the role of the French Army, cf. Edgar S. Furniss Jr, *De Gaulle and the French Army: A Crisis in Civil–Military Relations* (New York: The Twentieth Century Fund, 1964) and Orville D. Menard, *The Army and the Fifth Republic* (Lincoln, Nebraska: University of Nebraska Press, 1967).

44. X, 'À propos des bases étrangères en France', *Revue de défense nationale*, 22, 5 (May 1966), 897.

45. Arthur M. Schlesinger Jr, *A Thousand Days: John F. Kennedy in the White House* (Boston: Houghton Mifflin, 1965), p. 872. Cf. Louis Heren, *No Hail, No Farewell: The Johnson Years* (London: Weidenfeld and Nicolson, 1970), pp. 128 and 203; also Ball, 'Slogans and Realities', pp. 624–5.

46. Kolodziej, *French International Policy*, pp. 42–4.

47. Alain C. Enthoven and K. Wayne Smith, 'What Forces for NATO? And from Whom?', *Foreign Affairs*, 48, 1 (October 1969), 91.
48. Fontaine, 'What is French Policy?', p. 73.
49. Quoted in Dean Acheson, 'The Practice of Partnership', *Foreign Affairs*, 41, 2 (January 1963), 251–2.
50. Henry A. Kissinger, 'Unsolved Problems', p. 518.
51. XXX, 'La politique européenne des Etats-Unis', p. 384.
52. Pierre M. Gallois, 'La politique générale et l'armement', *Revue de défense nationale*, 23, 8 (August–September 1967), 1365.
53. Pierre M. Gallois, 'La nouvelle stratégie américaine et ses contradictions', *Politique étrangère*, 26, 4 (1961), 320.
54. Kolodziej, 'Patterns of French Policy', p. 37.
55. *L'Année politique 1965*, p. 261.
56. *Ibid.*, p. 277.
57. Kulski, *De Gaulle and the World*, p. 182.
58. Kolodziej, *French International Policy*, p. 144.
59. Cf. *Vers l'Armée de métier*, pp. 33, 88.
60. Press conference, 11 April 1961.
61. See Maillard, 'La défense nationale de nos jours', p. 778; Maillard was Minister Plenipotentiary and Deputy Secretary General for National Defence at the time he was writing.
62. Pierre M. Gallois, 'Les conséquences stratégiques et politiques des armes nouvelles', *Politique étrangère*, 23, 2 (1958), 168.
63. See discussion in Kulski, *De Gaulle and the World*, pp. 121–2.
64. Kohl, *French Nuclear Diplomacy*, pp. 361–2.
65. Groupe de travail, 'Puissances moyennes et armement nucléaire: Un groupe de travail', *Politique étrangère*, 34, 5–6 (1969), 516–20.
66. Robert J. Lieber, 'The French Nuclear Force: A Strategic and Political Evaluation', *International Affairs*, 42, 3 (July 1966), 428.
67. Kissinger, 'Unsolved Problems', p. 533.
68. Cf. Judith H. Young, 'The French Strategic Missile Program', Adelphi Paper no. 38 (London: Institute for Strategic Studies, July 1967); Wolf Mendl, 'Perspectives of Contemporary French Defence Policy', *The World Today*, 24, 2 (February 1968); and Groupe de Travail, 'Puissances moyennes et armement nucléaire'.
69. Carnéade, 'La défense "tous azimuts" et "l'art du réel et du possible"', *Revue des deux mondes* (15 May 1968), pp. 172–3.
70. Kulski, *De Gaulle and the World*, p. 113.
71. *Ibid.*, p. 114.
72. J. Brest, 'L'U.R.S.S. face à la guerre nucléaire', p. 828.
73. Kulski, *De Gaulle and the World*, p. 112; also Mendl, 'Perspectives', pp. 52–3.
74. For an official exposition of the 'trigger' theory, see Pompidou's speech to the National Assembly and Senate, 13 April 1966.
75. Kissinger, 'Unsolved Problems', pp. 532–3.
76. Kissinger, 'Strains on the Alliance', *Foreign Affairs*, 41, 2 (January 1963), 277–8.
77. André Beaufre, *Dissuasion et stratégie* (Paris: Armand Colin, 1964).
78. Beaufre, *NATO and Europe*, p. 85.

79. Quoted in Edward A. Kolodziej, 'French Strategy Emergent – General André Beaufre: A Critique', *World Politics*, 19, 3 (April 1967), 435.

80. K. J. Holsti, *International Politics*, p. 120.

81. François de Rose, 'Atlantic Relationships and Nuclear Problems', *Foreign Affairs*, 41, 3 (April 1963), 482.

82. Raoul Girardet, 'Autour du "Grand Débat" ', *Revue française de science politique*, 14, 2 (April 1964), 343–4.

83. Wolf Mendl, *Deterrence and Persuasion: French Nuclear Armament in the Context of National Policy, 1945–1969* (London: Faber and Faber, 1970), pp. 173–4.

84. Kohl, *French Nuclear Diplomacy*, pp. 30–1, 161–2; Mendl, *Deterrence and Persuasion*, p. 107.

85. See Jean Planchais, 'La cassure de l'Armée', *La Nef*, 25, 33 (February–April 1968), 115–23.

86. Aron, *Peace and War*, p. 490.

87. *Ibid.*, p. xiii.

88. Kohl, *French Nuclear Diplomacy*, pp. 248–50; Newhouse, *De Gaulle and the Anglo-Saxons*, pp. 245–6.

89. Kohl, *French Nuclear Diplomacy*, p. 81; Kulski, *De Gaulle and the World*, pp. 138, 184.

90. For details of the MLF proposals and the French reasons for rejecting them, see Kolodziej, 'Patterns of French Policy', pp. 31–2, 36–7.

91. Furniss, *De Gaulle and the French Army*, pp. 213–16.

92. Gilpin, *France in the Age of the Scientific State*, pp. 336–41.

93. Kolodziej, *French International Policy*, pp. 94–5.

94. Mendl, *Deterrence and Persuasion*, p. 178.

95. Gilpin, *France in the Age of the Scientific State*, p. 217; cf. also Marceau Long, 'L'incidence des dépenses des Armées sur l'économie', *Revue de défense nationale*, 24, 6 (June–July 1968), 987, and Maurice Schumann, 'La politique scientifique de la France', *ibid.*, p. 975.

96. See Young, 'The French Strategic Missile Program'.

97. 'The French Space Programme' (London: Ambassade de France, Press and Information Service, document B/29/7/6); Général R. Aubinière, 'Réalisations et projets de la recherche spatiale française', *Revue de défense nationale*, 23, 10 (November 1967), 1736; and Aubinière, 'La CNES et la politique spatiale de la France', *ibid.*, 24, 10 (December 1968), 1791.

98. Cf. Gilpin, *France in the Age of the Scientific State*; Morse, *Foreign Policy and Interdependence*, pp. 170–5; and Kohl, *French Nuclear Diplomacy*, ch. 5.

99. Morse, *Foreign Policy and Interdependence*, ch. 4, 'Welfare versus Warfare'.

100. Général M. Fourquet, 'La politique d'armement à long terme', *Revue de défense nationale*, 23, 5 (May 1967), 745; Carnéade, 'La défense "tous azimuts" '; Général André Martin, 'Armée de l'air d'aujourd'hui', *Revue de défense nationale*, 23, 1 (January 1967), 5; and Edmond Combaux, Défense tous azimuts? Oui, mais. . .', *ibid.*, 24, 9 (November 1968), 1600.

101. Young, 'The French Strategic Missile Program', p. 9.

102. Kolodziej, *French International Policy*, p. 105.

103. On the organisation of French conventional forces and their relationship to the overall defence structure, see 'France and her Armed Forces' (London: Ambassade de France, Press and Information Service, document B/30/10/6);

on their financing, see Young, 'The French Strategic Missile Program', pp. 6–7; on their strategic role, see André Beaufre, *Strategy for Tomorrow* (London: Macdonald and Jane's, 1974). On expenditure, Morse, *Foreign Policy and Interdependence*, p. 159; Contrôleur Général Heidt, 'Le budget des Armées pour 1969', *Revue de défense nationale*, 25, 2 (February 1969), 203; Heidt, 'Le budget de la défense nationale pour 1970', *ibid.*, 26, 1 (January 1970), 17; on relative Alliance contributions, see Enthoven and Smith, 'What Forces for NATO? And for Whom?', p. 90.

104. Gilpin, *France in the Age of the Scientific State*, pp. 299–300.

105. *Ibid.*, pp. 300–1.

106. Couve de Murville, *Une politique étrangère*, p. 61. Cf. also Kolodziej, *French International Policy*, pp. 104–5; on the question of civil–military relations, cf. Furniss, *De Gaulle and the French Army* and Planchais, 'La cassure de l'Armée'.

107. Aron, *Peace and War*, p. 507.

108. 'La doctrine du Général s'exprime en peu de mots: la France n' aurait jamais dû s'écarter de la politique continentale de Richelieu, de l'établissement d'un Etat fort et ferme au centre de frontières solides.' Tournoux, *La tragédie du Général*, p. 308.

109. Tint, *French Foreign Policy since the Second World War*, pp. 163ff.

110. Press conference, 10 November 1959.

111. La Gorce, *De Gaulle entre deux mondes*, p. 610.

112. See comments on Malraux's visit to China and India (August 1965), *L'Année politique 1965*, p. 286.

113. See Tournoux, *Le tourment et la fatalité*, p. 138; Newhouse calls French recognition of China an attempt 'to extend the conflict with the Americans to the roomy terrain of East Asia', p. 251.

114. Devillers, 'La politique française et la seconde guerre du Vietnam', pp. 569ff.; La Documentation Française, *La politique étrangère de la France: Textes et documents 1966* (Paris: La Documentation Française, 1967), p. 29.

115. Paul Balta, 'Dix ans de politique étrangère: 1958–1968', *Revue de défense nationale*, 24, 5 (May 1968), 827–8; cf. also Guy Feuer, 'Le conflit israélo-arabe et l'action des puissances: la politique de la France', *Revue française de science politique*, 19, 2 (April 1969), 414; Bernard Vernier, 'Les deux grands et le conflit israélo-arabe', *ibid.*, 6 (December 1969), 1247; and Paul Balta and Claudine Rulleau, *La politique arabe de la France de de Gaulle à Pompidou* (Paris: Sindbad, 1973).

116. In the context of a Soviet resolution in the UN: Kolodziej, 'Patterns of French Policy', p. 49.

117. Consider the claim that France's role in Africa – its civilising mission – was comparable to that of Rome in Gaul: Georges R. Manue, 'Réalités et perspectives de la francophonie', *Revue de défense nationale*, 23, 2 (February 1967), 226–7.

118. For figures, see Kolodziej, *French International Policy*, pp. 450–1; for comparative figures, see 'Aid: Who's Dragging their Feet', *The Economist*, 26 December 1970, p. 74. For structure, cf. Louis Dollot, *La France dans le monde actuel* (Paris: Presses Universitaires de France, 1964).

119. Cf. 'The United Nations Conference on Trade and Development: Statement of French Policy' (London: Ambassade de France, Press and Information

Service, document B/12, 1964); also 'France and the Second United Nations Conference on Trade and Development' (London: Ambassade de France, Press and Information Service, document B/45/5/8, 1968).

120. 'Most enlightened Indians are convinced that, in the field of aid to under-developed countries, de Gaulle has shown himself to be bolder than other Western countries. The "decline" of Gaullism (in the 1965 French presidential election) found rueful comments in New Delhi that were shared by most of the diplomatic representatives of other Southeast Asian countries and possibly even more by the countries of Africa. The independent posture of France is also meaningful to those states who seek to be neutralist in their policies.' Howard C. Reese, 'Beyond de Gaulle' (McLean, Va.: Research Analysis Corporation, 1966), p. 4. Also cf. Theresa Hayter, 'French Aid to Africa – Its Scope and Achievements', International Affairs, 41, 2 (April 1965), 236.

121. Cf. Feuer,'Le conflit israélo-arabe et l'action des puissances' and Debré's remarks (as Foreign Minister) in 1968 and 1969 on the French policy of pursuing a 'Big Four' settlement there, in La Documentation Française, La politique étrangère de la France: Textes et documents 1968 and 1969 (Premier semestre) (Paris: La Documentation Française, 1969).

122. Cf. Kulski, De Gaulle and the World, pp. 383–5; D. Pickles, 'French Foreign Policy', p. 210; Devillers, 'La politique française et la seconde guerre du Vietnam', pp. 584–5; Press conference, 4 February 1965; and discussion in Ch. 6, above.

123. See Henri Grimal, La décolonisation 1919–1963 (Paris: Armand Colin,1965).

124. Consider the withdrawal of various ex-colonies from the central franc zone banking arrangements in the early 1970s, the conflict with Algeria over oil agreements, the anti-French upheavals in such previously model ex-colonies as Malagasy, etc.

125. Kohl, French Nuclear Diplomacy, p. 253.

126. E.g. Jouve, Le général de Gaulle et la construction de l'Europe (1940–1966), pp. 213ff.

127. See Sydney N. Fisher (ed.), France and the European Community (Columbus, Ohio: Ohio State University Press, 1964).

128. Couve de Murville, Une politique étrangère, p. 350.

129. Speech to the National Assembly, 25 January 1963.

130. Ambrose, Rise to Globalism: American Foreign Policy 1938–1970.

131. Max Beloff, The United States and the Unity of Europe (London: Faber and Faber, 1963), p. 52.

132. Grosser, La IVᵉ République, pp. 292–4.

133. See Samuel P. Huntington, The Common Defense: Strategic Programs in National Politics (New York: Columbia University Press, 1961).

134. William Y. Elliot (ed.), The Political Economy of American Foreign Policy: Its Concepts, Strategy and Limits (New York: Henry Holt, 1955), p. 324, quoted in Beloff, United States and Unity of Europe, p. 85.

135. E.g. Ball, 'Slogans and Realities'.

136. See Stanley Hoffmann, Gulliver's Troubles; or, The Setting of American Foreign Policy (New York: McGraw-Hill, 1968).

137. Couve de Murville, Une politique étrangère, pp. 100–1.

138. André Marchal, 'Les problèmes du Marché Commun', Politique étrangère, 35, 1 (1970), 9–10.

139. Cf. Gabriel Kolko, 'The United States and World Economic Power', in Milton Mankoff (ed.), *The Poverty of Progress: The Political Economy of American Social Problems* (New York: Holt, Rinehart and Winston, 1972), pp. 152–74; also R. C. Edwards, M. Reich and T. E. Weisskopf (eds.), *The Capitalist System: A Radical Analysis of American Society* (Englewood Cliffs, N.J.: Prentice-Hall, 1972), ch. 10, 'Imperialism'.

140. Jean-Jacques Servan-Schreiber, *The American Challenge* (London: Hamish Hamilton, 1968), p. 8.

141. Cf. Kulski, *De Gaulle and the World*, p. 255, and Gilpin, *France in the Age of the Scientific State*.

142. See discussion in Morse, *Foreign Policy and Interdependence*, pp. 222–3; also Kolodziej, *French International Policy*, pp. 183–210.

143. Joseph M. A. H. Luns, 'Independence or Interdependence?', *International Affairs*, 40, 1 (January 1964), 8.

144. Paul-Henri Spaak, 'A New Effort to Build Europe', *Foreign Affairs*, 43, 2 (January 1965), 199.

145. Spaak, quoted in the *International Herald Tribune*, 28 March 1968.

146. *The Complete War Memoirs*, p. 557.

147. See Susanne J. Bodenheimer, *Political Union: A Microcosm of European Politics, 1960–1966* (Leiden: Sijthoff, 1967).

148. Couve de Murville, *Une politique étrangère*, pp. 347–8.

149. Kolodziej, *French International Policy*, p. 47.

150. Paul-Henri Spaak, 'Hold Fast', *Foreign Affairs*, 41, 4 (July 1963), 611.

151. See John Newhouse, *Collision in Brussels: The Common Market Crisis of 30 June 1965* (New York: Norton, 1967).

152. La Gorce, *De Gaulle entre deux mondes*, p. 714.

153. XXX, 'La politique européenne des Etats-Unis', p. 387; also cf. Tournoux, *La tragédie du Général*, pp. 656–7.

154. Tint, *French Foreign Policy since the Second World War*, p. 88.

155. Philippe de Saint-Robert, *Le jeu de la France* (Paris: 1967), p. 159, quoted in Hassner, 'Détente à la française', p. 48.

156. Vernant, 'L'O.T.A.N.', p. 902.

157. On French policy towards Germany on nuclear questions, see Pierre Messmer's interview on Europe No. 1, 7 October 1967; for more general background, see William B. Bader, 'Nuclear Weapons Sharing and "The German Problem"', *Foreign Affairs*, 44, 4 (July 1966), 693. A list of areas of divergence can be found in D. Pickles, *The Uneasy Entente*, pp. 50–3; a more useful survey is Alfred Grosser, 'France and Germany: Divergent Outlooks', *Foreign Affairs*, 44, 1 (October 1965), esp. 28–35.

158. See Pisani's remarkable account of the June 1965 meeting between de Gaulle and Erhard, in Pisani, *Le Général indivis*, pp. 90–2.

159. Cf. Kai-Üwe von Hassel, 'Détente through Firmness', *Foreign Affairs*, 42, 2 (January 1964), 184, and von Hassel, 'Organising Western Defence', *ibid.*, 43, 2 (January 1965), 209.

160. Cf. Siegfried Schwarz, 'The Events of August 1961 and their Effect on West German Foreign Policy', *German Foreign Policy* (DDR), 5, 5 (August 1966), 372; also Kurt L. Shell, 'Berlin and the German Problem', *World Politics*, 16, 1 (October 1963), 137.

161. See Galtung, *The European Community*, ch. 6, 'The European Community and the Third World Countries'; also Franz Ansprenger, 'Die Bedeutung von de Gaulles Politik für das Überleben Balkanisierter Staaten des Ehemals Französischen Afrikas', *Zeitschrift der Deutschen Vereinigung für Politische Wissenschaft*, 11, 2 (1970), 473.

162. See the statement by the Egyptian Foreign Minister, Mr Mahmoud Riad, 6 January 1971, *The Times*, 7 January 1971.

163. Kolodziej, *French International Policy*, pp. 129–30.

164. Newhouse, *De Gaulle and the Anglo-Saxons*, p. 59.

165. Numerous other examples occur in domestic politics: his flight to London on 18 June 1940; his resignation in 1946; his part in the *coup d'état* of 13 May 1958; and his mysterious disappearance and dramatic return in the midst of the May Events in 1968 – all of which are standard fare for biographers such as Tournoux.

166. Quoted in Tournoux, *La tragédie du Général*, p. 485.

167. Kolodziej, 'Patterns of French Policy', p. 38.

168. The description which follows of the gradual withdrawal process is based on *ibid.*, pp. 38–9; an abridged version of this section can be found in Kolodziej, *French International Policy*, pp. 130–1.

169. *Ibid.*

170. Quoted in *ibid.*

171. *L'Année politique 1965*, pp. 262, 277.

172. *Ibid.*, p. 323.

173. *Ibid.*, p. 261.

174. *Ibid.*

175. *Ibid.*, p. 303.

176. Press conference, 22 February 1966.

177. See discussion in Kolodziej, 'Patterns of French Policy', pp. 40–1.

178. The documents are available in La Documentation Française, *La politique étrangère de la France 1966*.

179. *Ibid.*; cf. Kolodziej, 'Patterns of French Policy', pp. 40–1.

180. *Ibid.*, pp. 41–2.

181. *Ibid.*

182. Louis Heren, *No Hail, No Farewell: The Johnson Years* (Weidenfeld and Nicolson, 1970), pp. 157–8.

183. On American views of her NATO role, see William T. R. Fox and Annette B. Fox, 'The Role of the United States in NATO', in Francis A. Beer (ed.), *Alliances: Latent War Communities in the Contemporary World* (New York: Holt, Rinehart and Winston, 1970), pp. 143–57.

184. Enthoven and Smith, 'What Forces for NATO? And for Whom?'

185. See the cogent criticisms of this view (especially of the views of George Ball), in Frank Church, 'U.S. Policy and the "New Europe"', *Foreign Affairs*, 45, 1 (October 1966), 50.

186. Kolodziej, *French International Policy*, p. 132.

187. *L'Année politique 1966* (Paris: Presses Universitaires de France, 1967), p. 239.

188. Heren, *No Hail, No Farewell*, p. 157.

189. Pompidou, speech before the National Assembly and Senate, 13 April 1966; cf. remarks in Heren, *No Hail, No Farewell*, p .253.

190. See *L'Année politique 1968* (Paris: Presses Universitaires de France, 1969), p. 279.

191. George Gallup, 'De Gaulle's Policy Turns Americans Against French', *International Herald Tribune*, 7 February 1968.

192. Pompidou, speech, 13 April 1966.

193. Couve de Murville, interview on ORTF, 17 March 1966. For an American justification of the Gaullist viewpoint on this issue and others, see the book by the former *New York Times* Paris correspondent: John L. Hess, *The Case for de Gaulle: An American Viewpoint* (New York: William Morrow, 1968).

194. Couve de Murville, *Une politique étrangère*, pp. 80–1.

195. It is with such distinctions in mind that early academic attempts to approach the 'convergence' question must be treated, e.g., Daniel Bell, *The End of Ideology: On the Exhaustion of Political Ideas in the Fifties* (New York: Free Press, 1962), or Walt Whitman Rostow, *The Stages of Economic Growth: A Non-Communist Manifesto* (London: Cambridge University Press, 1962); consider the critique in Noam Chomsky, *American Power and the New Mandarins* (Harmondsworth, Penguin, 1969).

196. Kolodziej, *French International Policy*, pp. 52–3.

197. 'Let every nation know, whether it wishes us well or ill, that we shall pay any price, bear any burden, meet any hardship, support any friend, oppose any foe to assure the survival and success of liberty.' John F. Kennedy, Inaugural Address, 20 January 1961, in Edmund S. Ions (ed.), *The Politics of John F. Kennedy* (London: Routledge and Kegan Paul, 1967), p. 50.

198. Cf. Heren, *No Hail, No Farewell*, p. 158.

199. Thomas S. Kuhn, *The Structure of Scientific Revolutions* (Chicago: University of Chicago Press, 2nd edn, 1969), p. 176.

200. Couve de Murville, Interview on ORTF, 17 March 1966.

Chapter 9
Convergence and reconciliation 1966–9

1. Harland van B. Cleveland, 'NATO After the Invasion', *Foreign Affairs*, 47, 2 (January 1969), 257.

2. C. L. Sulzberger, 'Johnson and de Gaulle', *International Herald Tribune*, 24 June 1968.

3. Article by Ronald Koven, *International Herald Tribune*, 31 January 1968.

4. Harland Cleveland, *NATO: The Transatlantic Bargain* (New York: 1970), cited disapprovingly in Elliot R. Goodman, *The Fate of the Atlantic Community* (New York: Praeger, 1975), p. 107; the latter book is, as regards de Gaulle, a detailed elaboration of the State Department line.

5. *L'Année politique 1966*, p. 243; Newhouse, *De Gaulle and the Anglo-Saxons*, p. 350.

6. Bromke, *The Communist States at the Crossroads: Between Moscow and Peking*.

7. Couve de Murville, *Une politique étrangère*, p. 227.

8. XXX, 'La politique européenne des Etats-Unis', pp. 394–5.

9. *Ibid.*, and Couve de Murville, *Une politique étrangère*, p. 228.

10. Bartlett, *The Rise and Fall of the Pax Americana*, p. 92.

11. Buchan, *The End of the Postwar Era*, pp. 233–4.

12. Arthur M. Schlesinger Jr, speaking in Norwich, *The Guardian*, 15 May 1968.

13. *International Herald Tribune*, 26 April 1968.

14. Charles Gati, 'Another Grand Debate? The Limitationist Critique of American Foreign Policy', *World Politics*, 21, 1 (October 1968), 146.

15. 'The Limits of Commitment: A TIME–Louis Harris Poll', *Time*, 2 May 1969.

16. Louis J. Halle, 'The Conduct v. the Teaching of International Relations', in Institut Universitaire de Hautes Études Internationales de Genève, *Les relations internationales dans un monde en mutation* (Leiden: Sijthoff, 1977), p. 36.

17. Cf. *Le Monde*, 1 April 1969, and *L'Express*, 2–8 March 1970.

18. Nixon, press conference, 4 March 1969, *The New York Times*, 5 March 1969.

19. *Time*, 9 March 1970.

20. Graham Allison, Ernest May and Adam Yarmolinsky, 'U.S. Military Policy: Limits to Intervention', *Foreign Affairs*, 48, 2 (January 1970), 247.

21. Buchan, *The End of the Postwar Era*, pp. 79–80.

22. Couve de Murville, *Une politique étrangère*, pp. 54–5.

23. Quoted in Kolodziej, *French International Policy*, pp. 143–5.

24. Goodman, *The Fate of the Atlantic Community*, p. 112.

25. Goodman states that full cancellation of overflight rights was seen by the French as a potential sanction against American obstruction or reprisals: *ibid.*

26. *Ibid.*, pp. 114–15.

27. Cf. *L'Année politique 1966*.

28. Couve de Murville, *Une politique étrangère*, pp. 84–5.

29. Goodman, *The Fate of the Atlantic Community*, p. 116.

30. Interview in *Le Monde*, 30 March 1966, quoted in *ibid.*, p. 115.

31. Thomas Barman, 'Britain and France, 1967', *International Affairs*, 43, 1 (January 1967), 37.

32. See *L'Année politique 1966*, p. 279.

33. Kolodziej, *French International Policy*, p. 143.

34. Goodman, *The Fate of the Atlantic Community*, pp. 121–3.

35. *Ibid.*

36. Kolodziej, *French International Policy*, p. 143.

37. Quoted in Goodman, *The Fate of the Atlantic Community*, pp. 121–3.

38. Kolodziej, *French International Policy*, p. 144.

39. *The Guardian*, 27 December 1968, and *L'Express*, 3–9 February 1969.

40. Quoted in, e.g. Kohl, *French Nuclear Diplomacy*, p. 266; cf. *The Guardian*, 6 December 1968. In 1970, French effectives were less than West Germany's, although France had 40,000 more regular troops (Germany having 233,000 more reserves). In terms of the percentage of GNP devoted to defence, France was second only to Britain in Western Europe: *The Military Balance, 1970–1971* (London: Institute for Strategic Studies, 1970), p. 112.

41. Quoted in *The Times*, 1 December 1970.

42. Press conference, 14 January 1963.

43. Kolodziej, *French International Policy*, pp. 128–9.

44. *Ibid.*, p. 149.

45. P. Maillard, 'Défense nationale et esprit de défense', *Revue de défense nationale*, 23, 3 (March 1967), 370.

46. *L'Express*, 20–6 January 1969.
47. *L'Express*, 2–8 June 1969; the polls may not be exactly complementary, as they emanated from very different organisations; the source does not specify the exact questions asked. The first was a standard IFOP poll, the second by Cofremca for the Association française pour la Communauté atlantique.
48. Général Ailleret, 'Défense "dirigée" ou défense "tous azimuts" ', *Revue de défense nationale*, 23, 11 (December 1967), 1923.
49. *Paris-Match*, 15 March 1968.
50. *International Herald Tribune*, 30 January 1968.
51. Carnéade, 'La défense "tous azimuts" et "l'art du réel et du possible" '; pp. 161–2.
52. See Combaux, 'Défense tous azimuts? Oui, mais. . .', p. 1600.
53. See Général d'Armée Aérienne M. Fourquet, 'Emploi des différents systèmes de forces dans le cadre de la stratégie de dissuasion', *Revue de défense nationale*, 25, 5 (May 1969), 757. Fourquet was Ailleret's successor. Various programmes necessary for the *tous-azimuts* policy were abandoned, including ICBMs, MIRVs and hunter-killer submarines: *Strategic Survey 1970* (London: Institute for Strategic Studies, 1971), p. 23.
54. Groupe de travail, 'Puissance moyennes et armement nucléaire: un groupe de travail', p. 535.
55. Couve de Murville, *Une politique étrangère*, p. 142.
56. *The Financial Times*, 7 November 1968; American backing of the French position in the November 1968 monetary crisis did not hurt, Kohl, *French Nuclear Diplomacy*, p. 263.
57. Francis Cassell, *Gold or Credit? The Economics and Politics of International Money* (London: Pall Mall Press, 1965), p. 148, quoted in Morse, *Foreign Policy and Interdependence*, p. 229.
58. For the history of the Franco-American compromise on monetary policy, see *ibid.*, pp. 231–50; the French official version is in Couve de Murville, *Une politique étrangère*, pp. 142–54.
59. Philip Windsor, 'West German Foreign Policy', pp. 249–50; Alfred Grosser, 'France and Germany: Less Divergent Outlooks?', *Foreign Affairs*, 48, 2 (January 1970), 235–44.
60. Devillers, 'La politique française et la seconde guerre du Vietnam', p. 596.
61. Cléry, 'Les objectifs extérieurs de la Chine', p. 889.
62. 'French–Chinese Relations Are at a 4-year Low Point', *International Herald Tribune*, 10 July 1968.
63. Ronald Koven, 'De Gaulle and Russia: The Limits of a Policy', *International Herald Tribune*, 12 March 1968.
64. Cf. press conference, 27 November 1967; also Raymond Aron, 'De Gaulle et les Juifs', *L'Express*, 18–24 March 1968, and the remarks of Couve de Murville, *Une politique étrangère*, pp. 469–70.
65. See especially Balta and Rulleau, *La politique arabe de la France de de Gaulle à Pompidou*; on economic ties, see pp. 65–74. Also *Newsweek*, 16 February 1970; *L'Express*, 8–14 September 1969; and *The Times*, 7 December 1967.
66. Kolodziej, *French International Policy*, pp. 507–8.
67. Couve de Murville, *Une politique étrangère*, pp. 229–30.
68. Kolodziej, *French International Policy*, p. 134.

69. *Ibid.*, pp. 137–8.
70. See *L'Express*, 15–21 April 1968 and 3–9 November 1969; also *The Guardian*, 15 November 1969.
71. Servan-Schreiber, *The American Challenge*, p. 14.
72. O. R. Holsti, *et al.*, 'Bloc Structure and Intra-Alliance Conflict: France and China as Alliance Mavericks', in Holsti, *et al.*, ch. 6, esp. pp. 160–1, 181–187 (incl. tables 3 and 4), and 207–213 (incl. tables 14 and 15).
73. Tournoux, *La tragédie du Général*, p. 496.
74. Buchan, *The End of the Postwar Era*, p. 227.
75. Galtung, *The European Community*, p. 12.
76. Buchan, *The End of the Postwar Era*, pp. 69–75.
77. *Ibid.*, pp. 77–8.
78. *Ibid.*, pp. 80–3; also Walter L. Barrows, 'Speculations on a Multipolar 1984', in Louis J. Mensonides and James A. Kuhlman (eds.), *The Future of Inter-Bloc Relations in Europe* (New York: Praeger, 1974), pp. 191–214, esp. pp. 196–7; and Beaufre, *Strategy for Tomorrow*, p. 3.
79. Aron, *Peace and War*, p. 382.

Chapter 10
The impact of Gaullist policy on political change

1. E.g. Hoffmann, 'Paradoxes', pp. 20–1.
2. Kissinger, *A World Restored*, p. 326.
3. Cf. P. G. Cerny, 'The French Presidency: The Role of the Chief Executive in the Fifth Republic' (Gambier, Ohio: Kenyon College, unpublished paper, 1967), and François Goguel, *Les institutions politiques françaises* (Paris: Institut d'Études Politiques, 1966), p. 42.
4. Stanley Hoffmann, 'Heroic Leadership: The Case of Modern France', in Lewis J. Edinger (ed.), *Political Leadership in Industrialised Societies* (New York: Wiley, 1967), p. 118.
5. E.g. David Thomson, *Democracy in France since 1870* (London: Oxford University Press, 5th edn, 1969), p. 277.
6. Marxist historians still have problems in 'explaining' Boulangism.
7. Duroselle, 'Changes in French Foreign Policy', p. 309.
8. Hoffmann, 'Heroic Leadership', pp. 116–17; cf. also Michel Crozier, *The Bureaucratic Phenomenon* (London: Tavistock, 1964).
9. Murray Edelman, *The Symbolic Uses of Politics*, p. 94.
10. For a particularly lucid analysis of this process, see W. Lance Bennett, *The Political Mind and the Political Environment: An Investigation of Public Opinion and Political Consciousness*, chs. 3 and 4.
11. Edelman, *The Symbolic Uses of Politics*, p. 75; also cf. Tucker, 'Theory of Charismatic Leadership', p. 740.
12. Jean Charlot, *Le phénomène gaulliste*, p. 43.
13. Tucker, 'Theory of Charismatic Leadership', p. 739.
14. Charlot, *Le phénomène gaulliste*, p. 44.
15. *Ibid.*, p. 47.
16. Schweitzer, 'Theory and Political Charisma', p. 172.
17. Charlot, *Le phénomène gaulliste*, pp. 46–7.
18. André Malraux, *Les chênes qu'on abat...*(Paris: Gallimard, 1971), pp. 21ff.
19. Charlot, *Le phénomène gaulliste*, p. 49 (fig. 4) and p. 48.

20. Cf. Philip Converse and Georges Dupeux, 'Eisenhower et de Gaulle. Les généraux devant l'opinion', *Revue française de science politique*, 12, 1 (March 1962), 58–64.

21. Charlot, *Le phénomène gaulliste*, pp. 51–2.

22. Institut Français d'Opinion Publique, *Les Français et de Gaulle*. This book, edited and with text by Jean Charlot, is a critical summary and review of opinion surveys appertaining to de Gaulle over the period 1944–69 by the IFOP organisation (the French Gallup institution). Specifically, 'seven Parisians out of ten wanted a constitution which would give "extended powers" to the President of the Republic, and as much for the Council of Ministers; as for Parliament, on the other hand, they hesitated and were divided on the advisability of giving it more or less power than before the war', p. 103.

23. *Ibid.*, pp. 31–3.

24. *Ibid.*, p. 103.

25. *Ibid.*, pp. 34–5.

26. *Ibid.*, pp. 37–8.

27. Cf. John Ardagh, *The New France: A Society in Transition, 1945–1973* (Harmondsworth: Penguin, 1973); Pierre Sorlin, *La société française*, vol. II, *1914–1968* (Paris: Arthaud, 1971); Georges Dupeux, *French Society 1789–1970* (London: Methuen, 1976); Harvey Waterman, *Political Change in Contemporary France: The Politics of an Industrial Democracy* (Columbus, Ohio: Merrill, 1969); and Peter Coffey, *The Social Economy of France* (London: Macmillan, 1973).

28. Jean Charlot, 'Les élites politiques en France de la IIIᵉ à la Vᵉ République', *Archives européennes de sociologie*, 14, 1 (1973), 78–92.

29. Philip E. Converse and Georges Dupeux, 'Politicisation of the Electorate in France and the United States', in Giuseppe di Palma (ed.), pp. 41–63.

30. David R. Cameron, 'Stability and Change in Patterns of French Partisanship', *Public Opinion Quarterly*, 36, 1 (Spring 1972), 19–30.

31. For the concept of the 'catch-all' party, see Otto Kirchheimer, 'The Transformation of the Western European Party Systems', in Joseph La Palombara and Myron Weiner (eds.), *Political Parties and Political Development* (Princeton, N.J.: Princeton University Press, 1966), pp. 177–200.

32. Cf. Charlot, *Le phénomène gaulliste*, pp. 67–76, and IFOP, *Les Français et de Gaulle*, pp. 109–29.

33. François Goguel, *Modernisation économique et comportement politique* (Paris: Armand Colin, 1969).

34. Cf. Gérard Adam, 'Introduction à un débat sur la nouvelle classe ouvrière', *Revue française de science politique*, 22, 3 (June 1972), 509–28.

35. Charlot estimates solid working-class Gaullist support at around 30 per cent of all workers (*Le phénomène gaulliste*, p. 73), which would be similar to working-class support for the Conservative Party in Britain: cf. Peter G. J. Pulzer, *Political Representation and Elections in Britain* (London: Allen and Unwin, 1967), p. 102.

36. See François Goguel, 'Combien y a-t-il eu d'électeurs de gauche parmi ceux qui ont voté le 5 décembre 1965 pour le général de Gaulle?', *Revue française de science politique*, 12, 1 (February 1967), 65–9.

37. Charlot, *Le phénomène gaulliste*, pp. 84–5.

38. For an early discussion of this point, cf. François Goguel, 'Quelques

remarques sur le problème des institutions politiques de la France', *Revue française de science politique*, 14, 4 (February 1964), 7, and Georges Vedel, 'Vers le régime présidentiel?', in *ibid.*, p. 20.

39. Nettl, *Political Mobilisation*, pp. 327–8.

40. See the comments of Jean-Luc Parodi in François Goguel (ed.), *L'élection présidentielle de décembre 1965* (Paris: Armand Colin, 1969), p. 536.

41. Avril, *U.D.R. et gaullistes*, pp. 10–16.

42. Quoted in *ibid.*, p. 52.

43. Cf. James MacGregor Burns, *The Deadlock of Democracy: Four-Party Politics in America* (Englewood Cliffs, N.J.: Prentice-Hall, 1963), and Robert A. Dahl, *Democracy in the United States: Promise and Performance* (Chicago: Rand McNally, 1972), pp. 134–9, 390.

44. In the United States, the 'complementarity' of presidential and congressional parties is less important because of the greater separation of powers; different branches can be controlled by different parties without paralysing policy-making of a non-innovative kind as well as day-to-day administration. The dual responsibility of the French Prime Minister would make such a situation highly problematic in the Fifth Republic.

45. See Institut Français d'Opinion Publique, *Quand la gauche peut gagner. . .: Les élections législatives des 4–11 mars 1973*, ed. by Jean Charlot (Paris: Ed. Alain Moreau, 1973).

46. Jack Hayward and Vincent Wright, ' "Les Deux France" and the French Presidential Election of May 1974', *Parliamentary Affairs*, 27, 3 (Summer 1974), 208–36.

47. Jack Hayward and Vincent Wright, 'Presidential Supremacy and the French General Elections of March 1973', Part II, *Parliamentary Affairs*, 26, 4 (Autumn 1973), 402.

48. Consider President Giscard d'Estaing's press conference of 22 April 1976. Thus far in the Fifth Republic, parliamentary coalitions have broadly resembled presidential coalitions: cf. Vincent Wright, 'Presidentialism and the Parties in the French Fifth Republic', *Government and Opposition*, 10, 1 (Winter 1975), 24–45. However, the internal balance and structure of each coalition has shifted significantly over the past five years, with the 1978 parliamentary elections marking a new stage in which the four major groups – RPR (ex-UDR), UDF (Giscardians), Socialists and Communists – split the major-party popular vote almost evenly, thus giving Giscard more leverage in executive–legislative relations.

49. *Le Monde*, 9 and 10 June and 16 July 1976.

50. Rosenau, *National Leadership*, p. 357.

51. Girard, 'Sondages d'opinion', pp. 34–5.

52. With the major exception of spending on the FNS, which was, however, largely financed by cutbacks in spending for conventional forces with the end of the Algerian War and the virtual elimination of France's role as a colonial power.

53. Shils, 'Consensus', pp. 13–14.

54. The extent, nature, penetration and intensity of such divisive beliefs among the various social strata is still a fertile area of controversy among historians of the entire post-Revolutionary period: cf. J. P. Mayer, *Political Thought in France from the Revolution to the Fifth Republic* (London: Routledge and

Kegan Paul, 1961); Barrington Moore Jr, *Social Origins of Dictatorship and* *Democracy*; Theodore Zeldin, *France 1848–1945* (London: Oxford University Press, 1973), vol. I; Hoffmann, 'Paradoxes'; Dupeux, *French Society 1789–1970*. National values were always present to counteract those with a more fragmenting effect. However, the symbolic perpetuation of the very belief in the divisive nature of ideological beliefs themselves – especially at elite level – has been a dominant feature of French political culture: cf. P. G. Cerny, 'Cleavage, Aggregation and Change in French Politics', *British Journal of Political Science*, 2, 4 (October 1972), 443–55.

55. *Ibid.*, pp. 445–7.
56. Laurence Wylie, 'Social Change at the Grass Roots', p. 232.
57. Guy Michelat and Jean-Pierre Hubert Thomas, *Dimensions du nationalisme: Enquête par questionnaire (1962)* (Paris: Armand Colin, 1966), p. 119.
58. *Ibid.*, p. 115.
59. IFOP, *Les Français et de Gaulle*, p. 76.
60. *Ibid.*, pp. 76–7.
61. *Ibid.*, pp. 261 and 267.
62. *Ibid.*, p. 78.
63. *Ibid.*, pp. 81–3, 276.
64. *Ibid.*, pp. 278–9.
65. *Ibid.*, p. 53.
66. *Ibid.*, pp. 83–4; cf. *L'Année politique 1966*, pp. 58–9.
67. IFOP, *Les Français et de Gaulle*, p. 120.
68. Goguel, *L'élection présidentielle de décembre 1965*, pp. 284, 275–6.
69. IFOP, *Les Français et de Gaulle*, pp. 86–8, 272–4.
70. *Sondages*, 30, 2 (1968), 41.
71. IFOP, *Les Français et de Gaulle*, p. 45. 'The Gaullism index applied to different categories of population has been calculated from replies to the question: "Are you satisfied or dissatisfied with General de Gaulle as President of the Republic?" This calculation was carried out in the following manner:

$$\frac{\text{Satisfied–dissatisfied}}{\text{Total replies}} \times 100 = \text{Gaullism index}$$
(satisfied plus dissatisfied)

Example: Gaullism index of the whole French sample in 1960.

$$\frac{69 \text{ p.c. satisfied} - 22 \text{ p.c. dissatisfied}}{91 \text{ p.c. who gave one reply or the other}} \times 100 = +51$$

Theoretically the index can have any value between +100 and −100. It is positive when the proportion of "satisfieds" is higher than the proportion of "dissatisfieds" and negative when the proportion of "dissatisfieds" is the greater.' *Ibid.*, p. 332; see also tables, pp. 333–9.

72. *Ibid.*, p. 46.
73. *Ibid.*, p. 47.
74. Charlot, *Le phénomène gaulliste*, pp. 55–60, and IFOP, *Les Français et de Gaulle*, pp. 101–7 (on stability).
75. Charlot, *Le phénomène gaulliste*, p. 55, table 6, and, even more strikingly, *Sondages*, 32, 1–2 (1970), 13.
76. Charlot, *Le phénomène gaulliste*, p. 56.
77. *The Complete War Memoirs*, p. 677.
78. *Mémoires d'espoir*, vol. I, 'Le renouveau', p. 39.

79. Rosenau, *National Leadership*, p. 352.
80. Rémond, *The Right Wing in France from 1815 to de Gaulle*, p. 342.
81. *L'Année politique 1966*, p. 23.
82. *Ibid.*, p. 34.
83. Consider the analysis of Annie Kriegel, 'Rôle du mouvement ouvrier français dans l'élaboration de la politique étrangère', in Léo Hamon (ed.), *L'élaboration de la politique étrangère*, pp. 107–9.
84. Kolodziej, 'Patterns of French Policy', p. 33. On censure motions, only those voting for the motion (i.e. against the Government) actually vote, and an absolute majority of the total membership of the National Assembly is required for the success of the motion; thus abstentions (for whatever reason) virtually count as votes in favour of the Government.
85. La Gorce, 'De Gaulle entre deux mondes', pp. 696–7.
86. Cited in Morse, *Foreign Policy and Interdependence*, p. 193.
87. Lawrence Scheinman, 'The Politics of Nationalism in Contemporary France', *International Organization*, 23, 4 (Autumn 1969), 847–8.
88. Morse, *Foreign Policy and Interdependence*, pp. 191–4.
89. Quoted in *L'Année politique 1966*, p. 30.
90. *Ibid.*, p. 37.
91. *L'Express*, 4–10 May 1970.
92. See Converse and Dupeux, 'Politicisation of the Electorate'.
93. Greenstein and Tarrow, 'The Study of French Political Socialisation'; this is a review article discussing the findings in C. Roig and F. Billon-Grand, *La socialisation politique des enfants* (Paris: Armand Colin, 1968).
94. O. R. Holsti, *et al.*, *Unity and Disintegration in International Alliances: Comparative Studies*, p. 158.
95. Frankel, *National Interest*, p. 121. Cf. note 49, above.
96. IFOP, *Les Français et de Gaulle*, pp. 29, 189–92.
97. It was cold war politics, after all, which eased the position of Truman faced with a hostile Republican Congress in the late 1940s; it was a foreign policy issue – the Cuban missile crisis – which prevented the election of a hostile Congress for Kennedy in November 1962; and it was a *breakdown* of bipartisanship in foreign policy which led to the greatest clashes between the American President and Congress since the 1930s – the Cambodian Affair of the early 1970s, which involved significant clashes over appropriations between Nixon and Congress (as well as over the President's war-making powers) – and paved the way for both Nixon's tactics in the 1972 elections and congressional hostility when the Watergate Affair fully blossomed in 1973–4.

Conclusions
The legacy of grandeur

1. Edelman, *Politics as Symbolic Action*, pp. 157–8.
2. Nettl, *Political Mobilisation*, p. 100; cf. Quincy Wright, *A Study of War* (Chicago: Chicago University Press, 1942), vol. II, p. 999, quoted in Deutsch, *Nationalism and Social Communication*, p. 23.
3. Couve de Murville, *Une politique étrangère*, pp. 483–4.
4. Herz, 'The Territorial State Revisited: Reflections on the Future of the Nation-State', p. 89.

Select Bibliography

I. WORKS BY GENERAL DE GAULLE

La discorde chez l'ennemi (Paris: Berger–Levrault, 1944), originally published 1924.

Le fil de l'épée (Paris: Berger–Levrault, 1961), originally published 1932.

Vers l'Armée de métier (Paris: Presses-Pocket, no date), originally published by Berger–Levrault, 1934.

La France et son Armée (Paris: Union Générale d'Editions, no date), originally published by Plon (Paris), 1938.

Trois études, with an introduction by Lucien Nachin (Paris: Berger–Levrault, 1945).

The Complete War Memoirs of Charles de Gaulle (New York: Simon and Schuster, 1967), original French edition, 3 vols., published by Plon (Paris), 1954, 1956 and 1959.

Mémoires d'espoir, vol. I, 'Le renouveau' (Paris: Plon, 1970), and vol. II, 'L'effort' (Paris: Plon, 1971).

II. COLLECTIONS OF DE GAULLE'S SPEECHES, ETC.

The essential work is:

Discours et messages, ed. by François Goguel (Paris: Plon, 1970), 5 vols.

English translations of many of de Gaulle's major speeches, statements, etc., are available from the French Embassy Press and Information Service (London and New York), either as individual publications, or, in the case of his earlier speeches, in *Major Addresses, Statements and Press Conferences of General Charles de Gaulle, May 19, 1958–January 31, 1964* (New York: Ambassade de France, Press and Information Service, no date).

III. USEFUL OFFICIAL SOURCES

The various publications of la Documentation Française are the best sources of public documents: *Articles et documents: Chroniques étrangères; Notes et études documentaires; Moniteur officiel de commerce et industrie*; but most important, covering the period from the beginning of 1966, is *La politique étrangère de la France: Textes et documents*, which normally appears twice a year.

IV. FURTHER ESSENTIAL READING

The memoirs of Maurice Couve de Murville, *Une politique étrangère 1958–1969* (Paris: Plon, 1971), are a fundamental source (though guarded and at times superficial) by de Gaulle's right-hand man, first as Foreign Minister (1958–68) and then as Prime Minister (1968–9); his master's voice truly speaks.

Biographies of de Gaulle are not good, on the whole, as so much of his private life was effectively hidden from scrutiny. The best is Paul-Marie de la Gorce, *De Gaulle entre deux mondes* (Paris: Fayard, 1964), although this does not cover his later years in power.

The best of the general surveys of French foreign policy under de Gaulle (the others vary considerably in quality) is Edward A. Kolodziej, *French International Policy under de Gaulle and Pompidou* (Ithaca, N.Y.: Cornell University Press, 1974).

A content analysis of de Gaulle's speeches from 1958–65 can be found in Jean-Marie Cotteret and René Moreau, *Le vocabulaire du général de Gaulle: Analyse statistique des allocations radiodiffusées 1958–1965* (Paris: Armand Colin, 1969).

A large body of essential material about de Gaulle's relationship with the French people can be found in the survey and critical review of 25 years of Gallup polls (1944–69) about attitudes to de Gaulle and related matters: Institut Français d'Opinion Publique (IFOP), *Les Français et de Gaulle*, ed. and with commentary by Jean Charlot (Paris: Plon, 1971).

Basic background on the political, social and economic context of the Fifth Republic can be found in Stanley Hoffmann, Charles P. Kindleberger, Laurence Wylie, Jesse R. Pitts, Jean-Baptiste Duroselle and François Goguel, *In Search of France* (Cambridge, Mass.: Harvard University Press, 1963), which covers the problems with insight and depth as well as breadth.

Stanley Hoffmann has written many acute articles on de Gaulle and related aspects of French politics over the years, and most of these have been recently collected into one volume: Stanley Hoffmann, *Decline or Renewal? France since the 1930s* (New York: Viking, 1974).

The works of Jean-Raymond Tournoux are in a class by themselves. They are real behind-the-scenes glimpses of de Gaulle and the Gaullist elite, full of semi-official 'leaks', 'off-the-record' comments succinctly paraphrased, and insights from extensive interviews. The only one available in English is his *Pétain and de Gaulle* (London: Heinemann, 1966). Others, equally essential, are all published by Plon (Paris): *La tragédie du Général* (1967); *Le mois de mai du Général* (1969); *Jamais dit* (1971); and *Le tourment et la fatalité* (1974). Tournoux has a strong sense for drama and symbol, too.

A highly detailed but analytically superficial chronicle of the membership and the rituals of the Gaullist elite can be found in Pierre Viansson-Ponté, *The King and his Court* (Boston: Houghton Mifflin, 1965), which is a translation of *Les gaullistes* (Paris, 1963).

Other very useful books include: on the development of the Gaullist party to 1969, though somewhat obsolete in view of developments in the 1970s, see Jean Charlot, *The Gaullist Phenomenon* (London: Allen and Unwin, 1971); on a variety of problems concerning decision-making and general contextual factors in French foreign policy, see Léo Hamon, ed., *L'élaboration de la politique étrangère* (Paris: Presses Universitaires de France, 1969); for a most unusual and well-argued pro-Gaullist viewpoint by an American correspondent (for the *New York Times*) in Paris, see John L. Hess, *The Case for de Gaulle: An American Viewpoint* (New York: William Morrow, 1968); a monumental work on de Gaulle's approach to Europe is Edmond Jouve, *Le général de Gaulle et la construction de l'Europe (1940–1966)* (Paris: Librairie Générale de Droit et de Jurisprudence, 1967); and the most detailed work on the nuclear question is Wilfrid L. Kohl, *French Nuclear Diplomacy* (Princeton, N.J.: Princeton University Press, 1971).

Index